Keep this book. You will need it and use it throughout your career.

About the American Hotel & Lodging Association (AH&LA)

Founded in 1910, AH&LA is the trade association representing the lodging industry in the United States. AH&LA is a federation of state lodging associations throughout the United States with 11,000 lodging properties worldwide as members. The association offers its members assistance with governmental affairs representation, communications, marketing, hospitality operations, training and education, technology issues, and more. For information, call 202-289-3100.

LODGING, the management magazine of AH&LA, is a "living textbook" for hospitality students that provides timely features, industry news, and vital lodging information.

About the American Hotel & Lodging Educational Institute (EI)

An affiliate of AH&LA, the Educational Institute is the world's largest source of quality training and educational materials for the lodging industry. EI develops textbooks and courses that are used in more than 1,200 colleges and universities worldwide, and also offers courses to individuals through its Distance Learning program. Hotels worldwide rely on EI for training resources that focus on every aspect of lodging operations. Industry-tested videos, CD-ROMs, seminars, and skills guides prepare employees at every skill level. EI also offers professional certification for the industry's top performers. For information about EI's products and services, call 800-349-0299 or 407-999-8100.

About the American Hotel & Lodging Educational Foundation (AH&LEF)

An affiliate of AH&LA, the American Hotel & Lodging Educational Foundation provides financial support that enhances the stability, prosperity, and growth of the lodging industry through educational and research programs. AH&LEF has awarded millions of dollars in scholarship funds for students pursuing higher education in hospitality management. AH&LEF has also funded research projects on topics important to the industry, including occupational safety and health, turnover and diversity, and best practices in the U.S. lodging industry. For more information, go to www.ahlef.org.

Hotel Sustainable Development
Principles & Best Practices

Educational Institute Books

Hotel Sustainable Development

Principles & Best Practices

Edited by
A. J. Singh, Ph.D.
Hervé Houdré

American
Hotel & Lodging
Educational Institute

Disclaimer

This publication is designed to provide accurate and authoritative information in regard to the subject matter covered. It is sold with the understanding that the publisher is not engaged in rendering legal, accounting, or other professional service. If legal advice or other expert assistance is required, the services of a competent professional person should be sought.
   —*From the Declaration of Principles jointly adopted by the American Bar Association and a Committee of Publishers and Associations*

The author or authors of each chapter are solely responsible for the contents of this publication. All views expressed herein are solely those of the authors and do not necessarily reflect the views of the American Hotel & Lodging Educational Institute (the Institute) or the American Hotel & Lodging Association (AH&LA).

Nothing contained in this publication shall constitute a standard, an endorsement, or a recommendation of AH&LA or the Institute. AH&LA and the Institute disclaim any liability with respect to the use of any information, procedure, or product, or reliance thereon by any member of the hospitality industry.

Contents

Part IV: Operating Perspectives

Foreword

Treating Earth As If We Intended to Stay

by John Elkington

GENERALLY, THE LAST THING ON MY MIND as I walk into a new hotel on my travels around the world is how it performs against the triple bottom line—which spotlights the economic, social, and environmental value created (or destroyed) by an enterprise. Instead, like most other travelers, I'm likely to be tired, in need of a shower, and keen that I'm not fobbed off with a room next to the waste facilities or a noisy elevator shaft. Still, it's weird how you can detect the quality of "green" thinking and management in such places almost as soon as you step through the door. When "green" is at the bottom of the pecking order in a hotel, the sustainability agenda boils down to cost efficiencies, whereas toward the other end of the spectrum it's more likely to be cultural, part of the hotel's DNA.

When you see the near-ubiquitous sign encouraging you to reuse your towels in a cheaper hotel, you know the managers want you to cut their overhead costs—and I have no problem with that, as long as it also cuts their hotel's energy, carbon, and water footprints. In better hotels, I often treat the sign as an invitation to a wider conversation—though it's extraordinary how often your towel is removed day after day, even when you follow all the instructions on how to signal your concern to protect the environment. Different notions of quality are at war here, it seems.

But real progress is being made. True, with honorable exceptions, the travel, tourism, and hotel sectors were slow to respond to the sustainable development agenda that began to build from 1987, when the World Commission on Environment & Development—better known as the Brundtland Commission—launched its report, *Our Common Future*. But it wasn't long before we saw organizations like the International Hotels Environmental Initiative (IHEI) taking a lead by identifying, collating, and disseminating best practices.

I have had the privilege to work with most sectors of the hospitality industry on sustainability issues since the early 1970s. At times progress has been frustratingly—sometimes agonizingly—slow. Progress, when it comes, has often followed a major accident or incident, as when the discovery of the Antarctic Ozone Hole in 1985 led to the eradication of the then widely used CFCs worldwide. Or—one decade later, in 1995—when Shell tripped up twice in the same year, in the North

Sea and in Nigeria, and grabbed onto the triple bottom line agenda as a North Star navigational device.

That was then. The 2009 UN Conference on Climate Change (COP15) in Copenhagen may have ended in political disarray, but the broader sustainability challenge is now moving up the business agenda in various ways. One recent indication of the trend came when *The Economist* launched its *The World in 2010* survey, in which pretty much every article used the words "sustainability" and "sustainable," though they were often implicitly defined in a much narrower economic or financial sense. More significantly, perhaps, *The Economist* itself also recently published two briefs on the triple bottom line,[1] underscoring my strong sense that the concept is now enjoying a new lease on life.

And more important even than what such business media say is what major businesses are now doing. Growing numbers of the world's largest corporations—among them Walmart—have embraced the sustainability agenda and are working energetically to drive change through their extensive supply chains. The market, even if patchily, is switching on.

In various ways, business leaders are trying to signal their growing concern about the potential future impact of energy, climate, and water security issues—and their interest in the solutions-based markets that will evolve as a result. Read *Vision 2050*, the latest futures report from the World Business Council for Sustainable Development (WBCSD), for example, and it is clear that the twenty-nine CEOs who signed off on this publication see the market opportunities created by the sustainability transition as very likely to dwarf those that flowed from the creation of the Internet.

Indeed, the agenda for the hotels sector has moved on tremendously since Julia Hailes and I published our book *Holidays That Don't Cost the Earth* in 1992, following up on the success of our 1988 book, *The Green Consumer Guide*, which ended up selling around one million copies worldwide. At the time, even leading hotel groups had yet to adopt environmental auditing—whereas today the best of them talk comfortably about energy efficiency, water footprints, sustainable fish, and the like.

Probe behind the scenes in some parts of the world, however, and it soon becomes clear that there is a lot more talk than action. One reason for this is that, despite the best will in the world, hotel board members and managers genuinely don't know exactly what is expected of them. They trained in a world where sustainability issues were marginal at best, and their minds (and their networks) are as yet poorly attuned to detecting the early, weak signals of change.

They will have no such excuses when they have read *Hotel Sustainable Development: Principles & Best Practices*, with its in-depth coverage of critical management issues in the regulatory, policy, development, architectural, financial, and operational areas of hotel sustainability. My hope is that they will be hooked by the challenges and opportunities presented. What makes the book particularly valuable is the fact that the chapters have been contributed by leading experts from a wide variety of disciplines and organizations, including consulting firms,

---

[1] www.economist.com/business-finance/management/displaystory.cfm?story_id=14301663.

government entities, legal practices, hotels, development companies, asset management firms, architectural firms, supply companies, certifying entities, and universities.

My warm congratulations go out to the American Hotel & Lodging Educational Institute and to the several other leading associations and their leaders for initiating and collaborating on this important, timely project. These include the International Society of Hospitality Consultants (ISHC), *The* School of Hospitality Business at Michigan State University, the World Travel and Tourism Council (WTTC), the Hospitality Asset Managers Association (HAMA), the Hotel Sales and Marketing Association International (HSMAI), the U.S. Green Building Council (USGBC), the Green Meeting Industry Council (GMIC), and the National Association of Hotel & Lodging Engineers (NAHLE). Furthermore, the voluntary contribution of several industry executives, consultants, and leading subject-matter experts is a testament to the growing passion for sustainability in the lodging industry and the importance of a collaborative effort to make sustainable development ubiquitous within the industry.

That said, the original invitation to contribute this foreword came from someone who I consider the hotel sector's pre-eminent champion of sustainability and the triple bottom line, Hervé Houdré. While a sustainable lodging enterprise is the result of a cohesive effort of several stakeholders, it is the hotel General Manager with a clear vision of sustainability and a passion for execution who can convert the vague idea of sustainability into a value-creating proposition for the owners and shareholders. While managing the legendary Willard InterContinental in Washington, D.C., Hervé exemplified the twenty-first century "Citizen Hotelier" who must, I believe, be triple-bottom-line focused by blending the three P's of People, Planet, and Profit. He has continued in his sustainability efforts at his new hotel, the InterContinental New York Barclay.

Our sense of hospitality will expand significantly in the coming decade. My hope is that what follows in *Hotel Sustainable Development* will help spur a new generation of talent to pick up the torch and use it to light the way in an ever-expanding range of organizations in the hotels sector. Over time, what are too often seen today as soft citizenship issues will become true competitive differentiators in tomorrow's quality- and sustainability-obsessed markets.

John Elkington was the co-founder of Environmental Data Services (1978); Sustain-Ability (1987); and Volans (2008), where he is currently Executive Chairman. He launched the triple bottom line agenda in 1994, making it central to his 1997 book Cannibals with Forks: The Triple Bottom Line of 21ˢᵗ Century Business *(Capstone/ John Wiley, 1997/98). His latest book, co-authored with Pamela Hartigan, is* The Power of Unreasonable People: How Social Entrepreneurs Create Markets That Change the World *(Harvard Business School Press, 2008).*

Part I

Historical Context— Local and Global Perspectives

The Evolution of Sustainable Development in the Hotel Industry: Drivers Shaping the Sustainability Agenda

By Hervé Houdré and A. J. Singh

*One of Europe and America's most respected hoteliers, **Hervé Houdré** began his current position as Regional Director of Operations & General Manager of the InterContinental New York Barclay in October 2009. Prior to this, beginning in 2004 he was the General Manager of the Willard InterContinental. Through his efforts, the Willard InterContinental was honored with the 2009 Condé Nast Traveler World Saver Award, the 2009 DC Mayor's Award for Environmental Excellence, and the DC Chamber of Commerce 2009 Business of the Year award, among others.*

Mr. Houdré is recognized for introducing operational and other refinements that impact profit and increase market share and was named "2006 Independent Hotelier of the World" by HOTELS magazine's readers. Prior to joining the Willard InterContinental, he managed such properties as the Hôtel de Crillon and Hôtel Plaza Athénée in Paris and held the position of Chief Operating Officer for Kempinski Hotels and Resorts. A native of France, he was born to the industry – literally. He was born and raised in a small inn in the Loire Valley that his parents owned. He has lived in several countries throughout the world, including a three-year period as Executive Assistant Manager with the Hôtel Plaza Athénée in New York, which he opened in 1984.

Under Mr. Houdré's leadership, the InterContinental New York Barclay is undergoing a sustainable transformation. The hotel's sustainable progress is being reported on regularly by Condé Nast Traveler's Truth.travel blog. The hotel's program, "Sustainability in the City," is based on the triple bottom line of Economic Viability, Social Responsibility, and Environmental Protection, and is comprised of interwoven sustainability projects designed to provide guests with a luxurious urban hospitality experience in harmony with social and ecological consciousness. Sustainability projects to date include the "adoption" of two local schools; the achievement of 100-percent wind energy through the purchase of RECs (Renewable Energy Certificates), a sustainable purchasing program; installation of CFL and LED bulbs throughout the hotel; an employee well-being program; a Natural Power Breakfast for guests comprised solely of local, natural, and organic products; and integrated charitable initiatives whenever and wherever possible. Wishing to ensure accountability and to track progress, Mr. Houdré put into place a five-year roadmap that defines and quantifies the hotel's sustainability goals.

In 2006, Mr. Houdré published a white paper entitled Sustainable Hospitality©: Sustainable Development in the Hotel Industry, *which was updated for Cornell University's Center for Hospitality Research in 2008. He was a contributor for HotelNewsNow.com on sustainable hospitality. His sustainability efforts have been noted in numerous magazine articles, including cover stories in such publications as* HOTELS *and* Lodging. *Mr. Houdré has been a featured speaker on the subject of sustainable hospitality at a variety of forums and for a variety of organizations, including Relais & Châteaux, PRSA (Public Relations Society of America), the International Franchise Association, the University of Florida in Gainesville, the International Society of Hospitality Consultants, the Green Jobs expo in Washington, D.C., Roundtables on Sustainable Hospitality at Cornel University, Michigan State University, New York University, the National Park Service Advisory Board, and AMFORHT (the World Association for Hospitality and Tourism Education and Training). He was also a speaker on Condé Nast Traveler's "World Savers: The Conversation" panel in the spring of 2010.*

Mr. Houdré serves on the Board of Directors of the New York Hotel Association, NYC & Company, and the Global Sustainable Tourism Council. Through 2009, he was a member of the Board of Directors of the Washington Downtown Business Improvement District and the Restaurant Association of Metropolitan Washington. From 1991 to 1999, he served on the Board of The Leading Hotels of the World. In 1999, he served as President of Comité Montaigne, Paris, an association of deluxe companies established in Avenue Montaigne that includes such well-established entities as Dior, Chanel, and Harry Winston.

Mr. Houdré studied at the Hotel School of Paris and holds an MBA from Reims Management School, France. He lives in New York with his wife and is the proud father of three.

A. J. Singh, *Ph.D., is an Associate Professor in* The *School of Hospitality Business at Michigan State University and focuses on international lodging, finance, and real estate. Dr. Singh was jointly responsible for the establishment of The Hospitality Business Real Estate and Development Specialization at Michigan State University. He has more than fifteen years of hospitality business experience in various management positions in the United States and India. He has worked for Oberoi Hotels, Stouffer Hotels, and Hyatt Hotels. In 1999, he taught financial management at Centre International de Glion in Switzerland. He has also conducted many real estate market and feasibility studies while working as a consultant for Laventhol & Horwath.*

Dr. Singh earned his undergraduate degree from the University of Delhi in India, his M.S. from Purdue University in Hotel Restaurant and Institutional Management, and his Ph.D. in Park, Recreation, and Tourism from Michigan State University. He is an active member of the Hospitality Asset Managers Association; the Council on Hotel, Restaurant, and Institutional Education; the Association of Hospitality Financial Management Educators; the International Society of Hospitality Consultants; and the Urban Land Institute. The National Institute of Standards and Technology appointed him to the 2006 Board of Examiners for the Malcolm Baldrige National Quality Award. He received the Richard Lewis Award for Quality and Innovation in 2006. He currently conducts two study-abroad programs to India, Dubai, Thailand, Hong Kong, Macau, and Southern China.

Authors' Acknowledgments

Chapter research was conducted by Ms. Rabiga Omarova and Ms. Emily Lustig. Ms. Omarova recently graduated with a degree in Finance from the Eli Broad College of Business at Michigan State University, and Ms. Lustig is a recent graduate of The *School of Hospitality Business at Michigan State University.*

The authors are grateful to the resource guidance provided by Professor David Stipanuk of Cornell University, whose historical research and sharing of resources greatly assisted with the writing of this chapter.

MANY FACTORS HAVE SUBSTANTIALLY ACCELERATED environmental degradation over recent decades. We are now at a point where we consume more of the Earth's resources than it can regenerate. While the lodging industry does not have the same environmental impact as the extractive and manufacturing sectors, it is nonetheless an important contributor to environmental problems.

The lodging industry's growing awareness of its impact—influenced by the changing public consciousness of environmentalism, regulatory changes, and the more practical benefits of cost savings—persuaded the lodging industry to take its first steps toward sustainability several years ago. However, sustainability in the hotel industry as we know it today has had a long evolutionary path and faces perhaps an even longer process to improve further.

This chapter presents a brief history of sustainable development in the hospitality industry, including some of its main drivers during different eras of the evolutionary process. The chapter references secondary publications on the subject and, to a large extent, relies upon the work done by Professor David Stipanuk of Cornell University on the subject. As such, the chapter will set the stage for subsequent chapters in the book that address in detail the current programs, projects, initiatives, and issues associated with sustainable development in the hotel industry.

The Early Years

There was not much interest in environmental management in the hospitality industry until the development of the International Hotels Environment Initiative (IHEI), which was launched by the Prince of Wales in 1992.[1] The sustainable development in the lodging industry as we know it today originated from the environmental movement in the tourism sector—widely known as "eco-tourism"—which in turn developed from global corporate sustainability initiatives. Yet historically, the tourism industry has been quite slow to take positive action on sustainability.[2]

The origins of environmentalism in the tourism industry can be traced as far back as the late nineteenth to early twentieth centuries, when many protected areas around the world were modeled after the U.S. national park system. Under this model, boundaries were drawn around specific areas to preserve them in their natural state and free them of direct use. Authorization by the U.S. Congress to use these national parks to serve as "pleasure grounds" for public visitors linked national parks to tourism from their inception.[3] The first such place was Yosemite National Park in California, established in 1890 by John Muir and Robert Johnson, who shortly thereafter officially joined forces to create the Sierra Club, one of the first environmental protection groups in the United States.[4]

In the late 1920s, Professor Frank H. Randolph, the founder of the hotel engineering program in the hotel management program at Cornell University, prepared

"Hotel Engineering Bulletins," a collection of material from a variety of sources, and bound them for his students' use. Included in this material was a copy of Randolph's article "How May the Hotel Reduce Cost and Waste in the Engineering Department?," which won an award from the Northwestern Hotel Association for the best essay submitted on one of four important topics.[5] The article focused on fuel efficiency in boiler-room operations, water conservation, methods to reduce fuel usage with better operational and maintenance procedures, and the possible relation of lamp maintenance to reducing energy costs of lighting. The article and related research show early evidence of the environmental management initiatives originating at that time in the hospitality industry, but with a primary focus on cost, resource control, and air quality management.

Professor Stipanuk's historical research refers to the period between 1930 and 1950 as a relatively slow time for development and innovation in the lodging industry due to the events related to the Great Depression and World War II.[6] He also points out, however, some of the positive effects that resulted from the stringencies of depression and war in the industry that today would be considered as green initiatives. Massive reuse of various everyday products, recycling, and reducing fossil fuel usage at that period are some examples. Despite the unpopularity of eco-terms, such as "environment" or "green," articles from the 1930s indicate that sustainable issues were still a great concern to the industry managers and educators. The environmental issues raised and solutions discussed, however, were mostly focused on specific activities and efforts, rather than on broad environmental implications. As the industry grew, this property-specific focus on sustainability gradually gained a broader perspective.

Mid-Century to 1970

The post–World War II period ushered in a growth and expansion of international hotel development as part of the American imperative for economic development of lesser-developed countries in Latin America and the Caribbean. This was coupled with reconstruction efforts of the war-torn economies of the Continent, which saw a growth of air transportation and hotels.[7] According to the estimations of the World Tourism Organization (WTO), the number of stay-over international tourist arrivals increased from 25 million in 1950 to about 750 million in 2004.[8]

The increase in the number of tourist travelers during that period was largely due to growth in demand/supply relationships between North American tourists and Caribbean basin destinations, as well as between European visitors and emerging destinations of the Mediterranean and Indian basins. Despite the potential economic and social benefits of increased lodging and tourism revenues in these regions, the environmental implications of this growth became a concern. These environmental concerns contributed to the emergence of the "cautionary platform," which basically argued that unregulated tourism development eventually results in unacceptably high environmental, economic, and sociocultural costs for the residents and destinations.[9]

The U.S. hotel industry began to consider environmental matters in different areas of hotel operations as early as the 1950s. A 1954 article titled "The Hotel that Research Built" contained detailed instructions on how the process of facility building might become more environmentally sound based on the example of the Statler Hotel facilities. Stipanuk summarizes the article, stating, "The urban hotel described in this 1954 article seems to have been designed with a conscious consideration of recycling, use of daylight for lighting of restaurant space, reuse of guest-room linens, a minimization of materials consumption in construction, and reductions in energy use. While the prime motivation may have been to control costs and save money, these are nevertheless all issues on today's environmental agenda."[10]

A greater emphasis on environmental sustainability associated with property economics, design, and development is also evident in later works, such as the 1967 *Cornell Hotel and Restaurant Administration Quarterly* article on Caneel Bay in the U.S. Virgin Islands (opened in 1956), which describes Laurence Rockefeller's efforts in relation to "conservation, the preservation of beauty, and the creation of job opportunities in our areas," while building and operating the hotel facility on the Virgin Islands.[11]

McEwen and Eberhard cite 1960 data for ten Sheraton hotels in which water use dropped to an average seventy-two gallons per occupied room per day.[12] Their article is a good example of existing environmental concerns associated with property building. The authors discuss water supply of the hotels, and its pollution and treatment, listing a variety of potential pollutants including infectious agents, different organic chemical exotica, and other mineral, chemical, and radioactive substances. The article noted that the chemicals involved were relatively new and thus possessed a possibility of negative effects on the health of human beings and animals. The authors suggested the industry take up the cause of water conservation in a public-spirited way in order to gain favorable national publicity.

The lodging industry in the 1960s considered such environmental issues as air purification, natural resources, radiation, ventilation, waste management, water supply control, and sound control methods. Stipanuk notes, however, that "specific environmental issues were of interest to the industry but the environmental label was not yet in use to describe them."[13]

In the late 1960s, U.S. businesses and the hotel industry also turned their attention to the social aspects of sustainability. This fact is evident from the various academic sources that could be classified as early works on corporate social responsibility, mostly focused on customer relationships and employer responsibilities. One example is the first nationwide study of black employment in the hotel industry, conducted in 1968 by The Wharton School of the University of Pennsylvania, which revealed employment opportunities for black people in the hotel industry in big cities of the United States.[14]

In 1972, the (then) American Hotel & Motel Association's board of directors adopted a new code of operating practices reflecting an explicit concern for the social conduct of its member hotels. Growing public pressure and the growing conviction within the business community itself were the most apparent drivers of the extension of corporate social obligations far beyond simple financial operation.[15]

1970 to 1990

Rachel Carson's *Silent Spring* was published in 1962, giving a detailed exposition on the dangers of environmental pollution to human health. It fundamentally altered the way Americans perceived the environment and the dangers of toxins. Carson's book marked the beginning of modern environmentalism. This created a foundation for a new wave of green-activist movements and a massive formation of environmental protection organizations in the United States and other developed countries, as the activists began to link the destruction of the natural environment to the complex interplay of new technology and corporate, political, and economic powers in the late 1960s and early 1970s.[16]

As public pressure increased, a shift from legislative to administrative environmental regulation also occurred. President Nixon's plan for creating the Environmental Protection Agency (EPA) was submitted to Congress in July of 1970 and received no opposition. The EPA began operating on December 2, 1970, bringing in its first sixty days of operation five times as many enforcement actions as the agencies it inherited had brought during any similar period before. The U.S. government also enacted numerous environmental acts and pieces of legislation concerning air, water, and wildlife protection during that period.[17]

In the 1970s, the advent of wide-bodied, high-speed airplanes fueled growth in the number of global travelers. The subsequent boom in tourism industry development and its fast penetration into underdeveloped regions, as well as the growing political influence of the environmental movement, contributed to the emergence of the aforementioned cautionary platform. In the middle of the 1970s, 8 percent of all vacationers traveled from the developed to the developing countries. By the mid 1980s, this number had jumped to about 17 percent, and by the mid 1990s, it had increased to about 20 percent.[18]

As the global community has recognized the environmental costs of tourism, the increasing ecological costs of rapid hotel development have also been noticed. Most resort developments were criticized for being unattractive and not well assimilated into the surrounding area.[19] High-rise hotels along the coastal zones of Atlantic City and Miami, for example, were perceived by many as visual pollution. Hawaii was one of the first tourist destinations in the United States to experience this problem, prompting articles about it as early as 1969. In one such article, Becker argues that "Statehood and the jet airliner have transformed the Hawaiian capital from a picturesque crossroads to something approaching an outpost of Southern California."[20]

By this time, the amount of research and literature related to environmental protection and sustainability had increased exponentially in volume and sophistication as the idea of "sustainability" had gained further recognition.[21] Stipanuk refers to the "acclimatization" category used in the bibliography of the *Cornell Hotel and Restaurant Administration Quarterly* in 1971–1974 as the publication's first category to be closely aligned with the term "environment."[22] This category was later replaced by the categories of "environmental engineering" and "environmental law."

Starting in the early 1970s, the (then) American Hotel & Motel Association had an environmental concerns committee operating within its institutional framework. An environmental survey conducted by the committee contained questions on outdoor air pollution with a decided focus on outside environment, recyclable and disposable materials, and issues surrounding energy supplies and energy conservation.[23] These issues are the same ones that were to be perceived by the public as environmental issues in the 1990s.

As the energy crisis of 1973/74 alarmed the American public and shortages of oil etched into the American experience the natural limits of human consumption, the escalating costs and energy supply became a great concern for business players, including lodging industry managers. Synthetic hydrocarbon and alternative fuels like solar and wind energy started developing, and the extension of daylight savings time and a total ban on the sale of gasoline on Sundays were some of the proposed solutions.[24] Numerous articles appeared in the industry press at this time, focusing on energy-use reduction for cost-cutting purposes.[25] Two examples of such articles are "Facing the Energy Shortfall"[26] and "Utilities Management: Part I—'Shedding Light'"[27] (part of the "Saving Energy Dollars" series) from the *Cornell Hotel and Restaurant Administration Quarterly* February 1974 and May 1975 issues, respectively. It was also in the 1970s that public awareness, the environmental sciences, ecology, and technology began to consider topics such as ozone depletion, global climate change, acid rain, and genetically modified organisms.

With the growth of mass tourism and harmful physical and sociocultural effects of destination stress resulting from overdevelopment in the 1970s, the environmental consciousness in tourism gained momentum. One of the consequences of this was the rise of the "alternative tourism" concept, which emerged as a possible route toward sustainability in the tourism industry.[28] Alternative tourism was thought of as the best medium to attain conservation of natural areas in order to maintain resource sustainability, avoid environmental damage, maintain resource quality, and bring in new economies to local people. It was also associated with benefits to the local communities, educational value for tourists, and a foreign exchange earner for the struggling developing countries.[29, 30]

The concept of alternative tourism was derived from the broader discourse on the idea of "sustainable development," which, according to Bramwell and Lane,[31] emerged in the early 1970s and gained further momentum through the 1980 World Conservation Strategy.[32] The most generally used definition of "sustainability" was christened by the World Commission on Environment and Development (now known as the Brundtland Commission), established by the United Nations in 1983. It was published in a 1987 report called *Our Common Future*, better known as the *Brundtland Report*, named after the commission's chairwoman and Prime Minister of Norway, Gro Harlem Brundtland. The *Brundtland Report* defined sustainability as "development that meets the needs of the present without compromising the ability of future generations to meet their own needs."[33]

Weaver points out that the *Brundtland Report* curiously made no mention of tourism or the lodging industry, despite the fact that the development of tourism had already attained its "megasector" status by the mid 1980s.[34] Nevertheless, the environmental concerns that emerged following the *Brundtland Report* had a major impact on the way that businesses were structured and operated in the next decade.[35]

Sustainable Development: 1990 to the New Millennium ——

As a result of the *Brundtland Report*, a greater awareness of the environment started to evolve. Environmental organizations, government protocols, and agreements continued to heighten this awareness, as well as that of environmental degradation. Included among these were the UN Earth Summits, the United

Nations Framework Convention on Climate Change, and Agenda 21, which offered a global environmental policy. In December 1997 a high-profile event, The Kyoto Protocol, was launched. The Kyoto Protocol is an international agreement that sets binding targets for thirty-seven countries and the European community to fight global warming by reducing greenhouse gases.[36] The Protocol entered into force on February 16, 2005, and as of November 2009, 187 states had signed and ratified the protocol. Noticeably missing from the signatory list is the United States.

These global initiatives resulted in a heightened awareness and discussion within the tourism and hospitality business sectors. The Travel Industry Association of America (now the U.S. Travel Association) issued a report suggesting that the hospitality industry was at a crossroads with an opportunity to be a global environmental leader rather than a reluctant follower. The American Hotel & Lodging Association administered a survey about managers' attitudes toward environmental issues in October of 1994. The results demonstrated that the industry's increasing globalization might be one factor that is contributing to the development of environmental activities. Another result of the survey provided evidence that generational gaps produce different attitudes with regard to environmental issues.[37]

In anticipation of the growing importance of sustainable development for business, leaders from several hotel companies formed the International Hotels Environment Initiative (IHEI) in 1992. The purpose of the organization was to create a collaborative forum to improve sustainability standards for hotels and, later, tourism-related companies. After twelve years, the organization changed its name to the International Tourism Partnership, in order to have a broader mandate and appeal.[38] Its programs have a strong education and informational focus to inspire and show companies how to develop and operate a sustainable enterprise.

In response to the recognition that a growing segment of travelers values conservation and preservation, another important organization was launched that provided further impetus to hospitality organizations to increase their sustainability quotient. The International Ecotourism Society was established in 1990 as a means to create a network to promote sustainable travel, educate both consumers and travel professionals, and influence tourism businesses to incorporate principles of ecotourism into their operations and policies.[39] The World Tourism Organization considers ecotourism to be the fastest-growing market in the tourism industry. The Travel Industry Association of America conducted a study in which 38 percent of U.S. travelers claimed they would pay more to use hospitality firms that strive to maintain and preserve the environment; additionally, of those travelers, 61 percent said they would be 5–10 percent more likely to stay with those companies.[40]

As the decade progressed, the sustainability discussion and dialogue broadened to include economic development and a social agenda. In the late 1990s, initiatives included issues associated with employment, training, elimination of poverty, and eradication of sexual exploitation. Several global organizations held conferences during this period focused on these issues, including the World Tourism Organization (WTO), World Travel and Tourism Council (WTTC), and the United Nations Commission on Sustainable Development.

A logical extension of the increase in discussion and dialogue between related entities, such as governments, non-governmental organizations, private sector hospitality firms, suppliers, and destination marketing organizations, was the formalization of partnerships between these entities to achieve sustainable development goals. The late 1990s and the beginning of the new millennium saw several partnerships develop. For example, in 1997 the Caribbean Hotel & Tourism Association (CHTA) launched a program called Caribbean Alliance for Sustainable Tourism (CAST) to demonstrate the collaborative nature of its activities. In 2000, the United Nations Environment Programme (UNEP) launched the Tour Operators Initiative for Sustainable Tour Development (TOI) to assist tour operators with information about sustainability and preserving the sensitive ecosystems of a destination. These and several other partnerships highlighted the importance of working jointly to promote sustainability.

As the environmental movement evolved from preservation and conservation to incorporate a broader agenda of sustainable development, some of the leading hotel companies were quick to adopt the same view. A few of these companies incorporated sustainability into their overall mission and were able to make a case for value creation by aligning the economic benefits of adopting sustainability with the fact that it was the right thing to do. The Saunders Hotel Group in the United States was a pioneer in this area, implementing a paper recycling program in 1989 and encouraging employee engagement in sustainability programs. The Accor Group, a French company, in 1994 was one of the first hotel corporations to embrace an environmental program and has continued to grow its programs. Scandic, a hotel company based in Sweden, was a leader in sustainably designed and operated hotels; through a comprehensive training program called the "Environmental Dialogue," it incorporated sustainability through establishing policies, regularly meeting with employees, creating specific action plans, and maintaining an environmental barometer to objectively measure its environmental program.[41] Another company that adopted this broader agenda was InterContinental Hotels & Resorts, which committed funds to support the World Travel & Tourism Council's environmental programs in 1996 and introduced several environmental initiatives in their hotels. Fairmont, Taj, Marriott, and Hilton were also committed to supporting sustainable development. As evidenced by the practices of these companies, it appears that by this point the phrase "corporate social responsibility" had entered the lexicon of the hotel industry.

Further into the new millennium, several hospitality firms formed synergistic partnerships in order to ensure success for implementing eco-friendly programs. For example, in July 2008 Kimpton Hotels & Restaurants announced partnerships with Kerstin Florian, Inc., a producer of sustainable, organic, and natural spa products, and with *Cooking Light,* a wellness magazine that offers readers discounted rates at Kimpton hotels. In April 2008, the Fairmont Washington, D.C., teamed up with the World Wildlife Fund to educate students at a local high school about plants and gardening in honor of Earth Day; the event includes meeting science students and teachers, cleaning school property, and planting trees, flowers, and shrubs. This type of partnership not only directly affects the environment, but also strengthens the Fairmont brand because it shows that the company is focused on engaging the community in a good way. Marriott International, Inc., partnered with various organizations such as Amazonas Sustainable Foundation (FAS), Conservation International, International Tourism Partnership, ENERGY STAR, and

Clean Up the World in efforts to offset its carbon footprint and protect the Juma rainforest in the state of Amazonas, Brazil. Marriott has already donated $2 million and urges its guests to make donations of any size to help fund various projects that will help monitor the Juma rainforest and preserve it from illegal farming and logging, as well as implement a school and education curriculum, medical facility, community center, and more.

Given the nascent stage of sustainable development and the lack of uniform legislative codes requiring businesses to become sustainable, there have been several voluntary codes and a growth of eco labels, standards, and certification programs created in the past ten years. These include guiding principles of sustainable development by the World Travel & Tourism Council; a consumer awareness campaign for responsible travel by the International Ecotourism Society; and the "Responsible Tourism" guidelines by the Association of Independent Tour Operators.

In addition, as hospitality companies increased their measurement, reporting, and communication of their sustainable efforts, several certification programs were created to assist them. Some of the notable certifications include LEED (for design efficiency in buildings), Green Globe (for carbon footprint calculation), Green Seal (for product labeling), and Blue Flag (for beach tourism).

Sustainable Development Today: The Triple Bottom Line

This chapter has documented the story of sustainable development from its narrow base of cost containment and waste reduction to its current and much broader multi-stakeholder conceptualization. As the chapter notes, sustainable development principles have been applied by companies for many years to various degrees without labelling them as such. Some companies, following their corporate leadership agenda, may have focused more on environmental issues, while others focused on social responsibility issues. Some companies may have developed activities around these two issues, but rarely did companies incorporate both issues into programs as an integral part of their strategy. Very few executives understood that it could become not only a part of their company's strategy, but actually the foundation of it, until John Elkington translated sustainable development as a concept into a tangible business model. He introduced this to the corporate world through a paradigm of the triple bottom line (TBL), which he initially presented in a book, vividly titled *Cannibals with Forks.*[42] The foundation of the triple bottom line is a holistic approach to developing business through a strategy based on three pillars, sometimes called Profit—People—Planet:

- *Economic prosperity (profit).* Businesses are meant to make a profit and improve their bottom lines year after year, but they should conduct their business with total transparency toward all stakeholders and with ethics.

- *Social responsibility (people).* While conducting business, companies must take care of the surrounding communities, starting, obviously, with their own employees, followed by the local community, the national community, and the international community.

- *Environmental protection (planet).* The impact that any business has on the environment must be assessed and reduced as much as possible. This will have two positive immediate consequences: it will reduce the carbon footprint of the company and, by measuring and improving energy expenses, it will improve the economic bottom line.

A triple bottom line strategy is not just an opportunity, but also a true responsibility, for hotels.

A hotel consumes a lot of energy, whether it is a small resort on an island or a major urban hotel, and therefore develops a substantial carbon footprint. The U.S. Environmental Protection Agency determined that the hotel industry's energy bill came fourth in the United States after buildings, retail, and education in 2006. Additionally, hotels create much waste either directly (e.g., food, old equipment) or indirectly (e.g., customers' trash left in rooms). Being very visible actors in a city, hotels take considerable business advantage of the local community and are an integral part of its life. These points underline the fact that sustainable hospitality must become the way forward for our industry. Not only does such a strategy help hotels to better manage their costs by focusing on minimizing their impact on nature, it also helps increase their revenue. As some hotels have started to recognize, hotel clients, particularly corporations, are now more willing to offer their business to "sustainable" hotels rather than to properties that do not apply those principles.

An anticipated future scenario would be that hotel companies and the hotel industry as a whole define a common language when addressing triple bottom line objectives and the measurements necessary to benchmark their efforts. It may take another few years to get to that point, but progression is being made in that direction. Hotel companies that are starting or have recently started this journey should remember, however, that change is never easy. Sustainable development involves not merely a few programs labelled as "green," but a paradigm shift in the culture of business.

Hotels that practice sustainable development can accrue benefits including cost containment, revenue enhancement, and a positive public image, not to mention employee satisfaction. All evidence indicates that sustainable development is here to stay, as more and more stakeholders become increasingly committed to sustainable development. If the customers want it, governments require it, employees find pride in being associated with it, and certifications and standards provide measures of performance for it, can hotel companies and owners afford to be too far behind?

Endnotes

1. David Kirk, "Environmental Management in Hotels," *International Journal of Contemporary Hospitality Management* 7:6 (1995): 3–8. Accessed January 4, 2010, www.emeraldinsight.com/Insight/viewContentItem.do?contentType=Article&hdAction=ln kpdf&contentId=867136.)

2. Martha Honey, *Ecotourism and Sustainable Development: Who Owns Paradise?*, Second Edition (Washington, D.C.: Island Press, 2008).

3. Ibid.

4. Douglas H. Strong, "Milestones in California History: The Birth of the Sierra Club," *A Century of Environmental Action: The Sierra Club, 1892–1992* 71:2 (1992). Accessed April 1, 2010, www.jstor.org/stable/25158624.

5. David. M. Stipanuk, "The U.S. Lodging Industry and the Environment: An Historical View," *Cornell Hotel and Restaurant Administration Quarterly* 37:5 (1996): 39–45.

6. Ibid.

7. Chuck Yim Gee, *International Hotels: Development and Management,* Second Edition (Lansing, Mich: American Hotel & Lodging Educational Institute, 2008).

8. David Weaver, *Sustainable Tourism: Theory and Practice* (Burlington, Mass.: Butterworth-Heinemann, 2006).

9. Ibid.

10. Stipanuk.

11. Ibid.

12. L. McEwen and J. P. Eberhard, "Hotels and the Water Crisis," *Cornell Hotel and Restaurant Administration Quarterly* 4:2 (1963): 43–57.

13. Stipanuk.

14. Harold E. Lane, "The Corporate Conscience and the Role of Business in Society," *Cornell Hotel and Restaurant Administration Quarterly* 23:3 (1982): 9–18.

15. Ibid.

16. William Cronon, foreword to *DDT,* Silent Spring, *and the Rise of Environmentalism: Classic Texts* (Seattle: University of Washington Press, 2008).

17. Jack Lewis, "The Birth of EPA," *EPA Journal* (Nov. 1985). Accessed June 14, 2010, www.epa.gov/history/topics/epa/15c.htm.

18. Weaver.

19. J. Clarence Davies and Sarah Cahill, "Environmental Implications of the Tourism Industry," Resources for the Future discussion paper (2000). Accessed April 9, 2010, www.rff.org/Publications/Pages/PublicationDetails.aspx?PublicationID=17125.

20. Jim Becker, "Look What Happened to Honolulu!" *National Geographic* 136:4 (1969): 500–531.

21. Weaver.

22. Stipanuk.

23. According to Stipanuk, with over 700 questionnaires distributed, the survey drew a response rate of over 26 percent (185 respondents). With only 11 percent of those polled responding to a similar AH&MA survey in 1994, this could indicate more interest on the part of the industry in the environment in 1977 than in the 1990s.

24. James Howard Kunstler, *The Long Emergency: Surviving the Converging Catastrophes of the Twenty-First Century* (New York: Grove Press, 2006), 22–60.

25. Stipanuk.

26. Jack J. Clark, "Facing the Energy Shortfall," *Cornell Hotel and Restaurant Administration Quarterly* 14:4 (1974): 2.

27. Jack J. Clark, "Utilities Management: Part I—'Shedding Light'," *Cornell Hotel and Restaurant Administration Quarterly* 16:1 (1975): 19–23.

28. Azilah Kasim and Cezar Scarlat, "Business Environmental Responsibility in the Hospitality Industry," *Management* 2:1 (2007): 5–23.

29. E. Boo, "The Ecotourism Boom: Planning for Development and Management," Wild Lands and Human Needs Technical Paper Series (Washington, D.C.: World Wildlife Fund, 1992).

30. K. Brandon, "Ecotourism and Conservation: A Review of Key Issues," Environmental Department Working Papers 33 (Washington, D.C.: The World Bank, 1996).

31. Bill Bramwell and Bernard Lane, "Sustainable Tourism: An Evolving Global Approach," *Journal of Sustainable Tourism* 1:1 (1993): 1–5.

32. International Union for Conservation of Nature (IUCN), United Nations Environment Programme (UNEP), and World Wildlife Fund (WWF), "The World Conservation Strategy: Living Resource Conservation for Sustainable Development" (Gland, Switzerland: 1980).

33. Philip Sloan, Willy Legrand, and Joseph S. Chen, *Sustainability in the Hospitality Industry* (New York: Butterworth-Heinemann, 2009).

34. Weaver.

35. Victor T. C. Middleton and Rebecca Hawkins, *Sustainable Tourism: A Marketing Perspective* (Burlington, Mass.: Butterworth-Heinemann, 1998).

36. See http://unfccc.int/kyoto_protocol/items/2830.php.

37. David M. Stipanuk and Jack D. Ninemeier, "The Future of the U.S. Lodging Industry and the Environment," *Cornell Hotel and Restaurant Administration Quarterly* 37:6 (1996): 74–83.

38. See www.tourismpartnership.org.

39. See www.ecotourism.org.

40. Karyn Strauss and Derek Gale, "The Growth of Green," *Hotels* (May 2006).

41. Paulina Bohdanowicz, Branko Simanic, and Ivo Martinac, "Environmental Training and Measures at Scandic Hotels, Sweden," Research paper presented at B.E.S.T. Sustainable Tourism Think Tank IV, "Sustainability and Mass Destinations: Challenges and Possibilities," July 1–4, 2004, Esbjerg, Denmark.

42. John Elkington, *Cannibals with Forks: The Triple Bottom Line of 21st Century Business* (Oxford: Capstone Publishing Limited, 1997).

2

Trends in Sustainability Regulation

By Jared Eigerman

*Based in Boston, **Jared Eigerman** is Senior Counsel at Goulston & Storrs, P.C., which also has offices in New York City, Washington, D.C., and Beijing, China. Mr. Eigerman focuses his practice on real estate development and land use law, with particular focus on complex urban projects and sustainable development. Prior to joining the firm, Mr. Eigerman practiced in San Francisco, first as a Deputy City Attorney and later representing the developers of large infill projects. His memberships include the American Planning Association, the Urban Land Institute, and the state bars of California and Massachusetts. Mr. Eigerman co-chairs the Legislation & Public Policy Committee of the Boston Bar Association's Real Estate Section. He also serves on the board of directors for Boston Street Lab, a nonprofit producer of temporary cultural and civic programs in Boston, including the new Chinatown Storefront Library.*

Mr. Eigerman holds a J.D., cum laude, *from the University of California, Hastings College of the Law, where he concentrated in public interest and served as an editor of the* Hastings West-Northwest Journal of Environmental Law and Policy. *He holds a Master's degree in city planning from the Department of City & Regional Planning at the University of California, Berkeley, where he concentrated in land use; and an A.B,* cum laude, *from Harvard College.*

The author thanks his Goulston & Storrs colleagues Matthew J. Kiefer, Esq., and Philip Tedesco, Esq., for proofreading this chapter and suggesting several improvements.

Once motivated by altruism, the sustainable development and operation of hotels in the United States today is driven increasingly by market conditions and mandated by law. While other contributors to this book examine the business case for sustainability in the hospitality industry, this chapter focuses on regulatory trends regarding sustainability. The most striking current trend in sustainability regulation appears to be its increasing focus on addressing climate change. One conclusion is that proactive hotel owners and operators may wish to consider managing their energy supplies more carefully and increasing the energy performance of their individual assets.

Hotels provide various services in a physical facility that must already comply with regulatory requirements such as zoning ordinances, building codes, health codes, environmental laws, consumer protection laws, and securities regulations. If sustainability regulations cover the same elements, what do they really add? Perhaps it is a broader and longer viewpoint: regulators often understand sustainability as an overarching policy to manage the interaction of people with their entire environment, not just the natural environment, with a long-term view of the future.

As famously defined in the 1987 United Nations' *Report of the World Commission on Environment and Development*, "Sustainable development is development that meets the needs of the present without compromising the ability of future generations to meet their own needs." Sustainability in this sense presumes that human needs in the near term can have lasting effects on human needs in the long term. For example, filling in wetlands to create more developable land in the short term could lead to increased long-term flooding that is not easily reversed. Sustainability regulation thus aims to minimize the long-term harmful impacts of human activity. In the case of the hospitality industry, sustainability regulations require the operators of hotels and resorts to avoid the impacts of travel and lodging on future generations.

The Impact of Climate Change Legislation on Environmental Regulations

In recent years, the perceived dangers of climate change have come to dominate regulators' understanding of sustainability. From a regulator's perspective, the general premise is that greenhouse gases (GHG) contribute significantly to unwelcome changes in the world climate; human behavior, especially the burning of fossil fuels, contributes significantly to GHG emissions;[1] and the development and operation of buildings, including heating, cooling, and electricity, contributes significantly to the burning of fossil fuels.[2]

Once that logical sequence regarding climate change is posited, the regulatory consequences to the hospitality industry come into focus. In the future, for all aspects of their businesses, hotel companies should expect laws to discourage their use of fossil fuels and to encourage substitutes, including renewable energy sources and greater energy efficiency. These laws can affect not only bricks and mortar and the delivery of services to guests, but all points on the supply chain.

Mandatory reporting laws may regulate large hotel chains, or at least individual hotels that emit very large quantities of greenhouse gases. The Securities and Exchange Commission recently advised that public companies should disclose risks associated with climate change regulation. In part to better prepare for future regulations, some U.S. companies have been begun asking their suppliers and partners to report their "carbon footprints."

Meanwhile, many major U.S. cities and states and, to some degree, the federal government have adopted policies and laws to promote sustainability. Most notably, they have mandated reductions of GHG emissions. Some of the largest U.S. cities now require new construction and major renovation projects to obtain "green building" certifications of some kind, which may involve not just GHG reductions, but also other aspects of sustainability, such as water management.

While the LEED certification system is the most widely known and used, regulators are already turning to other tools. In a conscious attempt to reduce fossil fuel consumption, most states have begun tightening their building codes to demand ever-greater energy efficiency in new construction and after major renovation. Some cities, most notably New York, have begun to devise regulations for energy consumption in existing buildings, which typically are grandfathered.

Finally, while the federal government continues to debate major energy and climate change legislation, many northeastern and western states have already set up cap-and-trade regulations for the largest greenhouse emitters, such as power plants and heavy industrial processing. At present, the clearest effect on the hospitality industry is likely to be higher energy prices. Conceptually, "carbon taxes" could be imposed on every type of emitter.

Three Broad Categories of Regulatory Tools

As new information becomes available, the regulatory context for sustainability is expected to continue to evolve. Although climate change issues dominate at present, other issues around sustainability, such as storm water pollution, merit attention and could take on greater relative importance. Today, the range of regulatory tools promoting sustainability can be understood in three broad categories:

1. Reporting and disclosure

2. Development regulations

3. Carbon pricing

Within the space of this chapter, it is possible to outline only the broad trends within each of these three categories. The hope is to give hotel owners and operators enough direction to take the next steps in evaluating the associated risks.

Reporting and Disclosure

Although climate change is a global issue, municipalities were the first level of government to take it on, soon followed by states, beginning with a commitment to reduce GHG emissions. To meet their goals, governments have begun to require certain business sectors and/or large individual GHG emitters to register and report their emissions. The federal government has hinted that it may require disclosure as well. Because buildings account for a significant proportion of GHG emissions in cities, some localities have also begun to require the owners of larger commercial buildings to measure and report energy consumption at the building level. Apart from regulation, there appears to be growing pressure in the marketplace for companies to voluntarily disclose their total GHG emissions to investors and the public.

GHG Accounting Protocols. Hotels, like most commercial real estate operations, are not accustomed to complying with complex air pollution regulations. The first issue, of course, is how to calculate emissions. Although a hotel manager may have ready access to a year's worth of utility bills, he or she probably has no sense of how many gallons of fuel were burned at the property that year, let alone how many short tons of CO_2e (carbon dioxide or its equivalents) were emitted as a result.

There is no single government-mandated protocol for calculating GHG emissions. Instead, regulations may rely on a few protocols that have been developed for voluntary registration and reporting. For example, Massachusetts regulations require registrants to use the General Reporting Protocol promulgated by The Climate Registry, a nonprofit collaboration among many U.S. states and Canadian provinces.[3]

Typically, GHG accounting standards seek to measure three mutually exclusive categories of GHG emissions. *Scope 1* covers all direct GHG emissions generated by sources that the reporting entity owns or controls, such as emissions from boilers, furnaces, and vehicles. *Scope 2* covers indirect GHG emissions from the consumption of purchased electricity, heat, or steam. Whereas Scope 1 emissions occur on-site, Scope 2 emissions physically occur off-site where the electricity, heat, or steam is produced. *Scope 3* covers all other indirect GHG emissions, including employee business travel and commuting, waste disposal, and the production and transportation of supplies and services.

Because GHG emissions associated with employee travel and lodging may be included in Scope 3, hotels that are unable or unwilling to measure and report the GHG emissions may risk losing customers interested in Scope 3 emissions. Furthermore, this reporting is sometimes required by meeting planners. Therefore, one could expect companies that report their Scope 3 emissions to choose to do business with the hospitality companies able to report lower GHG emissions than their competitors.

In addition to the costs and effort necessary to reduce GHG emissions—much of which, as discussed later, being likely to be offset by energy-cost savings—compliance with mandatory registration and reporting schemes, like that in Massachusetts, can itself entail significant effort and cost. The General Reporting Protocol, for example, is an intimidating document, weighing in at over 200 pages, plus updates and clarifications.

Municipal and State Mandates. In the United States, local governments have taken the lead in addressing climate change. In 2005, the U.S. Conference of Mayors unanimously endorsed a Climate Protection Agreement.[4] Signatories committed to strive to reduce GHG emissions by at least 7 percent below 1990 levels by 2012 through actions ranging from smart growth policies to public information campaigns, and to urge their states and the federal government to enact similar policies and programs. Hundreds of mayors have signed on, and most major U.S. cities have adopted reduction targets beyond what the agreement requires. For example, New York City committed in 2006 to reduce GHG emissions by 30 percent from 2005 levels by the year 2030.[5]

Some U.S. states followed suit, commissioning studies, adopting policies, and passing legislation to require statewide reductions in aggregate GHG emissions over time. California's landmark Global Warming Solutions Act of 2006 (Assembly Bill 32)[6] required the adoption of statewide targets to reduce GHG emissions to 1990 levels by the year 2020. Analogous legislation and/or executive orders have followed in a few states, including New Jersey's Global Warming Response Act of 2007, Massachusetts' Global Warming Solutions Act of 2008, and Maryland's Greenhouse Gas Emissions Reduction Act of 2009.

At this point, the practical effects of this activity have mainly involved developing plans to achieve ambitious reduction goals and empowering the state governments to require at least the largest emitters to report their GHG emissions regularly to the state. Massachusetts provides a useful example. Beginning in 2009, facilities that emitted more than 5,000 short tons of CO_2e during 2008 had to register with the state. Beginning in 2010, registrants had to submit annual certified reports of emissions during the previous year. A very large hospitality complex, perhaps over 1.5 million square feet, could conceivably cross the yearly threshold, for example, by burning 83.1 million cubic feet of natural gas or 442,000 gallons of No. 2 fuel oil.[7]

Federally Mandated Reporting. Although the federal government has recently become more active in regulating GHG emissions, pending federal regulation is unlikely to affect hospitality facilities directly. The federal government was slow to regulate GHG emissions, largely due to resistance by the administration of President George W. Bush.

In 2009, the U.S. Environmental Protection Agency (EPA) used its authority under the Clean Air Act to require emitters of at least 25,000 metric tons of GHG per year to collect and report data to the federal government.[8] This reporting requirement is expected to cover approximately 10,000 facilities, which together account for 85 percent of GHG emissions in the United States. With such a high threshold, the U.S. EPA's mandatory reporting system is unlikely to capture any hospitality facilities.

Nevertheless, publicly traded hotel companies may be required to report their GHG emissions for a different reason. In February 2010, the Securities and Exchange Commission (SEC) issued guidance in which it applies federal disclosure rules to climate change matters. The SEC reasoned that regulatory and legislative developments regarding climate change could have a significant effect on operating and financial decisions.[9] Even companies not directly affected by climate change regulation, the SEC advised, could be indirectly affected by changing prices for goods or services provided by other companies that are affected.

Building Benchmarking. Although energy use in buildings is only one contributor to the overall GHG emissions of any given company, buildings are responsible for large portions of municipalities' total GHG emissions and are therefore the logical target of regulation for municipal regulators. Perhaps at the extreme, New York City—which has nearly one million buildings containing over five billion square feet—has found that buildings account for 70–80 percent of the city's total GHG emissions.[10] Consequently, New York and other jurisdictions have begun to require the auditing and reporting of energy consumption at the building level, often called *benchmarking*.

Adopted with three other energy-related ordinances in December 2009, New York City's Benchmarking Energy and Water Use Ordinance requires annual benchmarking of energy and water use using the EPA's Portfolio Manager tool for, among other classes of buildings, all non-city buildings that exceed 50,000 gross square feet. Covered non-city buildings have until May 1, 2011, to comply.[11] By September 1, 2012, the city will begin posting data on the Internet, starting with 2011 benchmarking data from non-residential buildings.

Portfolio Manager is an interactive energy management tool used to track and assess energy and water consumption online.[12] For many facilities, Portfolio Manager can generate a percentile score of one to 100 on the EPA's national energy performance rating system. The score is based on how the building's performance compares to similar facilities inventoried in the EPA's Commercial Buildings Energy Consumption Survey (CBECS). A score of 75 or higher means the buildings' energy performance surpasses that of 75 percent of comparable facilities and may qualify the building for the ENERGY STAR label, also administered by the EPA.[13]

New York City's ordinance was actually anticipated by statewide legislation passed in California in 2007, commonly known as Assembly Bill 1103.[14] Starting in 2011, the California law requires the owners of nonresidential buildings to release their Portfolio Manager data and ratings for the previous twelve months to parties in any commercial real estate transaction involving the sale, lease, or financing of a whole building.[15] Hotels are treated as non-residential buildings, with compliance deadlines that vary depending on whether they are owner-occupied. Washington State has also adopted a law similar to California's.[16]

As already mentioned, benchmarking energy performance can entail significant costs. Moreover, buildings that consume large amounts of energy will be the logical targets of regulatory mandates in the future. Perhaps most importantly, hotels that report their energy consumption open themselves to unaccustomed scrutiny. Even if the government does not impose penalties on the facilities that perform relatively poorly, appraisers might, thereby affecting the availability and/or cost of equity and debt. Additionally, savvy potential customers might also seek out energy benchmarking data to make their hotel choices.

Voluntary Disclosure to the Marketplace. Market pressure appears to be outstripping government reporting and disclosure regulations in the United States. Large companies, including many in the hospitality industry, face a trend in the market toward voluntarily disclosing current emissions and creating "green" strategies. Several non-profit organizations have fostered and led this market, along with powerful individual market actors like Walmart and the federal government. Exhibit 1 illustrates how a number of major hospitality companies are disclosing their emissions and internal green strategies.

An important influence is the U.K.-based Carbon Disclosure Project (CDP), which claims to maintain the largest database of corporate climate change information in the world.[17] CDP obtains its data by sending questionnaires annually to thousands of companies on behalf of 534 institutional investors holding $64 trillion in assets under management and about sixty large purchasing organizations. Last year, CDP received responses from about 2,500 companies worldwide, including 500 U.S. companies, a ten-fold increase since 2003. More than two-thirds made their reports available to the public.

Similarly, Ceres, a non-profit group dedicated to sustainability issues, announced in March 2010 that investors had filed a record ninety-five climate change resolutions against companies in various sectors, including entertainment giants MGM Mirage and Wynn Resorts. Most were filed by large public pension funds, as well as labor, foundation, religious, and other institutional investors.

Exhibit 1   **Hospitality Company Disclosures**

Company Name	Disclosure Activity
Grand Targhee Resort	Carbon Registry • Member
InterContinental Hotels Group	Carbon Disclosure Project • Answered questionnaire • Disclosed total and Scope 2 emissions
Las Vegas Sands Corp.	Ceres • Disclosed green strategy
Marriott International, Inc.	Carbon Disclosure Project • Answered questionnaire • Disclosed total, Scope 1, and Scope 2 emissions Ceres • Disclosed Scope 1 and Scope 2 emissions • Disclosed green strategy
MGM Mirage	Ceres • Disclosed green strategy
The Rezidor Hotel Group	Global Reporting Initiative • Published a report on sustainability performance
Sol Meliá Hotels & Resorts	Global Reporting Initiative • Published a report on sustainability performance
Starwood Hotels & Resorts Worldwide, Inc.	Carbon Disclosure Project • Answered questionnaire, but did not publicly disclose emissions Ceres • Disclosed green strategy
TUI AG	Global Reporting Initiative • Published a report on its sustainability performance
Disney	Carbon Disclosure Project • Answered questionnaire • Disclosed total, Scope 1, and Scope 2 emissions
Wyndham Worldwide Corp.	Carbon Disclosure Project • Provided some information but did not complete questionnaire or disclose emissions

Many of the investors are part of the Investor Network on Climate Risk (INCR), an alliance of more than ninety institutional investors with collective assets totaling more than $9 trillion, formed by Ceres.

Nevertheless, while the numbers climb, the relative share of real estate companies reporting their energy consumption, let alone their GHG emissions, remains relatively low. A recent survey of publicly traded and private real estate funds and companies worldwide, conducted on behalf of three major European pension investors, found that just 19 percent of respondents report their energy consumption; 16 percent report water consumption; and 14 percent report GHG emissions. Respondents based in Australia and Europe (especially in Sweden and the United Kingdom) were much more likely to report than U.S.-based respondents. Two strong performers in the United States, in terms of both disclosing emissions and implementing green policies, included Normandy Real Estate Partners and USAA Real Estate Company, both of which hold hotels.[18]

Some individual actors are having significant effects on the marketplace. Wal-Mart Stores, Inc., for example—which controls 8,416 retail units in fifteen different countries, employs more than 2.1 million people worldwide, and reported sales in fiscal year 2010 of $405 billion—has formally committed to be supplied entirely by renewable energy, to create zero waste, and to sell products that sustain people and the environment.[19] In February 2010, Wal-Mart pledged to eliminate 20 million metric tons of GHG emissions from its global supply chain in five years. To serve its sustainability goals, Wal-Mart has not only been measuring and acting to reduce its own GHG emission, but has also been making efforts to influence its own vendors to reduce their greenhouse gas emissions.

The federal government plays a similarly influential role. The federal government owns approximately 445,000 buildings with a total floor space of over three billion square feet, and it leases another 57,000 buildings with approximately 374 million square feet. It is also the single largest energy consumer in the United States, having spent more than $24.5 billion on electricity and fuel in 2008 alone. The federal government has an untold number of suppliers.

In October 2009, President Barack Obama issued Executive Order 13514 to establish an integrated strategy toward sustainability within the federal government itself and specifically to prioritize the reduction of GHG emissions by federal agencies.[20] Various deadlines under the order have now passed, and noticeable effects on commercial real estate can be expected to take hold soon. Among other things, the order requires that each federal agency undertaking new construction or major renovation building projects must comply with five "guiding principles" of sustainability, including optimizing energy performance.

By the end of 2010, the order affected all federal vendors and contractors. By early June 2010, all federal agencies were required to submit their targets to reduce Scope 3 GHG emissions by 2020. Again, Scope 3 includes indirect emissions, not covered by Scope 2, from sources not owned or directly controlled by a federal agency but related to agency activities, such as vendor supply, delivery services, and employee travel and commuting. Mandates for federal employees will affect the hotel industry, as federal employees' Scope 3 emissions will include the emissions of hotels where federal employees choose to stay.

Development Regulations

Development regulations, which typically take the form of zoning and building codes and mandatory reviews of the environmental impacts of new developments, may directly affect where and how hotels are built and how they are operated. New regulation, for example, may favor new hotel construction near existing infrastructure, or require the use of certain materials and systems within hotel buildings. New regulations can also affect how hotels are operated, and require the minimization or optimization of certain inputs, like fuel oil or potable water, or outputs, like solid waste and wastewater.

In the past several years, many major U.S. cities have come to require green building certification as a condition of project approval under their planning or zoning codes.[21] Currently, while planning and zoning codes are largely administered by planning staff and commissions acting in their discretion through public hearings, non-governmental third parties certify green buildings, although this unusual regulatory approach to ensure sustainable development may soon change. Green building certification may also exert market pressure on the hospitality industry to "green" their operations, as private certification organizations, as well as the federal government, seek to promote green hotels.

So-called green building codes are an alternative to certification, as they can address the same broad range of sustainability issues covered by third-party green building certification systems. Unlike certification systems, however, green building codes are applied during the review of a building permit application, which typically comes after the project has been conceptually approved under the planning and zoning codes, and without the involvement of third-party certification bodies.

Smart growth policies may incentivize mixed-use, higher-density development near existing public transportation infrastructure. Nevertheless, the stronger trend in the United States currently is to address buildings individually, rather than to mandate compact development patterns.

Green Building Certification. The dominant U.S. player in green building certification is Leadership in Energy and Environmental Design (LEED), which the U.S. Green Building Council (USGBC) created in 1993 in anticipation of sustainability regulation. The LEED Green Building Rating System has become the de facto market standard for a project developed with sustainable principles. According to USGBC, as of this writing more than 25,000 projects are currently registered for LEED certification.

LEED is a scoring system in which achieving a minimum number of "credits" entitles a project to different levels (silver, gold, etc.) of certification. There are six different categories of LEED credits, from the generally quantitative Energy and Atmosphere to the more subjective Innovation in Design. After project completion, a USGBC affiliate reviews documentation from the project proponent before deciding whether to grant certification, and at what level.

The LEED system does not mandate or offer credits that are directly tied to the reduction of GHG emissions. USGBC, however, echoes the importance placed by regulators on the problem of climate change, asserting that "the green building movement has an unprecedented opportunity to make a major contribution to new global carbon reduction targets."[22] In March 2009, the USGBC signed a memorandum of understanding with many of the largest green building organizations worldwide, including the BRE Trust, to develop a "common carbon metric."[23]

Outside the United States, there are dozens of green building certification systems that dominate specific countries, including BRE's Environmental Assessment Method (BREEAM) in the United Kingdom and CASBEE in Japan. USGBC's LEED system is the best known in the United States. In the last few years, local ordinances in several major hotel markets, such as Boston, New York, and Washington, D.C., have required new developments and major renovations to obtain LEED certification as a condition of project approval. There is no current or proposed LEED standard specific to hospitality uses as there are for other types of development. Some competing standards *are* specific to lodging, including Green Globes' Green Building Initiative and Audubon International's Audubon Green Leaf Eco-Rating Program. Others, such as Green Seal, are tailored to food service.

The Green Leaf Eco-Rating Program audits members' facilities to determine which ones exhibit environmental best practices in the areas of energy efficiency, environmental management, pollution prevention, and resource conservation. Green Leaf–rated facilities then may enter into a licensing agreement to display the Green Leaf seal on their promotional materials.[24] The group iStayGreen, an online travel website similar to Orbitz.com, features Green Leaf–rated hotels and allows customers to search only hotels that have received Green Leaf certification. Many hotels have sought this certification, including a dozen in the Orlando area alone.[25]

Likewise, the EPA has publicly encouraged travelers to stay in hotels that have received an ENERGY STAR label.[26] ENERGY STAR, which is administered by the EPA, is a relative, rather than an absolute, rating. Whereas LEED and Green Leaf rate each building individually to determine whether it is sufficiently "green," the EPA's system tracks the energy performance of hotels in its Commercial Buildings Energy Consumption Survey (CBECS) database, and awards the ENERGY STAR label to those in the top quartile. LEED standards can become more stringent as USGBC changes its standards, while ENERGY STAR can only become more stringent as hotels improve overall.

In the absence of a common regulatory standard for "green building," several major U.S. cities, including Boston and San Francisco, have incorporated LEED by reference in their zoning or building codes.[27] However, completing the LEED certification process, or even just completing a LEED checklist as Boston requires, can be expensive and time-consuming. Despite severe economic pressure and skepticism about climate change, 92 percent of respondents to the 2010 Green Building Survey felt that it is worth the time and effort to build green projects. Yet, only 62 percent thought that LEED certification was worth the time and effort, down from 77 percent two years ago.

Energy Codes. Another way for regulators to ensure that new construction is designed to operate sustainably is to adopt mandatory energy codes. For example, state building codes commonly incorporate by reference the International Energy Conservation Code (IECC), which is promulgated by the non-profit International

Code Council (ICC). Model codes promulgated by the ICC, such as the International Building Code (IBC), are used in most states as well as the District of Columbia.

The IECC affects the building shell; windows and doors; heating, ventilation, and air-conditioning; and electrical power and lighting systems. The IECC is updated every three years and becomes stricter each time. Compliance with the 2009 IECC is expected to improve energy performance by approximately 12–15 percent compared to the 2006 edition. Commercial buildings also have the option to comply with the 2009 IECC by complying with Standard 90.1 of the American Society of Heating, Refrigerating and Air-Conditioning Engineers (ASHRAE).[28]

The federal government has been using a combination of carrots and sticks to encourage states to adopt the latest editions of the IECC (2009) and ASHRAE 90.1 (2007), which are both updated every three years. Under Section 410 of the American Recovery and Reinvestment Act of 2009 (ARRA), for example, a state established its eligibility to accept certain grants from the U.S. Department of Energy (DOE) by giving written assurance that it would, among other things, adopt a commercial building energy code that met or exceeded Standard 90.1-2007.[29]

All fifty states submitted the required letters to the DOE and are well on their way to adopting the latest editions of the IECC and/or ASHRAE 90.1, or their equivalent, even if they had not used those model codes before. For example, new construction codes for the District of Columbia based on ASHRAE 90.1-2007 and exceeding the 2006 IECC by about 30 percent took effect in late December 2009.[30] Likewise, the State of New York has begun procedures to adopt the 2009 IEEC and ASHRAE 90.1 in 2010.

Although building codes tend to be uniform statewide, some states have enabling statutes that allow local jurisdictions the option of adopting more stringent energy performance requirements, called *stretch codes*, than the base energy code. Since 2009, for example, Massachusetts cities and towns have been allowed to adopt a stretch code that requires commercial buildings to perform about 20 percent better than under the IECC.[31] Because the IECC and ASHRAE 90.1 become more stringent every three years, the stretch code essentially moves up the timetable.

The incremental cost of compliance with stricter energy codes is unsettled. Some studies suggest that it is relatively small,[32] but their accuracy and particular relevance to hotels is not clear.

Based on the prevailing climate change science, regulators generally accept that there is a finite period, perhaps a few decades, in which the reduction of GHG emissions can make a difference.[33] Because new construction accounts for only about 2 percent of U.S. commercial building stock in any one year,[34] it is necessary to address existing buildings. For example, New York City has projected that approximately 85 percent of the city's energy consumption in 2030, one of its target years for GHG reductions, will come from buildings that exist today.[35] Therefore, in December 2009, New York City adopted ordinances to regulate *existing* buildings, and other cities have taken note.

Under the New York City Energy Conservation Code (NYCECC), all existing buildings must now comply fully with the Energy Conservation Construction Code of New York State (ECCCNYS) for those portions of a building or building system being added, altered, renovated, or repaired. The ECCCNYS would otherwise only apply to existing buildings when an alteration leads to the replacement within a twelve-month period of at least 50 percent of a building system.[36]

A second New York City ordinance requires private buildings that exceed 50,000 gross square feet[37] to conduct energy audits of the "base building" every ten years, and to recalibrate, or "retro-commission," building systems for optimal performance.[38] Energy efficiency reports based on decennial audits and retro-commissioning will be phased in over a period of ten years, beginning in 2013. Some deferrals are available for newer buildings, for renovated buildings that meet the new NYCECC, and based on financial hardship.

In a nod to third-party certification systems, New York's audit and retro-commissioning ordinance also exempts from mandatory audits those buildings that have carried the EPA's ENERGY STAR label for at least two of the previous three years, or that are certified under the LEED for Existing Buildings: Operations & Maintenance (LEED-EB:O&M) system. Likewise, retro-commissioning is not required for buildings that have been certified LEED-EB:O&M within two years of filing the building's energy efficiency report.[39]

As originally proposed, the audits and retro-commissioning bill would have required energy retrofits with a five-year payback at privately owned buildings. Strong opposition from owners fearful of capital costs in an era of uncertain financing led to the amendment of this provision to require reasonable capital improvements with a seven-year payback only at city-owned buildings. Even without it, the ordinances represent the most aggressive requirements applicable to existing buildings in the United States. While other regulators continue to study mandatory energy and water audits and re-commissioning, New York City—the largest U.S. market—has them in place.

A third New York City ordinance requires, with limited exceptions, non-residential buildings that are subject to the auditing and retro-commissioning ordinance to meet the NYCECC by upgrading their lighting systems at the time of renovation, and, in any case, by January 1, 2025. This ordinance also requires building owners to sub-meter for electrical use all floors larger than 10,000 gross square feet with at least one tenant space and all tenant spaces (on one or more floors) larger than 10,000 gross square feet, both excluding dwelling units.

Green Building Codes. By definition, energy codes address only that one aspect of green building. Early in 2010, the International Code Council (ICC) and the American Society of Heating, Refrigerating and Air-Conditioning Engineers (ASHRAE) each published model "green building codes" that set objective standards on the broader front addressed by green building certification systems.

The ICC's new International Green Construction Code (IGCC)[40] meshes with the ICC's other model codes, including the previously discussed IECC. While the IECC regulates energy issues, the IGCC, like the LEED green building certification systems, addresses non-energy issues, such as the use of water, indoor environment quality, and reduction in greenhouse gas emissions.

Just as one path to compliance with the IECC is through adherence to ASHRAE's Standard 90.1, compliance with the IGCC is also possible by adhering to an ASHRAE model code, Standard for the Design of High-Performance, Green Buildings (Standard 189.1),[41] which was released by ASHRAE shortly before the release of the IGCC.

No jurisdictions so far appear to have adopted the IGCC or ASHRAE Standard 189.1. California, however, has incorporated similar green building standards in its building code effective 2011 through adoption of the 2010 California Green Building Standards Code (CALGreen). In addition to regulating energy performance, CALGreen requires a 20 percent reduction in indoor water use, a diversion of at least half of construction waste from landfills, and the use of low pollutant–emitting interior finish materials.[42] In this way, while it is less exacting than the IGCC and ASHRAE Standard 189.1, CALGreen is nearly as broad.

ASHRAE, the ICC, and the USGBC worked together to develop both the IGCC and ASHRAE Standard 189.1, and the USGBC already uses ASHRAE standards in LEED. All three groups assert that the new green building codes will complement the LEED systems, not compete with them. For their part, USGBC officials describe the IGCC as setting a higher regulatory "floor" for green buildings that allows USGBC to continue to raise the "ceiling" through LEED.[43]

Hospitality companies may come to welcome the advent of green building codes. Permit-approving agencies may find them to be sufficiently strict to take the place of requiring projects, such as hotels, to achieve LEED certification, which can be costly. Moreover, with a code in place, agencies and applicants alike can apply objective, enforceable standards adopted and administered through governmental processes, rather than relying on private third parties like USGBC, which are not subject to due process requirements. Finally, postponing detailed review of a project for its "green" credentials until the building permit phase could avoid costs for projects that are rejected at the conceptual stage during planning and zoning review.[44]

On the other hand, the new green building codes could impose heavier burdens and requirements on hotel developers and owners than do LEED or the Green Leaf Eco-Rating Program. Although major cities already reference LEED for major project approvals, on either a mandatory or elective basis, until California's adoption of CALGreen there had been no requirements imposed statewide. Just as the incremental costs to hotels from stricter energy costs remains unclear, so too do the costs from CALGreen, the IGCC, and ASHRAE 189.1.

Environmental Impact Review. U.S. jurisdictions began mandating environmental impact reviews of private development in the 1970s, after the federal government adopted the National Environmental Policy Act of 1970 (NEPA).[45] The development or major renovation of hospitality facilities, like all significant development, is likely to require environmental impact review at some level of government.

NEPA and its state analogues, such as the California Environmental Quality Act (CEQA), actually regulate permit-approving agencies, not permit applicants, by requiring government decision-makers to become fully informed of the potential environmental effects resulting from permit approval. Although such laws normally require the reviewing agency to impose mitigation or make special findings on projects expected to lead to significant environmental affects, permit approval is generally still allowed.

Environmental laws are increasingly requiring specific review of issues regarding climate change, with a particular emphasis on greenhouse gas emissions. For example, CEQA has provisionally required such analysis for several years, and, after an extensive comment process, comprehensive amendments to the CEQA regulations to account for climate change and GHG emissions went into effect in March 2010.[46] In February 2010, the federal government issued draft NEPA guidance directing federal agencies to consider climate change issues, at least for those projects reasonably anticipated to cause direct emissions of at least 25,000 metric tons of CO_2e annually.[47]

Smart Growth. Years before the terms *sustainability* and *climate change* found their way into zoning codes and state law, government regulators had been promoting *smart growth.* Smart growth is an urban planning approach that favors compact, mixed-use development proximate to existing urbanized areas, often including affordable housing, in place of the dispersed, auto-oriented development patterns commonly known as urban sprawl.[48]

Smart growth policies endure in many major states and cities, and the Obama Administration has embraced them at the federal level.[49] The apparent trend, however, is for smart growth to enjoy lesser emphasis than building-by-building regulations. Smart growth regulations can take many forms, including locally imposed urban growth boundaries beyond which non-commercial development or utility service will not be provided,[50] and statutes that incentivize redevelopment within existing urban cores.[51] Carrots are more common than sticks.[52]

Smart growth relates to climate change, too. Roughly one-third of GHG emissions come from transportation, mostly in the form of tailpipe emissions from private automobiles. Dense, transit-oriented development tends to reduce automobile trips. For example, New York City's per capita GHG emissions are less than one-third of the U.S. average,[53] and they account for only 22 percent of citywide emissions. More than 60 percent of New York City commuters use public transit or walk, a far higher proportion than in most U.S. cities.[54] Also, extending electrical service to areas far from generation leads to increased GHG emissions because some power is inevitably lost when transmitted over lines.[55] More compact development minimizes "line loss."

California is thought to have the most aggressive smart growth policies tied to climate change. Adopted in 2008, Senate Bill 375 requires the California's Air Resources Board (ARB) to set regional targets for 2020 and 2035 for automobile emissions, in order to help the state achieve its goals under Assembly Bill 32, described previously.[56] To hit those vehicle emissions goals, Senate Bill 375 requires metropolitan planning organizations, in conjunction with the ARB, to make planning and funding choices to reduce vehicle trips. The law has had few real results so far.[57]

Some green building certification systems also tackle smart growth. In 2009, USGBC, the Congress for the New Urbanism, and the Natural Resources Defense Council introduced LEED for Neighborhood Development (LEED-ND). LEED-ND integrates principles of green building, the New Urbanist design movement, and smart growth.[58] Likewise, the new green building codes require "greenfield" development to be proximate to transit and/or services.[59]

Smart growth policies can be a positive or a negative for a hospitality company, depending on its particular strategy. For example, government aid may be available to construct or redevelop hotels located in downtown neighborhoods, where other complementary uses likely already exist and where transit density is likely to be highest. On the other hand, hotel chains that emphasize outlying locations may find it more difficult to obtain land use approvals in jurisdictions with smart growth policies. Likewise, lodging that taps convention business benefits from agglomerations; isolated resorts (including ecotourism, ironically) do not.

Carbon Pricing

An obvious way for regulators to discourage GHG emissions is to increase the cost associated with them, often called *carbon pricing*. So far, carbon pricing regulations have targeted only the very largest emitters. Hotels are unlikely to experience carbon pricing directly; rather, the likely effect on the hospitality industry from carbon pricing is an increase in the cost of energy.

Carbon Tax. Some economists argue that the most economically efficient approach to carbon pricing would be to impose a tax on the emission of each unit at a value equal to the harm it does to the climate.[60] In this perfect world of internalized costs, buying a gallon of gasoline, for example, would entail paying a tax on the amount of CO_2e associated with its production and consumption. To date, governments in the United States have not attempted carbon taxation meaningfully. Nevertheless, carbon taxes remain part of policy debates.

Cap and Trade. Carbon pricing does exist in the form of *cap-and-trade* systems. Currently, the largest carbon trading system in the world is the European Union's Emission Trading System (EU ETS), started in 2005. EU ETS covers more than 10,000 installations in the energy and industrial sectors, which are collectively responsible for almost 40 percent of its total GHG emissions.[61]

Under cap-and-trade, the government sets a total cap on GHG emissions by all regulated emitters for a given period of time.[62] It then allocates *allowances* for the trading period to each regulated facility. At the end of the period, each facility must surrender allowances equivalent to its actual emissions during that period. The government can influence the system by manipulating the cap and the allowances, both of which decrease over time.

To keep their emissions balanced with allowances, facilities subject to cap-and-trade regulations may reduce their emissions, perhaps by investing in more efficient technology or using less carbon-intensive energy sources, and/or buying extra allowances on the regulated market. A facility with fewer emissions than allowances can sell (trade) its excess on a regulated market.

For decades, the United States has used a cap-and-trade system to regulate air pollutants that contribute to acid rain, such as sodium dioxide.[63] In summer 2009, the U.S. House of Representatives passed a bill that would create a national cap-and-trade system for other greenhouse gases, including carbon dioxide.[64] As of this writing, the U.S. Senate is considering the matter.

Several U.S. states also have cap-and-trade systems in place. Formed in 2007, the Western Climate Initiative includes seven U.S. states (including California) and four Canadian provinces.[65] The Regional Greenhouse Gas Initiative (RGGI), involving ten northeastern and mid-Atlantic states (including New York) and three Canadian provinces, led to the first auction of allowances in member states during September 2008.[66]

Neither the existing regional cap-and-trade systems nor the various federal proposals affect individual hotels. Rather, the required participants have been the biggest GHG emitters, such as power companies and certain industrial concerns like cement manufacturers. A cap-and-trade system could be designed and implemented to include a much broader set of companies.

In April 2010, the United Kingdom began its new Carbon Reduction Commitment (CRC) Energy Efficiency Scheme. The scheme is compulsory for organizations that consumed over 6,000 mWh of half-hourly metered electricity during 2008, which equates to a yearly electricity bill of approximately $750,000. It is thought that this will capture approximately 5,000 of the United Kingdom's largest organizations, including supermarkets, banks, property management companies, government departments, hotel groups, food retail chains, and local authorities.

The United Kingdom's new scheme is consciously designed to regulate low energy–intensive emitters of greenhouse gases that are not captured by the EU ETS. In the United States, federal and state regulators are watching the CRC with interest, and hospitality companies should as well. In addition to compelling large emitters of GHG gases to report their emissions to the federal government, the EPA has asserted its authority under the Clean Air Act to regulate such emissions, perhaps under a cap-and-trade system. To date, the EPA has taken extraordinary steps to ensure that only the very largest emitters will be covered.[67]

Voluntary Markets. As with the disclosure of sustainability practices, especially GHG emissions, the private market is somewhat ahead of the regulators in the field of carbon pricing. Founded in 2003, two years before the EU ETS, the voluntary Chicago Climate Exchange (CCX) is today the largest market for trading carbon allowances in North America.[68] CCX members make voluntary but legally binding commitments to meet annual GHG emission reduction targets. As in any cap-and-trade regime, emitters who reduce emissions below their targets have surplus allowances to sell or bank. Those who emit more than their targets must buy tradeable packages of allowances and offsets. Some CCX members are involved in hospitality, including the Aspen Skiing Company.

Conclusion

Sustainability is about more than just mitigating climate change. Meeting "the needs of the present without compromising the ability of future generations to meet their own needs" can also require regulating economic activity to ensure a host of other public goods, such as clean air and water, adequate food supply, and even social equity. Nevertheless, what is most remarkable about sustainability *regulation* in the United States is its central concern with climate change. Moreover, regulators tend to favor addressing climate change by focusing on greenhouse emissions.

For now, carbon pricing tools, like cap-and-trade, and government mandates to report greenhouse emissions have yet to target hospitality companies or hotel assets. Nevertheless, there is a significant risk of indirect effects on the industry from carbon pricing in the form of increased energy costs. Also, larger (especially publicly traded) hospitality companies are likely to feel pressure to disclose their GHG emissions voluntarily, especially if a significant share of their guests are employed by companies that disclose their emissions.

Meanwhile, agencies regulating major markets, including California and New York City, have begun to require the owners of large commercial properties, including hotels, to measure and report their energy consumption. Some laws require energy consumption data to be collected and made public at regular intervals. Others require owners to disclose the information to prospective buyers, investors, lenders, and occupants.

This trend can be expected to continue, especially as the market becomes more sophisticated in terms of evaluating energy consumption at buildings to predict operational costs, GHG emissions, and, eventually, asset value. The presumption is that buildings that consume comparatively less energy are not only less costly to owners and occupants, but have less of an impact on the environment because they have fewer GHG emissions, and so are more sustainable.

Development regulations have direct effects on the hospitality industry, just as they do on all real estate sectors. Virtually every populous state in the United States has already or will soon adopt stricter energy performance codes, usually the International Energy Conservation Code and/or ASHRAE Standard 90.1, both of which become more exacting every three years. Again, the goal is to reduce energy consumption, thereby minimizing GHG emissions. More aggressive jurisdictions may adopt comprehensive "green building codes," such as the IGCC or ASHRAE 189.1

To protect against the risks posed by sustainability regulation, the most obvious action for hospitality companies is to investigate measurement and tracking of the energy consumption and greenhouse gas emissions associated with their businesses. Regardless of the business case for improving energy efficiency and reducing GHG emissions, regulatory trends appear to make these efforts worth the time and expense.

Endnotes

1. In 2008, over 85 percent of energy consumed in the United States came from petroleum, natural gas, or coal. See U.S. Energy Information Agency, *Renewable Energy Consumption and Electricity 2008 Preliminary Statistics*, Table 1: U.S. Energy Consumption by Energy Source, 2004-2008 (July 2009), available at www.eia.doe.gov/cneaf/alternate/page/renew_energy_consump/rea_prereport.html.

2. Worldwide, buildings consume approximately 30–40 percent of final energy use, and they account for approximately 40 percent of GHG emissions. See World Business Council for Sustainable Development, *Transforming the Market: Energy Efficiency in Buildings* (2009), 16, available at www.wbcsd.org/DocRoot/HtQXNjP1wUMPVlnQD-mDx/91719_EEBReport_WEB.pdf. "Final energy use" means consumptions by end users. In New York City, buildings are responsible for approximately 75 percent of

GHG emissions. See PlaNYC, *Inventory of New York City Greenhouse Gas Emissions: September 2009* (Sept. 2009), available at www.nyc.gov/html/planyc2030/downloads/pdf/greenhousegas_2009.pdf.

3. 310 C.M.R. 7.71(5)(c). See The Climate Registry, http://www.theclimateregistry.org/. In turn, The Climate Registry's protocol draws from the World Resources Institute and the World Business Council for Sustainable Development's Greenhouse Gas Protocol. The Climate Registry, *General Reporting Protocol* 32 (May 2008), available at www.theclimateregistry.org/downloads/GRP.pdf.

4. *The U.S. Mayors Climate Protection Agreement* (Chicago: 2005), available at http://usmayors.org/climateprotection/documents/mcpAgreement.pdf.

5. See PlaNYC's "Greenhouse Gas Emissions Inventory" at www.nyc.gov/html/planyc2030/html/emissions/emissions.shtml.

6. The full text of Assembly Bill No. 32 is available at www.arb.ca.gov/cc/docs/ab32text.pdf.

7. See the Massachusetts Department of Environmental Protection's "Mandatory Reporting of Greenhouse Gas Emissions to a Regional Registry" (Dec. 29, 2008), available at www.mass.gov/dep/service/regulations/771tsd.pdf.

8. See the Environmental Protection Agency's *Mandatory Reporting of Greenhouse Gases; Final Rule* 74, no. 209 (Oct. 30, 2009).

9. Securities and Exchange Commission, *Commission Guidance Regarding Disclosure Related to Climate Change* 75 (Feb. 8, 2010).

10. PlaNYC, *Inventory of New York City Greenhouse Gas Emissions: September 2009* (Sept. 2009), available at www.nyc.gov/html/planyc2030/downloads/pdf/greenhousegas_2009.pdf.

11. Where a non-residential rental space is separately metered, the building owner must ask for and the tenant must provide annual energy use data for the rented space.

12. See Energy Star's "Portfolio Manager Overview" at www.energystar.gov/index.cfm?c=evaluate_ performance.bus_portfoliomanager. Many hotel companies participate in the ENERGY STAR program. See also the EPA's *ENERGY STAR® Building Manual*, Chapter 12: Facility Type: Hotels and Motels.

13. See "The Energy Star for Buildings & Manufacturing Plants" at www.energystar.gov/index.cfm?c=business.bus_bldgs.

14. California Public Resources Code §25402.10 (2007).

15. Assembly Bill 531 (2009) charged the California Energy Commission to establish the deadline. See the California Energy Commission's *Draft Regulations Implementing AB 1103 (2007)* (2009), accessed at www.energy.ca.gov/2009publications/CEC-400-2009-011/CEC-400-2009-011-SD.pdf.

16. See Chapter 423, Washington Laws of 2009 (Senate Bill 5854), available at http://apps.leg.wa.gov/documents/WSLdocs/2009-10/Pdf/Bills/Session%20Law%202009/5854-S2.SL.pdf. The statute also bars state agencies from entering into a new lease or lease renewal for a building with a National Energy Performance Rating System score below 75 unless a preliminary audit has been conducted within the last two years, and the owner agrees to perform an investment grade audit and implement cost-effective energy conservation measures within the first two years of the lease agreement. (ibid. §8(7).)

17. See the Carbon Disclosure Project's website at www.cdproject.net/en-US/Pages/HomePage.aspx.

18. N. Kok, P. Eichholtz, R. Bauer, and P. Peneda, "Environmental Performance: A Global Perspective on Commercial Real Estate" (Maastricht University, Netherlands: 2010), available at www.uss.co.uk/Documents/Launch%20of%20Report%20PPT%20NK%20(2).pdf. One hundred ninety-eight funds and companies responded out of 700 surveyed. Author Professor Nils Kok has acknowledged that the percentages might have been even lower with a higher response rate. *(Investments & Pensions Europe,* Jan. 22, 2010.)

19. See Wal-mart's website at http://walmartstores.com/AboutUs/.

20. See "Federal Leadership in Environmental, Energy, and Economic Performance" *Federal Register* 74 no. 194 (Oct. 5, 2009), available at http://edocket.access.gpo.gov/2009/pdf/E9-24518.pdf.

21. For a survey of this trend nationwide, including case studies, see the American Institute of Architects' *Local Leaders in Sustainability: Green Building Policy in a Changing Economic Environment* (2009), available at www.aia.org/aiaucmp/groups/aia/documents/document/aiab081614.pdf.

22. The USGBC elaborates on its blog: "As the built environment accounts for 40 percent of global carbon emissions, the green building movement has an unprecedented opportunity to make a major contribution to new global carbon reduction targets. USGBC will continue to be actively involved with government delegations and non-government organizations to better understand how we can work together to show that green building represents one of the most direct, immediate and cost-effective opportunities to help tackle climate change." From the entry "COP 15 - United Nations Climate Change Conference; Dec. 7–18; Copenhagen, Denmark," *Buildings & Climate Change International Blog,* www.usgbc.org/DisplayPage.aspx?CMSPageID=2124.

23. The USGBC's November 11, 2009, press release is available at www.usgbc.org/News/PressReleaseDetails.aspx?ID=4237.

24. See Audubon International's website at http://greenleaf.auduboninternational.org/.

25. See "12 Hotels in Orlando Have Now Been Awarded the Prestigious Green Eco-Leaf Rating," *The Earth Times* (May 26, 2010), www.earthtimes.org/articles/show/12-hotels-in-orlando-have,1317011.shtml.

26. See ENERGY STAR, Buildings & Plants News Room, accessed May 2010 at www.energystar.gov/index.cfm?c=news.nr_news&news_id=http://www.energystar.gov/cms/default/index.cfm?LinkServID=E77FB9F2-96D9-EAAD-6B3C6ECF0D9E4808#c_CAE9217A-1EC9-2E06-C1F262079566962E.

27. See Boston Zoning Code, Article 37 (Green Buildings), www.bostonredevelopmentauthority.org/pdf/ZoningCode/Article37.pdf, and San Francisco Building Code, Chapter 13C (Green Building Requirements), www.amlegal.com/library/ca/sanfrancisco.shtml.

28. For a detailed comparison, see D. Conover, R. Bartlett, and M. Halverson, *Comparison of Standard 90.1-2007 and the 2009 IECC with Respect to Commercial Buildings* (December 2009), available at www.energycodes.gov/publications/research/documents/codes/90-1_iecc_comparison_final_12-16-2009.pdf.

29. See ARRA Funding Opportunity Number DE-FOA-0000052 (2009).

30. See 55 D.C. Register 013094–013493 (Dec. 26, 2008), available at http://newsroom. dc.gov/show.aspx/agency/os/section/37/release/15772/year/2008/month/12.

31. See 780 CMR Appendix 120 AA "Stretch Energy Code," available at www.mass.gov/ Eeops/docs/dps/inf/appendix_120_aa_jul09_09_final.pdf.

32. One example is the Southwest Energy Efficiency Project; *Increasing Energy Efficiency in New Buildings in the Southwest* (August 2003) is available at www.swenergy.org/ publications/ieenb/.

33. For an example, see the United Nations Environment Programme's *UNEP Year Book: New Science and Developments in Our Changing Environment* (2009), available at www.unep.org/yearbook/2009/PDF/UNEP_Year_Book_2008_EN_Full.pdf.

34. G. V. R. Holness, "Improving Energy Efficiency in Existing Buildings," *ASHRAE Journal* (Jan. 2008), available at http://findarticles.com/p/articles/mi_m5PRB/is_1_50/ ai_n25376330/.

35. PlaNYC, *A Greener, Greater New York* (April 22, 2007): 106, available at www.nyc.gov/ html/planyc2030/downloads/pdf/full_report.pdf.

36. A copy and description of this and the other New York City ordinances described in this section is available on the PlaNYC website at www.nyc.gov/html/planyc2030/ html/news/news.shtml.

37. Approximately 2 percent of the buildings in New York City (22,000) exceed 50,000 gross square feet, but together they account for nearly half of total floor space, approximately 45 percent of energy consumption, and a correspondingly high share of city-wide GHG emissions. See PlaNYC, "Greener, Greater Buildings Plan" (Dec. 2009): 4, available at www.nyc.gov/html/planyc2030/downloads/pdf/greener_greater_build-ings_final.pdf.

38. The base building excludes systems owned or maintained by tenants (other than very long-term lessees); condominium unit owners or cooperative unit shareholders, or a system for which a tenant bears maintenance responsibility; and that is within and/or exclusively serves the tenant's leased space.

39. The EPA maintains a list of state and local policies that leverage the ENERGY STAR tool at www.energystar.gov/ia/business/government/State_Local_Govts_Leveraging_ES.pdf.

40. See the "International Green Construction Code" at www.iccsafe.org/cs/igcc/pages/ default.aspx.

41. See www.ashrae.org/publications/page/927.

42. The energy-related provisions are strict, too. For example, similar to regulations in the European Union, CALGreen mandates inspections of energy systems for nonresidential buildings over 10,000 square feet to ensure they are operating at their maximum capacity according to their design efficiencies. See "Draft 2010 California Green Buildings Standard Code," available at www.documents.dgs.ca.gov/bsc/documents/2010/ Draft-2010-CALGreenCode.pdf.

43. "Standard 189 Integrated into New Green Construction Code," (April 1, 2010), www.buildinggreen.com/auth/article.cfm/2010/3/15/Standard-189-Integrated-into-New-Green-Construction-Code/.

44. Naturally, some green building code provisions have to be considered during conceptual design, most notably site selection.

45. See 42 U.S.C. §§4321 et seq at www.apfo.usda.gov/Internet/FSA_File/nepa_statute.pdf.

46. The updated regulations, Title 14, § 15000 et seq are available at www.ceres.ca.gov/ceqa/docs/FINAL_Text_of_Proposed_Amendemts.pdf. Massachusetts is another innovator amongst the states. The Greenhouse Gas Emissions Policy and Protocol dates from 2007, when the state determined that "damage to the environment" regulated under the Massachusetts Environmental Policy Act (MEPA) includes GHG emissions caused by projects subject to MEPA review. The protocol is available at www.env.state.ma.us/mepa/downloads/GHG%20Policy%20FINAL.pdf.

47. Nancy H. Sutley, Chair, U.S. Council on Environmental Quality, "Draft NEPA Guidance on Consideration of the Effects of Climate Change and Greenhouse Gas Emissions" (Feb. 18, 2010), available at http://ceq.hss.doe.gov/nepa/regs/Consideration_of_Effects_of_GHG_Draft_NEPA_Guidance_FINAL_02182010.pdf.

48. See "Smart Growth Principles," at www.epa.gov/smartgrowth/about_sg.htm.

49. See the "HUD-DOT-EPA Partnership for Sustainable Communities," at www.epa.gov/dced/partnership/index.html

50. One of the best known examples of an urban growth boundary is administered by the regional government for metropolitan Portland, Oregon. See "Urban Growth Boundary," at www.oregonmetro.gov/index.cfm/go/by.web/id=277.

51. For example, see M.G.L. Chapter 40R (adopted 2004) and Chapter 40S (adopted 2005) at www.mass.gov/?pageID=ehedterminal&L=3&L0=Home&L1=Community+Development&L2=Community+Planning&sid=Ehed&b=terminalcontent&f=dhcd_cd_ch40s_ch40s&csid=Ehed.

52. For a useful critique of Maryland's carrot-based approach since 1997, see R. Lewis, G.J. Knapp, and J. Sohn, "Managing Growth with Priority Funding Areas: A Good Idea Whose Time Has Yet to Come," *Journal of the American Planning Association* 75, no. 4 (2009). In 2009, Maryland adopted stronger smart growth legislation; see S. Olivetti Martin, "Maryland's Second Generation of Smart Growth," Planning (March 2010).

53. "Inventory of U.S. Greenhouse Gas Emissions and Sinks: 1990-2007," (April 2009), available at www.epa.gov/climatechange/emissions/downloads09/InventoryUS-GhG1990-2007.pdf. These figures exclude GHG emissions from aviation and shipping.

54. PlaNYC, *Inventory of New York City Greenhouse Gas Emissions: September 2009* (Sept. 2009), available at www.nyc.gov/html/planyc2030/downloads/pdf/greenhouse-gas_2009.pdf.

55. See "High Temperature Superconductivity," *National Transmission Grid Study* (May 2002): 63, available at www.ferc.gov/industries/electric/indus-act/transmission-grid.pdf.

56. See California Senate Bill No. 375, Chapter 728, at www.calapa.org/attachments/wysiwyg/5360/SB375final.pdf.

57. See W. Fulton, "SB 375 is Only the Beginning," *California Planning & Development Report* (Aug. 26, 2008), available at http://www.cp-dr.com/node/2106; and M. Altmaier, E. Barbour, C. Eggleton, J. Gage, J. Hayter, and A. Zahner, "Make it Work: Implementing Senate Bill 375" (Berkeley: University of California, Oct. 4, 2009), available at http://sustainablecalifornia.berkeley.edu/pubs/SB375-FULL-REPORT.pdf.

58. U.S. Green Building Council, *LEED For Neighborhood Development*, www.usgbc.org/DisplayPage.aspx?CMSPageID=148.

59. For example, see CALGreen §A5.103 at www.documents.dgs.ca.gov/bsc/documents/2010/Draft-2010-CALGreenCode.pdf; IGCC §401 at www.iccsafe.org/cs/SBTC/Documents/drafts/IgCC_First_draft-v5.pdf; and ASHRAE Standard 189.1 §5.3.1 at www.ashrae.org/publications/page/927.

60. For example, see the Congressional Budget Office's *Policy Options for Reducing CO$_2$ Emissions* (Feb. 2008), available at www.cbo.gov/ftpdocs/89xx/doc8934/02-12-Carbon.pdf.

61. See http://ec.europa.eu/environment/climat/emission/index_en.htm.

62. Ibid.

63. See Clean Air Act Amendments of 1990, §§ 401–16, 42 U.S.C. §§ 7651–51o, available at www.epa.gov/oar/caa/title4.html.

64. H.R. 2454, 111th Cong. (2009). See http://thomas.loc.gov/cgi-bin/bdquery/z?d111:H.R.2454:.

65. See the Western Climate Initiative website at www.westernclimateinitiative.org/.

66. See the Regional Greenhouse Gas Initiative website at www.rggi.org/home. The clearing price per allowances has dropped by about 50 percent since the first auction, but the participating states have realized $600 million through the seventh auction on March 10, 2010.

67. See "Prevention of Significant Deterioration and Title V Greenhouse Gas Tailoring Rule; Proposed Rule" *Federal Register* 74 no. 206 (Oct. 27, 2009)

68. See the Chicago Climate Exchange website at www.chicagoclimatex.com/index.jsf.

An Overview of Sustainable Development Standards and Certifications

By Peggy Berg

Peggy Berg, CPA, CHA, is one of the hotel industry's leading experts on hotel franchising, market analysis, financial performance, and feasibility. She is the founder of The Highland Group, Hotel Investment Advisors, Inc., a national hotel consulting firm. Ms. Berg is a founder of the Extended Stay Council of AH&LA. She is on Advisory Boards for the School of Hospitality at Georgia State University and The School of Hospitality Management at Michigan State University. She is past Chairman of the Georgia Hospitality and Travel Association and past co-chair of the AH&LA Council of Inns and Suites.

Owner of Rosedale Enterprises, LLC, and Northlake 3400, LLC, Ms. Berg has acquired, renovated, and operated the Comfort Inn Augusta and the Hampton Inn Atlanta Northlake, where she has implemented many sustainability initiatives.

Ms. Berg has a Bachelor of Science in business from The School of Hospitality Management at Michigan State University and is a Certified Public Accountant and Certified Hotel Administrator.

T HE RAPIDLY ACCELERATING TREND toward the "greening" of hotels has been accompanied by a proliferation of standards and certifications offered by profit, non-profit, and government entities. According to the CMIGreen Traveler Study 2009, "Over 40 percent of respondents looked for third-party certification to verify that a travel supplier is truly 'environmentally friendly.' However, there are presently over 350 'green' travel or hospitality certifications—and 97 percent of respondents could not name any."[1]

More and more hotel managers are keen to communicate their green footprints to the traveling public and other interested stakeholders, so understanding these benchmarks is increasingly important. Further, standards and certifications for sustainability are in a formative stage of development. Despite discussion for more than two decades, there are not yet widely recognized or broadly adopted standards or certifications. Over the next several years, we anticipate that some certifications will become dominant. However, norms, requirements, standards, guidelines, processes, and every other aspect of evaluating sustainable development will remain under discussion and subject to ongoing revision. As practices and technologies improve with regard to sustainability, standards and certifications will continue to be upgraded.

There is broad agreement that the hospitality industry needs standards and certifications with regard to sustainable practices. It is reasonable to expect that this discussion will advance throughout the next few years. In the meantime, hotels and consumers are testing sustainable practices. They will readily adapt to some and reject others. As the process matures, sustainable practices will become easier to identify and understand. They will be more pervasive, resources will be readily available for implementation, and certification will become more standardized. However, in this period of transition, hotel operators and owners need unbiased guidance and resources to provide them with a basis upon which to decide which certifications are best for their properties. The purpose of this chapter is to assist hotel owners and operators in understanding the various choices available for green certification and related programs. Exhibit 1 defines many terms used throughout this chapter.

Guidelines for Selecting a Sustainability Certification Program

As a result of the diverse array of hotel owners and operating structures, and the diverse natures of hotels, the motivation for implementing sustainability programs is different for each hotel and company. Some hotels implement sustainable practices primarily to operate their buildings more efficiently and, therefore, to save money. Others (brands in particular) promote sustainability to meet corporate marketing objectives or consumer demand for green hotels. Still others are driven by the desire to become more responsible corporate citizens. Increasingly, environmental regulations at the municipal level are an influential driver. Whatever the reason, greener business is of growing interest to hoteliers. However, translating an interest in green business into sustainable business practices is a challenge. Subscribing to a formal program simplifies the process, shortens the learning curve, provides direction, establishes a measurement benchmark, and facilitates reporting and communication of sustainability results.

The example of an energy management system illustrates the value of benchmarking and reporting programs. When a hotel installs an energy management system, technicians set up the system and leave. Without benchmarking, management does not know if the system actually reduces energy use. It may increase energy use if it is not set properly. Over time, employees and guests use the system and may reset or disconnect the energy management features. Without ongoing reporting, management does not know to what degree the system is still operational, or how to adjust the system to gain the most benefit. Formal programs can help solve the problem by facilitating staff training, reporting, and benchmarking.

Most hotels implement sustainability measures either as a cost containment tactic or market penetration strategy. The current emphasis on positioning sustainability as a marketing differentiator will soon give way to a broader differentiation between hotels that are positioned for the future and those that are not. A recognizable sustainability certification program could well become a brand of quality in the eyes of a potential guest.

Exhibit 1 Terms and Definitions

Certification: Certification refers to the confirmation of certain characteristics of an object, person, or organization. This is usually provided by some form of external assessment. Common types of certification are professional (doctor, appraiser, or CPA, for example) and product, which specifies whether a product meets minimum standards. The National Commission for Certifying Agencies (NCCA) accredits certifying organizations to ensure that certification practices are acceptable (typically meaning that an organization is competent to test and certify third parties) and that the organizations behave ethically and employ suitable quality assurance. Not all organizations that offer certifications in sustainable practices are accredited.

Code: A building code is a set of rules and laws that specify the minimum acceptable level of safety for constructed objects. The purpose of building codes is to protect public health, safety, and welfare related to the construction and occupancy of buildings and structures. Building codes will increasingly reflect community concerns about sustainability. This will directly affect hotels during development and renovation.

Guideline: A guideline is a document that streamlines processes according to a set routine; it is never mandatory. Guidelines may be issued and used by any organization (government or private) to make the actions of constituents more predictable, and to strive for higher quality. The American Hotel & Lodging Association (AH&LA) has developed sustainability guidelines that are presented in this chapter. Guidelines have been a way for the industry to approach sustainability, though they will be superseded by stronger initiatives as sustainable development gains traction.

Regulation: Regulation includes legal restrictions by government and self-regulation by industry, such as through a trade association. Legal regulation seeks to produce outcomes that might not otherwise occur, produce outcomes more slowly or more quickly, or prevent outcomes altogether. Regulations regarding air quality and water use are examples already in place; there will be more and increasingly complex regulations regarding sustainability in the future. Some of these regulations are and will be national, while others are and will be local. The patchwork of regulations and inconsistencies from one jurisdiction to another, promulgated by any of more than 90,000 government entities in the United States, from the Environmental Protection Agency (EPA) to local health departments, will be a challenge to hotel operators.

Standard: A standard is an established norm or requirement. It is usually a formal document that establishes uniform engineering or technical criteria, methods, processes, and practices. In the hotel industry, brand standards promulgated by hotel chains define physical features and operating characteristics for many hotels and are a strong influence on others. Brand standards are beginning to address sustainability, though tentatively. Only a few brands, such as the Element brand from Starwood Hotels & Resorts, have sustainability built into their standards. It is likely that brand standards will shift toward sustainable development and operations because the market and consumer preference are moving in that direction.

Sustainability programs and products run the gamut from pure green washing to highly rigorous certifications, so it is a challenge for hotel management to select an appropriate program. Features that differentiate the various programs in the market today include (1) profit or non-profit status, (2) who performs the certifications, (3) the participation in and size of a program, (4) the existence and nature of sponsoring or supporting entities, (5) the practicality of a program, and (6) the benefits derived from a program.

Some programs, such as Green Globes, are for-profit ventures owned and operated by public or privately held companies. Alternatively, the U.S. Green Building Council (USGBC), which provides Leadership in Energy and Environmental Design (LEED) certification, is a 501(c)(3) non-profit program, as are several others. Some non-profit organizations use for-profit entities to handle their inspections or parts of their programs. ENERGY STAR is a public program sponsored by the EPA and paid for with tax dollars. It is unclear whether public, private, or non-profit providers will ultimately dominate standards and certifications for sustainability. It is possible that a mixed endeavor will take the lead. Considerations in this area include credibility and cost, both of which can be affected by profit versus non-profit legal status.

Most programs begin with self (first-party) review, followed by documentation (second-party) review, then an external (third-party) audit. First-party certification is self certification. In these programs, the hotelier uses an evaluation metric provided by the certifying entity to evaluate its operation. For example, Green Key certification begins with an online assessment that hotel management accesses and completes in-house, then submits online. First-party processes are important educational tools, and are useful means of establishing a starting point and gathering information about how to proceed with sustainable development. However, first-party methods tend to be less robust as rating or certification systems than other methods.

Second-party certification includes formal completion of criteria with documentation. For example, the second phase of Sustainable Tourism Eco-Certification Program certification from Sustainable Travel International is to submit specified documentation about the property's operation. This documentation is then used to determine certification. Documenting sustainable practices is part of ongoing performance measurement and is a critical part of a successful and effective sustainability program. Second-party certification formalizes these practices. It can be an effective tool to move property management toward sustainable processes and to establish good business practices for a sustainable operation. Second-party certification is more robust than first-party certification, but does not have the credibility of third-party certification.

Third-party certification includes an on-site audit and inspection by a trained and qualified inspector whose report is submitted as part of the certification process. For example, the final stage of attaining a Green Globes rating is third-party inspection. Third-party certifications carry the costs of travel and skilled personnel. However, they are likely to be the most credible form of certification.

The size of a program and its distribution drive recognition. None of the certification programs has the kind of distribution that drives consumer recognition yet. Eventually, one or a few will become dominant and command consumer attention A few already have professional recognition. LEED, for example, has gained traction among institutional investors in office buildings and is becoming a qualifier for investment by these companies. Florida's state program has wide distribution throughout the state, and has become a selection factor for hotel guests, government travelers, groups, and referral sources. Eventually, certification will have the potential to affect such factors as qualifying for business, ability to obtain financing, and the prices at which hotels are bought and sold. However, it is unclear which certifications will have this strength.

The entities supporting a program contribute to that program's credibility and potential dominance. The United Nations (UN) played a role in Global Sustainable Tourism Criteria (GSTC), for example, while the Building Owners and Managers Association (BOMA) and the Jones Lang LaSalle real estate firm back Green Globes in Canada. Considerations in evaluating sponsorship include whether the entity has the financial strength to survive and thrive in a competitive and emerging arena, the scope to promote itself successfully nationally or internationally, and the credibility to generate consumer trust in the program.

Sustainability programs carry two kinds of costs. There are the direct cost of paying for participation in the program and the ongoing cost of meeting the sustainability criteria the program demands. Fees and inspection costs vary widely from one program to another, though they are relatively straightforward to assess. Costs of meeting the criteria to qualify for certification are more difficult to evaluate. They may run upward of hundreds of thousands of dollars for some programs. One reason these programs are still in flux is that it has been difficult to hammer out requirements that are beneficial from a sustainability perspective, but that can still be implemented as a practical matter.

The triple bottom line—yielding benefit to people, benefit to the planet, and profits for the company—is the stated goal of most sustainability programs, but it is elusive. It is important for the individual evaluating a program to be clear about the benefits and priorities targeted for a given hotel. For example, if saving money is a priority, reducing utility costs is the most likely strategy. Certification is probably not a priority in this case, but the systems, processes, and measurement tools available through sustainability programs might be excellent resources to use when reducing utility costs. Alternatively, if a green program with high visibility to guests and team members is a priority, a certification that has high public recognition and includes criteria like recycling and use of green-labeled products is likely a good choice.

Overview and Discussion of Sustainability Programs

This section presents an overview and brief description of fifteen programs (fourteen of which are summarized in Exhibit 2). State and city programs are not described individually, but are listed in Appendix A of this chapter.

ENERGY STAR

ENERGY STAR for Hospitality is a voluntary government program that provides free tools and resources for hotel owners and operators.[2] The program, sponsored

Exhibit 2   Summary of Select Sustainability Programs

Program	Cost	Certification	Website
AAA Eco Program	Listing fee	Icon in TourBook	www.aaa.com
AH&LA Green Guidelines	Free	None	www.ahla.com
ASHRAE	In development	Building Energy Quotient	www.ashrae.org
Audubon Green Leaf™ Eco-Rating Program	Annual fees vary by property size and program year	Green Leafs	greenleaf.auduboninternational.org
EcoRooms & EcoSuites	$150 application and $200 directory fees	EcoRooms listing	www.ecorooms.com
ENERGY STAR	Free	ENERGY STAR label	www.energystar.gov/hospitality
Green Globe	$750 to $5,000 annually	Green Globe	www.greenglobe.com
Green Globes	$500 to $1,000, plus $4,000 to $5,000 for assessment	Green Globes	www.thegbi.org
Green Meeting Standards (APEX)	Not yet defined	Not yet defined	www.conventionindustry.org
Green Key Eco-Rating Program	$600 annually	Green Keys	www.greenkeyglobal.com
Green Seal	$1,450 to $3,000 annually	Gold, Silver, and Bronze	www.greenseal.org
ISO 14001	Individualized	ISO	www.iso.org
LEED	$900 to $1,200, plus $0.01 to $0.045 per square foot	LEED	www.usgbc.org
Sustainable Tourism Eco-Certification Program	$300 to $2,400, plus on-site audit	Eco certification	www.sustainabletravelinternational.org

by the EPA and the Department of Energy (DOE), offers benchmarking services to encourage hotels to improve their energy efficiency. It also designates top energy performers nationwide.

The ENERGY STAR Portfolio Manager tool gives hotels a 1 to 100 score based on energy performance. To receive a score, a hotel operator provides certain operational characteristics of his or her hotel and monthly energy usage from utility bills. To score the hotel's energy efficiency, the ENERGY STAR model constructs a predicted average energy usage, then compares the hotel's actual energy usage to this prediction. The program currently relies on a construction based on the DOE's 2003 Commercial Buildings Energy Consumption Survey (CBECS). Its dataset of 142 old CBECS observations spans 178 hotel brands and 20,000 independent hotels (and their differentiated energy use) across varied climates in the United States. This makes accuracy and relevance a challenge for ENERGY STAR.

ENERGY STAR recommends a seven-step process for proper energy management:

1. Make commitment
2. Assess performance
3. Set goals
4. Create action plan
5. Implement action plan
6. Evaluate progress
7. Recognize achievements

To promote these objectives, the program's website offers details and tools, including the Energy Program Assessment Matrix. The program also offers opportunities for national recognition. Hotels that earn a score of seventy-five or higher (the top 25 percent) on the ENERGY STAR scale are eligible to apply for the ENERGY STAR label and earn a listing on the program's website. ENERGY STAR had 4,711 hotels participating as of September 2009. As of that date, 410 facilities (fewer than 9 percent of participants) had pursued recognition.

The potential importance of ENERGY STAR can be understood when one considers that energy usage is the area of sustainability getting the most attention and offering the most immediate financial return for hotels. According to the American Society of Heating, Refrigerating and Air Conditioning Engineers (ASHRAE), buildings use 40 percent of energy in developed countries. For environmental, economic, and geo-political reasons, the United States and other nations are offering tax credits and encouraging new technologies as two of several initiatives to promote energy conservation.

ENERGY STAR's prominence is demonstrated by the fact that governments in cities like Austin, Washington, D.C., San Francisco, Portland, Seattle, Louisville, Chicago, Albuquerque, and Denver, and in states like California, Hawaii, Michigan, Washington, New Mexico, New Jersey, and Pennsylvania specify ENERGY STAR or its Portfolio Manager tool in campaigns, incentive programs, and legislation. With Assembly Bill 1103, California was the first state to require the sharing of energy data with potential purchasers, financers, and leasers for select non-residential buildings. Beginning in January 2009, California utilities were required to make energy data available in a format compatible with the ENERGY STAR Portfolio Manager; many utilities automatically upload information to the tool. Energy reporting is spreading to other jurisdictions, which means that excellent benchmarking data is becoming more available. If the EPA changes its model to use these large samples of accurate and up-to-date utility data, ENERGY STAR ratings could be both relevant and valuable to participating hotels, especially because ENERGY STAR is a qualifier for some certification programs.

LEED

The LEED green building rating system is a program of the USGBC, a 501(c)(3) non-profit community of leaders "working to make green buildings available to everyone within a generation."[3] LEED comes in two versions applicable to hotels. *LEED NC* is for new construction and major renovations; *LEED EB* is for existing buildings. *LEED CI* is also available for commercial interiors; it is prevalent in the tenant improvement arena, although it may occasionally be used for hotels.

The USGBC has penetrated more deeply into the American market than any other green building program, with chapters and affiliates across the country. The USGBC's LEED reference guides and training materials are available online and in bookstores and are widely used in university, technical, and corporate settings. LEED offers some of the most in-depth technical guidance and information available. The program certifies projects and accredits professionals, extending its reach and recognition through communities of such stakeholders as architects, construction executives, contractors, building materials suppliers, and developers. As a result of its educational and technical outreach, as well as its broad-based consensus approach to ratings development, LEED is perhaps the most credible and recognized brand and resource in sustainability in the United States.

LEED is maintained through an open, consensus-based process led by committees that rely on input and review from a cross section of building and construction industry members, technical advisory groups, and other stakeholders. It is a third-party certification program and a nationally accepted benchmark for the design, construction, and operation of high-performance green buildings. LEED promotes a whole-building approach to sustainability by recognizing performance in five areas of human and environmental health:

1. Sustainable site development and management
2. Water use
3. Energy efficiency
4. Materials selection
5. Indoor environmental quality

LEED has a Hospitality Adaptations Working Group developing improvements to LEED standards applied to hotels. LEED standards are available on the USGBC website at no cost.

The USGBC develops and maintains the LEED rating system, while the Green Building Certification Institute (GBCI) administers the LEED certification program. GBCI works with nearly a dozen world-class "certification bodies" or firms accredited to International Organization for Standardization (ISO) standards to certify products and services. These certification bodies manage the review process, ascertain a building's compliance with LEED standards, and determine the level of certification for which the building qualifies. GBCI conducts independent audits to ensure the quality and consistency of certification reviews. All LEED certification applications are submitted through LEED-Online.

The GBCI also administers the LEED professional credentialing program, including exam development, application, registration, and delivery, with the goal of achieving American National Standards Institute (ANSI) accreditation. ANSI is a private, non-profit organization that oversees the development of voluntary consensus standards within the United States. It also coordinates American and international standards so that American products are viable in the international market. ANSI compliance will allow LEED rating systems to be more easily adopted by the federal government, military, and state and local governments. It will also position LEED as a national standard, which is important to many business decision-makers.

LEED membership costs $750 to $3,500. Project registration costs a flat fee of $900 for USGBC members and $1,200 for nonmembers. LEED offers free registration in the EB program for projects certified in the NC program. There is also a certification fee, based on membership status and building size, of $0.010 to $0.045 per square foot.

ASHRAE

ASHRAE publishes standards and best practices for its members and the industries in which they work. ASHRAE developed a Building Energy Quotient Program in which metrics measure both the energy a building is designed to use and the energy it actually consumes. The tool helps owners and operators to search for ways to understand their buildings' energy use and to select the most attractive targets for improvement. This third-party assessment uses trained ASHRAE member engineers, who assess commercial buildings using ASHRAE standards. The program applies solely to energy use; it does not address other aspects of sustainability. However, because of its sponsorship, this program has the potential to gain traction. It is likely to roll out most rapidly with office buildings and other large-scale commercial and government buildings.

Green Globe

Green Globe International, Inc., is a U.S.-based for-profit company; since 2008, it has been the exclusive worldwide owner of the Green Globe brand, which offers sustainability certification and benchmarking services, carbon footprint calculation and offset programs, and consulting services. The World Travel and Tourism Council (WTTC) holds 5-percent ownership in Green Globe International. Green Globe is an affiliate member of the United Nations World Tourism Organization (UNWTO) and originated at the 1992 United Nations Earth Summit. According to the Green Globe website, its accreditation "was established in 2002 to maintain quality of assessment services offered through certification bodies including SGS (worldwide), AJA (worldwide), Groupa Mendez (Mexico) and GT Certification (South America). Assessors are trained on four continents to deliver local assessments."[4]

Green Globe is ISO/IEC 17021-compliant, which means that certification is verified and audited by accredited third-party auditors. Certification is offered in five languages and draws on 248 standards, which are applied by type of certification, geographic area, and local factors. Certification is available for a variety of travel-related businesses, including hotels. Standards cover three areas: environment and energy (70 percent), corporate social responsibility (20 percent), and conservation (10 percent).

Green Globe standards are reviewed and updated to international standards twice per calendar year. Certifications can be obtained from the following Green Globe Alliance members:

- TÜV Rheinland (Europe)
- Heritage (South Africa)
- Avireal (Middle East)
- Chattanooga Green Lodging Program (United States)
- EC3 Global (Asia Pacific)
- Green Globe Mexico

Green Globe uses web-based tools for a paperless certification process. The Green Globe Index provides an immediate measuring tool. On average, a Green Globe certification takes from thirty to sixty days. Green Globe certification is based on the following documents:

- Global Partnership for Sustainable Tourism Criteria (STC Partnership)
- Baseline Criteria of the Sustainable Tourism Certification Network of the Americas
- Agenda 21 principles for sustainable development, endorsed by 182 governments at the United Nations Rio de Janeiro Earth Summit in 1992
- The Mohonk Agreement
- ISO 9001 / 14001 (International Standard Organization)
- Green Globe Standards

Annual certification fees range from $750 to $5,000 in the United States, plus third-party audit fees. Green Globe also offers a variety of fee-based marketing opportunities for its certified properties.

The Green Globe Alliance in North America includes the American Automobile Association (AAA), Travelocity, and the Chattanooga Green Lodging Program of the Greater Chattanooga Hospitality Association. Operating under the Alliance, international and regional certification organizations—including their certified hotels, resorts, tour operators, and attractions—have agreed to a universal set of certification standards. In the United States, Green Globe–certified hotels include the Crowne Plaza Atlanta Perimeter at Ravinia, Fairfield Inn & Suites Chattanooga South, Hilton Garden Inn Chattanooga, Residence Inn and Conference Center Chattanooga, Taj Campton Place in San Francisco, Taj Boston, and The Langham Boston. Green Globe is also a certification partner with the Los Angeles Green Business Certification Program.

Green Globes

Green Globes is an environmental assessment, education, and rating system. In the United States, Green Globes is owned and operated by the Green Building Initiative (GBI). In Canada, the version for existing buildings is owned and operated by BOMA Canada under the brand name BOMA BESt. All other Green Globes

Exhibit 3   Green Globes Certification Rating System

Score	Rating	Description
85–100 percent	Four Green Globes	Reserved for select buildings that serve as national or world leaders in reducing environmental impacts and in efficiency of buildings.
70–84 percent	Three Green Globes	Demonstrates leadership in energy and environmentally efficient buildings and a commitment to continual improvement.
55–69 percent	Two Green Globes	Demonstrates excellent progress in reducing environmental impacts by applying best practices in energy and environmental efficiency.
35–54 percent	One Green Globe	Demonstrates movement beyond awareness and a commitment to good energy and environmental efficiency practices.

Source: Green Building Initiative, Portland, OR.

products in Canada are owned and operated by ECD Jones Lang LaSalle. The Canadian federal government uses Green Globes; it is also the basis for the BOMA Canada Go Green Plus program.

Green Globes is a green management tool and software suite that includes an assessment protocol, rating system, and guide for integrating environmentally friendly design into both new and existing commercial buildings. It consists of the following areas:

- Green Globes New Construction, which is designed for architects, engineers, and builders for use with such projects as offices, multi-family structures, and institutional buildings such as schools.

- Green Globes Continual Improvement of Existing Buildings, which is used by owners and managers to evaluate and improve buildings' environmental performance. Based on an assessment of environmental performance, policies, and procedures, Green Globes identifies improvements to reduce energy consumption, conserve water, and minimize greenhouse gases, solid waste, emissions, and effluents.

Projects that score 35 percent or higher (on a 1,000-point scale) on the self-assessed Green Globes Continual Improvement of Existing Buildings or the Green Globes New Construction scales can schedule an independent third-party assessment that could qualify them for Green Globes rating/certification. Green Globes rating/certification is a tool that lets property owners recognize, communicate, and market the designing, building, or managing of commercial buildings in an environmentally responsible manner. See Exhibit 3 for the Green Globes certification rating system.

To complete the third-party assessment, an authorized and Green Globes–trained assessor reviews data submitted online. Using the building's construction documents, analysis documents, management policies, facility records, and other support material, the assessor reviews the completed Green Globes online questionnaire and confirms that the score is supported by documented evidence. Assessors also make site visits to walk through buildings, review additional documentation, and interview relevant staff; then, they make necessary adjustments. Users can engage a Green Globes assessor immediately following completion of the questionnaire. Buildings can claim a Green Globes rating or certification only after they have completed the two-stage process (paperwork and on-site walk-through). GBI has a personnel program that certifies its assessors, who are subject to a quality assurance protocol.

Green Globes has certified approximately 100 buildings of all types. It has not yet certified a hotel in the United States, but is interested in doing so. GBI is in the final stages of approval for a new protocol to get buildings designed and rated with an ANSI-approved standard. Green Globes affiliates include ENERGY STAR, ASHRAE, BOMA, and the American Institute of Architects (AIA).

Subscriptions, which include software and access to the Green Globes tool, data entry for the building, self evaluation on a scale of 0 to 1,000, and a report with recommendations, cost $500 for a new construction building, and $1,000 for an existing building. The tool also lets building operators evaluate the impact green initiatives would have on their Green Globes scores. The third-party assessment carries a separate fee.

Green Key Eco-Rating Program

The Green Key Eco-Rating Program is a graduated rating system that recognizes hotels, motels, and resorts committed to improving their fiscal and environmental performance. The system was developed by the non-profit Hotel Association of Canada and launched in 1997. Its design was based on input from hotel operators, engineering firms, corporate hotel brands, and the government. Designed primarily by hoteliers for hoteliers, Green Key uses language that is simple and understandable. It is a program for green operations, not materials or construction. More than 1,300 hotels in Canada, including over 90 percent of branded hotels, are reportedly participating in Green Key, and it is used as a guideline by the Canadian government. Green Key launched in the United States in August 2009; it is rapidly gaining distribution, rating thirty hotels in about six months.

The Green Key Eco-Rating Program is administered online. Once hotels register, they gain access to the audit, tools, and resources in a members' only area of the program's website. The audit's approximately 150 multiple-choice questions cover five areas (corporate environmental management, housekeeping, food and beverage operations, conference and meeting facilities, and engineering), and delve into nine aspects of sustainable hotel operations:

1. Energy conservation
2. Water conservation
3. Solid waste management
4. Hazardous waste management
5. Indoor air quality

6. Community outreach

7. Building infrastructure

8. Land use

9. Environmental management

Each question has a numeric value reflecting the environmental and social impacts of an action and its associated impact on guests, employees, management, and the local community. (Scoring for limited-service hotels is adjusted to take into account the absence of food, beverage, and meeting facilities.) Once the audit is complete, the applicant presses "submit." The system generates the hotel's Green Key rating of one to five, and sends the applicant an e-mail. This is followed by a property-specific report with performance highlights and recommendations for improvements, such as advice on reducing operating costs and environmental impacts through employee training, supply chain management, and reduced energy consumption. A plaque with the hotel's rating is also provided.

The Green Key Eco-Rating Program is a voluntary, self-administered audit designed to help a hotel determine its environmental footprint. Use of the results is at the hotel's discretion. On-site inspections are performed at no additional cost. In the United States, Green Key is a joint partnership between the Hotel Association of Canada and LRA Worldwide, a research and consulting firm that performs the on-site inspections on an independent basis.

Hoteliers might find that participation in the Green Key Eco-Rating Program offers benefits beyond the ability to assess their operations' environmental friendliness. Green Key Global has partnered with Travelocity to recognize green hotels and resorts. Travelocity includes Green Key members in its Green Hotel Directory, and tags these hotels with an "Eco Friendly Hotel" symbol in the website's hotel shopping path. Green Key is also negotiating with other services and brands, including Accor North America, which piloted Green Key in twenty hotels in 2010. Fairmont Hotels & Resorts has joined the Green Key program in the United States, while the state of Indiana is adopting the Green Key Eco-Rating Program as its official statewide environmental initiative for the lodging industry, becoming the first state to make this designation.

Audubon Green Leaf Eco-Rating Program

The Audubon Green Leaf Eco-Rating Program, which began in 1998, offers assurance that audited lodging facilities have met environmental standards. The program is jointly managed by Audubon International and GreenLeaf Environmental Communications (GEC), a for-profit partner. GEC manages membership and assigns ratings on a scale of one to five Green Leafs (with input from Audubon International), while Audubon International handles educational materials and some on-site verification. Ratings indicate a hotel's commitment to water quality, water conservation, waste minimization, resource conservation, and energy efficiency.

The Audubon Green Leaf Eco-Rating Program is based on eco efficiency, with the premise that what is good for the environment can be good for business. The

Exhibit 4   Steps to Audubon Green Leaf Certification

Stage 1: Self-Evaluation	Familiarize yourself and your staff with the program and the key aspects of environmental management for lodging facilities. Conduct a review of your current practices and identify areas to improve. When you are ready, complete the Green Leaf Survey.
Stage 2: Green Leaf Assessment	Audubon Green Leaf staff will review your survey and prepare an environmental performance report with suggestions about how to improve. Completed surveys and reports are confidential and only accessible to you and program staff.
Stage 3: Green Leaf Eco-Rating Awarded	An eco-rating is awarded based on your overall survey score. Eco-rated hotels enter into a licensing arrangement that authorizes the facility to display the trademarked Green Leaf on marketing materials.
Stage 4: Verification	Within a year of awarding your eco-rating, Audubon Green Leaf staff will direct an independent verification of your facility to assess its environmental best practices.
Stage 5: Continuous Improvement	You can increase your eco-rating! Tools are available to help you implement and expand environmental practices, including online resources and fact sheets.

Source: Audubon International, Selkirk, NY.

program combines environmental awareness and education with best management practices tailored to hotels, motels, inns, and bed-and-breakfasts. The Eco-Rating Criteria categories are: energy efficiency, resource conservation, pollution prevention, and environmental management. Steps toward achieving certification (as defined by the program) are outlined in Exhibit 4. In addition to ratings, participants receive tools that help them incorporate their environmental commitment into marketing strategies.

The program costs $100 per year for hotels with fewer than 101 rooms and $200 per year for larger hotels. Within three years of enrollment, each facility must complete the Eco-Rating process, which requires an upgraded level of membership. After completing the process, a hotel can market itself as a Green Leaf facility, paying $350 to $1,500 (pro-rated by hotel size) for the first year, and pro-rated annual costs of $175 to $750 for the second and third years. The three-year fee cycle starts again in the fourth year, when the facility is Eco-Rated again. There are fifty-three Green Leaf–rated hotels in the United States and Canada.

In conjunction with the New York State Governor's Green Hospitality & Tourism Initiative, the Green Leaf Eco-Rating Program for hotels has been selected by the New York State Hospitality & Tourism Association (NYSH&TA) as the premier environmental evaluation program for hotels, motels, inns, and bed-and-breakfasts throughout New York State.

Green Seal Environmental Leadership for Lodging Properties Program

Green Seal is an independent non-profit organization that works with manufacturers, industry sectors, purchasing groups, and governments to "green" the production and purchasing chain. Green Seal seeks to inform stakeholders about how environmental efforts can both improve their bottom lines and benefit the environment. Using a life-cycle approach, Green Seal evaluates a product or service, beginning with material extraction, continuing with manufacturing and use, and ending with recycling and disposal. Products become Green Seal–certified only after testing and evaluation during on-site visits.

To qualify for Green Seal's GS-33 certification—its environmental standard for lodging properties—a hotel must demonstrate sustainable practices in the following areas:

- Waste minimization, reuse, and recycling
- Energy efficiency, conservation, and management
- Management of freshwater resources
- Wastewater management
- Hazardous substances
- Environmentally sensitive purchasing

Certification requires an initial evaluation by Green Seal, including an on-site audit of the property, and annual monitoring to ensure ongoing compliance. Green Seal auditors are ISO 9001–certified and work directly for Green Seal. The GS-33 standard recognizes three levels of environmental achievement:

1. Bronze—Entry level, meets essential environmental leadership elements; available for only one year, after which a hotel must move up to Silver.
2. Silver—Meets a more comprehensive level of required leadership and operations.
3. Gold—Meets additional criteria demonstrating the hotel is at the forefront of environmental leadership.

Bronze certification costs $1,450 to $1,950, while Silver and Gold certifications cost $1,950 to $3,000, depending on total number of rooms. The cost of the on-site audit, except for travel expenses, is included in the certification fee.

Fifty-five hotels in seventeen states and Washington, D.C., are Green Seal–certified. The city of Chicago in particular has embraced the program, sponsoring a Green Hotels Initiative that challenges hotels to obtain Green Seal certification. As part of this initiative, twenty-five hotels were audited, and five were recently awarded Green Seal Silver certification. Twenty additional hotels have been audited and are working toward Green Seal certification. The initiative has been so successful that Chicago now has the most Green Seal–certified hotels in the nation. In addition, the Los Angeles Convention and Visitors Bureau, known as LA INC, is implementing a Green Lodging Program based on certification of local hotels to Green Seal's GS-33 standard.

STEP

Founded in 2002, Sustainable Travel International (STI) is a 501(c)(3) non-profit organization that promotes sustainable development through responsible travel. It does this by providing programs that help travelers, businesses, and destinations protect the environment, preserve cultural heritage, and promote economic development. In 2007, STI launched STEP (the Sustainable Tourism Eco-Certification Program), which it developed after consulting stakeholders from around the world. The program certifies travel companies at five levels. STI is a member of the steering committee of the GSTC partnership, and has integrated the GSTC baseline criteria (mentioned later in this chapter) into STEP.

To earn certification, applicants complete a four-step process.

- **Self Assessment.** The STEP self-assessment tool is a set of standards and related questions with weighted point values. It applies to businesses of all sizes, from large hotel chains to small bed-and-breakfasts. The self-assessment tool provides guidelines for each STEP criterion and guides applicants through the process of building and implementing a sustainability framework in the following areas:

  - Sustainable business plan and policy
  - Guest education
  - Internal support, education, training, and communications
  - Waste
  - Chemical management
  - Water management and wastewater
  - Construction
  - Purchasing and supply chain management
  - Energy and climate management
  - Ecosystem preservation
  - Community impacts and support

- **Eco Assessment.** To be eco assessed, hoteliers give STI copies of their completed self-assessment applications and documentation for the required criteria. Those who complete and submit their self assessments are eligible for a one- or two-star rating and corresponding logo.

  Eco-assessment criteria are grouped into three rows (*Incubator, Initiative,* and *Integrated*) that are awarded one, three, or nine points. Eco-certified status requires compliance with one criterion per row, as well as required criteria. Complying with more criteria increases a hotel's star rating.

- **On-Site Audit.** Following the eco assessment, a hotelier can request an on-site audit. STEP-certified assessors undertake on-site audits to verify performance and document and compare their findings with the information provided by applicants in their self assessments.

- **Evaluation and Eco Certification.** A volunteer third-party evaluation committee reviews the assessor's report and awards eco certification. Successful applicants receive "Professionally Audited" eco-certified status, three- to five-star ratings, and corresponding logos.

The self-assessment application costs $150; application processing costs range from $300 to $2,400, depending on an organization's size. Becoming eco certified incurs the additional cost of an on-site audit. Twelve hotels have been eco certified through STEP worldwide, and hundreds more are completing the STEP self-assessment process. In addition to STEP, STI offers a Luxury Eco-Certification Program (LECS), which recently certified its first hotel and has ten more in process.

EcoRooms & EcoSuites

EcoRooms & EcoSuites is a private company that lists hotels meeting criteria for ecologically responsible hotel products, practices, and principles. The company offers a self-certification program in which applicants earn certification by meeting the following criteria:

- Using Green Seal–certified (or equivalent) cleaning products in guestrooms.

- Using Green Seal–certified (or equivalent) paper products (facial and bathroom tissue) in guestrooms.

- Offering amenity dispensers or small amenity sizes in bathrooms; in the latter case, encouraging guests to take remainders home or donate them to homeless shelters.

- Implementing a linen and towel reuse program.

- Providing separate, easily identified receptacles and/or bags in which guests can deposit recyclables.

- Placing energy-efficient lighting in every applicable area.

- Using high-efficiency plumbing (1.6 or fewer gallons-per-flush for toilets, and 1.5 or fewer gallons-per-minute for sinks with water-efficient aerators).

- Designating the hotel 100-percent smoke-free.

To be considered for certification, each potential member pays a $150 application fee and a $200 directory listing fee. The EcoRooms board of advisors developed criteria for the list after considering the results of surveys completed by eco-conscious consumers. (Survey results are available on the company's website.)

APEX

Through the Convention Industry Council (CIC), the meeting and convention industry is working on best practices and standards regarding sustainability. The Accepted Practices Exchange (APEX) is the council's initiative to design voluntary standards. The initiative includes a process of gathering input from more than 2,500 stakeholders and to develop standards in nine areas.

GSTC

GSTC involves a coalition of more than forty organizations working to foster increased understanding of sustainable tourism practices and the adoption of universal sustainable tourism principles. The partnership began with the Rainforest Alliance, the United Nations Environment Programme (UNEP), the United Nations Foundation, and the UNWTO. The GSTC partnership is developing baseline criteria organized around four pillars of sustainable tourism:

1. Effective sustainability planning
2. Maximizing social and economic benefits to the local community
3. Reduction of negative impacts to cultural heritage
4. Reduction of negative impacts to environmental heritage

To develop these criteria, the partnership consulted with sustainability experts and members of the tourism industry, and reviewed more than sixty certification and voluntary sets of criteria around the globe. In all, more than 4,500 criteria have been analyzed; the resulting draft criteria have received comments from more than one thousand stakeholders.

ISO 14001

The ISO is the world's largest publisher of international standards, being a network of the standards institutes of 161 countries. Its ISO 14001 family of standards, which deals with environmental management, includes more than 18,000 standards on a variety of subjects; new standards are published every year. Several standards focus on sustainability, including standards regarding building construction, service life planning, and indoor environments. It is reasonable to expect that, over time, the ISO will issue additional standards regarding sustainability.

AAA Eco Program

To help travelers identify environmentally friendly lodging, AAA created the "eco" label. AAA does not establish environmental criteria or evaluate a property's environmental practices. Instead, its Eco Program identifies AAA-approved lodgings that are eco certified by designated government and private programs like Audubon Green Leaf, Green Globe, Green Key, LEED, ENERGY STAR, Green Seal, and select state certifications.

AAA reports a property's status as a service to members who consider sustainability when selecting lodgings. Since 2010, the "eco" icon has been highlighted in AAA's TourBook guides and in listings on the AAA website. The icon provides notice of properties certified by one or more of the AAA-recognized programs. Travelers can initiate a lodging search using the eco certification criterion on the AAA website.

AH&LA Green Guidelines

At this is being written, the AH&LA has not endorsed any sustainable development program or rating system for the hotel industry. Instead, it has established eleven minimum guidelines for going green, based on existing certification

Exhibit 5   American Hotel & Lodging Association's Green Guidelines

1. Form an Environmental Committee that is responsible for developing an Environmental Green Plan for energy, water, and solid waste use.

2. Manage the hotel's environmental performance by monitoring the electric, gas, water, and waste usage information on a monthly and annual basis.

3. Replace incandescent lamps with compact fluorescent lamps wherever possible.

4. Install digital thermostats in guestrooms and throughout the hotel.

5. Implement a towel and/or linen reuse program.

6. Install 2.5-gallons-per-minute showerheads or less in all guestroom baths and any employee shower areas.

7. Install 1.6-gallon toilets in all guestrooms.

8. Implement a recycling program—including public spaces—to the full extent available in your municipality; document your efforts.

9. Implement a recycling program for hazardous materials found in fluorescent bulbs, batteries, and lighting ballasts through licensed service providers.

10. Purchase ENERGY STAR–labeled appliances and equipment.

11. All office paper products should have 20 percent or more post-consumer-recycled content.

A comprehensive description of the eleven guidelines and fifty-eight additional guidelines can be found in the AH&LA's Green Resource Center (www.ahla.com/green.aspx). In addition, the resource center provides case studies, statistics, and related resources.

Source: American Hotel & Lodging Association, Washington, D.C.

programs like Green Seal, Green Globe, Green Key, LEED, and state programs. According to the AH&LA, its guidelines are actions hotels "should take to stake their claim as an eco-friendly establishment." The purpose of these guidelines is to provide hotel owners and operators with a framework to reduce operating costs and environmental impacts. Using these guidelines, hotels can create action plans to reduce energy, create waste reduction programs, train employees, and create more responsible purchasing programs. The guidelines are defined as "minimum" to set a low threshold for participation. Ideally, as the industry becomes greener, the guidelines would be expanded to encompass a broader range of sustainability initiatives and updated to reflect current sustainable practices. The eleven guidelines are summarized in Exhibit 5.

Conclusion

Certification is likely to be a growing feature of the sustainability movement. Currently, there is no clear direction for sustainability certification. However, a number of contenders are in operation, and the movement is gaining momentum. It is reasonable to expect that standards and certifications will move in a clear direction as they are more widely adopted and become a common feature of hotel industry operations.

Endnotes

1. CMIGreen, *Green Traveler Study 2009* (San Francisco: CMIGreen, 2009).

2. http://www.energystar.gov/hospitality.

3. "Welcome to USGBC," www.usgbc.org.

4. "Green Globe History," www.greenglobe.com/about.html.

Appendix A:

State and City Programs

More than twenty states now have some form of a green lodging program, and several cities, including Chattanooga, Los Angeles, and Chicago have programs as well. Some are full certifications with on-site inspections, while others are test programs or no more than websites with information about reducing energy use. Some are specifically designed for hotels, while others are broadly defined for commercial properties. Several state and city programs use other certifications as well, including Green Key, Green Seal, and Green Globe.

Florida's Green Lodging Program, through the Department of Environmental Protection, is the largest program in the country, with more than 614 designated Green Lodging properties. Florida originally had a robust program with on-site inspections; this was reduced to a self-certification (level 1) program. The largest and most successful government programs encourage or require State agencies to use hotels certified for sustainable practices through that state's program. Following are links to select state and city programs.

States

California:	www.travel.dgs.ca.gov/lodging/greenlodging
Connecticut:	www.ct.gov/dep/greenlodging
Delaware:	www.dnrec.delaware.gov/p2/Pages/GreenLodging.aspx
Florida:	www.dep.state.fl.us/greenlodging/
Georgia:	www.p2ad.org/documents/pp_home.html
Hawaii:	www.hawaii.gov/dbedt/info/energy/resource/greenbusiness
Illinois:	www.stayillinois.com/Green_overview.cfm
Maine:	www.visitmaine.com/travel-resources/environment/
Maryland:	www.visitmaryland.org/green/Pages/Home.aspx
Michigan:	www.michigan.gov/greenlodging
Missouri:	www.lodgingmissouri.com/green.asp
New Hampshire:	www.nhslp.org/
New York:	www.dec.ny.gov/chemical/58045.html
North Carolina:	www.p2pays.org/hospitality/
Oregon:	www.obbg.org/green.html
Pennsylvania:	www.dep.state.pa.us/dep/deputate/pollprev/Industry/hotels/
Rhode Island:	www.dem.ri.gov/programs/benviron/assist/grncert/index.htm
South Carolina:	www.greenhospitalityalliance.com/
Vermont:	www.vtgreenhotels.org/
Virginia:	www.deq.virginia.gov/p2/virginiagreen/lodging.html
Wisconsin:	www.travelgreenwisconsin.com/consumer/index.htm

Cities

Buffalo:	www.visitbuffaloniagara.com/meetingplanners/green/
Chattanooga:	www.chattanoogagreenlodging.com/

Appendix B:

Contact Information for Green Standards, Guidelines, and Certifying Organizations

American Automobile Association
1000 AAA Drive MS 50
Heathrow, FL 32746
407.444.7000
www.aaa.com

American Hotel & Lodging Association
1201 New York Avenue, NW, Suite 600
Washington, DC 20005-3931
202.289.3100
www.ahla.com

American Society of Heating, Refrigerating and Air-Conditioning Engineers
1791 Tullie Circle, NE
Atlanta, GA 30329
404.636.8400
www.ashrae.org

Convention Industry Council
http://www.conventionindustry.org/StandardsPractices/APEX.aspx/

Global Sustainable Tourism Criteria
www.sustainabletourismcriteria.org

Green Building Certification Institute
2101 L Street NW, Suite 650
Washington, DC 20037
800.795.1746
www.gbci.org

Green Building Initiative
2104 SE Morrison
Portland, OR 97214
877.424.4241
www.thegbi.org

Green Globe Certification Headquarters
703 Pier Avenue Suite B286
Hermosa Beach, CA 90254
800.915.7920
www.greenglobe.com

Green Key Eco-Rating Program
888.752.7061
www.greenkeyglobal.com

GreenLeaf Environmental Communications, Inc.
171 Nepean Street, Ste 400
Ottawa, ON K2P 0B4 Canada
613.247.1900 x 222
http://greenleaf.auduboninternational.org

GreenSeal, Inc.
1001 Connecticut Ave NW, Suite 827
Washington, DC 20036
202.872.6400
www.greenseal.org

Pineapple Hospitality, Inc. (EcoRooms® & EcoSuites™)
5988 Mid Rivers Mall Drive
St. Charles, MO 63304
636.922.2285
www.ecorooms.com

Sustainable Travel International
835 SW William Drive,
White Salmon, WA 98672
800.276.7764
www.sustainabletravelinternational.org

U.S. Green Building Council
2101 L St NW, Suite 500
Washington, DC 20037
www.usgbc.org

LEED and the Growth of Green Building in Lodging

By Marc Heisterkamp

Marc Heisterkamp is a Vice President at Bank of America focused on sustainability within corporate real estate. Marc is responsible for the sustainability of Bank of America's diverse leased portfolio of almost forty million square feet, including large offices, small offices, and banking centers. Having worked on green lease issues and been the creator and lead developer of the industry guide "Green Office Guide: Integrating LEED into Your Leasing Process," Marc is considered a leader in the field of green leases and landlord and tenant collaboration on green building.

Previously, Marc served as Director of Commercial Real Estate at the U.S. Green Building Council. In his work at USGBC, Marc managed the LEED volume certification pilot, directed outreach and relationship management with all commercial real estate vertical markets, and built relationships with major companies who collectively brought over one billion square feet of LEED registrations to the green building movement. Marc pioneered the adoption of green building practices in numerous new market sectors, including hospitality. He created the hospitality industry's first green interior design competition, Sustainable Suite, and successfully worked with key hotel brands on the integration of green design into their hotel prototypes.

Marc is a frequent speaker and has brought the green building and sustainable business message to thousands through a broad range of industry conferences and private company events.

As CONSUMER AWARENESS ON CLIMATE CHANGE and other environmental issues has increased, another trend has also occurred. The real estate sector, an area of significant environmental impact that has historically been overlooked, has started to make dramatic and largely voluntary reductions in environmental impact. In the past, real estate has seen far less environmental regulation than other more notorious sectors such as transportation and manufacturing. Yet residential and commercial buildings combined represent almost 40 percent of primary energy use in the United States—a significant and largely unregulated contributor to the climate change issue. The absence of tailpipes and smokestacks from buildings allowed real estate to avoid regulation and public scrutiny at a level that matches its impact. As we become more sophisticated about understanding all the different emissions reductions we need to make, buildings are increasingly recognized as a critical sector.

With such a significant impact on the environment, buildings pose a unique opportunity to quickly reduce carbon emissions. Unlike the transportation industry, which lacks a way to improve existing vehicles and must instead replace old, inefficient technology on an ongoing basis, buildings can be extensively improved without starting over. Since buildings are investments with lifespans of decades, if not a century or more, constant retrofitting is already a necessity to keep them relevant and performing at a high level. This provides a unique opportunity for the industry to improve upon the practices of the past, while also making sure that buildings built today are designed for higher performance.

In other environmental impacts, building construction and renovation consumes over 40 percent of raw materials globally, and 13.6 percent of all potable water gets used in the daily operation of our buildings. Virtually all non-industrial waste is generated in buildings, either during their construction or in ongoing operations. Lodging properties, which constitute 7 percent of the overall non-residential building stock and up to 18 percent of overall annual construction, are a substantial part of this impact. Green building strategies within the lodging industry provide a real opportunity to reduce this impact in a highly visible real estate sector.

Green Buildings as a Sustainable Business Solution

Green building has been adopted by many major companies across the real estate industry because, in addition to reducing environmental impact, the fundamentals of green building practices have positive financial outcomes. Reducing energy use, water use, and waste and improving building indoor air and environmental quality all have direct or indirect financial benefits. Additionally, the broader market trends show that to compete in a carbon-constrained economy, hotels will need to adapt to changing customer preferences and lower operating costs, as well as prepare for a future market- or government-imposed cost on carbon.

Operating Costs

The fundamental business case for green building begins with lower operating costs. Hospitality financial metrics are focused on revenue, specifically RevPAR (revenue per available room), yet overall profit can be increased through lower operating costs, particularly in terms of energy, water, and waste. Green buildings often reduce energy costs by 25–50 percent, consume 30–40 percent less water, and produce 50–95 percent less waste from construction and ongoing operations. Furthermore, a study done by the U.S. General Services Administration on their own green buildings showed that green buildings have 13 percent lower maintenance costs in addition to the utility savings.

The focus on lower operating costs makes green building one of relatively few triple bottom line (people, planet, profit) solutions to help mitigate climate change. The financial benefits of green building allow for widespread adoption and scalability in the marketplace. While the lodging industry tends to emphasize financial metrics surrounding revenue, opportunities to increase profit through lower operating costs are sometimes missed.

Guest Demand

The top-line financial impact of green hotels can also be compelling. There is much discussion in the industry about whether consumers will prefer or even pay more for green building. While in the past many hotel companies thought that having a green hotel or room would not appeal to guests and might even signify a lack of service or amenities, there are now numerous examples of hotels that have married green with luxury to offer full-service levels in a more environmentally sound way. Furthermore, studies and numerous anecdotal examples show that certain consumers prefer green hotels and may even pay more for them. A TripAdvisor study released in early 2009 that surveyed 1,200 travelers found that 33 percent would be willing to pay more for a certified green hotel. Yet the credibility of the green hotel is critical, as 72 percent of that same sample indicated that they felt that hotels were more likely to be merely marketing green ("greenwashing") than truly incorporating green practices.[1]

The most common question around the business case for green building is "Will a guest pay more?" But is this really the right question? By focusing simply on average daily rate (ADR), hotels might miss the overall financial benefit of a green hotel. While some guests might *not* be willing to pay more for a green hotel, they may choose that hotel over a competitor. This is particularly true with group travel, where the decision might also be driven by a company's environmental commitments. A green hotel may find that its occupancy level and overall performance improves, even if ADR does not increase.

Currently, the largest demand for green hotels comes from corporate meetings and group travel. Requests for Proposals (RFPs) for meetings and conferences now often include questions about the company's sustainability efforts, both environmental and social, as well as specific information about the performance of properties. Based on informal dialogue with six major hotel companies, corporate sales teams are seeing approximately 15–30 percent of all RFPs ask questions about overall company positioning on sustainability. A higher proportion, 30–60 percent of RFPs, includes questions about hotel environmental performance. In some cases, the hotels see wide differences among their clients; some account managers receive frequent questions about environmental performance, while some account managers never encounter these requests. For some companies, 10–30 percent of the RFPs are asking for specific metrics and certifications, such as the U.S. Green Building Council's (USGBC) Leadership in Energy and Environmental Design (LEED) program. This indicates that, while there is a trend toward verified performance, many customers are still satisfied with more general commitments to green. This is likely to change as the Convention Industry Council APEX standards for green meetings are released and used in the marketplace.

The relatively new focus on green meetings is promoted by groups such as the Green Meetings Industry Council and is spurring hotel brands and owners to offer solutions for energy, water, and waste management. Also, the USGBC has released a resource, the *Green Venue Selection Guide*, which helps meeting planners evaluate the environmental performance of a hotel or convention center.[2] Meant to be complementary to the more detailed green meeting standards, this guide helps planners pick the best facility to host a green meeting. After all, the greener a facility already is, the more successful a meeting planner can be in reducing the environmental impact of the event.

Competitive Advantages

In the office market, where green practices have progressed at a more rapid pace than in the lodging industry, the differentiation and success of green buildings has already put non-green buildings at a disadvantage. There is wide speculation that non-green buildings will actually lease at a discount compared to market rates because of their higher energy costs and lower overall marketability. While the same is not yet true for lodging properties, the strong business and leisure travel demand for green hotels may quickly put the market in a similar position.

In the office market, it is now commonly said that a building can't truly be "Class A" unless it is LEED-certified. Based on recent surveys by the American Hotel & Lodging Association (AH&LA), it appears that top-tier lodging properties may be headed in the same direction. AH&LA's 2008 Lodging Survey[3] of existing hotels showed that 32 percent of luxury and 59 percent of upper-upscale properties planned to incorporate parts of LEED in the subsequent twelve months. While the proportion of lower-service-level properties incorporating LEED was much lower, at 9–18 percent, several hotel brands have green prototypes available for new mid-scale and economy hotels. The opening of numerous new green hotels in those segments in the coming years would quickly create an impetus to improve sustainability for existing properties at those service levels. As a result, non-green buildings may become functionally obsolete if they are unable to incorporate green practices, improve performance, and make capital improvements as necessary to maintain high performance levels. Ultimately, lower financial performance of a hotel will affect the valuation of the physical asset, which should be a consideration for any developer, including developers who plan to sell the asset after it has stabilized in the market. In the past, developers with short-term ownership plans largely didn't see the financial rationale for investing in measures that would pay back in lower long-term operating costs. However, owners of non-green properties may increasingly find that buyers have lower demand for their properties, particularly as established real estate funds make environmental performance a standard part of their due diligence. Already, major investors such as Principal Global Real Estate Investors, J.P. Morgan, and General Electric have well-capitalized green investment funds or specific environmental criteria used for all potential investments and acquisitions.

Carbon, Codes, and Regulations

Although voluntary adoption of green building practices has increased greatly in recent years, there is still a critical role for green building codes and regulation to ensure that appropriate minimum standards are in place for green buildings. In the United States as of early 2010, 34 states, 36 counties, and 164 cities and towns have LEED-related legislation, executive orders, resolutions, ordinances, or policies. In many cases, jurisdictions began by mandating that all public-sector buildings needed to pursue LEED standards. Impacts on private sector owners and developers can include incentives such as expedited permitting, density bonuses, technical assistance, or tax abatements. A few jurisdictions have started requiring LEED certification for new developments by for-profit companies. This has led to some confusion in the market, as LEED is meant to be a leadership standard; it was not designed or intended to serve as building code.

In order to provide a better solution for building codes, since 2006 the American Society of Heating, Refrigerating and Air-Conditioning Engineers (ASHRAE), the Illuminating Engineering Society of North America, and the USGBC have been collaborating on a new standard, written in code language, for adoption by code jurisdictions. The new standard, geared to help provide an enforceable and holistic approach to green building code, was released in February 2010 as Standard 189.1, "Standard for the Design of High-Performance Green Buildings Except Low-Rise Residential Buildings."

Improving and better enforcing building codes is one critical way to change design and construction practices. However, codes are not a great mechanism for improving the performance of existing buildings. Government jurisdictions looking to create changes in existing buildings are largely turning to the concept of building performance labeling, in which building owners are required to benchmark the energy performance of their buildings and make that information available to potential buyers or lessees of the building. While this approach does not indicate a minimum required performance level, it does create greater transparency and, presumably, competitive pressure on owners to improve efficiency. Building performance labeling is expected to become more common in coming years, particularly in urban areas where buildings are commonly responsible for more than 80 percent of a jurisdiction's carbon footprint.

The Role of LEED Certification

While the environmental impact of buildings is now much better known and regulatory efforts have increased, the green building movement is largely still voluntary in nature. The USGBC, a non-profit organization founded in 1993, has fostered this transformation primarily through its internationally recognized third-party green building certification system, LEED. Created in 1999, LEED has become the predominant national and global certification for green building design, construction, and operations. LEED is a flexible program based on the five major environmental impact areas of buildings: site selection and management, energy, water, material use and disposal, and indoor environmental quality. An additional category captures innovation and regional priority credits. Some of these areas have minimum requirements, called prerequisites, to ensure that basic environmental performance in such areas as energy efficiency and waste management is achieved. Beyond the prerequisites, each building team has a choice about where to focus their efforts. An office building may put a greater emphasis on energy efficiency to reduce operating costs, whereas a school may choose to focus on indoor environmental quality in order to provide a stimulating and healthy learning environment for children. Similarly, in the hospitality market, an upscale property may choose to focus on strategies that will be visible and marketable to guests such as furnishings with high recycled content and Forest Stewardship Council–certified wood. By contrast, an economy property might focus more attention on energy efficiency in order to reduce operating expenses and increase profit while maintaining the same average daily rate. Due to the point totals required to achieve certification, most properties end up with numerous achievements in each credit category.

LEED sub-programs and certification criteria vary depending on the scope and use of the building. Most hotels and lodging properties will use the LEED for New Construction or LEED for Existing Buildings: Operations & Maintenance programs. Major renovations typically use the new construction rating system. All LEED rating systems work on a 100-point scale, with 10 additional points available for innovation and environmental areas that are particularly important to each U.S. geographic region. There are four levels of certification: 40 points for Certified, 50 points for Silver, 60 points for Gold, and 80 points for the highest level, Platinum.

LEED as a Market Transformation Tool

LEED is a voluntary market transformation program. While the program recognizes and certifies specific top-performing buildings, including offices, retail, schools, convention centers, and all types of lodging properties, the true purpose of the program is not simply recognition of top performers. The purpose is to create economies of scale and competitive pressures to pull the rest of the market closer to this higher level of performance. By using market pressures to increase the use of green building processes and technologies among leading companies in the industry, these solutions become more prevalent and cost-effective for everyone to use. As the market finds solutions and significantly lowers the environmental impact of buildings, the LEED program will need to adapt and use more stringent criteria. Over time, achieving LEED certification will require progressively higher performance levels, while recognizing that the goal is for the program to stay in lockstep with the performance levels that are possible and cost-effective in the market. While lower-performing buildings may never achieve LEED certification, the intention is that market forces created by certified properties will help all properties incorporate green strategies in an easier and more cost-effective way.

Third-Party Verification and Credibility

The widespread use of LEED in the real estate market has also increased the awareness and value of third-party verification. Similar to other non-environmental areas, where the thorough review and endorsement by a third party helps ensure transparency and credibility, third-party verification of green building practices helps with employee accountability as well as communication with executive leadership, employees, investors, and other stakeholders. While a building or hotel can achieve high levels of environmental performance without seeking certification through LEED or a similar program, it is less credible to discuss these unverified accomplishments publicly.

Even more important than third-party verification is the substance of the certification standard. LEED strives to be performance-based in its approach in all possible areas: it's simply not good enough to have a green practice in place if you can't quantify the actual results. For example, the hospitality industry has long been criticized for the poor implementation of linen and towel reuse programs.

While this program makes a tremendous amount of environmental and financial sense, the poor execution and lack of measurable results are problematic. Furthermore, the true focus of a performance-based standard should be the measured overall performance, allowing for a variety of strategies to increase efficiency and decrease resource use. Some luxury properties have decided not to implement linen and towel reuse programs, but have instead concentrated on the energy and water efficiency of their laundry machines and washing practices. While they could be even more efficient by also doing a reuse program, their current measured performance is actually far better than that of facilities with sporadically effective reuse programs. Measured results, not prescriptive strategies, should be the focus of any green hotel efforts at the property level. Any certification standard used should measure performance wherever possible, not just offer strategies.

This same drive for high performance is leading the top innovators in the market to work toward an ambitious goal: a building with zero environmental impact. While LEED is positioned to help a larger portion of the construction industry utilize market-ready strategies and technologies, these newer efforts are focused on innovative practices that push current limits, and ultimately will create new strategies and ways to increase performance to an even greater degree. Several significant initiatives exist, including extensive work done by the U.S. Department of Energy through the Net-Zero Commercial Building Initiative. Its goal is to achieve marketable zero-energy commercial buildings by 2025. The International Living Building Institute has launched the Living Building Challenge, an effort to raise the bar and recognize projects that achieve zero impact or even regenerative results in all areas including site, water, energy, health, materials, equity, and beauty. These efforts will continue to push the innovators in the market to create new ideas and solutions to our building challenges. Performance-based certification systems such as LEED will help provide the competitive advantage and scalability for mainstream adoption of financially viable ideas.

Framework for Improved Building Performance

LEED also helps project and management teams by providing a framework for the key areas and performance metrics that a project should address. The rating system has gone through several iterations over its ten-year existence, and the latest version, LEED 2009, serves as an improvement in making sure project teams focus on the highest-impact areas of buildings. The rating system is organized into six main environmental impact areas, and in LEED 2009, these areas are weighted according to the urgency and importance of these environmental impacts, with areas related to climate change given the highest point totals. The six impact areas are:

- *Sustainable Sites.* The Sustainable Sites credit category encourages site selection and building management practices that minimize a building's impact on ecosystems and waterways, promote regionally appropriate landscaping, reward smart transportation choices, control stormwater runoff, and reduce erosion, light pollution, heat island effect, and site maintenance-related pollution.

- *Water Efficiency.* The goal of the Water Efficiency credit category is to encourage smarter use of water, both inside and outside the building. Water reduction is typically achieved through more efficient appliances, fixtures, and fittings inside and in water-wise landscaping outside.

- *Energy Efficiency.* The Energy and Atmosphere credit category encourages a wide variety of energy strategies and measures overall energy performance. It includes commissioning; energy-use monitoring; efficient design and construction; efficient appliances, systems, and lighting; the use of renewable and clean sources of energy, generated on-site or off-site; and other innovative practices.

- *Materials and Resources.* This Materials and Resources category encourages the selection of sustainable materials, including those that are harvested and manufactured locally, contain high recycled content, and are rapidly renewable. It also promotes the reduction of waste through building and material reuse and construction waste management, as well as ongoing recycling programs.

- *Indoor Environmental Quality.* The Indoor Environmental Quality credit category promotes strategies that can improve indoor air quality and overall environmental health through low emitting–materials selection and increased ventilation, as well as promoting access to natural daylight and views.

- *Innovation in Operations.* The Innovation in Operations credit category provides additional points for projects that use new and innovative technologies, achieve performance well beyond what is required by LEED credits, or utilize green building strategies that are not specifically addressed elsewhere in LEED. This credit category also rewards projects for including a LEED Accredited Professional on the team to ensure a holistic, integrated approach to operations and maintenance.[4]

Interdependence and Flexibility of Credits

While it is tempting to simplify the environmental performance of a building into a checklist, the complexity of building design and operations makes that a significant challenge. In reality, the discrete credits within LEED are interdependent and possibly contradictory at times. For example, there are many ways that a particular material purchase can contribute to LEED materials and resources credits. However, a project may find that it is not possible to get a locally manufactured product that is also high in recycled content. Similarly, there is a well-known trade-off between increasing ventilation and energy efficiency due to the increased heating and cooling load for additional intake air. Tough choices often need to be made, and the flexibility of LEED allows for this market reality. The rating system is designed with prerequisites that must be achieved for every project, ensuring that basic environmental performance levels are met in every area. Beyond the prerequisites, the most important environmental considerations are the areas where achievement is the most cost-effective or provides the greatest financial return.

LEED-certified buildings will often excel in different areas. Two projects may have identical LEED scores, but very different means of achieving them. For example, a hotel project focused on long-term operating costs might emphasize an investment in low-flow water fixtures and a sophisticated irrigation system that cuts water use. Conversely, a property seeking to cater to environmentally conscious travelers might put a greater emphasis on environmental products that are extremely visible to guests and invest in indoor air quality in order to market the health aspects of the hotel. As long as all prerequisites are met, these strategies and other similar combinations that earn enough points in the rating system are options for LEED certification.

In terms of the critical area of energy performance, the prerequisite is set at a level that no LEED-certified property can ignore. In new construction, for example, whole-building design simulations demonstrating an efficiency of 14 percent beyond ASHRAE 90.1-2007 are required to meet the prerequisite. In existing buildings, properties must demonstrate an ENERGY STAR score of 69 or greater, indicating that they are in the top 31 percent of similar properties in the United States.

Design and Construction Considerations

Green building and LEED have spurred a key evolution in the way that the market designs and constructs buildings. The concept of integrated design has become much more prevalent. Integrated design is a much more holistic approach to development, as it emphasizes the active involvement of all stakeholders and contributors at all key steps in the process. This multidisciplinary approach has numerous benefits, including a greater alignment with the ultimate operators of the building, and continuous opportunities to adjust systems and designs based on other decisions. In a more traditional development approach, the steps of the development process are discrete, with hand-offs between architects, engineers, contractors, and other involved teams. The fragmented nature of that approach often leads to contradictory decisions or overcompensation in design due to a lack of awareness about decisions by other teams. While LEED certification can be accomplished without a fully integrated design process, the holistic approach of integrated design will likely produce the best short- and long-term results, due to the integration of building systems and efficiencies that can occur through collaboration.

Integrated design also serves as a key factor in the ultimate cost of developing a green building. Through integrated design, projects often see the potential cost premiums of green design evaporate in response to collaborative decision-making. For example, focusing on energy efficiency in relation to the building envelope and lighting may reduce the size and cost of the chiller plant. This saves up-front costs that, often more than not, make up for any incremental costs incurred for other energy efficiency measures. While real estate and construction professionals tend to overestimate the costs of green building by 300 percent, there are numerous examples of LEED-certified buildings coming in at typical budgets or at a small cost premium that will be easily recouped through savings in ongoing operational budgets.

It is important to keep in mind that the vast majority of a building's environmental impacts will occur during the operation of the building, not the initial development. There are critical areas of the development process that are one-time occurrences, such as the selection of building materials and the disposal of construction waste. However, much of the development of a green building involves infrastructure decisions that will have a long-term impact on the performance of the building, particularly in energy and water consumption. Furthermore, efficient design decisions do not always equate to efficient operational practices. While integrated design has helped the market considerably, there often remains a disconnect between the design and construction teams and the operational managers of those facilities. Therefore, it is critical that future operators of buildings be involved early in the process to ease the transition, particularly as it relates to new building systems, automation, or technologies the building employs. Furthermore, it's important to remember that LEED for New Construction certifies only a building's design and construction. A truly green facility should employ measures that will enable it to operate at a high performance level; put into place green operational practices for janitorial services, pest management, and waste management; and ultimately recertify under LEED for Existing Buildings: Operations and Maintenance.

Operations and Maintenance

While new hotels might seem the obvious place to try out new green practices, the bigger environmental and financial opportunities involve improving the performance of existing hotels. The essential first step to greening an existing hotel is to measure the current environmental performance of the property. Far too often, the race to green a property drives the implementation of strategies that might not be the optimal choices or highest-impact opportunities for a property. Many properties don't have a current or historical perspective on energy consumption, water use, or waste management metrics. All of these are essential to evaluate current performance and to decide which strategies will yield the greatest results.

Standard Operating Practices. Regardless of current performance, a number of practices are now widely available. The LEED for Existing Buildings rating system includes areas such as green cleaning, integrated pest management, and exterior and landscape management. Improvement in these areas will come through an overhaul in the building's standard operating practices. A large number of vendors will have products or practices that will meet the LEED requirements at zero or minimal additional cost. While there are possibilities for capital improvements in areas such as landscape irrigation, most improvements of this type can be done within a property's standard operating budget. There are many low- and no-cost ways to improve performance.

Waste Management. Many properties have found success in conducting a waste audit, providing them a measureable perspective on their overall waste stream and the largest opportunities for diversion. Waste diversion goes beyond recycling soda cans and office paper. In a hotel, the larger opportunities are often with food waste and other back-of-house waste streams. Additionally, a hotel should create a comprehensive waste management plan that includes a process for future renovations of the property. A room or restaurant renovation will result in a large amount of construction waste, of which 50–100 percent can be recycled in most areas.

In many ways, changes to waste management will also be changes to standard operating practices. In some cases, small investments may help launch a new or enhanced program. The biggest investment related to a basic waste diversion program is usually staff training and ongoing measurement as the infrastructure investment in recycling bins and receptacles is likely not a significant expenditure (provided that there is sufficient space on the property to collect recyclables for disposal). A food waste diversion program, such as composting, may have additional expenditures to ensure a solid infrastructure and avoid health code violations or related issues.

Energy Efficiency. In terms of system efficiency, an important first step is to perform retro-commissioning or a basic ASHRAE energy audit. These practices will help gauge the opportunities available, including low- and no-cost measures with strong financial returns. A typical energy audit could uncover extensive renovation options, such as chiller or window replacement, as well as relatively straightforward and cost-effective measures such as variable speed drives, reduced operating hours, or other parameters for immediate implementation. Often these reports uncover areas in which building systems aren't being operated as designed or have degraded in performance over time. LEED credits related to ventilation and indoor air quality should also be evaluated in this process, since energy efficiency and indoor air quality are so intertwined with the performance of the building envelope and mechanical systems.

There are also no-cost practices that can be integrated into staff training. Housekeeping staff that work in guestrooms every day can be trained to identify opportunities, such as lights left on by guests, open or leaking windows, or heating units that are operating inefficiently.

Some brands, such as Marriott, have made compact florescent bulbs (CFLs) a brand standard. This low-cost, high-return activity can actually save maintenance in the long term due to the longer life of CFLs. Furthermore, light-emitting diodes (LEDs), based on semiconductor technology, are improving significantly in quality and becoming cheaper as an easy retrofit option. The AH&LA 2010 Lodging Survey revealed that properties using energy-efficient lighting jumped from 68 percent in 2008 to 88 percent.[5]

Water Efficiency. While changing fixtures is generally a capital expense, there are simple areas of indoor water use that can result in quick savings. Faucet aerators and effective low-flow showerheads are low-cost solutions that can drastically cut water use. Water use is significant in hotel food and beverage operations. Staff training is of utmost importance to ensure careful use of water in back-of-house operations.

Capital Expenditures

Greening operations becomes significantly more challenging when the measures require capital investment. Although many green operations measures have a strong return on investment, it is often hard to secure the necessary capital outside of a planned renovation cycle. For this reason, an interior renovation or repositioning project can be an ideal opportunity to make investments that improve energy efficiency and water conservation. Built into an existing capital budget, many of the upgrades can add little to no incremental cost beyond replacement products or equipment that was already going into the space, similar to the opportunity during initial design and construction.

Off-cycle capital expenditures for greening the operations of an existing hotel can be compelling opportunities for quick financial returns, depending on the current state and performance of the building. In many cases, the highest-return items will be identified through a comprehensive retro-commissioning or energy audit process. Through a comprehensive look at the building systems and infrastructure, capital can be targeted at the most opportune investments, while making sure that the full system is considered.

Market Trends and the Future of Green Hotels

In LEED's short history, there have been some notable changes in the user base of the system. Originally, LEED was used by public-sector organizations, such as universities and governments, with long-term ownership of their buildings; they have a greater capacity to benefit from the long-term operating savings of a green building. Over time, private-sector owners of buildings, such as hoteliers, have become a larger proportion of the LEED user base, with 2007 being the year when privately owned LEED buildings surpassed the number in the public sector (see Exhibit 1). Market-wide, 67 percent of all building square footage in the United States is owned by a for-profit entity, making private-sector adoption essential for market transformation. Current LEED metrics reflect this reality, with 72 percent of all square footage registered for LEED under private sector ownership.

The lodging industry has historically been a laggard in terms of overall project registrations for LEED, but the past two years have changed those numbers dramatically. At the beginning of 2008, only 285 lodging properties had registered for LEED. By 2010, this figure had more than tripled, with just over 1,000 properties registered. Currently there are approximately 50 lodging properties with a LEED certification.

However, lodging still lags behind all other major commercial real estate asset classes with the exception of warehouses and distribution centers (see Exhibit 2). Office buildings were the initial adopters of LEED and continue to be a large proportion of registered and certified projects. Retail, multi-family, and public-sector buildings have outpaced the lodging market in terms of sheer growth. However, the past two years of early success on individual projects for brands and owners is leading to fundamental market shifts that may change these numbers dramatically in the near future.

Brand Commitments

Major drivers, such as corporate social responsibility and the repositioning of brands to appeal to a younger, more eco-conscious consumer, are creating fundamental market trends that are not yet captured in the LEED activity data. While individual property owners may be greening their new or existing properties, changes at the brand level have the opportunity to greatly affect market

Exhibit 1   Private Sector vs. Public Sector Cumulative LEED Registrations

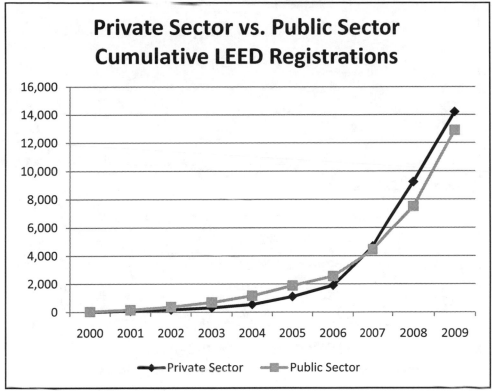

Source: U.S. Green Building Council.

adoption. Retailers such as Starbucks, Kohl's, and Darden (Olive Garden, Red Lobster) have made company-wide announcements about pursuing LEED certification for all new properties. Rather than building one or two flagship green stores, these companies have built green design into their standard prototype, making it typical practice. This is driving economies of scale in their implementation. A similar trend is starting to happen in the hospitality market, with Starwood requiring LEED certification for its relatively new extended-stay brand, Element. Marriott is offering a green prototype for its Courtyard brand as an option, with similar options for its other mid-scale brands. While hotel construction is sluggish due to the economy, these companies are well positioned to lead the green pack once the economy picks up.

The business model and players among full-service hotels and the lower number of new projects makes it somewhat harder to achieve the same type of commitment, but new companies or brands such as "1" and Candela Hotels have built their brand and reputation around delivering green hotels to the market. Additionally, baselining efforts, such as those undertaken portfolio-wide by InterContinental Hotel Group and Hilton, position those companies to seek

Exhibit 2   Cumulative LEED Registrations by Space Type

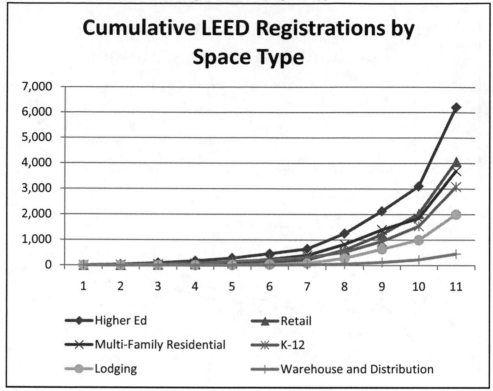

Source: U.S. Green Building Council.

certification on a large number of existing hotels across service levels that meet the performance criteria. This large-scale commitment to green building is fundamentally altering the green building movement as we know it, and will lead to significant competitive pressures for non-green hotels in the future.

Conclusion

Although the hospitality industry started its adoption of high performance building practices later than other building sectors, it is quickly catching up. A solid business case for operational savings, the demand for green hotels from conference and event planners, and the emergence of a more environmentally oriented consumer class have fueled tremendous momentum toward sustainability. Strong commitments from brands will lead the way and drive individual properties to begin competing on sustainability, as well as on service and rate. LEED has been adopted by many of these companies as a way to credibly showcase high-performance buildings, and it is expected that registration and certification of hotels will continue to increase. As economic prosperity returns to our nation, ever more newly constructed hotels will seek LEED certification, and competitive pressures will only increase the focus of existing hotels on achieving similar performance levels. There remains much to do to improve the environmental performance of the hospitality industry, but both the momentum and commitment are strong.

 Endnotes

1. TripAdvisor press release, April, 2009, at http://www.tripadvisor.com/PressCenter-i235-c1-Press_Releases.html.

2. *Green Venue Selection Guide* is available at www.usgbc.org/venueguide.

3. American Hotel & Lodging Association, 2008 Lodging Survey.

4. This bullet list is drawn from www.usgbc.org/DisplayPage.aspx?CMSPageID=1989.

5. American Hotel & Lodging Association, 2010 Lodging Survey.

5

Redefining Sustainable Travel and Tourism in the Twenty-First Century: A Global Context

By Ufi Ibrahim

Ufi Ibrahim is the Chief Executive of the British Hospitality Association, which she joined in July 2010. Previously, she was Chief Operations Officer of the London-based World Travel & Tourism Council (WTTC), where she worked with governments and industry across the world advising on policymaking and the development of planning frameworks for the long-term success of travel and tourism. Ms. Ibrahim was instrumental in the establishment of the Global Travel & Tourism Summit, the annual meeting of world leaders to discuss and agree upon key priorities for the industry. Before joining WTTC in 2000, she was in charge of the American Express Global Passport and Visa Unit for five years.

Ms. Ibrahim studied at the London Metropolitan University, graduating with a B.A. in Leisure and Tourism Management, and has recently graduated with distinction in her MBA from the Open University.

THE NINETEENTH-CENTURY WESTERN CONCEPTS of business development that focused on competitiveness, profit, and growth were updated in the late twentieth century with the incorporation of sustainability as a key motivator and indicator of successful organizational performance. At the beginning of the twenty-first century, when a global community demands, has access to, and responds dynamically to information and trends, sustainability as we know it is being actively redefined. This chapter discusses the public and private sector context within which travel and tourism needs to reinvent itself to face the new challenges and take advantage of the emerging opportunities.

Are We Paying Attention to Climate Change?

A recent report commonly called the Stern Review stated:

> No one can predict the consequences of climate change with complete certainty; but we now know enough to understand the risks. Mitigation—taking strong action to reduce emissions—must be viewed as an investment, a cost incurred now and in the coming few decades to avoid the risks of

very severe consequences in the future. If these investments are made wisely, the costs will be manageable, and there will be a wide range of opportunities for growth and development along the way. For this to work well, policy must promote sound market signals, overcome market failures, and have equity and risk mitigation at its core.[1]

Supported by international scientific evidence that links anthropogenic activity with climate change, the Stern Review has come to inform much public debate, particularly in the United Kingdom and the European Union. At the United Nations Framework Convention on Climate Change (UNFCCC) in Copenhagen, the governments of the United States, China, India, Brazil, and South Africa agreed on (but did not adopt) an international accord that underlined the need for "strong political will to urgently combat climate change in accordance with the principle of common but differentiated responsibilities and respective capabilities."[2] Despite mounting evidence indicating the negative effects of climate change, governments continue to grapple with the task of identifying an international policy framework that is meaningful, feasible, fair, and acceptable for both developed and developing nations. Therefore, in this context of urgency, should the lack of an international policy framework for a low-carbon economy delay the progression of a sustainable travel and tourism industry? Does the lack of leadership from government in the short term offer industry an opportunity to take the lead?

The Travel and Tourism Industry's Impact on Sustainability

Relative to many other industries, travel and tourism, like technology and telecommunications, is a young sector. Taking off in the 1950s with the development of the jet engine, which made air travel possible and within the means of the mass population, travel and tourism activity has quickly grown to become one of the world's largest industries. Comprising diverse and interdependent sectors, travel and tourism collectively represents 10 percent of global gross domestic product and 8 percent of employment worldwide.[3] Travel and tourism activity is largely accepted in today's global society as a contributor to the quality of human life. The "right to travel" is a strong factor in the social fabric of our world. In addition to an ever-stronger leisure market, business travel and trips to see friends and family have become activities inextricably linked to the global society in which we live. The magnitude of the impact on the environment is reflected in the sheer volume of international trips, recorded at 880 million in 2009,[4] together with a significantly higher number of domestic tourist trips (estimated at 1.7 billion trips in China alone in 2008).[5]

Tourism Industry Taking the Lead to Combat Climate Change

Businesses across many industries have taken the lead and started investing in sustainable technologies, resources, processes, and infrastructure. This is reflected by the fact that major stock market indexes like the FTSE, NASDAQ, and Dow Jones have created sustainability indexes because of increased demand from investors for information on companies' environmental records and green products.

Travel and tourism investors are no exception. Many are responding to and helping drive the re-engineering of organizations toward sustainable low-carbon enterprises. In this regard, strategies focused on the "triple bottom line" (i.e., financial, environmental, and social development and reporting) are becoming commonplace. Like other industries, travel and tourism's transformation is not limited to products designed specifically to tap into the responsible consumer market, such as "eco-resorts" and "eco-vacations." Rather, it extends throughout the sector and throughout organizations, helping to create business competitiveness of a new form. "Just five or six years ago, the term 'green building' evoked visions of tie-dyed, granola-munching denizens walking around barefoot on straw mats as wind chimes tinkled near open windows," said Charles Lockwood in the *Harvard Business Review*. "Today, the term suggests lower overhead costs, greater employee productivity, less absenteeism, and stronger employee attraction and retention."[6]

Travel and tourism businesses are realizing a range of opportunities in this area, from conservation, energy efficiency, and carbon mitigation to community benefit programs. These organizations continue to identify and develop their own strategic spaces within the sustainability sphere. In fact, many are pursuing several opportunities at once. InterContinental Hotels Group, Marriott International, Wilderness Safaris, Six Senses Resorts & Spas, Air New Zealand, British Airways, Boeing Commercial Airplanes, Rolls-Royce Engines, Whitbread, Scandic, and TUI are just a few of the organizations in travel and tourism that are driving product differentiation and cost reduction, redefining markets, and managing environmental risk within the new paradigm of sustainable organizations. By leading re-engineering efforts toward sustainable enterprises, industry leaders hope to increase their chances of readiness and responsiveness to policies that will be set and to proactively influence the policy agenda in ways favorable to the viability of their organizations and beneficial to their various stakeholders.

Many of the industry's leading companies recently joined forces to influence a wider market change in travel and tourism and to convince governments of the need for progressive and supportive policies. In 2009, more than forty of the world's largest travel and tourism organizations united to establish a common vision and commitment to reduce carbon dioxide emissions (with 2005 as the base year) by no less than 50 percent by 2035. An interim target was set to cut emissions by 30 percent by 2020, assuming the existence of an international agreement on global emission reduction, or by 25 percent by 2020 in the absence of such an agreement.[7]

Consumers Driving the Industry Shift to Sustainability ———

A primary impetus for the travel and tourism industry's increasing progress toward sustainable dynamism (embracing planning, design, management, and operations at every level) is linked to the consumer profile shift from "globe-trotters" to "value-trotters."[8] This term reflects the changing mass market (no longer just the niche) that increasingly seeks trips offering "good value."

The term "good value" in this instance refers to more than an amiable balance between price and product/service. Aided by the Internet and access to information regarding the huge range of services and products at similar prices across the world, value-trotters are seeking more than a saving spree. As globally aware, environmentally conscious, technologically savvy, time-poor individuals spoiled by a wide range of choices and considerations, who want to see themselves as good world citizens, value-trotters seek responsible travel options that have minimal impact on the natural and cultural environments they visit. They also demand experiences enhanced through engagement with local communities and natural habitats. More and more, these value-trotters communicate with a global audience through social media, influencing decisions made by other consumers, organizations, communities, and the public at large. They are the consumers of the twenty-first century.

In 2009, the Maryland University Program on International Policy Attitudes (PIPA) undertook the World Public Opinion survey.[9] The findings, which included results from 18,000 people from more than nineteen countries, revealed clearly the rising environmental ethic and priorities of the public at large.

- 73 percent of all surveyed wanted higher priority for climate change.

- 77 percent of British citizens wanted greater government intervention on climate change.

- 44 percent of American citizens wanted climate change to be a major preoccupation of the Obama administration.

- 94 percent of Chinese citizens supported the need for government to keep climate change on the front burner.

- 59 percent of Indian citizens wanted their government to make climate change a top priority.

Already, many travel and tourism companies have made great strides toward meeting and satisfying value-trotters' expectations; some groundbreaking initiatives are even exceeding them. Such brands are actively engaged with local communities, making definite and verifiable efforts toward carbon mitigation and poverty alleviation. They are embracing dynamism and engaging in new levels of dialogue with employees, consumers, and communities across the world helping drive sustainability as a new cultural paradigm.

As businesses re-engineer to fully embrace twenty-first century dilemmas, new opportunities will emerge through the learning that will increasingly take place at all levels of an organization, and the creativity and innovation that will prosper from dialogue with the wider group of stakeholders engaged collectively in dynamic sustainability. These stakeholders include the new line of investors demanding "green credentials," procurement teams demanding sustainable supplies throughout the value chain, local communities and operators, and consumers and businesses. Social networking sites, trip advisors, and other global communication tools will accelerate the speed with which information can be gathered and dialogue enhanced, not only with consumers, but also with the wider range of stakeholders.

So why are governments and intergovernmental organizations yet to form a basis for dialogue with the travel and tourism industry? Why are industry leaders pushing for more government leadership in setting an international regulatory framework that will condition the new sustainability context?

Travel and Tourism—Undervalued and Disconnected

Despite being a major contributor to wealth generation, employment, international cultural exchange, and the overall quality of life for millions of people, tourism is undervalued and disconnected in most public policy debates. The primary reason is that most governments do not record or measure the industry's full impact on their economies. The standard measure of Tourism Satellite Accounting (accredited by the United Nations Statistical Commission) has yet to be adopted by most countries. Therefore, most governments rely on a narrow definition of traffic counts and airport enplanements/deplanements. By excluding many major sectors of tourism, such as aviation and transport, they assign low priority to the sector and do not recognize the industry's full value. Furthermore, most economies, both developed and developing, do not have high-ranking administrators leading this important sector. In fact, few governments have announced travel and tourism as a key strategic priority for their overall economic development and subsequently acted upon this claim. The few governments who have done so include China, the United Arab Emirates, and Japan.

Similarly, travel and tourism's inextricable link with the natural environment could be harnessed in tackling deforestation and adding value to land conservation efforts.

It is possible to attain a more comprehensive assessment of travel and tourism's impact by considering the industry's overall effect on society, the economy, and the environment. After all, for the travel and tourism industry, sustainable dynamism is not limited to carbon mitigation. Social and cultural issues and degradation of natural environments are equally important. Just as the balanced scorecard gives business leaders a more informed basis for decision making, a new comprehensive representation of travel and tourism is necessary.

The Strategic Approach to Framing Public Policy

Certainly, there is much room for sustainable dynamism to grow throughout the industry. For many large enterprises, the current approach to sustainability is based on faulty assumptions. Some businesses try to capitalize on the premise that the Earth is sick and, therefore, profits can be obtained by finding ways to return it to good health. Other businesses take the opposite stance that there really is no return to health, and thus no need for such futile investments. The correct approach is to make environmental investments because those investments deliver positive returns or reduce risks. Managers need to go beyond the question, "Does it pay to be green?" and instead ask, "Under what circumstances do particular kinds of environmental investments deliver benefits to shareholders?"[10]

Similarly, the question that governments should ask themselves is not whether businesses need to step up to the challenge or whether they need new technology or innovations. Rather, the question should focus on ways in which governments can motivate markets to produce the innovation and attract the venture capital and investment needed to create a low-carbon, sustainable economy. These questions should be addressed at local, national, regional, and international levels of government. Three examples of areas in which government action could have a progressive impact on sustainable travel and tourism dynamism are as follows.

- Consider the lack of market mechanisms that enable fair access to sustainable products and services for travel and tourism businesses. According to some experts, government legislation can drive more effective and speedier transformation. "The biggest obstacle for developers is the lack of a complete and well structured value chain that can put sustainable products in the market at a price the consumers can and will pay."[11] This is happening quickly because pressure from legislators, the media, the public, and consumers is strong enough to make it happen.

- International aviation policy is another example. While technological developments in the industry continue to progress, and business operators seek optimal ways to increase fuel/carbon efficiency, international governmental collaboration is critical for advancing emissions trading schemes, shortening routes, and developing an improved air navigation infrastructure.

- It is estimated that 80 percent of the global travel and tourism industry consists of small- to medium-sized enterprises. Many of these are families and entrepreneurs actively serving international travel and tourism consumers, thereby generating much-needed foreign income for their local economies. Government assistance in enabling access to know-how, resources, or opportunities to invest in sustainable, low-carbon activities could help boost the sustainable viability and dynamism of these enterprises and their communities.

Conclusion: The Way Forward for Governments ————————

A timely response to the challenge of climate change is not only essential, but feasible and achievable. As set out in this chapter, international political cooperation and global policies are pivotal to travel and tourism sustainability. Numerous travel and tourism businesses have reframed their missions and value statements accordingly, embracing sustainability throughout their organizations. Many are going a step further, intensifying their efforts by harnessing the dynamism offered by the twenty-first century consumer and by global communication tools and technologies. However, the disconnect between industry development and the observations of government and others in the public domain limits the full potential of travel and tourism as an engine for sustainable dynamism in a global sense.

Like businesses, local and national governments should consider the right strategic fit of policies for their own destinations, as well as for the global context. Sustainable dynamism is not restricted to private sector operations or development, particularly in the travel and tourism arena. Much can be shared between public and private sectors, including the overall approach to address sustainability. The triple bottom line is just as applicable to government policy as it is to commercial policy. For governments, the three pillars of a sustainable destination should consider collectively the society, the economy, and the environment. Just as each organization will benefit from identifying its own sustainability drivers based on the organization's unique context, culture, capabilities, and resources, governments too should identify the right policy frameworks for the unique natural and cultural attributes of their destinations, as well as the means and capabilities of their societies and economies (including the industry operators active within their jurisdictions).

Like businesses, governments will also benefit from extended dialogue with the changing population, business operators, and other stakeholders. Only in this way can a dynamic approach be taken to ever-evolving challenges and opportunities. Some governments are already leading the way in this regard. Let us hope that others will embrace this twenty-first century approach to policymaking, thereby assuming leadership on sustainable dynamism for travel and tourism.

Endnotes

1. Nicholas Stern, *The Economics of Climate Change: The Stern Review* (Cambridge: Cambridge University Press, 2007).

2. United Nations Framework Convention on Climate Change, "The Copenhagen Accord" (Copenhagen, 2009): 1.

3. World Travel & Tourism Council, "Travel & Tourism Economic Impact 2010" (London, 2010).

4. United Nations World Tourism Council, "International Tourism on Track for a Rebound After an Exceptionally Challenging 2009," *UNWTO World Tourism Barometer 8*, no. 1 (2010): 1, 5–7.

5. "Domestic Tourism in 2008 May Reach 1.7 Billion People with 1.14 Trillion Incomes,"*China Financial Daily*, January 8, 2009, www.chinafinancialdaily.com/financial/news/2009/01/08/3178/domestic-tourism-inbound-tourism-and-outbound-tourism-of-china.html.

6. Charles Lockwood, "Building the Green Way," *Harvard Business Review 84*, no. 6 (2006): 129–137.

7. World Travel & Tourism Council, "Leading the Challenge on Climate Change" (London, 2009).

8. Ufi Ibrahim, "The Rise of the Value-Oriented Traveler," *Hotel Year Book 2009*.

9. See www.worldpublicopinion.org.

10. Forest L. Reinhardt, "Bringing the Environment Down to Earth," *Harvard Business Review 77*, no. 4 (1999): 148–158.

11. Miguel Ruano, 2009.

Part II

Development and Investment Perspectives

Developing and Operating Sustainable Resorts: A Case Study of Maho Bay Camps and Estate Concordia Preserve

By A. J. Singh and Adrian Davis

A. J. Singh, Ph.D., is an Associate Professor in The School of Hospitality Business at Michigan State University and focuses on international lodging, finance, and real estate. Dr. Singh was jointly responsible for the establishment of The Hospitality Business Real Estate and Development Specialization at Michigan State University. He has more than fifteen years of hospitality business experience in various management positions in the United States and India. He has worked for Oberoi Hotels, Stouffer Hotels, and Hyatt Hotels. In 1999, he taught financial management at Centre International de Glion in Switzerland. He has also conducted many real estate market and feasibility studies while working as a consultant for Laventhol & Horwath.

Dr. Singh earned his undergraduate degree from the University of Delhi in India, his M.S. from Purdue University in Hotel Restaurant and Institutional Management, and his Ph.D. in Park, Recreation, and Tourism from Michigan State University. He is an active member of the Hospitality Asset Managers Association; the Council on Hotel, Restaurant, and Institutional Education; the Association of Hospitality Financial Management Educators; the International Society of Hospitality Consultants; and the Urban Land Institute. The National Institute of Standards and Technology appointed him to the 2006 Board of Examiners for the Malcolm Baldrige National Quality Award. He received the Richard Lewis Award for Quality and Innovation in 2006. He currently conducts two study-abroad programs to India, Dubai, Thailand, Hong Kong, Macau, and Southern China.

Adrian Davis grew up in the foothills of North Carolina and graduated from the University of North Carolina at Charlotte. He held management positions in the manufacturing and retail industries before joining Maho Bay Camps on St. John in 2005. His background and years as general manager prepared him well for his current position of Vice President for Maho Bay Camps, Harmony Studios, and Estate Concordia. Together these properties employ more than seventy employees who oversee 168 guest accommodations, two restaurants, two retail stores, and the Recycled Art Center and Gallery, as well as activities and classes for guests. "Many of our guests have visited multiple times and we love that they return feeling a part of our Maho and Concordia family," Adrian says. "It's exciting that we now have two and three generations of one

family making us their choice for vacations. It really shows how special our properties are. I'm proud to be a part of this company."

Adrian is married to his college sweetheart and they welcomed their first son, born on St. Thomas, in September 2008. "We love the Virgin Islands and having our son born here makes it an even more special place for us."

Authors' Acknowledgments

This material is primarily based on internal documents provided by Maho Bay Camps, published articles and reports, and a visit by A. J. Singh to Maho Bay Camps during which he interviewed the owner, Stanley Selengut, and several key executives. Jake Abrahamson, a student in *The* School of Hospitality Business at Michigan State University, assisted the authors with the compilation and synthesis of data for the chapter.

V<small>IRTUALLY ALL RESORT DEVELOPMENT</small> in the United States and across the world is driven primarily by a profit motive. The extent to which these resorts comply with environmental preservation is influenced by external forces such as regulations, customer preferences, and community compatibility. It is rare to find resorts driven primarily with a conservation and preservation ethic that are profitable as well. These resorts are typically developed by innovative entrepreneurs with a strong environmental ethic.

The Maho Bay Camps and Estate Concordia Preserve resort complex is a special case, as it was one of the earliest examples of a hospitality enterprise's efforts to incorporate the triple-bottom-line philosophy of value creation through a balance of ecological, social, and economic goals. The founder of Maho Bay Camps is Stanley Selengut, a civil engineer by training, entrepreneurial and innovative by nature, and environmentally avant-garde. He foresaw in 1975 a sustainable future for affordable, environmentally friendly, and comfortable resort accommodations that are close to nature. Selengut's philosophy for his resorts is best captured in his statement, "I don't see why human comfort and environmental sensitivity can't be compatible."

The purpose of this chapter is to share Maho Bay Camps' and Estate Concordia Preserve's journey and identify lessons and best practices for the resort development and investment community. Furthermore, our hope is that the chapter will inspire hospitality students to consider Selengut's tenets of sustainable development and operations if they should design, develop, and/or operate resorts in the future.

Background: Overview of the U.S. Virgin Islands and St. John

The U.S. Virgin Islands is a group of islands in the Caribbean that is part of the United States. These islands lie within the Caribbean Sea and the Atlantic Ocean and are located about forty miles east of Puerto Rico, immediately west of the British Virgin Islands. The U.S. Virgin Islands consist of the main three main islands of St. Croix, St. John, and St. Thomas. The total land area of the territory is

133.73 square miles. The resident population of the islands in 2009 was 117,011, of which St. John accounted for only 4,500.[1] This is not surprising, as it is the smallest of the three main islands, and two-thirds of the island is a national park. The 7,200-acre park is a sanctuary of mangroves and subtropical forest. The park was a gift from Lawrence Rockefeller in the 1950s. Cruz Bay, the island's main town, is a twenty-minute ferry ride from St. Thomas.

On average, the temperature reaches a high of 79°F (26°C) and varies 6°F (3.3°C) between summer and winter. Typically an arid island, St. John receives about forty inches of rainfall a year. The island has many woodland trails that end on a high plateau.

Because of its proximity to the United States (which provides a ready supply of travelers) and its lush natural surroundings, the U.S. Virgin Islands' primary economic activity is tourism. The islands hosted 2.2 million visitors in 2009.[2] While most visitors to the islands are cruise passengers, eco-travelers are a niche segment who are attracted by the natural beauty of the islands. The United States represents approximately 80 percent of the tourist market, with U.S.V.I. residents at about 9 percent and Europe, Canada, South America, the West Indies, and Puerto Rico making up the rest.

The islands have a limited agricultural sector, so most food products are imported. The manufacturing sector consists of petroleum refining, textiles, electronics, rum distilling, pharmaceuticals, and watch assembly. Due to the high cost of transportation, a fragile ecosystem, and the high cost of waste disposal, conservation and waste management are critical for the islands.

Maho Bay Camps is located in Maho Bay on the northern tip of St. John. Since opening its first canvas-sided eco-tents to its first visitors in 1976, Maho Bay Camps has remained one of the most popular Caribbean vacation destinations and one of the world's best-known resorts. Over the years the resort has grown from its initial eighteen tents to 168 units, found in Maho Bay Camps (with two types of accommodations, Maho Tent Cottages and Harmony Studios) and Estate Concordia Preserve (also with two types of accommodations, Concordia Eco-Tents and Concordia Eco-Studios)—each of these resort areas serving a specific market niche. As it has grown, this resort complex has maintained its identity as a vacation destination that provides an outdoor, close-to-nature experience combined with basic human comforts. How this all came about is a story worth sharing.

Maho Bay Camps: Humble Beginnings

Stanley Selengut was introduced to Maho Bay in 1972 while working for the Rockefeller Foundation and fell in love with its pristine beauty. In 1974, Selengut secured a thirty-seven-year ground lease on fourteen acres of a commercially zoned "in-holding" (a privately owned piece of land within a government-owned park or other public, protected area) within the large national park on St. John. These acres were located just above a white sand beach along coral reefs filled with endangered turtles and abundant marine life. The superintendent of the Virgin Islands National Park was concerned at first about any type of resort construction within the boundaries of the park. Resort development in the 1970s typically consisted of bulldozing the land, building what was needed, then landscaping around the newly constructed resort, virtually eliminating the land's existing value as a natural habitat. The superintendent's concerns were not at all lessened when he learned that Selengut was from New York. He met with him and explained that resort development could potentially ruin the existing landscape, beaches, and coral reefs. This conversation stimulated in Selengut a true understanding of the value of nature.

"I was just a kid from the Bronx who did Boy Scouts for a while. I knew the value of nature, but the idea that what you put on the land is secondary to what is already there—that was new to me," Selengut said in an interview with *Audubon* magazine.[3] A quick learner, he took this early lesson to heart, and the idea of the sustainable Maho Bay Camps was born.

Influenced by an innovative elevated walkway he had experienced as a housing developer in Fire Island National Park near New York City, and by structures he had seen on a trip to Africa, Selengut worked with the U.S. National Park Service at Maho to design similar walkways to protect plants and avoid erosion. Selengut not only worked extensively with the National Park Service, he worked with the local Virgin Islands government. Because Maho Bay Camps obtained U.S. Virgin Island Industrial Development Commission IDC benefits[4] (initiated in 1977), the camp was able to continue with the constant upgrading and improvements it needed, not only to compete in an increasingly competitive tourism market, but to develop a resort that could continue to pioneer environmentally responsible methods of building in fragile environments. The IDC benefits afforded the opportunity to construct elevated walkways throughout the entire hillside and construct bright, airy, cloth-covered cottages between the existing vegetation.

Sustainable Site Plan, Design, and Construction

Sustainable design balances human needs (rather than human wants) with the carrying capacity of the natural and cultural environments. It minimizes environmental impacts, the importation of goods and energy, as well as the generation of waste. To protect the site's valuable natural resources and unique environmental amenities, innovative environmental preservation and design guidelines were set up throughout the various stages of Maho Bay Camps' development.

The project started small with only eighteen units and a modest cash investment. The first tent cabins were designed by Maine architect Jim Hadley. They were made of translucent, water repellent fabric and built on 256-square-foot (sixteen foot by sixteen foot) wooden platforms supported by beams cantilevered over the hillside. The tents had a sleeping area with twin beds; a sitting area with a couch; a small cooking area with a propane stove, dishes, and utensils; and an outside deck with lawn furniture. The units cost $3,400 to build in the 1970s. These light, inexpensive units were designed to fit within the existing trees and plants and were connected via a network of elevated walkways. The walkways rested on hand-dug footings. The walkways (totaling over 21,000 feet) were built for approximately $15 per linear foot. Construction materials were wheeled along the walks and carried into place. No heavy construction equipment was required or used. All utility lines, including pipes and electrical cables, were hidden under the walkways rather than buried in trenches. The finished walkways flowed naturally through the landscape; they avoided rock outcroppings and mature trees, and left untouched as much valuable flora as possible.

This design minimized the environmental impact and site preparation costs associated with typical resort development. The impact of guests was also minimized, as they could traverse the resort's steep hillside without trampling the ground. The resort minimized its environmental impact with its low density of eight units per acre, which yielded the added benefit of guest privacy. The elevated walkways have remained an important aspect of the sustainable nature of the resort, and have allowed Maho Bay Camps to minimize on-site soil erosion throughout its history. Addressing the need for water conservation on an arid island such as St. John, water conservation devices were installed on all fixtures, and water use guidelines were communicated to guests.

The central dining facility was the focal point of the resort. Designed as an open-air structure, the facility has beautiful views of the surrounding Caribbean islands and is the gathering spot for guests during the three cafeteria-style meals. The dining facility's construction components were chosen from recycled materials such as composite beams made from wood scraps and decking made from recycled tires. While today these building materials have become more standard, at the time these were real innovations. Other facilities at the resort include a store to provide daily essentials for guests and a recreational equipment rental facility.

"When I finished building the place, it looked like it had grown there," Selengut said. Today, the support buildings and tent cottages are hidden in the foliage; to guests, most of the resort appears to be situated in the trees. Maho's design, with its elevated wooden walkways linking tent cabins, has since been emulated by eco-resorts throughout the world.

To reduce the structural damage caused by hurricanes, every structure built within the resort was designed to be frangible. The benefit of this to Maho Bay Camps was that high winds would blow off the building skin and thereby reduce the potential for greater structural damage. This also added the benefit of modest redevelopment costs to restart operations after a storm, versus higher costs for other kinds of structures. Maho Bay Camps is usually the first resort in the Caribbean to be up and running after a hurricane, which gives it a strong competitive advantage.

One principle that guided Maho's development was that every parcel of land has a historical point when it reached its height as a balanced ecosystem. Once this point is identified, then there is a clear path to its restoration. The Virgin Islands reached its height as a native habitat before the land was farmed and grazed, and heavy rains depleted the topsoil. On St. John, much of the land is degraded forest with eroded topsoil, and alien species have replaced native plants and animals. Confronted with this condition, Selengut was led to the theory of ecological restoration. As the Maho Bay Camps' tent cottages and walkways were built, alien species were removed (such as vines that were choking the indigenous trees) and native plants re-introduced. There was a feral animal population of stray cats, wild donkeys, goats, and mongooses on St. John. These had devastated indigenous plants and native animals such as lizards and frogs. With the help of park professionals, the resort's staff regulated the number of these feral animals and re-introduced land-nesting birds and other native wildlife. The resort was repopulated with iguanas and now, on most days, guests see iguanas resting throughout the camp. This type of landscaping and wildlife management in harmony with nature had a tremendous impact on the guest experience. Imagine the marketability of a campground where walls open up to cactus and turpentine trees, draped with orchids and air plants alive with iguanas and Bananaquit birds.

The Development of New Accommodations at Maho

As the word spread about this unique resort, Maho Bay Camps attracted more guests than the eighteen tent cottages could accommodate. Slow development progress occurred in the 1980s, but another development impetus occurred after November 1991, when the U.S. National Park Service hosted a workshop on sustainable design at Maho Bay to establish guidelines for construction within national parks. It was attended by more than sixty renowned architects, engineers, landscape architects, and naturalists. They addressed solar design, the use of recycled building materials, energy from wind power, and responsible waste disposal. They also produced a document entitled "The Guiding Principles of Sustainable Design."[5]

After participating in the workshop, Selengut decided to put these concepts to work, both in his existing property as well as in a totally undeveloped property. At Maho Bay Camps, he used the park service guidelines to build twelve apartment studios called Harmony Studios. These became the first resort structures in the world to be built according to the new park service guidelines. They were built from recycled materials and incorporated energy-efficient appliances and solar panels for heating water and generating electricity. While Maho Bay Camps' spartan dwellings, public bathhouses, cold-water showers, and simple amenities are popular with younger and more adventuresome travelers, other guest markets existed that agreed with Maho's eco principles but were interested in a greater degree of comfort; Harmony Studios were built to appeal to these markets. With the cooperation of the Virgin Islands Energy Office and the Southwest Technology Development Institute, computer systems were installed in the studios that were designed to display each studio unit's energy generation and usage, and to provide user-friendly tutorials on topics such as renewable energy, conservation, and recycling. Harmony Studios were promoted as education centers where visitors could leave with practical ideas for sustainable living at home. The development cost for the studios was approximately $100,000 per unit; these studios are Maho Bay Camps' most profitable units.

Being the first to experiment with and market such untested concepts had both advantages and disadvantages. Some of the early experiments in the studios adversely affected guest comfort and had to be eliminated. In other instances, new products did not work as anticipated and had to be replaced. However, most of the innovative design features were successful, such as tiles made from recycled light bulbs and beams made of wood scrap. As a result, the Harmony Studio project received tremendous media coverage and free publicity. Within twelve months of its opening in 1993, Harmony was featured in seventeen national magazines, eighteen special interest magazines, fourteen newsletters, eighteen major newspapers plus wire services, four TV programs, seven foreign publications, and eight radio programs. Suppliers who learned of Maho's willingness to experiment with new products began to provide special purchasing deals.

The overall feedback from guests who upgraded from the more spartan Maho tent cottages to Harmony Studios was positive. However, these guests did miss the closer-to-nature experience of the tents, where they "could see the moon through their roof, hear the crickets, and see a sting ray glide by from their tents."[6] As a result of this feedback, Selengut's next innovation was to identify a resort product that combined comfort with a back-to-nature experience.

Estate Concordia Preserve: Eco-Tents and Eco-Studios ———

In the 1970s Selengut purchased vacant land on the southeast corner of St. John with the thought of someday building a residence there and other housing for a community of like-minded people. The land was accessible by potholed dirt roads and was a degraded forest with eroded topsoil. Alien species had replaced native plants and animals. He contributed some of the land he had purchased to a joint venture with a reputable, well-financed and experienced developer. A small condominium project that protected the valuable fauna was designed and partially constructed. But the developer ran out of funds, the bank foreclosed, and the project lay unfinished for several years. Upon reacquiring his land from the bank, Selengut realized that his interests were no longer in condominiums.

He finished the buildings and began a program of constructing self-sufficient eco-tents that offered more amenities than the Maho tent cottages. The twenty-five eco-tents, connected by elevated pedestrian walkways, provided living space that was totally supported by renewable technologies. "Responsible energy" is what the resort calls its approach to reducing energy waste. Units are equipped with renewable electric power as well as solar power. Each unit is energy self-sufficient and collects solar energy through photovoltaic cells to energize a refrigerator, fans, a water pump, and electric lights.

A cistern, solar hot water heater, and a composting toilet add bathroom convenience without environmental impact. The composting toilets are located underneath the walkways and save the environment from potential pathogens that would be discharged from normal flush toilets. The compost is a great asset to the land because of the nutrients it contains. Odors can be an issue, however; this problem is addressed by placing the composting toilets downwind from the tents and keeping them out of the sun as much as possible.

The eco-tents' space-age fabrics provide great strength and come in colors that blend into the landscape. The super-reflective roof fabric maintains a temperature 14°F (10°C) cooler under the fabric than on the surface, and provides a perfect surface for water collection. The floors are made of recycled plastic and wood. The units have a barometer that provides weather information, a thermometer and meter to show water temperature and water usage, and a gauge that shows guests how much power their unit is generating. To help guests keep power usage to a minimum, timers were put on appliances and guests are urged to shut them off when not in use. A gauge is located in each tent to allow guests to monitor battery levels and use their power accordingly. Water is easily available in cisterns attached to each unit to collect rainwater runoff from the roof; guests are able to pump this rainwater into a container over the shower that provides water pressure and acts as a water heater.

The object of the Concordia eco-tents was to offer an affordable, close-to-nature vacation experience with almost no intrusion into the environment. The tents were constructed at an elevation that provides clear and unobstructed views of the bay. Each tent maximizes the value of the natural landscaping and faces in a direction to capture the sunrise in the morning and moonrise at night.

Selengut's creativity in sustainable design is seen in the natural synergies he has produced in each of his development projects. An example of this is seen in a particular feature of the eco-tents: the natural slope of the landscape promoted water flow to help grow aromatic flowers around the tents, which attracted hummingbirds. The flowers and hummingbirds provide a delightful, natural experience for guests sitting on their tents' balconies. Because of their location, unique design features, and inimitable ambience, the eco-tents have high occupancy. When combined with low maintenance costs, the eco-tents provide a strong financial payback.

As the lease for the original Maho project is due to expire and its future is uncertain, the development of Estate Concordia Preserve ensures a continuation of Selengut's vision of providing affordable and sustainable resort accommodations. Selengut has continued to invest in Estate Concordia Preserve by adding a dining facility serving healthy cuisine, a swimming pool using a natural process of chlorination (by separating chlorine and sodium), and a solar-operated pool pump. A multi-use pavilion deck was constructed with gabion baskets filled with rocks gathered from the site; the glass blocks in the pavilion were created using recycled glass from the Maho Bay Art Center. Since water is scarce on the island, underground tanks were constructed to harvest rainwater for guest usage.

Recent Sustainable Elements

The latest development at Estate Concordia Preserve as of this writing is a pod of four highly energy-efficient eco-studios. Their elevated location, which overlooks Salt Lake Pond and the U.S.V.I. National Park, provides guests with an excellent view from their rooms and balconies. In many ways, these studios are a distillation of more than thirty years of innovation and learning at Maho Bay Camps, and incorporate innovative, energy-efficient features. Some of these features include the following:

- Cogeneration of power using photovoltaic cells.

- Panels with an extremely high R-rating used for the construction of the studios. These panels are similar to the material used in walk-in coolers. The studios are then wrapped in aluminum foil and covered with planks.

- The studios feature solar water heaters, cork floors (quiet to walk on, and easily forested), Energy Star–rated appliances, rainwater catchment, and sustainable purchasing of building materials.

- The new studios showcase the use of recycled art created at the Maho Bay Art Center. Each unit features handmade glass countertops, glass tiles, and lampshades; batiked, recycled fabric wall hangings; and clay sconces.

Because the design and development of the eco-studios have incorporated energy-efficient building, the studios are eligible for LEED certification, the Island Builders Association's green certification, and Energy Star certification. These certifications will add value through public relations exposure.

From a financial perspective, development of the eco-studios made perfect economic sense. The U.S. Department of Energy rebates offset 50 percent of the costs associated with purchasing various equipment and fixtures for the studios. For example, the wind generator for the studios cost $12,000, but the rebate reduced the cost to $6,000. In addition, there were other tax credits and rebates. A rough calculation indicated a payback of three years for each eco-studio.

From an operating perspective, the cost of electricity for the studios is at or near zero due to cogeneration, and the cost of water is at or near zero due to the studios' rain catchment features that reuse rain water. The only operating cost for the units is housekeeping and supplies, as utility costs are virtually free. To provide context for these savings, currently Maho Bay Camps spends $250,000 per year to buy water and $150,000 for power. For the eco-studios, these costs are substantially reduced or eliminated and the resulting savings go directly to the bottom line.

Sustainable Resort Operations and Innovative Sustainable Best Practices

Given the fragility of an island eco-system, resorts that operate in such sensitive environments need to develop operational practices that intelligently and creatively balance the use of resources on the island. These operational practices must be developed with an understanding of the complete life cycle of any product the resort uses, from the time the product is purchased to its eventual disposal. This type of "cradle-to-grave" analysis requires the tabulation of energy consumed and the environmental impacts of the material used in each product. At Maho Bay Camps, several systems have been developed to not only reduce, reuse, and recycle products on the island, but also profit from the processes developed.

The registration desk is where guests first encounter Maho Bay Camps. The orientation given there stresses the importance of recycling and minimizing waste. It is there that guests are informed of the resort's recycling program and encouraged to assist in Maho's efforts by separating their trash for recycling. During the checkout process, registration personnel encourage guests who are interested to donate their $30 security deposit to the Friends of the Virgin Islands National Park. This nonprofit organization, based on St. John, raises funds for activities such as research, advocacy, and educational programs in the park.[7]

Sometimes at the end of their stays guests have items that they don't wish to take home with them for various reasons. In the continuing effort to reduce the amount of waste the resort produces, Maho set up the "Help Yourself Shelf," where guests can leave items that others might be able to use. As the saying goes, "One person's trash is the next person's treasure." Guests at the resort are instructed to help themselves to anything they like in the designated cabinet and refrigerator. What might have ended up in a landfill becomes an unexpected "gift" for another guest. While traditional business thinking might see the use of a help-yourself shelf as reducing sales from the resort's general store, Selengut views this invitation to generosity as having two practical benefits. It creates goodwill among guests when they see that the resort is actually helping them save money, while at the same time helping the environment. Furthermore, the cost of hauling left-behind items off the island would end up costing the resort more than the marginal reduction of its store sales.

In its housekeeping operations, Maho Bay Camps utilizes 100-percent biodegradable laundry detergent and keeps the amount of bleach used to a minimum. Old towels are cut into strips and used as cleaning rags, which not only extends the life of these items, but eliminates the use of paper towels for cleaning purposes.

Innovative Reuse and Recycling Programs

One characteristic of Maho owner Stanley Selengut is his ongoing innovation. In 1997, Mark Koenings, then the U.S.V.I. National Park superintendent, initiated an aluminum recycling program on the island, and Maho contributed to the purchase of a can crusher. Not only did Maho send all of the resort's cans to the crusher; the resort's employees did much of the actual crushing. Then Maho started its own recycling center, with a glass crusher to condense the resort's waste glass. Maho used the crushed glass bottles for backfill and as aggregate for non-structural concrete, offering it free to contractors and home builders on St. John. This evolved into a center that manufactured objects from the resort's trash.

In 1998 a glass furnace and an annealing oven were purchased. A glass artisan, Larry Livolsi, was invited to Maho to teach the glass blowing craft. At first, easy products such as floor tiles, sun catchers, and paperweights were produced. As skill developed, glass was blown into objects such as mugs, bowls, and urns. Then glass art was created, using Heineken bottles for the color green, Schlitz bottles for brown, Arizona Iced Tea bottles for cobalt blue, and combinations of these materials for light bluish green. Next, a kiln was purchased to melt the waste aluminum cans and manufacture castings of coat hooks, door hooks, and coasters. A cardboard shredder was purchased for recycling.

This program eventually evolved into "Trash to Treasures," a recent chapter in Maho's efforts to design and operate an ecologically sensitive resort that can serve as a model for sustainable development in the hotel industry and elsewhere. The original "Trash to Treasures" program was envisioned to be a modest educational center where guests and staff might learn to produce craft objects from Maho Bay Camps' waste bottles, cans, cardboard, and paper, as well as from articles found during beach clean-ups. To equip the center for small-scale production, a glass furnace, an annealing oven, a cardboard shredder, a glass crusher, and pottery wheels, kilns, and hand tools were purchased. A visiting-artist program was established where potters, glassblowers, jewelry makers, metal workers, and other craftspeople were invited to make saleable art objects from the resort's trash stream.

Seating was built around the glass furnace so guests could watch the artists create beautiful glass objects. Some of the resort's staff members began producing craft objects in their spare time to earn extra income. Maho's waste bottles, cans, cardboard, pallet wood, etc., were used as raw material, and the finished items were sold from the Maho store with no intermediaries or gallery commissions, thus covering the cost of the glassblowers, equipment, and propane. Marketing was accomplished via the various craft workshops and by guests watching the glass art being made. Waste paper and cardboard were shredded and used for packing.

The art center has been a three-fold benefit to Maho Bay Camps: it recycles trash into treasures; it offers classes, which educate guests in recycling as well as providing entertainment; and it has created a profit center through the sale of products. New marketing programs include an online store, displaying items in guestrooms, expanding the wholesale operation, and the development of a joint program with cruise companies.

With sufficient capital and employment of creative talent, Selengut feels the "Trash to Treasures" program could be expanded to become a major economic development tool for communities by creating microenterprise ventures. At the same time, such a program would considerably reduce the amount of trash headed for landfills. A project of this scope would require a multilateral collaboration between public, private, and academic institutions, with funding from government or environmentally active foundations.

Sustainable Food and Beverage Operations

The Maho Bay Camps' restaurant and bar coordinated its ordering with the resort's store to keep camp-wide deliveries to a minimum. By keeping deliveries down and storing a majority of their supplies, they are able to lower the amount of fuel that is consumed on their behalf. Local providers and distributors are contracted for food and boutique items as much as possible. This not only reduces the distance items must be shipped (reducing the use of fossil fuels and packing materials), but also helps to bolster the local economy.

The resort's system of ordering significantly reduces the total amount of waste that is produced at the camp. Condiments are ordered in bulk and placed in centrally located, refillable containers. Reusable utensils, plates, and cups help in the effort to cut down on waste.

The resort's store carries numerous items from businesses that have demonstrated a commitment to environmental issues at the corporate level. For instance, Maho sells T-shirts made from organic cotton, as well as clothes that have been created at the camp. The store does not bag customer purchases; shipping boxes and other materials are reused when a customer requires a container to carry items. The store has stopped sales of small water bottles in order to minimize plastic waste. The temperature of store coolers and freezers is monitored on a regular basis in an effort to reduce energy consumption.

Through its various practices, Maho Bay Camps has been a trendsetter in waste management by its policies to reduce garbage, reuse items, save energy and water resources, and recycle waste. The resort has influenced practices at resorts and campgrounds around the world.

Maho welcomes comments and suggestions from its guests. The Eco Box serves as a vehicle by which guests can make suggestions to assist Maho in fulfilling its eco-friendly program. For example, Maho used to carry Fiji bottled water. When guests pointed out that Fiji water is shipped a very long distance (coming from Fiji in the Pacific), Maho discontinued selling it. The resort sells larger bottles of water in an effort to reduce the number of purchases and therefore plastic waste. Maho encourages guests to reuse their water bottles by filling them with water from the resort when empty rather than buying more water. Most guests understand and adjust.

Even though some guests are not eco-sensitive when they arrive, they have a better understanding of ecological issues by the time they leave. One evidence of this comes from an internal resort study that showed that its guests use many fewer gallons of water per person per day compared to a typical resort. Some guests (and employees) come to the resort with an environmental ethic already; others develop one as a result of their experiences at the resort.

Connections with the Community

Maho Bay Camps is very proactive about interacting with its surrounding community. Art and other demonstrations are conducted for local schools on St. John, St. Thomas, and St. Croix (both at Maho and at the schools); for tours conducted by the Virgin Islands Department of Tourism; and for resort visitors and guests. Maho offers art classes and workshops, conducted by the Maho staff and visiting artists, to community residents as well as to the resort's visitors and guests. The resort is also involved in community projects such as local clean-up events. As previously mentioned, if a security deposit is required for accommodations, guests have the option to donate the deposit to a local environmental group or to St. John's national park when they check out. The resort hires local residents whenever possible and invites locals to give evening talks and sell locally made handcrafts or gift items at the camp store. On Monday nights local musicians play at the resort's pavilion.

Marketing Maho Bay Camps: The Power of a Unique Story and Shared Values

The direct marketing expenses at Maho are much less than at a typical resort of its size. The marketing manager said the resort spends less than $15,000 per year on direct marketing. There are two reasons for this. First, Maho has a unique physical product; second, as a pioneer in sustainability its methods of operation are also unique. As a result, over its history Maho has received a huge amount of free media coverage in travel and special interest magazines, newsletters, newspapers, television programs, and Internet blogs. This does not include the free publicity from its loyal repeat guests, many of whom may be considered generational clients of the resort, as guests who first visited Maho as children are now bringing their young families to Maho.

This aspect of Maho's culture is perhaps its single most unusual attribute. Based on the author's personal experience from touring Maho Bay Camps and interacting with its guests, it was clear that these guests had a sense of ownership and proprietorship associated with the camp. It was evidenced by their sharing common experiences, planning repeat visits to the camp, and bringing their spouses and family members to share their experiences at Maho. As the author walked around the camp with Selengut, Selengut was stopped repeatedly by guests who thanked him for creating the resort (some hugged him as well). Selengut's comment after the walk was that many resorts, including his, make money, but he has the added benefit of the genuine appreciation the guests have for Maho. The strength of this emotional bond with Maho was seen when Hurricane Hugo battered St. John in 1989. Several guests who had expertise in various aspects of construction, development, facilities, etc., volunteered their time and money to come and repair the resort's facilities. Some even donated equipment and other things in kind.

This kind of guest involvement in a property is virtually unheard of in regular hotels. It reveals the ownership that guests feel about Maho Bay Camps—"their camp." This sentiment resurfaced recently when guests learned that the lease for Maho was due to expire and the camp may close for good. Many of them publicly lobbied to keep the camp open and contributed money to a fund created to buy the land on which Maho is built. Ultimately, this type of feeling for a hotel, resort, or campground can only be created if there is a sense of shared values between the facility's owner and its guests. In Selengut's case at Maho, the shared values happen to be preservation, conservation, and the simple appreciation of nature.

Summary and Lessons Learned

When asked in a closing interview at Maho to summarize his operation at Maho, Selengut said that he follows a "green" variation of the KISS principle, which is: "Keep it Simple and Sustainable." While the idea of ecotourism became popular in the late 1970s, Selengut had already started to implement its principles years earlier in the sustainable design and development of his project at Maho. Maho Bay Camps and Estate Concordia Preserve have provided several valuable ideas, lessons, and principles for resort developers and operators around the world. These include: (1) the creative use of resources to minimize the resort's impact on the environment; (2) developing resort projects that are in harmony with their natural surroundings; (3) the promotional power of a unique sustainability story; (4) the creation of a loyal fan following by establishing a culture in which guests, employees, and resort owners share a common set of values; and (5) the responsibility of eco-sensitive resorts to not only entertain their guests but educate them to become better environmental stewards. Most importantly, Maho Bay Camps has shown through its consistent performance over three decades that by employing innovation, creativity, and a passion for sustainable development it is possible to be environmentally conscious and profitable at the same time. Finally, the Maho Bay Camps story may serve as an inspiration for hotel industry leaders to incorporate principles of the triple bottom line and adopt a balanced concern for people, planet, and profit in their businesses.

Addendum: The Future of Maho Bay Camps

Unfortunately, the future of Maho Bay Camps is uncertain at the time of this writing. The resort was built on a site leased from a private owner, Giri Giri Corp. The lease, which was originally set to expire in January 2012, received a six-month extension. A non-profit land conservation organization, the Trust for Public Land (TPL), is in serious negotiations to acquire the land and allow the resort to remain open.[8]

Mr. John Garrison, the field office director for TPL covering South Florida and the Caribbean, said[9] that TPL had recently finished a land acquisition for most of a 419-acre land parcel adjacent to the U.S.V.I. National Park, called Estate Maho. (One owner of 38 acres within the parcel has not yet sold them, although TPL is still in discussions with the owner over a potential sale. TPL now owns 381 acres at the Maho Bay beachfront, and plans to turn it over to the National Park Service.) With this purchase, TPL shares a common boundary with Maho Bay Camps.

TPL is also negotiating to buy the Maho Bay Camps parcel, Mr. Garrison said. If the purchase of the land on which Maho rests is successful, TPL plans to keep the resort operating, conduct bidding to determine its future operator (which could include Mr. Selengut), and make changes to further reduce the ecological footprint of the resort's structures and operations. While it is still too early to tell if the negotiations will be successful, Garrison indicated that the vast public support that Maho Bay Camps enjoys, its economic impact on the community, and its large number of loyal guests are advantages in the negotiations. He said that more than 17,000 resort guests have indicated their willingness to donate cash to support the purchase of the land.

Endnotes

1. Data from U.S.V.I. Bureau of Economic Research, www.usviber.org.

2. According to statistics from the U.S.V.I. Bureau of Economic Research.

3. Jane Braxton Little, "Camp Caribbean," *Audubon*, November/December 2007, p. 64.

4. For more information, see http://www.usvi.net/usvi/taxes.html.

5. United States National Park Service, "Guiding Principles of Sustainable Design," a document available at http://www.nps.gov/dsc/d_publications/d_1_gpsd.htm.

6. Author A. J. Singh's private conversation with Mr. Selengut.

7. For more information, see http://www.friendsvinp.org/about.htm.

8. For more information, see the Trust for Public Land's website at www.tpl.org.

9. Information is based on interviews of Mr. Garrison conducted by A. J. Singh.

Designing and Developing Sustainable, High-Performing Hotels: An Architectural Perspective

By Steve Galbreath and Laura Galbreath

Steve Galbreath, *AIA, ISHC, LEED AP, is a Vice President with RTKL, the international architecture, planning, and design firm. With almost two decades of experience around the globe, Steve's focus has been exclusively on the design of hospitality, gaming, and mixed-use projects with a particular expertise on sustainable design and LEED-certified projects.*

Galbreath is currently a board member of the ISHC (International Society of Hospitality Consultants) and is a frequent speaker at industry events, including multiple engagements at the International Society of Hospitality Consultants annual conferences; the Tourism Conference at InfoMax/ProInversion, Lima, Peru; the Hotel Developer's Conference in Palm Springs, CA; the BITAC Hotel Luxury Conference in San Juan, Puerto Rico; the XIII Congreso International de Arquitectura in Monterrey, Mexico; and the HD (Hospitality Design) Expo in Las Vegas.

Steve has published articles and been quoted in numerous industry journals, including Forbes.com, Hotel & Motel Management, Texas Architect, The Hotel Yearbook, Hotel Interactive, Hotel Design, and a number of others.

Laura Galbreath, *AIA, LEED AP, is a Principal in RTKL's Dallas office and a seasoned project manager with experience in hospitality and mixed-use projects. In the last decade, Laura has emerged as a recognized expert in the planning and design of sustainable hospitality environments. She is currently a member of the United States Green Building Council's LEED for Hospitality Adaptations Working Group.*

Laura's work has been recognized by such organizations as the Southface Institute and Condé Nast. Her work on The Lodge & Spa at Callaway Gardens, one of the first LEED-certified hotels in the world, helped earn the project the International Restaurant & Hotel's Green Award; while her involvement in the extensive renovation of the Ritz-Carlton Palm Beach contributed to that project being named as a Gold Key Awards Finalist by the International Hotel/Motel & Restaurant Awards in 2009.

After graduating from Ohio State University with a Bachelor of Science in Architecture degree, Laura went on to earn her Masters of Architecture at Texas A&M University. Laura is a registered architect in Texas, a LEED-accredited professional, and is a member of the American Institute of Architects and Texas Society of Architects.

Authors' Acknowledgments

The authors wish to thank the following people for their contributions to this chapter: Thom McKay, Vice President, RTKL Associates Inc.—Washington, D.C.; Wendy Mendes, IIDA, LEED AP, Vice President, RTKL Associates Inc.—Miami, Florida; Jason Litt, Principal, RTKL Associates Inc.—Dallas, Texas; William O'Donnell, P.E., Managing Principal DeSimone Consulting Engineers—Miami, Florida; and Kelly Thomas, Stone Source—New York, New York.

WITH ENERGY COSTS, CONSUMER EXPECTATIONS, AND GOVERNMENT MANDATES for sustainability on the rise, the opportunity—and the competitive advantage—of implementing eco-friendly design and operational practices is clear and present as the hotel industry begins to rebound. According to a March 2010 Ernst & Young report on the global hospitality industry, green initiatives are a key way with which successful operators will differentiate themselves in this increasingly competitive market. While developers and owners will certainly admit the issue is important to them, very few project sponsors appreciate the benefits green initiatives can offer.

One of the contributing factors to this attitude is the industry's fragmented nature and multiple stakeholders (owners, lenders, operators, consultants, and suppliers). The heterogeneous nature of hotel products, combined with hotels' varied locations and renovation cycles, also makes sustainable property development appear costly and negative-value-added. Finally, a hotel's complex operational model, especially in the full-service and resort segments, places greater demand on materials and systems, making sustainable renovation of hotels more logistically challenging than sustainable renovation of other commercial real estate properties.

For these and other reasons, we believe the hospitality industry lags behind other industries in defining itself as truly green, but there is no shortage of proven innovations in related sectors from which to learn. For example, RTKL is a leader in the design of cruise ship interiors. This industry has out of necessity developed creative approaches to the use of space, lighting, energy, and materials—all of which have sustainable currency applicable to land-based hotels. Throughout the past decade, the cruise industry has made significant strides toward reducing water use (e.g., toilets use one-third of a gallon per flush) and energy use (e.g., compact fluorescent and LED lighting have replaced incandescent lighting, reducing energy consumption and heat loads). Some vessels even have composting programs.

This chapter explores the salient principles and best practices of designing a sustainable hospitality project from the perspective of the designer/architect. The following pages present a framework we have found to be integral to the success of any sustainable hospitality project, regardless of location, scale, or budget.

The framework begins with all stakeholders making the commitment to develop sustainably. Next, stakeholders should incorporate sustainability into the project's conceptual design and planning, then select the right team and assign roles and responsibilities to each team member. We hope this chapter encourages developers and project sponsors to vigorously embrace sustainable practices on all fronts, taking sustainability beyond the guestroom card request for reused towels and toward a fully integrated system of sustainable operations.

Commitment to Create a Sustainable Hotel

While green design practices and third-party certifications like Leadership in Energy and Environmental Design (LEED) have moved into the mainstream over the past several years, there remains a lingering sense that "designing green" adds cost and not value to a project. This seems especially true in the hospitality industry, which is so devoted to the guest experience that many architects and designers are reluctant to raise the issue, fully expecting developers or operations experts to declare, "It can't be done." We believe it can.

The process starts with the development team (investor, developer, architect, and consultant team) committing to clear, articulated sustainability goals. These goals should form the basis of a written document that sets out targets, responsibilities, and a specific scope of work. This document may change over the course of a project, but once it is established, the team can come to an understanding regarding time and cost considerations, as well as each goal's longer-term operational impact. Project meetings should include time for discussing and monitoring progress toward each goal, especially when dealing with issues like long-lead activities that might affect schedule, budget, or operations and management. Teams should define their goals beyond the simple checklist mentality of third-party certification systems like LEED, Green Globe, Green Seal, or the Green Key Eco-Rating Program, the latest certification tailored for the hospitality industry. Goals should clearly identify the general direction for sustainability management and maintenance throughout the project's lifetime.

Sustainability Starts Early in the Process

While it is tempting to define sustainable design in its simplest terms (as "bricks and mortar" or "systems and materials"), a broader approach sees opportunity across the entire development cycle—from site selection and contract negotiations to design and ongoing facilities/property management. Choosing a hotel operator and ensuring that the operator's expectations dovetail with the client-ownership group is critical to a sustainable hotel project's success.

Site selection and building orientation may be hardest to control, but often have the greatest impact on a hotel or resort's overall energy use. Energy modeling, along with wind and solar studies, which developers usually see as avoidable or unnecessary up-front costs, typically pay for themselves many times over through energy savings in the area of 4 to 8 percent annually. Similarly, basic master planning issues like building massing (a building's three-dimensional volume), on-site transportation, storm water run-off management, and irrigation requirements all affect a property's carbon footprint and should be assessed from a sustainability perspective long before shovels break ground. A slight change to a building's orientation or its layout on a drawing is much less expensive to implement than a massive cooling system needed to offset design flaws.

Select the Right Team

Having a dedicated team that is knowledgeable, creative, and persuasive on sustainability issues is critical. This starts at the top, and assumes the client team (investor/developer and operator) has committed to sustainability principles. However, from a design perspective, hotels and resorts generally require the expertise of myriad consultants, so it helps to have a team that not only commits to sustainability goals, but brings tested experience and a willingness to share best practices. Fortunately, because of the trend toward green design, many consultants in North America and Europe—from front-of-house designers to more technical back-of-house consultants—are gaining expertise in sustainability. Properties in climate-intensive locales (like most resorts) or with system-intensive amenities (like spas) require specialized help from consultants with proven expertise in sustainable practices. Additionally, some locations might need a practiced hand at sourcing local products and materials.

In terms of sustainable design, perhaps the most overlooked team member is the contractor, whose role, understanding, and commitment to the project are essential, especially in areas like recycled waste and systems testing. With a contractor committed to the project's sustainable design features, the commissioning agents and the entire team will have a relatively easy journey toward certification. A proactive contractor can do the following: help develop a plan for handling construction waste and defining on-site protocols and conditions; address air quality, recycling, and material procurement; and monitor the amount of recycled content a project uses. The contractor can also help manage pre-occupancy air quality, and integrate its testing into opening schedules. Air duct filter maintenance and regular air tests can save considerable time and prevent anxiety at a project's completion.

Roles and Responsibilities. Team efforts are most successful when roles and responsibilities are clearly defined from the earliest stages. While cross-pollination is always recommended, responsibility and accountability carry the day. It is important to instill a protocol for decision-making and to communicate this protocol to the entire team. RTKL uses a spreadsheet to monitor key issues and project decisions, tracking each issue from when it first surfaces, determining who is responsible for resolving it, noting the manner in which it was resolved, and dealing with schedule or budgetary implications. A searchable spreadsheet or database seems simple, but helps greatly with information flow. The "issues" list becomes an integral part of the project's meeting agendas and serves as a quick prompt on latest developments and outstanding tasks.

A single member of the team should be designated the sustainability coordinator. This person will monitor progress and salient issues, as well as documentation and filing requirements. The assignment is especially critical when a project pursues third-party certifications that rely on systems of points or checklists.

Having a single, experienced professional maintaining these responsibilities improves the odds of achieving a project's sustainability targets. The sustainability coordinator might be an existing member of the consultant team or someone with specific qualifications brought in to fulfill this requirement.

Low-Impact Design Collaboration. While the goal is to have a truly sustainable and, in many cases, certified project, how the team gets there is just as important as the finished product. Whether due to the pressures of a challenging economy or the nobler pursuit of green practices, we have all learned to think twice before printing stacks of paper and hopping on planes to consult with fellow team members. Today, face-to-face meetings and overnight couriers are becoming relics of an outmoded approach to communication. Instead, videoconferencing, electronic media, and online document management are tested methods of shrinking a project's carbon footprint while saving money on travel and other expenses.

It is important to communicate the architect's work process. In the past, an architect would send a set of plans or AutoCAD drawings to a mechanical, electrical, and plumbing (MEP) engineer. Now, the entire team can work from a central model updated in real time. For example, web-based meetings and advances in building information modeling (BIM) software let multi-disciplinary teams work on a single project model, with each consultant collaborating across secure lines. That said, teams will still need to meet face-to-face at critical junctures in the project's design process.

Sustainability Through Structural Optimization

A symbiotic relationship exists between the goals of sustainable practices and efficient structural design. All other things being equal, a reduction in construction materials will always result in a beneficial economic and environmental outcome. In this regard, good structural design, by definition, is sustainable design because it strives to achieve the most efficient use of materials. It stands to reason that encouraging and ensuring an optimal design will result in a sustainable design as well.

A variety of techniques can minimize the amount of structural materials used in a hotel's construction. The most effective techniques are broadly categorized as follows:

- Remove unnecessary conservatism from the design.

- Optimize the structural system using advanced analysis techniques.

- Consider alternate structural materials and systems.

The effort required to pursue these techniques ranges from simple to complex, and ultimately depends on the engineer's capabilities and commitment, as well as on the design schedule. Although some of these techniques require substantial effort on the part of the engineer, the potential economic and environmental benefits can far outweigh the associated expense. For example, cement production is a key source of global carbon dioxide emissions. Because the cement industry contributes about 5 percent to global carbon dioxide emissions annually, the benefits of minimizing its creation become obvious. When excess materials are used unnecessarily, a ripple effect is felt from production to placement (i.e., pollution to energy consumption to possibly feeding and housing the labor force needed to manufacture the construction materials).

Remove Unnecessary Conservatism

Conventional building codes are based on minimum design criteria that ensure a building's safety. These criteria are in a simple form to ensure ease of compliance and enforcement. Building codes are meant to cover a broad array of structures, shapes, locations, and materials, and their range typically transcends geologic and climatic boundaries. This one-size-fits-all approach is not intended to address the needs of a particular project in a particular location. Rather, it encompasses a broad range of possible design applications. This approach requires an "upper-bound" design philosophy that results in conservative designs for some structures, and bare minimum designs for others. The one-size-fits-all conservatism of many building codes leads to greater material usage and greater costs and therefore should be challenged when possible.

Optimize the Structural System Using Advanced Analysis Techniques

The level of detail and sophistication used in completing a structural analysis can have a significant impact on the required structural material quantities. Advances in analytical modeling have helped structural engineers develop highly refined and optimized designs. Although performance-based design (PBD) is the only legal method to avert some of the conservative code requirements, numerous techniques are available to minimize the impact of the prescriptive code provisions. Dynamic analysis, non-linear analysis, and finite element analysis are examples of advanced techniques that can help achieve design optimization.

The benefits of using advanced analysis techniques can be illustrated by comparing the various methods of assessing the stiffness of concrete elements for lateral analysis (see Exhibit 1). It is well-known that the stiffness of a concrete structure is sensitive to the degree of cracking, if any. Many design offices consider the effects of cracking by using some arbitrary reduced section properties (e.g., 50- to 70-percent stiffness for some portion of the building height). However, the only accurate method of assessing and modeling the true stiffness of these structures is to model their non-linear constitutive material relationships explicitly. Exhibit 1 illustrates a comparison of the three methods of stiffness modeling for a 125-meter slender tower. In this example, it can be seen that use of an arbitrary 70-percent reduced section modifier for half the building height would have resulted in an unnecessary over-design. Again, while such a detailed analysis is an intensive and time-consuming process for the engineer, the potential benefit to the owner and the environment justifies the effort.

Consider Alternate Structural Materials and Systems

Although theoretically an infinite number of structural systems exist for use on a given building, there are some limitations on materials and construction methods.

Exhibit 1   Comparison of Stiffness Assumptions for a Reinforced Concrete Tower

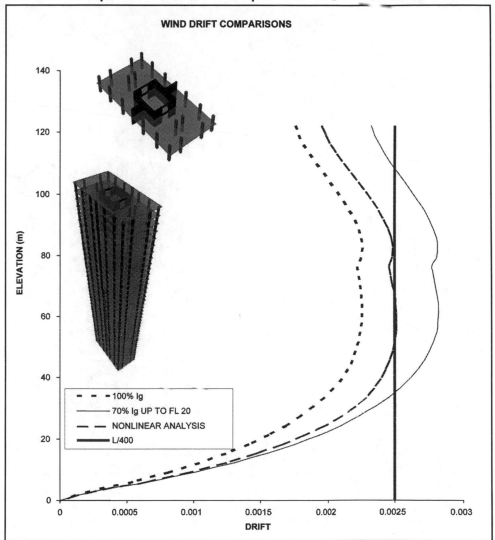

The prevalence of certain systems aligns with the availability of regional resources and historically engrained cultural perceptions of what is appropriate or required. In some areas, labor is abundant and inexpensive, while in others, labor is the limiting factor. With regard to sustainability, numerous structural systems can achieve effective material reductions, but must be considered within the context of local market conditions, including labor resources. Structural systems comprised of precast elements, post-tensioning, and lightweight materials all deserve due consideration. Ultimately, sustainable structural solutions must go beyond

Exhibit 2   Stiffness Comparisons for Typical High-Rise Shear Wall Systems

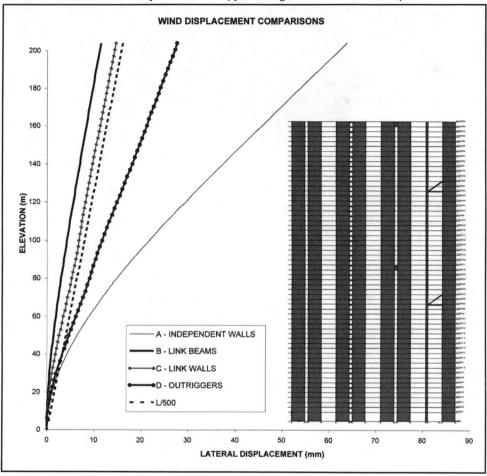

material choice alone and include innovative systems that achieve efficiency in a more global sense.

As an example, the lateral-force resisting system—the system of structural components that resist "sideways" loads, most often from wind and earthquakes—for tall concrete buildings typically uses shear walls at service cores and possibly at some demising walls. These wall arrangements vary from fully independent walls on either side of central corridors, to systems of interlinked shear wall groups combined with more flexible frames and outrigger systems that incorporate, and sometimes enlarge, some of the building's beams and columns. The process leading to selection of a building's lateral system can be complex. Shear walls are, without question, the stiffest and, therefore, most efficient means of transferring lateral loads down through a building to its foundation (see Exhibit 2). Additionally, they have the advantage of simple formwork. While sometimes requiring more concrete material, they are often most efficient with respect to the amount and simplicity of reinforcement required.

That said, shear walls are also the most obtrusive solution from the perspective of architectural and MEP distribution. When earthquake loads are of greater concern than loads from wind, shear walls actually increase the magnitude of the lateral loads needing accommodation. As a result, they can lead to additional "secondary" costs related to architectural and ductwork inefficiencies—both in terms of labor and materials—and to the increased lateral loads that must be accommodated by the building's foundation.

All these factors must be viewed as a matrix of competing advantages and disadvantages. This matrix, in turn, must be examined in the context of local materials and labor markets, local physical conditions (e.g., soil and groundwater conditions), and the building's required structural loading and performance. In the end, the right solution for a lateral system could end up being one that is, on the face of it, more complex, but that leads to simplification and cost savings in other areas or systems.

The Role of Government in Identification and Enforcement of Sustainable Structural Design

Where local construction practices or public perception resist sustainable structural design, government regulations can be an effective means either of compelling owners to pursue them or of providing substantial benefits for compliance. In this regard, governing authorities can exercise greatest control over a project's degree of sustainability by requiring and/or rewarding innovation in structural design. For example, a local building code could be amended to include more appropriate region-specific design provisions, and to value more detailed analysis procedures over conservative methods. Additionally, significant projects could be required to have a value engineering design review or a structural sustainability review conducted by an independent engineering firm or by the governing body itself. Although this might sound like a new and added expense, many projects already incorporate value engineering design reviews as a means of achieving the same goal, albeit for economic and/or legal reasons. With regard to a building's structure, the economic and sustainability benefits of reduced material quantities become mutual.

Common Features of Sustainable Interior Design

Perhaps more than for any other building type, hospitality interiors present some of the biggest challenges for sustainability designers. Yet nowhere is being green more important. Inevitably, interior designers must strike a balance between sustainability objectives and the so-called "guest experience," which touches virtually every aspect of hospitality design, from materials and systems to furniture, fixtures, and equipment (FF&E), colors, and carpeting. An infinite number of touchpoints serves as the measurement for good hospitality interior design, with each touchpoint offering an opportunity to incorporate sustainability.

Water consumption is one of the biggest challenges in this balancing act. Many guests use a property's bathrooms as a benchmark of its quality. At a certain tier, a robust shower, luxurious towels, and a soaking tub are requirements. A guest might not realize (or even care) that the toilet uses 1.28 gallons per flush or that the bathroom faucet's flow rate is 1.5 gallons per minute. However, the guest will almost certainly notice the shower's water pressure and use it as a quality measurement. Fortunately, several manufacturers have developed adjustable-flow shower heads with internal turbines that boost streams to give guests the feeling of ample flow, while still conserving water.

Other challenges have inspired creative and technologically sustainable solutions, especially in the area of lighting. Today's compact fluorescent bulbs have color temperatures of 2700 K and improved color-rendering indexes, offering the same quality as incandescent lamps at a fraction of the wattage consumption. The growing popularity of light-emitting diode (LED) lighting has also led manufacturers to develop a variety of decorative fixtures that are replacing the traditional incandescent lamp. LED lamps not only use far less wattage than incandescent lights, they also offer a lamp life of 50,000 hours, reducing the number of light bulbs that end up in landfills.

Related to lighting, control and monitoring systems are another technological approach to achieving sustainability objectives in a hospitality environment. While specific calculations are not available, the amount of energy used to condition or light unoccupied guestrooms is no doubt staggering. Features as basic as key card slots that activate room power—fairly prevalent in European properties—have significantly reduced electricity consumption. When a guest is away, the removed key card shuts down the room's systems. More elaborate control or monitoring systems can also be used, letting the front desk monitor everything from heating, ventilating, and air conditioning (HVAC) and lights to whether or not guests are in their rooms.

Beyond these elements, interior designers deal with an array of materials— fabrics, wall coverings, and floor coverings—that compose a majority of the overall green equation. Fortunately, advances in manufacturing have given designers access to an almost limitless choice of products with post-consumer content, low volatile organic compounds (VOCs), and other organic or eco-friendly components. Most quality manufacturers have whole-heartedly embraced the green movement; some are even reclaiming old product (carpeting, for example) and recycling it for new uses. Over the long term, these recycling programs have not only helped the environment, they have reduced raw material costs and, consequently, the costs of finished products.

The High Speed of Change and the Rise of the Smart Suite

How does technology factor into the sustainability equation? The key to a sustainable technology design lies in a flexible infrastructure that lets technology change over time. Today's technology is pushing further toward converged networks in which audiovisual, data/telecom, wireless, security, lighting, and HVAC control systems share common infrastructures. By sharing this converged network, a building does not necessarily work synergistically, but does reap reduced costs associated with cable, infrastructure, and labor.

Smart technologies are finding their way into suite designs that let guests feel like they would in their own homes, using technology to set their preferences. The primary interface for this so-called "smart suite" is a touch panel, either wall-mounted or wireless. The touch panel acts as the main portal to a variety of automated services, such as a digital concierge, HVAC control, lighting control, shade control, and other guest amenities. Some hotel brands have used televisions as portals to these services; however, while flat-panel power consumption rates are improving, a flat-panel television is still one of the largest power consumers in a guestroom.

The ideal smart suite incorporates HVAC control, lighting control, shade control, energy modeling, building amenities, audiovisual applications, security features, and smart appliances. These systems can be more holistic and incorporate real-time interaction and reporting into the building's management systems. In this way, the building comes closer to an integrated building technology (IBT) design model.

The current goal is to develop an open language that would let a room's systems "talk" to one another. For example, a light sensor could measure the amount of light entering a room and automatically adjust the shades. Occupancy sensors would determine whether someone was in the room and, if so, adjust the thermostat to a preferred setting. If the room was unoccupied, the system would switch to a dark mode in which the temperature adjusted, the shades closed, and the lighting and electronic devices turned off. As soon as the guest re-entered the room, the system would return to its previous state. Guests could also set a "green" mode in which the suite operated at optimal settings (e.g., water flow, lighting, HVAC) for a sustainable stay. Guests could monitor their energy use through a meter at the bottom of the control system touch panel.

This approach requires a shift in thinking for designers and engineers. They need to ask themselves how their systems affect or interact with other systems in the suite. The primary roadblock to this transition involves the different system languages and interfaces these legacy systems use. In other words, the various system software applications cannot talk to one another. The solution comes in the form of browser-based applications and software with relational capabilities, like Extensible Markup Language (XML) Application Programming Interfaces (APIs). Technology like this has cost implications, but with an ever-expanding database of financial return metrics and proof of energy conservation, these smart suites will eventually become the rule rather than the exception.

Currently, most third-party certifiers, including LEED, provide limited recognition of the use of technology to boost sustainability. These third parties could have an impact on light pollution reduction, optimization of energy performance, measurement and verification, controllability of systems, innovation in design, and various other areas.

What Makes a Product Sustainable?

Several opinions exist regarding which criteria make a product truly sustainable. Many architects and designers do not classify products as "sustainable" or "not sustainable." Instead, they ask questions: Is the product comprised of recycled materials? Can the material be recycled after its useful life? Is the product manufactured within 500 miles of the project? Does the manufacturer use sustainable practices, such as reusing water used in manufacturing, using solar power, recycling, and preserving the natural landscape when building manufacturing facilities?

Lifecycle vs. Recycle

Hospitality design requires frequent renovation to keep a space fresh, so it is critical to weigh lifecycle versus initial costs when selecting sustainable products. What good is a highly rated material if it does not endure a hotel's normal wear and tear? For example, while wheat board products might seem more "green" and are certainly cheaper than other products, their lifecycle endurance might actually work against the cause of sustainability. Using systems and products that extend the renovation cycle is one of the easiest ways to keep amenities out of landfills. Also consider a product's end-of-life attributes. Can it be reclaimed and recycled? Is it biodegradable? A product with a longer lifecycle not only reduces waste, but also (because shorter replacement cycles create more manufacturing and transportation needs) leads to lowered energy and pollution levels. Although green products sometimes cost more initially, they are usually replaced less frequently, lowering their long-term cost and environmental impact.

LEED and Third-Party Certifications

Today, many products come with third-party endorsements or certifications, and it's important to understand what all of these mean. Endorsed or certified products, materials, and systems are desirable because, for instance, they contribute to LEED certification, so architects and designers use them to guarantee the products they use are truly sustainable. What follows are just a few examples of "green" endorsements and certifications:

- *U.S. Green Building Council (USGBC).* The USGCB developed the LEED rating system to give building owners, developers, and architects a concise framework for identifying and implementing practical and measurable green building design, construction, operations, and maintenance solutions.

- *Rainforest Alliance.* The Rainforest Alliance certifies tourist-based enterprises (hotels and resorts) that achieve significant and measurable sustainability milestones.

- *Forest Stewardship Council (FSC).* The FSC promotes responsible management of the world's forests and sets the standard for organizations interested in responsible forestry, including timber harvesting and the production of paper products.

- *McDonough Braungart Design Chemistry (MBDC).* MBDC's Cradle to Cradle certification assesses a product's safety to humans and the environment. Focused on lifecycle issues, the certification is based on five categories of guidelines for materials that can be disassembled and recycled as technical nutrients in manufacturing or composted as biological nutrients.

Typical Sustainable Products for Hotel Projects

A wide range of sustainable materials aimed at the hospitality industry is available today. To make smart selections, architects and designers should understand the pros and cons of each.

Reclaimed Wood. Reclaimed wood is often harvested from unused barns and factories. Manufacturers turn the beams, rafters, barn boards, and other elements into wood fiber. This fiber can then be used in wood wall paneling, flooring, and millwork, which can then be recycled into other materials at the end of their useful lives. As with all products, reclaimed wood offers varying levels of sustainability, depending on the manufacturer's (or mill's) processes.

Recycled Porcelain Tile and Glass Tile. Many of today's porcelain and glass tile products contain post-industrial recycled material. Recycled porcelain is generally 40-percent recycled material, a level that will likely increase as technology improves. Glass tile can be 99-percent post-industrial or post-consumer waste.

Natural Stone. If a stone is quarried and manufactured within 500 miles of a project site, it may contribute to LEED certification, thereby giving the stone a sustainable quality. Other aspects that may qualify a natural stone as sustainable include the manufacturer's operations in the quarry, mill, and manufacturing facility. Have these operations been evaluated and do they meet the requirements for MBDC's Cradle to Cradle certification? What happens to the byproduct during manufacturing? In many cases, these products are reused as smaller stones or groundcover, or are ground into sand.

Engineered Wood. Engineered wood contains compressed wood fibers covered by a thin layer of wood. It may be considered sustainable if the fibers come from reclaimed materials. When deciding whether to use engineered wood in a project, designers should consider not only the material's composition, but also its longevity. High-quality engineered wood has a thick top layer, making the material more durable (depending on the species), even when subjected to heavy commercial traffic and consistent cleaning and maintenance.

Stains and Finishes. A wide range of stains and finishes are available for use on natural stone and reclaimed wood. When selecting finishes, look for low-VOC items or those that are water-based.

Other Products. The design industry is seeing more materials derived from non-traditional resources. The results are impressive. For example, agricultural byproducts, such as wheatgrass, corn husks, corn kernels, and sunflower seeds, are being infused with resin to create durable, versatile products.

Low-Impact Packaging. Beyond their efforts to research and develop new products, manufacturers are taking more pronounced approaches to sustainability by re-engineering their packaging. Styrofoam and similar types of packaging are wasteful and have a negative impact on the environment. Several alternative packing methods exist. For example, in the stone industry, wood crates support products during shipping and are frequently reused. Such sustainable packaging often helps the delivery process and can aid in some third-party certifications.

A Final Note on Sustainable Products. With all of today's marketing bravado, it is easy to be persuaded by lofty claims and checked boxes claiming sustainable design. Yet the true goal of sustainable design is to consider our professional role in the preservation of limited natural resources. In many cases, this requires a long-term vision that looks beyond checklists or the immediate needs of a project timeline or budget. It takes a mindset that questions and challenges traditional conventions, and endeavors to make more responsible decisions. Often, it makes good business sense, especially if lifecycle costs—so critical in hospitality development—are taken into account.

Educate the Guest

Guest profiles show a growing trend toward sustainability and eco-tourism, including a willingness to pay a premium for green or organic products. Because this trend—and the importance of the eco-tourism market—is likely to continue, if not grow, it is important to let guests play a role in the sustainability cause. Educating and informing guests through approaches like sustainability tours, in-room material, and co-branding are excellent ways of changing behavior and reinforcing a green ethos.

A prime example is The Lodge & Spa at Callaway Gardens in Georgia. From the project's inception, sustainability served not only as a design criterion, but as a means of fulfilling Callaway's mission to provide a living landscape where visitors could experience nature and cultivate a long-standing relationship with the environment. The most unique aspect of Callaway's sustainability efforts is the Building Education Program. Using various instructional methods, the Lodge & Spa educates the public about the benefits of green building and sustainable living practices. Signs throughout the property (see Exhibit 3 for one example) describe conservation tactics used on-site. Because many of these tactics are not immediately obvious, guests can take guided tours that illustrate and explain individual features. To lead tours, resort employees receive training on the building's sustainability initiatives.

Sustainable Hotels and the Power of LESS

In the world of hospitality, abundance—more service, bigger beds, higher status, infinite views, and ultimate privacy—is king. Traditionally, travelers judged hotels by the number of amenities offered. This, more often than not, translated into some fairly unsustainable practices. But what if a great hospitality experience

Exhibit 3   Educate Guests on Sustainability Efforts

A SUSTAINABLE SITE

Continuing Callaway's legacy of land stewardship and our commitment to environmentally sensitive development, many conservation techniques were used during the construction of this facility including:

- A sediment and erosion control plan was established and followed to prevent a loss of soil by wind erosion and/or stormwater run-off during construction and to prevent sedimentation of storm sewer and local receiving streams and rivers.

- An appropriate location was chosen for the building within the Callaway Gardens campus in order to reduce the environmental impact of the building.

- In addition to the shuttle services available to hotel guests, employees of Callaway Gardens who live in Pine Mountain are brought to and from work by shuttle bus in an effort to reduce pollution. Preferred parking for carpool vehicles are also provided in each of the parking areas.

- During the original development and later expansion of the parking area, special considerations were given to the characteristcis of the land. The site was developed in harmony with the natural surroundings, retaining the qualities and feel of a forest. The natural topography, drainage courses, and established trees were respected to reduce "heat islands" that normally occur in parking lots and to improve run-off rates and groundwater recharge.

- The disruption of natural water flows has been limited through the design of onsite filtration to increase the filtration of contaminants and to eliminate stormwater runoff.

- A parcel of land that is equal in size to twice the amount disturbed for this facility is being preserved within the Callaway Gardens campus as open space for the life of this building.

Please ask at the front desk about a tour of this facility to learn more about sustainable building and living practices.

were not defined by "how much" but by "how little"? What if the paradigm were reversed so that the object of a great stay was to minimize, not to maximize?

The Livable Environmentally Sustainable Suite (LESS), developed by RTKL, is a new concept in sustainable hospitality design. A LESS hotel invites guests to become active participants in the way their rooms function. Guests simultaneously control, learn, and benefit from the performance of various components in their rooms, all in a well-designed and completely green environment. Although still in a concept phase, LESS principles are capturing the attention of industry leaders across markets. Exhibit 4 illustrates the three intentions of the LESS research project: to educate, reduce, and reward, and, in turn, to inform the many aspects of hotel development and operation these intentions directly affect.

Exhibit 4   LESS—How Does It Work?

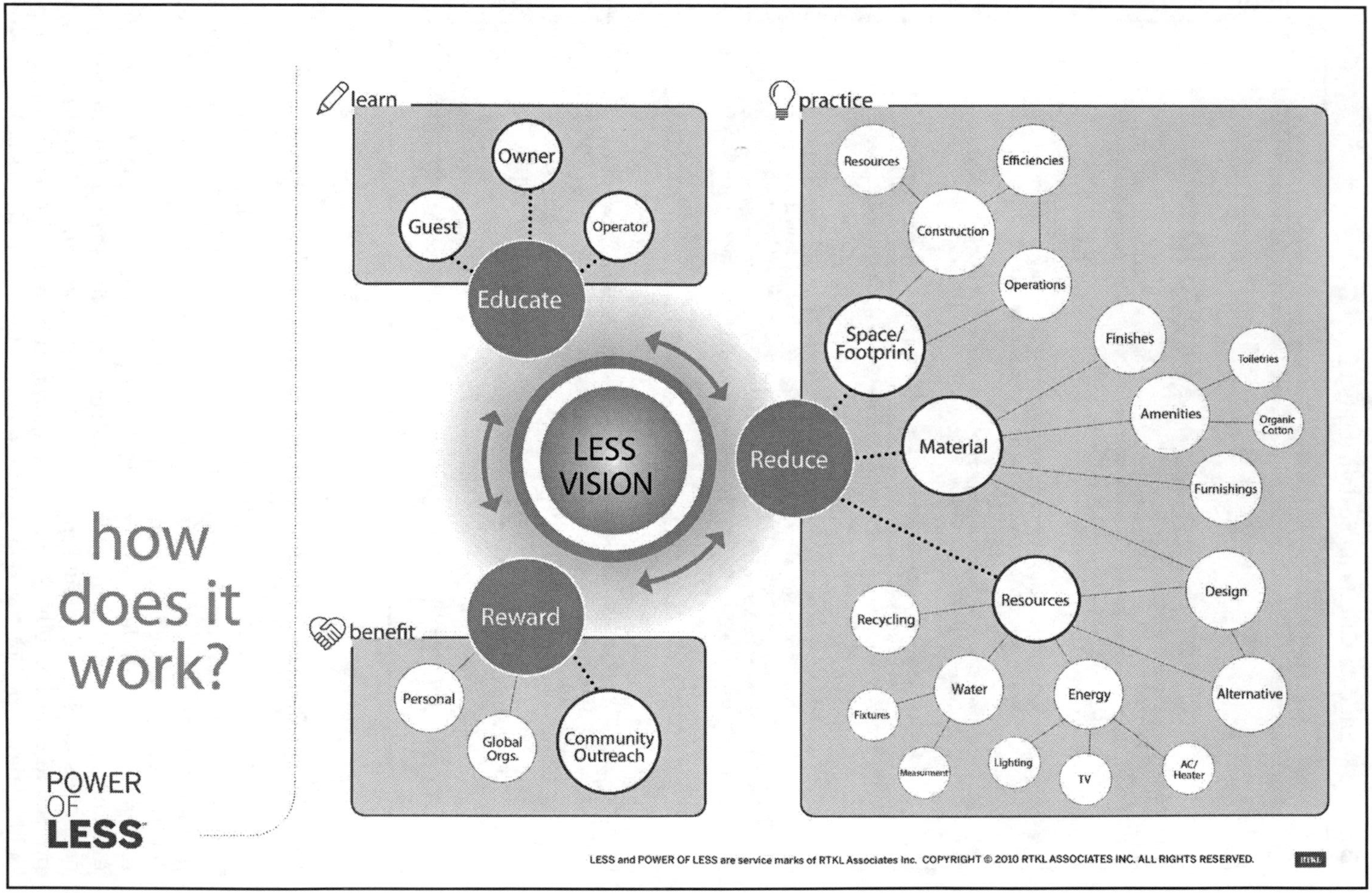

Exhibit 5   E-Concierge Homescreen

LESS Is More

True to the adage that "less is more," clear and quantifiable benefits arise from simplifying our environments. A LESS hotel invites guests to manage their energy consumption through an e-concierge, a digital interface as easy to use as an iPhone. The e-concierge encourages guests to define their own energy use by turning off the air conditioning and lights as often as possible. Each guestroom is sub-metered to measure and set a target for energy and water consumption per guest night's stay. Every kilowatt and gallon saved translates into points for the guest's END-LESS Benefits account. (The program rewards guests by offering additional nights and credits toward spa treatments or other amenities.)

A large LED panel in the center of the room is more than just a TV. It assembles all the information guests need for their stays. The remote control allows a guest to initiate a pre-programmed eco-profile, order room service, start a virtual yoga class, or offer an update of a guest's ENDLESS Benefits reward points (see Exhibit 5). No paper, no hassle, no waste.

LESS Is Less

A LESS hotel's guestrooms offer small, efficient footprints, maximizing the use of every square foot (see Exhibit 6). Throughout each room, dynamic information conveys material savings achieved through sustainable design and construction. For example, the 12-by-16-by-9-foot modules use ten standard sheets of drywall, as opposed to a typical guestroom's thirty-five sheets (of which at least 7 percent

Exhibit 6   LESS vs. Typical Guestroom

🖊 learn

Making drywall accounts for 1% of U.S. energy consumption and 25 billion pounds of CO in the air each year.

reduced materials

LESS
IS
LESS

Typical Guestroom Plan - 300 sf

L.E.S.S. Plan - 192 sf

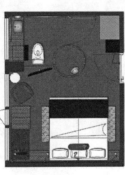

💡 practice

- **Reduce Resources**
  Less construction resources are utilized by building smaller.

- **Reduce Construction Waste**
  Less pollution lowers the impact on the environment by lowering construction waste.

- **12' x 16' x 9' Module**
  The **LESS** room module is 12' x 16' x 9' based on using ten (10) 9' high sheets of drywall to avoid waste. The typical room module requires thirty-five (35) sheets of drywall, of which at least 7% is wasted.

- **Reduced Carbon Footprint**
  A smaller room uses less energy to heat, cool and light, lowering the operating costs and carbon footprint of the hotel.

Build less. Use less.

The **POWER OF LESS** concept is evident through its holistic approach, involving the owner, the designer, the contractors, the end-user and ultimately the community in which it resides. In the process the design team, creates a new paradigm for a suite that uses less of everything...from size to resources. The mantra of "Build less, Use less" is carried throughout, resulting in lower operating costs, a more efficient use of the site, more revenue per square foot.

RTKL

are wasted). LESS guestrooms also improve on typical guestrooms by orienting both sleeping areas and bathrooms along exterior walls to maximize natural light and reduce energy costs.

LESS Is Cool

Current economic times have ushered in a new philosophy of "cool"—that we can acquire less, use less, and feel rich not through an abundance of things, but through a lack of them. Yet "cool" is not just the mindset of a new generation; it is also about putting function first. Current and upcoming generations of hotel guests expect more than image. They value function over fluff. They know when things work and when they're cool. From the key card to the HVAC system, a LESS hotel delivers solutions that work and offer a green aesthetic. Key to the LESS concept's design is the creation of a well-functioning environment that gets by with less (see Exhibit 7). Laying out a room into functional zones focuses on how a guest actually uses it, creating true efficiencies while using less space.

LESS Is Dual

Dual purposing is another tenet of the LESS concept. Hotels can reduce guestroom footprints and create maximum efficiency by combining uses for room features (see Exhibit 8). Dual functions not only save time, space, and budget, they also inform consumers that a hotel responds to cutting-edge design and socially responsible causes. Taking cues from small-footprint Japanese properties and cruise ship models, dual purposing can become cool. Flexible furnishings can be light and moveable so that guests can work, eat, rest, and recline wherever they choose. Different-size mattresses can offer flexibility; for example, housekeepers can place a pillow top across two twin mattresses to form a king mattress, converting the bed's arrangement based on guest needs.

LESS Is Life

The LESS concept is a philosophy carried through all a hotel's touchpoints to create a truly healthy environment. LESS provides options for a holistic, healthy setting, including locally grown foods, green building and finish materials, and organic toiletries. Guests also gain ENDLESS Benefits points by participating in recycling programs.

LESS Is Love

The LESS concept does not stop with the creation of a beautiful hotel. LESS influences, assists, and informs the community in which the hotel resides. ENDLESS Benefits sponsors programs to help commercial and community neighbors in need, while serving as an educational hub for local schools and green programs.

Conclusion

As an architect, designer, developer, operator, or even a student, you will encounter and have the opportunity to develop and implement sustainable solutions. Use

Exhibit 7 LESS Room Zones

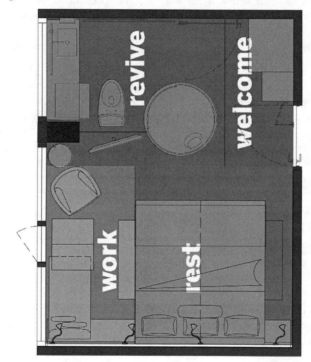

learn

In the average American home, a formal living room is 200 s.f. of wasted space. Hotel models are following residential trends.

an efficient plan

LESS IS COOL

A place for everything

The new generation of hotel guests expect more than image...they value function over fluff. They know ultimately when it works, it's cool. From the key card to the HVAC, the **LESS** concept delivers cool solutions that work and a green aesthetic for a totally new paradigm.

practice

- **Functional Zones**
  Shift how the room is planned away from the typical layout to zones focused on how the guest uses the room...creating real efficiencies and using less space

- **Small, But Enough**
  Even though spaces are smaller, The **LESS** concept provides enough space for everything the guest needs. The welcome center provides more function than a typical closet, the bathroom has space for the things we actually travel with... even the bed and chaise are designed so a standard sized wheeling luggage can be stored below them

- **Small, But Comfy**
  No one likes a small shower, but to make the room sustainable, smaller is a key factor...so a round shower takes away the feeling of being confined, and provides a more usable and comfortable experience

- **Less Furniture**
  No need for a bulky dresser or tv armoire... the welcome center wardrobe accomodates two drawers for folded clothing, and the tv pivots on a pole to provide the desired viewing angle, all using less furniture

Exhibit 8   LESS Dual Functions

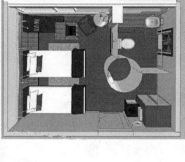
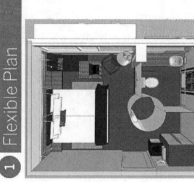

learn

The average size of a US hotel room is about 325 sf, while luxury hotel rooms typically average over 470 sf and over 550 sf in economy/extended stay hotel rooms.

practice

1   Efficient Bedding
Minimize the use of different mattress sizes with a bed that converts from a two twins to a king.   A pillow top placed over two twins converts them to a unified king mattress, and allows housekeeping to convert the bed arrangement based on the guest's needs.

2   Simple, Smart Arrangements
Flexible furnishings move around to meet the needs of the Guest - so they can work, eat, or rest and recline wherever they choose.

1 Flexible Plan

2 Flexible Furnishings

Multi-purpose. Multi-functional.

Dual functions are not only time, space and budget saving, they inform the consumer that their hotel responds to cutting-edge design and socially responsible causes. Taking cues from smaller footprint Japanese and cruise ship models, DUAL becomes CCOL.

dual
function

LESS
IS
DUAL

this knowledge to inform those with whom you do business. Encourage manufacturers to develop sustainable products and packaging. Use sustainable practices
in both the way you do business and in the projects on which you work. Push the
limits of what is possible with sustainability in every possible way. Many of us are
trying to ensure a more sustainable future for the planet. Collaboration between
students, architects, designers, developers, operators, and manufacturers can help
the industry make greater strides toward sustainability.

Sustainable Development: Converting Existing Historic Buildings into Hotels

By Maurice Robinson

Maurice Robinson, ISHC, CRE, ASA, *is President of the hospitality and real estate consulting firm Maurice Robinson & Associates LLC, based in El Segundo, California. Mr. Robinson has been structuring public-private partnerships and facilitating the development of full-service hotels and resorts in California for over thirty years. He has also served as the National Park Service's financial advisor, appraiser, expert witness, mediator, arbitrator, and lodging consultant on more than three dozen national park concessions and leases since 1991.*

PRESERVATION OF HISTORIC STRUCTURES is a cornerstone of sustainability. This chapter describes the benefits reaped, and the processes used, when historic buildings are converted into environmentally friendly modern hotels. The chapter provides a list of historic structures in the United States that have successfully become hotels, and describes a few notable conversions. The case study used to illustrate this process is the recent conversion of an entire historic district—the 100-year-old Fort Baker army post north of San Francisco—into Cavallo Point—The Lodge at the Golden Gate, which received Gold Certification through the U.S. Green Building Council's (USGBC) Leadership in Energy and Environmental Design (LEED) program.

The Benefits of Using Historic Buildings to Develop Hotels

Building a new hotel from the ground up affects the natural environment. The construction process requires substantial amounts of natural and manufactured resources, including water, energy, and building materials. It also creates waste products that end up in the air, water, and land. New development often degrades the natural landscape, pushes out urban boundaries, alters the ecosystem by creating impermeable surfaces and heat islands, and extends the infrastructure into previously undeveloped areas.

Redevelopment of existing structures can be substantially more environmentally friendly. Think of it as recycling architecture. If an existing building's former grandeur is restored by converting it into a hotel, its environmental impact can be significantly reduced. Incorporating sustainable features into the new design can lessen its impact even further. Best of all, from both the cultural and ecological standpoints, is the preservation of a historic structure. In many cities, the oldest and most historic buildings are on prime real estate. Often, public officials will provide streamlined entitlements, more accommodating zoning permits, and even public subsidies to save and restore these buildings.

Examples of Historic Structures Converted into Hotels

The chapter appendix contains a list of one hundred structures that have been converted from their original uses into modern hotels. These structures are on the National Park Service's (NPS's) National Register of Historic Places. Short descriptions of some of the more notable conversions follow:

- The 100-year-old Haslett Warehouse on Fisherman's Wharf in San Francisco is now the 260-room Argonaut Hotel. The historic building, built between 1907 and 1909 following the famous earthquake that destroyed most of the city, was once the largest fruit cannery warehouse on the west coast. The NPS owns the structure, and leases it to Kimpton Hotels, which undertook the award-winning conversion from 2000 to 2003.

- The 365-room *Queen Mary* was a British ocean liner that plied the waters from 1936 to 1967. It is more than one thousand feet in length, has twelve decks, and carried more than three thousand passengers and crew members on each of its one thousand transatlantic voyages. During World War II, it transported more than half a million military personnel, including as many as fifteen thousand troops at a time. Since 1971, it has been a hotel, docked in Long Beach, California.

- The 190-room Quaker Square Inn in Akron, Ohio, was built in the 1800s and served as a Quaker Oats grain silo, once holding 1.5 million bushels of grain. Its eight floors of guestrooms are perfectly round, and twenty-four feet in diameter.

- The 183-room Hotel Monaco in Washington, D.C., originally opened in 1842 as the all-marble General Post Office. Kimpton Hotels restored it from 1999 to 2002, marking the General Services Administration's first use of the National Historic Preservation Act of 1966 to lease a surplus historic building to a developer for renovation and conversion to a new hotel.

- The 193-room Aloft Dallas Downtown hotel was built in 1924, and served as a Santa Fe railroad freight terminal and commercial dry goods warehouse. Hamilton Properties Corporation and Sava Holdings, LTD, restored the eight-story structure from 2007 to 2009.

- The 336-room Ritz-Carlton hotel, located on Nob Hill in San Francisco, was built in 1909 as the headquarters of Metropolitan Life Insurance Company. More recently, it served as the home of Cogswell College.

- The 250-room Hotel Monaco in New Orleans was built in 1926 as a Masonic temple. From 2001 to 2006, Kimpton Hotels spent $34 million to renovate the eighteen-story Gothic tower.

- The thirty-four-room Hermosa Inn in Paradise Valley, Arizona, was a hacienda-style residence and studio hand-built in the 1930s by cowboy artist Lon Megargee. It was converted and opened as an inn in 2010, and features much of Megargee's original artwork.

- The 300-room Liberty Hotel in Boston's Beacon Hill area was once the Charles Street jail. Carpenter & Company, Inc., renovated the 160-year-old structure in 2007.

- The sixty-six-room Napa River Inn was built inside the Historic Napa Mill and warehouse in downtown Napa, California. For over one hundred years, the Historic Napa Mill stored fertilizers, feed, supplies, and Napa Valley wines for local vineyards. Napa Mill LLC handled renovation of the building, built in 1884 by Captain Albert Hatt.

- The 150-room Hotel Indigo in downtown Atlanta was the city's first skyscraper. Panther Hospitality renovated the twelve-story office building, which originally opened in 1929 as the Carnegie Building. It reopened as a hotel in 2010.

- The 221-room Hotel Monaco in Portland, Oregon, was built in 1912 and originally served as the Lipman-Wolfe & Company department store. Kimpton Hotels undertook a $25 million renovation of the historic building, which had been occupied by retailer Frederick & Nelson, and opened the hotel in 1996.

- The 131-room Harbor Court Hotel in San Francisco was once a 400-bunk YMCA building.

- The 116-room Hotel Teatro in Denver was built in 1911 as a trolley barn for the Denver Tramway Company.

In Europe, restoration and conversion of centuries-old buildings into hotels has become an art form. While this chapter discusses only American conversions, interested readers can explore Europe's architectural wonders at Historic Hotels of Europe (www.historichotelsofeurope.com), an organization that unites fifteen of Europe's hotel associations to promote the heritage, architecture, and cultural traditions of their countries. The group contains more than six hundred châteaux, manors, convents, palaces, monasteries, farms, townhouses, villas, post-houses, and family-owned residences, all of which have been converted into hotels.

Case Study—Fort Baker Becomes Cavallo Point

One of the most recent and notable conversions of historic buildings into a hotel involves a former military base, Fort Baker, in San Francisco. The United States Army established the fort in 1897 to support the many seacoast defense batteries around the north side of the Golden Gate Bridge. Most of the fort's structures were built between 1902 and 1910, and housed troops from the Coast Artillery Corps, stationed in the area to protect San Francisco Bay's northern entrance from invading watercraft. Seven batteries were built into the hillsides of Marin County, with cannons, bunkers, and numerous troops stationed there as the Bay Area's first line of defense against attacks from the sea and, later, the air. As armaments evolved throughout the twentieth century, anti-aircraft guns replaced the fort's cannons as primary defense weapons; Nike missiles eventually replaced the guns. (However, as far as anyone knows, no shot was ever fired at an enemy target from Fort Baker.) Fort Baker received relatively little use after the 1970s, and the number of troops dwindled dramatically from the fort's peak earlier in the century. By the early 1980s, Fort Baker was used only occasionally, primarily as a training station for reserve units. In 1995, the Department of Defense's Base Realignment and Closure (BRAC) process selected Fort Baker for decommissioning. The final reserve unit left in 2000, and in 2002 the base was decommissioned and turned over to the NPS.

In 1973, Fort Baker had become a National Historic District; twenty-one of its buildings, most in the Colonial Revival style, are on the National Register of Historic Places. In the mid-1990s, once the NPS knew it would eventually own the fort's buildings, it developed a renovation and re-use plan, reaching out to a non-profit "friends" group—the Golden Gate National Parks Conservancy—to start the process and determine what lay ahead, in the next century and beyond, for the then ninety-year-old buildings at Fort Baker.

The Planning Process

Planning began in 1996, not long after the Department of Defense announced that Fort Baker would be decommissioned. It involved a visioning process and highest and best use analysis that included many stakeholders. While planners explored various education-, culture-, and arts-related alternatives for the fort's historic buildings, a financial feasibility analysis determined that only a high-end hotel could pay for the relatively steep renovation costs. The concept of a mission-driven conference center and retreat house gained traction as a way of upholding the NPS's mission while keeping the site available to the general public. Forums solicited best practices that would shape future programming.

Eventually, what emerged from this visioning process was the Institute at the Golden Gate, a non-profit entity with top-quality educational programs focused on environmental sustainability and modeled after the Aspen Institute. The Fort Baker project would include formation of the institute and creation of a hotel that would accommodate both the Institute's meetings and outside guests. The institute would also become part of the hotel's overall branding. A financing plan was conceptualized using a creative public/private partnership to combine the public sector's assets of land, buildings, and location with the private sector's assets of money, management, and marketing.

To facilitate the use of Fort Baker for commercial purposes, in 1999 the NPS was granted authorization to lease the property to outside companies. Additional legislation in 2003 let the local park unit charge special visitor fees and keep the net income from those fees, instead of sending it to Washington, D.C., as other NPS concessions did at the time. Although the site was ten miles from downtown San Francisco, planners believed the buildings' historic nature, along with their location in the nation's largest urban national park, would attract visitors. It didn't hurt that the buildings had a spectacular view of the iconic Golden Gate Bridge as well.

In 1998, planners issued a request for qualifications (RFQ) that solicited proposals for the site's development. Many hospitality firms responded, along with a few non-profit organizations. In 1999, planners issued another RFQ to the top four respondents. After much internal debate and evaluation, in 2002 the NPS selected the Fort Baker Retreat Group (FBRG), which had submitted the most environmentally friendly proposal, as the winning team.

FBRG relied on separate development and operations firms for its work on the project. The developer would be Equity Community Builders (ECB), a San Francisco–based company that felt comfortable working with the NPS on long-term leases. In 1996, ECB had completed a $16 million conversion of sixteen historic buildings at the former Presidio army post (part of the Golden Gate National Recreation Area) into the ecologically friendly Thoreau Center for Sustainability. The Thoreau Center was a 150,000-square-foot renovation of the original Presidio's Letterman Army Hospital and medical office buildings, which became modern office space, including ECB's headquarters. FBRG's operator for the hotel at Fort Baker was Passport Resorts, which ran three world-class boutique luxury resorts with many sustainable features: Post Ranch Inn in Big Sur, California; the Jean-Michel Cousteau Fiji Islands Resort; and Hotel Hana-Maui in Hawaii. Bank of America provided the first mortgage debt, while initial equity funding came from Ajax Capital. The capital structure ultimately included fifty additional private investors, most of them based in the Bay Area or previous investors with ECB or Passport Resorts.

One of the earliest steps in the planning process was completion of an environmental impact report (EIR) on the proposed project and a few potential alternatives. Because the NPS did not know how large the future lodge would be, the EIR conservatively studied the impact a hotel with up to 350 rooms would have on the surrounding environment. As one might expect, a 350-room hotel can generate a lot of traffic, and citizens of neighboring Sausalito were concerned about the effect this traffic would have on their city. The NPS tried to assure them that the 350-room figure was not realistic or even desired, but the NPS could not commit to a size limit because, at that point, it had not yet selected a developer. Based on this concern, the City of Sausalito filed a lawsuit in 2001 to force the NPS to reduce the potential number of rooms (and the resulting traffic impacts). The district court rendered a summary judgment in favor of the NPS, but the city appealed to the federal appellate court. By the time the issue was settled, in early 2005, both parties agreed to a limit of 225 rooms.

This delay led to yet another round of site planning and financial projections, necessary due to the rapid run-up of construction costs after 2002. Certainly, the delays brought about by the lawsuit added to expenses. FBRG's original plan was for a 155-room lodge that would cost about $55 million. Over the next seven years, this ballooned to about $100 million.

Predevelopment activities from 2002 to 2006 included design work, engineering, and plans to restore the fort's structural and landscape elements. Crews refurbished the punched-tin ceilings in several buildings by removing, marking, and freezing each panel, then shaking it vigorously to remove layers of paint. Other restored features included bedroom fireplaces, crown molding, hardwood floors, and front porches (which had been missing for nearly fifty years). To maintain the integrity of the former chapel and gym within the site's historic landscape, developers used these buildings as meeting spaces instead of building a new meeting facility.

To preserve public access and reduce the burden FBRG would take on should it maintain responsibility for the property's forty-five acres, the NPS retained about fifteen acres, including the parking lots, many of the infrastructure systems and easements, and the public's favorite open space (the historic parade grounds). FBRG ended up with about thirty acres of land and twenty-nine buildings. The NPS gave two of the larger buildings—the former hospital and a barracks structure—to FBRG with ten-year "option periods," meaning FBRG could leave the buildings unoccupied for up to ten years. This flexibility was an important part of the lease, as it let the property grow organically into its optimal uses, rather than forcing FBRG to guess at the start of the project which facilities would be needed throughout the lease's sixty-year lifecycle.

Financing the Conversion

Structuring the legal and financial elements to create value and maximize all parties' gain involved complex ground and building leases with carve-outs, historic tax credits, annual room inventory set aside at per-diem rates for non-profit groups, and the creation of a voluntary fee for overnight guests that would go toward the project's sustainability initiatives.

In November 2006, at the height of the capital market frenzy, the project secured $102 million in financing in the form of debt, equity, and Federal Rehabilitation Tax Credits. The NPS obtained over $20 million in infrastructure funding from the House Defense and Interior Appropriations. The project spent these funds upfront during the construction period, a fact that greatly eased FBRG's financial burden. In total, Congress made eight appropriations to Golden Gate National Park to upgrade the fort's infrastructure. (Some of the money went toward improving infrastructure in other areas of the park as well.) The federal tax credits reimbursed 20 percent of the actual cost of qualified renovations to historic structures. In the case of Cavallo Point, renovation of twenty-one historic structures consumed about $65 million of the $102 million development budget, leading to $13 million in tax credits. The lender, Bank of America, purchased the historic tax credits, which made the funding and closing process go more smoothly. Construction of fourteen new buildings cost about $37 million, while the remainder of the budget ($20 million) went toward site infrastructure costs. The financial pro formas indicated a projected internal rate of return of 13.4 percent over the life of the lease. Financing included the sources of public and private debt and equity shown below:

Sponsor Equity (FBRG)	$ 6.5 million
Investor Equity	$33.5 million
Historic Tax Credit Equity	$13.0 million
First Mortgage Debt (Bank of America)	$49.0 million

Subtotal Private Sources	$102 million
Public Funds (infrastructure)	$20.0 million
Total Development Costs	$122 million

To get started, the Institute at the Golden Gate received grants, donations, and other tax-exempt funding, and continues to be subsidized in its early years of operation. The majority of its money comes from the Golden Gate National Parks Conservancy, though the NPS has contributed various grants. FBRG supports the institute's mission, and accommodates its activities. Cavallo Point sets aside 10 percent of its annual guestroom inventory at lower room rates for non-profit and government organizations. The Institute does its own part to generate revenue by attracting room night demand for the lodge.

The Lodge Opens

Parties signed the lease on December 7, 2006, and construction began immediately afterward. The construction/renovation/conversion period lasted from December 2006 through June 2008, though the lodge had a soft opening on May 1, 2008, when it accommodated its first group. At that point, only a few buildings had received their Certificates of Occupancy from the local government, and much of the site looked like a construction zone.

Cavallo Point's grand opening, with 1,800 people, took place on June 23, 2008. The community—once fearful of the redevelopment—embraced the hotel with open arms. Locals loved the fact that the parade ground was not part of the leased property, but instead was still open and accessible to the public. The building restorations—particularly exterior features like the long-neglected front porches—received positive feedback. (The lodge provides rocking chairs on its porches, with views of the Golden Gate Bridge and San Francisco.) The placement of fourteen new lodging buildings in the hills behind the main area allowed for outstanding views while having little impact on the site's overall density. In addition, the lodge's Murray Circle restaurant has been well received, earning a Michelin Gold Star its first year in operation. The Farley Bar, named after a character created by well-loved local cartoonist Phil Frank, is a popular watering hole, with standing-room-only crowds on most weekend evenings. The staff's quality service and friendliness have won over many of the project's former opponents. The lodge is truly seen as a community asset.

Sustainability Features of Cavallo Point

Cavallo Point was built with the highest ideals of sustainability in mind. The lodge earned Gold LEED certification from the USGBC, becoming the first hotel on the National Register of Historic Places to receive LEED certification, and the first new hotel in the national park system to achieve LEED Gold status. Cavallo Point has also received certification under the Green Seal Environmental Standard for Lodging Properties. Exhibit 1 contains a list of sustainability awards the hotel won during its first eighteen months of operation. The following sections list some of the environmental stewardship and community support features that led to those awards.

Exhibit 1   Sustainability Awards Won by Cavallo Point

Awards won by Cavallo Point in its first eighteen months of operation include:

- National Trust for Historic Preservation's National Preservation Honor Award
- California Governor's Environmental and Economic Leadership Award
- California Governor's Historic Preservation Award
- National Park Service's Cultural Resource Award
- California Preservation Foundation's Preservation Design Award
- National Housing & Rehabilitation Association's Award for Excellence in Historic Rehabilitation
- Preferred Hotel Group's Hotel of the Year
- HotelWorld Global Hospitality & Design's Sustainable Design Award
- *Real Estate & Construction Review*'s Green Building of America
- *Business Journal*'s Top Historic Restoration Project Award
- *Travel + Leisure*'s Top 10 New Green American Landmarks

Land, Sea, and Wildlife

- The lodge environs are home to the mission blue butterfly (*Icaricia icarioides missionensis*), which the federal government named an endangered species in 1976. To keep the habitat pristine and prevent intrusion from hikers, a post-and-cable fence surrounds the area.

- The lodge's designation as a historic landmark has implications for many of its features, including landscaping. All plants in the historic cantonment must conform to the site's "period of significance," which, for Fort Baker, was between 1905 and 1940, when the base was in full operation.

- Approximately 58,000 native plants have been grown from seeds collected within the Fort Baker watershed. These seeds were planted in the contemporary lodging area adjacent to the mission blue butterfly habitat, ensuring a genetic compatibility with the site's existing plants while eliminating impact on the sensitive butterfly habitat.

- For the site's historic core, foundation plants were chosen from a list of vegetation that has a recorded history at Fort Baker. In addition, the historic core's palette consists of ornamental plants resembling those that may have existed during the fort's period of significance. The site's native coastal scrub community is optimally suited for the local environment, and will likely consume much less water than the previous landscaping.

- The lodge maximizes open space to encourage wildlife habitation. While LEED standards consider a ratio of 50-percent open space to be adequate, Cavallo Point substantially exceeds this amount.

- Because light pollution affects wildlife behavior, the lodge conforms to a set of NPS guidelines (known as the "dark skies initiative") that seek to reduce it. Cavallo Point maintains low-level and minimal lighting outdoors, using, for example, safety lights to illuminate only steps and not entire pathways.

Water Conservation

- Instead of a typical drain system, which channels storm water into fast-moving storm sewers that flow into the ocean, depositing silt, soil, and other debris in the process, the lodge has an eco-sensitive storm water design. Six infiltration zones throughout the site let water percolate down, purifying it, reducing erosion, and protecting ocean waters.

- Based on the results of a two-year on-site study, the lodge uses water-efficient, drought-tolerant landscaping.

- Instead of using spray irrigation on its foundation plants, the lodge uses more-efficient drip irrigation, in which water trickles slowly onto a plant's roots.

- To irrigate its plants, the lodge uses gray water, which is left over from washing machines, bathtubs, showers, and sinks. Special purple piping, which code requires for use with gray water, has been installed throughout the site, and will facilitate upgrades to gray water systems in the future.

- Low-flow, dual-flush toilets conserve water by letting guests determine how much water to use when they flush.

- Typically, a hotel uses one-third of its water in the laundry room because linens like sheets and towels are continually being used. However, Cavallo Point expects to cut its water usage by 65 percent through use of a state-of-the-art water reclamation system.

Reduced Use of Energy, Chemicals, and Other Resources

- Chemical products used on-site meet the Green Seal sustainability standard. Also in keeping with the Green Seal standard, Cavallo Point uses a reduced level of chemicals.

- Low-voltage lighting and compact fluorescent lights, which consume less energy than traditional incandescent lights, are used wherever possible, especially in guestrooms.

- Tank-less water heaters heat water only when needed, providing savings over traditional storage water heaters, which waste money and energy by continuously heating water, even when it is not required.

- Windows in all of the lodge's contemporary rooms feature low e-glazing. This low-emittance (Low-E) coating reduces total heat flow through the window, making it more energy efficient.

- Staff members take steps to minimize the overuse of laundry detergent and related chemicals. Guests can help with these efforts during multi-night stays by displaying in-room cards that indicate when linen changes aren't necessary.

- Chlorine is not used in the basking pool or hot tubs. Instead, environmentally friendly ozone is used so that the water can be recycled as gray water and used to irrigate the landscaping.

- The lodge uses no fertilizers or pest management chemicals on its landscaping.

Waste Management and Use of Earth-Friendly Products

- Guest soaps and other in-room amenities are environmentally friendly; most are locally produced.

- Cavallo Point's premium nylon carpet contains 25-percent recycled content obtained through the recovery and use of over twenty million pounds of recycled nylon. This helped the lodge attain LEED certification.

- Many of the guestrooms' lighting fixtures are made from recycled items, like surveyor tripods and plumbing parts.

- All guestroom items, like wooden hangers and guestroom keys, are reusable. Guest amenities like shampoo and conditioner come in large, refillable bottles.

- Each guestroom has a collection bin for recyclables. The lodge has a comprehensive plan for recycling paper, plastic, aluminum, and other items, which it promotes property-wide, including in offices, the kitchen, and the restaurant.

- Instead of plastic, the lodge uses glass or paper products whenever possible. Each guestroom comes with a pitcher of filtered water and glasses that can be washed and reused.

- As an alternative to non-degradable plastic packaging, the lodge uses packaging products that are renewable, sustainable, compostable, and biodegradable. These include SpudWare (cutlery made from potatoes), BagasseWare (plates, platters, and bowls made from sugar cane fiber pulp), and other biodegradable products made from renewable resources.

- No tablecloths are used during meals.

- The restaurant uses local products and produce that is fresh and organic.

- Collateral material is printed on recycled paper; most inks are soy-based.

- The property's public restrooms provide cotton hand towels, not paper towels.

- Pest control products used on-site are non-toxic to humans and animals.

- The lodge's garbage collection company composts waste. (Composting cannot be done on-site because it affects the native habitat.)

Design and Construction of Green Buildings

- Cavallo Point renovated twenty-one historic buildings that had been abandoned and were deteriorating. Most of the materials in these buildings were reused. Nearly 100 percent of the building shells and approximately 75 percent of the buildings' interior elements, like walls and floors, were retained or repurposed. These efforts extended the lifecycle of existing building stock, conserved natural resources, retained cultural resources, and reduced waste and environmental impacts related to the manufacturing and transport of materials.

- Over 75 percent of the site's construction waste was diverted from landfills through reuse or recycling.

- Use of green building materials was a priority. These included products with a high recycled-materials content; products that were regionally extracted, processed, or manufactured (which minimized expenditures on transportation and energy while supporting indigenous resources); and products made from rapidly renewable materials like bamboo, wool, and cork. The contemporary structures' cabinetry and casework are made from bamboo and other rapidly renewable products, while recycled wood was used for many furniture and casework pieces.

- In the contemporary lodging structures, interior walls use recycled blue jean cotton insulation.

Energy Efficiency

- Energy systems (heating, ventilating, and air conditioning [HVAC] and lighting) in all buildings meet the stringent requirements for energy efficiency defined in Title 24, California's Energy Efficiency Standards for Residential and Nonresidential Buildings. However, Cavallo Point optimizes energy efficiency far beyond this. Not only do its buildings meet minimum requirements under Title 24, they exceed them, achieving nearly 20 percent additional energy cost savings in the new structures, and more than 10 percent in the historic structures.

- An extensive building system commissioning plan has been developed and implemented on all mechanical equipment, ensuring systems requiring energy are installed and operating at peak efficiency.

- State-of-the-art thin film photovoltaic panels were installed on twelve of the fourteen new buildings' south-facing standing-seam metal roofs. The system generates nearly all the electrical energy these buildings require. Electrical cost savings are estimated to be about $16,500 per year, with the system paying for itself by Year 11. Other benefits over a twenty-five-year period include the offset of three million pounds of carbon dioxide and 9,799 pounds of nitrogen oxide—the equivalent of taking sixteen cars off the road for twenty-five years, or planting twenty-six acres of trees.

- An energy measurement and verification plan monitors energy demand and provides ongoing accountability of system performance. This ensures energy-related systems perform as intended. Benefits include reduced energy use, lower operating costs, reduced contractor callbacks, better building documentation, and improved well-being of occupants.

- To help defray energy costs, the lodge buys renewable energy credits. This is achieved through contracts with grid-source, renewable energy providers in the form of renewable energy certificates that encourage delivery and usage of renewable energy technology on a net-zero pollution basis. Such green power comes from solar, wind, geothermal, biomass, or low-impact hydro sources.

Indoor Environmental Quality

- Cavallo Point is a no-smoking facility.

- The lodge takes advantage of its waterfront location by making extensive use of natural or energy-efficient ventilation, including ceiling fans and windows that open to cool breezes from the bay.

- Ninety-five percent of the lodge's rooms have no air conditioning.

- The property developed and implemented an indoor air quality management plan, which includes ways to prevent mechanical and ventilation parts from getting dusty, and requires the flushing of all rooms before occupancy to ensure guests' comfort and well-being.

- To reduce the quantity of indoor air contaminants that are odorous, irritating, and/or harmful to occupants, all buildings use materials—including adhesives, paints, sealants, coatings, and carpeting—that emit low amounts of volatile organic compounds (VOCs).

- Lighting and heating systems, including radiant heat on the floors of all contemporary lodging structures, maximize guests' comfort. Radiant heat ensures that particulates don't blow from ductwork into guests' breathing spaces.

- All spaces maximize the site's daylight and exceptional views.

Outdoor Environmental Quality

- When Fort Baker opened more than a century ago, environmental standards were less stringent than they are today. When Cavallo Point opened in 2008, it met or exceeded current requirements, some at great cost to the project. Site rehabilitation included: cleanup of lead-based paint in soil (due to paint flecks falling from walls as the buildings aged); removal of asbestos (which the Environmental Protection Agency banned in 1989) from flooring tiles and flue-pipe insulation; and elimination of underground fuel storage tanks and environmental contamination remaining from the fort's Army days.

Guest Outreach and Education

- Cavallo Point educates guests about its environmental efforts through printed materials, guided tours, reclamation activities, and demonstrations. The lodge provides information on the mission blue butterfly, the history of Fort Baker, green design, and LEED-related activities.

- Guests are encouraged to enjoy various activities, such as bird watching, nature walks, native plant nursery tours, and hikes in nearby park land.

- All meeting spaces are named for local endangered species, and include descriptions and photos so that meeting attendees can learn about these species and assist in their protection.

Employee Education and Incentives

- To help achieve the most sustainable project possible, the property had six design and consulting professionals accredited in "LEED—New Construction" on its team. Part of their role was to educate project team members about green building design and construction, and apply the LEED rating system early in the project's lifecycle.

- For both staff and guests, preferred parking is available for carpools and alternate-powered vehicles. Similarly, bicycle storage racks encourage bike riding.

- A significant percentage of the hotel's vehicles are low emitting and energy efficient, including its entire fleet of golf carts, which operate on electricity instead of gas.

- To encourage use of public transportation, a shuttle system links all major transit nodes, including the Sausalito ferry to San Francisco, and bus stops at the Golden Gate Bridge. This reduces the impact from automobiles, especially in the areas of traffic, air pollution, and land development.

Community Outreach and Education

- The Institute at the Golden Gate sponsors meetings, conferences, and programs related to the environment, with the goal of promoting its health, protection, and sustainability. The Institute accomplishes this through cross-sector dialogues, collaborative leadership training, action summits, and youth programs.

- Cavallo Point is a partner in The Good Night Foundation. The non-profit organization raises money to support local and global programs that focus on health, education, poverty, and the environment. Partner hotels add a four-dollar donation to each guest's nightly charge. (Guests who do not wish to participate may opt out by contacting the hotel's front desk.) At least 50 percent of The Good Night Foundation's proceeds stay in the communities in which they were collected, supporting local causes selected by hotel staff.

- Community-wide lectures and seminars are provided at low cost to the general public.

Summary and Lessons Learned

FBRG renovated twenty-one of Fort Baker's existing structures and built fourteen new structures, resulting in sixty-eight historic guestrooms and seventy-four newly built guestrooms. Cavallo Point also includes 14,000 square feet of meeting space; forty-four acres of restored landscape, including the fourteen-acre parade ground and ten acres of mission blue butterfly habitat; a Healing Arts Center & Spa; a cooking school and demonstration kitchen; and two miles of hiking trails. In addition, the project included creation of the Institute at the Golden Gate, which uses the lodge's meeting facilities to advance environmental preservation and global sustainability efforts.

Although the physical product turned out beautifully, more community involvement and buy-in on the front end might have shortened the pre-development process (and might have prevented the lawsuit), which would have lowered the project's overall cost. Renovation costs were quite high (about $860,000 per room); lower costs would have helped reduce the debt load. The Institute at the Golden Gate would have benefitted from more specific financing sources, which would have provided more financial stability for the non-profit entity.

Other lessons learned include the fact that the site's size made for an operationally complex property, especially regarding parking. The Murray Circle and Farley Bar have been so popular that the lodge might want to provide, in the near future, another, more casual food and beverage outlet. However, the success of the restaurant and bar has also created problems, like unexpectedly large utility expenses and periodic parking issues. Design-wise, unlike many other iconic National Park lodges, Cavallo Point's lobby contains no great room. In addition, the lodge has a shortage of office, storage, and back-of-house space.

Still, the conversion of historic Fort Baker into Cavallo Point—The Lodge at the Golden Gate was a win-win situation for the major stakeholders: FBRG, as the developer/lessee; Passport Resorts, as the hotel operator; NPS, as the landlord; Ajax Capital and the other private investors; Bank of America, the lender and historic tax credit buyer; local residents; employees; non-profit environmental groups and other users of the Institute at the Golden Gate; and hotel guests.

Chapter Appendix:

Historic Structures Preserved and Converted to Hotels

Hotel Name	City	State	Rooms	Year Built	Original Use
Lexington Birmingham	Birmingham	AL	200	1926	Bank
Hotel Monroe	Phoenix	AZ	144	1932	Office
Queen Mary	Long Beach	CA	365	1936	Ocean Liner
Napa River Inn	Napa	CA	66	1884	Mill
500 West	San Diego	CA	259	1924	YMCA
Courtyard San Diego Downtown	San Diego	CA	245	1925	Bank
Argonaut	San Francisco	CA	268	1907	Warehouse
Harbor Court	San Francisco	CA	131	1925	YMCA
Casa Madrone	Sausalito	CA	63	1885	Residence
Cavallo Point	Sausalito	CA	142	1905	Army Base
Cable Building	Denver	CO	240	1889	Power Facility
Courtyard Denver Downtown	Denver	CO	188	1927	Dept. Store
Magnolia Denver	Denver	CO	244	1860	Bank
Monaco Denver	Denver	CO	189	1909	Office
Teatro	Denver	CO	116	1911	Trolley Barn
Inn at Middletown	Middletown	CT	100	1810	Armory
Monaco Washington DC	Washington	DC	172	1839	Post Office
Comeau Renaissance	West Palm Beach	FL	162	1926	Office
Glenn	Atlanta	GA	110	1923	Office
Indigo	Atlanta	GA	150	1920	Office
Residence Inn Atlanta Downtown	Atlanta	GA	160	1929	Office
Mansion on Forsyth Park	Savannah	GA	126	1888	Residence
Burnham	Chicago	IL	122	1895	Office
Guest Quarters	Chicago	IL	321	1928	Office
Hard Rock Chicago	Chicago	IL	381	1929	Office
Hampton Majestic	Chicago	IL	135	1905	Office
Silversmith	Chicago	IL	143	1897	Office
Homewood Suites Indianapolis Downtown	Indianapolis	IN	92	1863	Warehouse
Cotton Exchange	New Orleans	LA	102	1921	Office
Hampton Inn & Suites New Orleans Convention Center	New Orleans	LA	288	1904	Warehouse
Hilton Garden Inn French Quarter/CBD	New Orleans	LA	155	1956	Office
International House	New Orleans	LA	110	1906	Bank
Maison Orleans Ritz-Carlton	New Orleans	LA	75	1909	Department Store
Marriott New Orleans Convention Center	New Orleans	LA	331	1800s	Mill

(continued)

Hilton New Orleans	New Orleans	LA	250	1926	Temple
Queen & Crescent Clarion	New Orleans	LA	129	1913	Office
Renaissance Arts New Orleans	New Orleans	LA	217	1850	Warehouse
Renaissance Pere Marquette	New Orleans	LA	280	1927	Retail Shops
Ritz-Carlton New Orleans	New Orleans	LA	452	1908	Department Store
Whitney Wyndham	New Orleans	LA	93	1890	Office
Hampton Inn & Suites Baltimore Inner Harbor	Baltimore	MD	116	1906	Office
SpringHill Suites Baltimore Downtown	Baltimore	MD	99	1900	Bank
Ames Hotel	Boston	MA	114	1893	Office
Hilton Boston Financial District	Boston	MA	362	1928	Office
Langham	Boston	MA	318	1922	Bank
Liberty	Boston	MA	298	1850	Jail
Marriott Customs House	Boston	MA	84	1847	Customs House
XV Beacon	Boston	MA	62	1875	Apartments
Residence Inn Minneapolis at the Depot	Minneapolis	MN	130	1899	Train Depot
W Minneapolis Forshay	Minneapolis	MN	229	1929	Office
Westin Minneapolis	Minneapolis	MN	214	1942	Bank
Courtyard Meridian	Meridian	MS	125	1929	Commerce/ Trade
Courtyard Kansas City Country Club Plaza	Kansas City	MO	123	1926	Residence
Drury Plaza St. Louis	St. Louis	MO	370	1920	Office
Hilton St. Louis Downtown	St. Louis	MO	195	1889	Bank
St. Louis Union Station Marriott	St. Louis	MO	517	1892	Train Depot
Sheraton St. Louis City Center & Suites	St. Louis	MO	288	1928	Warehouse
WS on Washington	St. Louis	MO	78	1901	Office
Bryant Park	New York	NY	129	1924	Office
Dylan	New York	NY	107	1903	Office
Regent Wall Street	New York	NY	144	1842	Office
Saugerties Lighthouse	Saugerties	NY	2	1869	Lighthouse
W New York Union Square	New York	NY	270	1917	Office
Quaker Square Inn	Akron	OH	190	1872	Grain Silo
Hyatt Regency Cleveland at the Arcade	Cleveland	OH	294	1890	Office
Indigo Columbus Downtown	Columbus	OH	117	1869	Commercial
Residence Inn Columbus Downtown	Columbus	OH	126	1927	Commercial/ Trade
Courtyard Tulsa Downtown	Tulsa	OK	118	1922	Office
Custom House	Portland	OR	82	1898	Federal
Kennedy School	Portland	OR	35	1915	School
Monaco Portland	Portland	OR	221	1912	Dept. Store
The Nines	Portland	OR	331	1908	Dept. Store
Courtyard Philadelphia Downtown	Philadelphia	PA	499	1926	City Hall

Le Meridien Philadelphia	Philadelphia	PA	202	1912	YMCA
Loews Philadelphia	Philadelphia	PA	583	1932	Office
Courtyard Pittsburgh Downtown	Pittsburgh	PA	182	1905	Bank
Renaissance Fulton Pittsburgh	Pittsburgh	PA	300	1906	Office
Radisson Lackawanna Station Hotel	Scranton	PA	145	1908	Train Depot
Hampton Inn & Suites Providence Downtown	Providence	RI	110	1945	Bank
Renaissance Providence	Providence	RI	216	1927	Temple
Embassy Suites Charleston	Charleston	SC	153	1830s	Arsenal
Sheraton Columbia Downtown	Columbia	SC	135	1913	Office
Crowne Plaza Chattanooga Downtown	Chattanooga	TN	142	1927	Office
Madison	Memphis	TN	110	1905	Office
Wyndham Union Station Hotel	Nashville	TN	125	1900	Train Depot
Aloft	Dallas	TX	193	1924	Train Depot
Magnolia	Dallas	TX	330	1921	Office
Ashton	Fort Worth	TX	39	1915	Office
Courtyard Houston Downtown	Houston	TX	191	1921	Office
Hotel Icon	Houston	TX	135	1858	Bank
Magnolia Houston	Houston	TX	314	1926	Office
Residence Inn Houston Downtown	Houston	TX	171	1921	Office
Drury Plaza San Antonio Riverwalk	San Antonio	TX	306	1913	Bank
Homewood Suites San Antonio Riverwalk	San Antonio	TX	146	1919	Office
Hampton Inn & Suites Ogden	Ogden	UT	137	1913	Office
Monaco Salt Lake City	Salt Lake City	UT	225	1924	Bank
Landmark	Charlottesville	VA	101	1910	Courthouse
Doubletree Arctic Club	Seattle	WA	120	1916	Social Space
Courtyard Seattle	Seattle	WA	262	1904	Bank
Residence Inn Milwaukee Downtown	Milwaukee	WI	131	1900	Dept. Store

Note: The author would like to express his appreciation to Ricah Marquez of the National Register of Historic Places for researching and verifying the historical authenticity of these hotels and for identifying key facts. To complete this project, she worked closely with student researcher Julia Allos of *The* School of Hospitality Business at Michigan State University.

Part III

Hotel Corporate and Property Perspectives

9

Sustainable Development Strategies and Best Practices: InterContinental Hotels Group

By David Jerome

David Jerome is the Senior Vice President for Corporate Responsibility at InterContinental Hotels Group based in the United Kingdom. IHG leads the industry in environmental innovation with its guide to sustainable hotel building, construction, and operations. IHG is also leading in community investment and local economic development, with over 4,200 hotels globally.

Before joining IHG in 2006, David led Corporate Affairs for AB InBev, the world's largest brewer. Prior to AB InBev, David worked for General Motors in a variety of staff and operational roles. He was head of GM Korea before assuming responsibility for GM's global reputation and corporate responsibility activities. David practiced law in Washington, D.C., before joining GM.

David and his wife and two children have lived in Asia, North America, and Europe.

INTERCONTINENTAL HOTELS GROUP (IHG) is an international hotel company with the goal of creating "Great Hotels Guests Love." The company operates seven well-known hotel brands: InterContinental, Crowne Plaza, Hotel Indigo, Holiday Inn, Holiday Inn Express, Staybridge Suites, and Candlewood Suites. Its Priority Club Rewards program has 48 million members.

With more than 645,000 rooms in over 4,400 hotels across more than 100 countries, it is the world's largest hotel group by number of rooms. Its guests make over 130 million stays in IHG hotels every year.

IHG's business model focuses on managing and franchising hotels, with business partners owning the bricks and mortar. Its hotel development pipeline is the largest in the industry, and currently stands at more than 1,400 hotels (over 210,000 rooms).

Exhibit 1 IHG Strategic Corporate Responsibility

Source: InterContinental Hotels Group.

Corporate Responsibility: Core Values, Vision, Mission, and Strategy

Corporate responsibility (CR) is an integral part of the way IHG does business, and it forms a central part of its business strategy. The company believes that being a responsible business helps it create value for the company and for society. As with other areas of the business, IHG's approach to CR is based on innovation and collaboration. The company looks for creative solutions to the environmental and social challenges it faces, working alongside partners to develop and implement new ideas. This idea is illustrated in Exhibit 1 and summarized by Gavin Flynn, senior vice president of strategy and corporate development: "We have placed corporate responsibility at the heart of our strategic thinking, embedded it in our strategic priorities across the business, and set up internal measurement and performance objectives."

Why Sustainable Development Is Part of IHG's Overall Strategy

IHG focuses its CR strategy on the two main areas where it believes it can make a difference. These are (1) the environment, including a commitment to reduce the company's carbon footprint, and (2) communities, in particular the creation of local economic opportunity.

Exhibit 2   IHG Steering Wheel

Source: InterContinental Hotels Group.

Within each of these areas, IHG looks for opportunities that will create value for the business and society, an approach that plays a key role in IHG's efforts to manage costs and drive revenue more effectively. This is why the company believes there is real competitive advantage in acting responsibly. The company's approach is illustrated in the IHG steering wheel (see Exhibit 2), which is used both on the corporate and hotel level as a business planning and performance measurement tool.

The way IHG has chosen to tackle carbon emissions is an example of this comprehensive approach. Rather than purchase carbon offsetting permits, the company works with partners such as hotel owners and suppliers to deliver emission reductions that are innovative and sustainable and that reduce costs.

Although IHG has been engaged in CR-related activities for years, corporate responsibility is a relatively new business discipline in the company. For that reason, over the past two years the team has concentrated on building a solid foundation of policies and measurement/management systems that will support IHG's CR strategy and activities.

Much of the company's CR work so far has involved applying systems developed to monitor and measure progress across the entire group of brands. With 86 percent of IHG's properties operating under brand franchises, the pace of progress is inevitably constrained. As systems are still being rolled out to franchised hotels, the company isn't yet in a position to deliver anything other than directional results for the business as a whole. However, IHG understands that it will achieve its CR goals only by bringing all hotels on board. To achieve this, the company is building a strong foundation with partners based on compliance with its CR policies, contracts, and statements of intent; and encouraging all hotels to follow the valued behaviors set out in the company's "Winning Ways" guidelines. These guidelines are: (1) aim higher, (2) show we care, (3) work better together, (4) celebrate difference, and (5) do the right thing.

With the groundwork in place, IHG is working on its CR priorities: defining the green hotel of the future, bringing new products to the marketplace, finding cost efficiencies for the company and its partners, and enhancing the value of IHG's brands. Some initiatives, such as Green Engage and the Innovation Hotel, are already starting to show how this will work in practice. These initiatives have feedback mechanisms that are helping IHG build a franchise community that genuinely shares the company's commitment to growth through sustainable innovation. Key initiatives include:

- Green Engage, an online sustainability tool that gives hotels the means to measure, manage, and monitor energy usage, water usage, and waste.

- IHG Academies, a public/private partnership in China that provides hospitality job training and employee skill-building while supplying the company's hotels with a sustainable source of talent.

- The Innovation Hotel (www.ihgplc.com/innovation), an online showcase of what green hotels might look like in the future. The site gives website visitors an opportunity to share their ideas, which inform the company's CR activities and services.

- Conservation partnership with Oxford University. IHG has pledged $1 million over five years to help the university map biodiversity hotspots and influence future hotel design and operations.

- Sustainably designed building for IHG's new headquarters in Denham, England. The company wanted the building to be sustainable in all ways, from the materials and suppliers used for the refurbishment, to the creation of an environment that supports the well-being of IHG employees and demonstrates environmental best practices. Measures adopted included using suppliers within twenty-five miles of Denham to reduce the project's environmental footprint; a 20 percent reduction in water consumption through energy and water saving measures; and reusing or recycling waste during the project, which prevented 400 tons of waste going to landfills.

Priorities for Action

IHG's CR priorities are to reduce its impact on the environment and support the communities where it operates. What follows is a discussion of some of IHG's climate change and local economic philosophies and initiatives.

Climate Change

Climate change presents significant challenges to businesses as they attempt to balance business growth with the expectations of a responsible business.

Some of the factors affecting the travel and tourism industry in general include increased electricity, water, and energy prices—all of which drive up operational costs; closer scrutiny of the environmental impact of the supply chain; and rising pressure on guests to reduce air travel. In addition, changing sea levels and climate patterns affect the availability of raw materials for construction, how and where hotels are built, and how guests travel to various locations.

IHG is committed to finding new and innovative approaches to building and running its hotels, in order to mitigate its impact on climate change and future-proof the business against rising carbon and resource costs. Defining what a green hotel is and how to achieve energy and carbon reductions is a central plank of the company's environmental strategy.

Day to day, IHG is encouraging its hotels to reduce the negative impacts that contribute to climate change by using resources such as energy and water wisely, minimizing waste, conserving ecosystems and biodiversity, and sourcing locally whenever possible. Progress is monitored through the Green Engage program. Green Engage is a tool IHG uses to innovate and focus on the practical measures it can take to reduce emissions through responsible design, construction, and operational activities.

Carbon Costs/Opportunities. As a global brand operating in over 100 countries, IHG is exposed to an increasing number of regulatory measures designed to encourage cuts in carbon emissions by enforcing monetary penalties and incentives on carbon emitters. These measures will increasingly have a direct impact on sectors such as the hotel industry. For instance, starting in 2010, IHG's operations in the United Kingdom had to comply with the Carbon Reduction Commitment (CRC). This carbon-trading scheme compels companies to monitor energy use and purchase carbon allowances corresponding to CO_2 emissions. This regulation has management and cost implications for franchise-based businesses based in the United Kingdom, and IHG is working to support its franchisees appropriately to address this new law. Failure to reduce emissions in IHG's owned *and* franchised hotels increases the risk of public censure as well as financial penalty.

In response to growing regulatory requirements, IHG set up a Carbon Strategy Team. The company's carbon strategy is reviewed regularly with the IHG CR

Board Committee and discussed with its independent owners' association, the IAHI, to make sure franchise business partners are fully engaged.

Taking a proactive approach to reducing carbon emissions helps the company comply with existing and emerging regulations. Rather than purchase carbon offsets, IHG works with partners to seek new ways to deliver real emission cuts across the business through tools like the Green Engage program. Objectives such as carbon regulation compliance and cost efficiencies led to the creation of Green Engage.

Energy Efficiency

Energy usage in hotels accounts for the largest proportion of IHG's carbon footprint and is the second largest cost to the hotels after staff. The average IHG hotel's carbon footprint is 130 pounds, roughly equivalent to the average U.S. home on a per-room-night basis. An independent emissions measurement exercise undertaken by the company showed that the environmental aspects of hotel activities, such as heating and ventilating design as well as air conditioning operations, could be better managed to lower energy use and carbon footprints. Using its green program, IHG set a target of achieving energy savings of 6–10 percent on a per-available-room-night basis over the three-year period of 2010–2012 in its owned and managed properties.

Local Economic Impacts

Despite the global economic downturn, international tourist arrivals are predicted to increase from 903 million in 2007 to 1.6 billion in 2020.[1] IHG's size and global market presence means it has a significant impact on the economies of the communities where it operates. The company believes that managing the issues that arise with tourism can help make the company's impact on local communities a positive one.

For IHG, responsible tourism means involving local people in tourism to generate greater well-being for their communities. The company's hotels support economic development by creating stable sources of income and providing opportunities for both local employment and local businesses, notably as employees of and suppliers to the hotel. In 2009, the economic downturn meant IHG focused on maximizing the benefits it brings to local economies via direct and indirect employment, taxes paid, local purchasing, and community support.

Looking to have a more positive impact on the communities in which it operates, the company is currently reviewing its community activities. A revised, more focused community strategy was launched in 2010. It was informed by the views of stakeholders, including guests and employees, who were consulted to find out what they consider important areas of community focus.

The company also supports communities by working with other organizations, such as InterContinental Hotels & Resorts' partnership with the National Geographic Society, an organization widely acknowledged as a leader in geotourism. Together they have developed a CR strategy that sets out to educate guests on responsible tourism and let them know how IHG supports these principles.

Availability of Local Skilled Staff. IHG has a large expansion program in place and is opening a hotel a day worldwide. But finding skilled staff to serve guests can be a problem. Often when a work force is available, potential employees lack the knowledge and skills they need, affecting the community's ability to attract tourism. To address this issue, the company works with local companies and organizations to train potential employees in local communities. Notably, it launched the IHG Academy in China in 2006.

Community Support

IHG has hotels and offices in more than 100 countries across six continents. Its approach to operating responsibly in local communities includes creating opportunities for local people, preserving local customs and traditions, and introducing guests to local cultures. It also supports communities through charitable donations. In 2009, IHG gave $813,908 in charitable donations.

In addition to corporate efforts, IHG hotels are directly involved in their communities through in-kind donations, grants, and volunteering programs. IHG surveys grassroots activity to monitor trends and seek synergies for its brands. This way of working enables IHG to share best practices throughout the company, communicate more effectively with guests, and make better-informed decisions about community support. As part of a revised community strategy launched in 2010, IHG is introducing criteria aimed at creating greater community impact through donations and making sure all donations are aligned with corporate objectives.

Specific Initiatives within IHG's Priority Areas

Green Engage

In March 2009, IHG launched its online sustainability tool Green Engage. The system enables IHG hotels to measure, manage, and report their key environmental and other CR impacts. It also helps them identify the most appropriate solutions to their local environmental risks by providing best practice information specific to the type of hotel and the climate in which they operate. Recommendations cover design, operations, and technologies aimed at reducing energy usage, water usage, and waste; cutting carbon emissions; improving guest health and comfort; reducing operating and maintenance costs; and raising guest and staff awareness of sustainability issues. More than 900 hotels have currently signed up to use the system.

What Is Green Engage? Green Engage tells both new and existing IHG hotels what they can do to be a green hotel and gives them the means to conserve resources and save money. This offers a significant advantage to owners in the current economic climate and in relation to future carbon taxes they may face. Green Engage enables hotels to more effectively measure, manage, and report on their hotel energy, water, and waste consumption, as well as their community impacts. Green Engage is a good example of IHG's commitment to innovation; for instance, the company chooses to tackle carbon emissions by making real cuts rather than offsetting.

How It Works. Hotels input their site data into Green Engage. The system automatically generates reports and benchmarks against similar hotels across the world. Green Engage then advises hotels on specific actions they can take to reduce their impacts, depending on their climatic location. Action lists are provided for both newly built hotels and existing hotels. Finally, reports are produced that allow IHG, as well as guests and corporate clients, to review an individual hotel's progress.

Green Engage provides owners with advice on every aspect of the hotel lifecycle, from picking a suitable site, to selecting the correct lighting for the hotel, to choosing responsible cleaning materials and providing staff training on sustainability. The return on investment, carbon reduction, and potential impact on guests is calculated for each action item suggested.

Benefits for Hotel Owners. IHG believes Green Engage gives its hotels a substantial competitive edge, making them the most cost-effective in the sector and allowing them to improve the value of the service they offer to guests. The system is already driving change across the business, with early trials of the system showing potential energy savings of up to 25 percent. If fully adopted by all hotels across all 4,438 properties in IHG's portfolio, it is estimated that the savings for hotel owners could reach $200 million. To date, 900 hotels have signed up for the system. Of those, the 600 IHG owned-and-managed hotels reduced energy use by up to 10 percent in 2009.

Consumer insight research conducted by the company showed that guests prefer to stay in a green hotel rather than a non-green hotel. Some Green Engage hotels are beginning to acquire new business because of their sustainability commitments. In one hotel, The Willard in Washington, this was estimated to be worth up to $1,000,000 in one year.

Integration with Existing Green Building Certifications. IHG's environmental policies were developed in consideration of existing global sustainability metrics, such as LEED, BREEAM, and Green Globe. Like these systems, IHG's system uses a point-based metric that establishes a minimum level of sustainability and outlines opportunities to exceed this minimum. The company's environmental policies are applied to existing hotels as well as newly built properties.

Cost Savings. The economic climate in 2010 meant IHG was under pressure to fast-track the launch of Green Engage. IHG's corporate responsibility and operations teams worked together to roll out this new approach to the company's hotels. Using the feedback it gets from its hotel and operations teams, the company is working to make the tool even easier to use. Further training is also planned.

The Next Stage in Green Management. The original Green Engage pilot went live in late 2009. It was quickly extended to all of IHG's owned-and-managed properties, and then opened up to any franchise hotel who wanted to participate. The uptake was positive, with nearly 900 hotels on board in a matter of months. The company hopes to maintain this momentum and will continue to roll out Green Engage to 100 percent of its owned-and-managed hotels, as well as expanding further into the franchised estate in all three regions.

IHG recognizes it is still learning how to make the most of the technologies and techniques introduced to achieve its corporate responsibility goals. The corporate responsibility section of its website has examples of how Green Engage is already bringing "early wins" for IHG and for individual hotels. The company plans to start quantifying these benefits on a group-wide basis within the near term.

IHG Academy

Social and Economic Background. Throughout the world, travel and tourism provides opportunities for economic development, new business, much-needed jobs, and technology transfer. As an industry, it is particularly important to the economies of developing countries, employing more than 235 million people worldwide and generating more than 9 percent of global gross domestic product (GDP).[2]

However, the tourism industry faced a number of significant challenges in 2010. The economic crisis, rising unemployment, and the swine flu pandemic meant that fewer people traveled—and those that did travel spent less while they were away. As a result, the revenue generated by international tourism fell by 8 percent in 2009, a drop that was felt not only by IHG but also by its business partners and the local communities in which IHG operates. Economic challenges remain, but IHG thinks the tourism industry is showing signs of recovery.

Against this background, IHG's size and economic success allows the company to support communities that have been affected by economic instability, and to continue to invest in long-term environmental and community initiatives. Community initiatives undertaken by the company include training potential employees in local communities and supporting work force development by working with local and regional chambers of commerce and trade, as well as industry associations. IHG also works with other companies and governmental bodies to identify and address work force issues such as working conditions, skills shortages, and infrastructure development in the countries where IHG has a substantial presence, particularly in developing countries. To ensure it acts responsibly and to the highest ethics, IHG has policies addressing human rights and has endorsed the UN Global Compact.

The company's business model, based on franchising its brands for use by third-party hotel owners, has further economic benefits. IHG partners with small-to medium-size enterprises, which are often local to the hotel location. With them, the company is committed to employing local people and supporting their career development, sourcing products and services locally, and encouraging tourists to experience local culture and use local services.

Helping to Build a Skilled Work Force in China. In many cases, the lack of a skilled work force prevents developing nations from tapping into the full economic benefits that travel and tourism offers. For instance, IHG is the largest international hotel operator in China, but has found it difficult to attract and retain talented employees in the region. For that reason, the company launched the IHG Academy, a public/private partnership with renowned educational institutes in several regions in China; the Academy teaches students the skills they need for a career in hospitality. First launched in Shanghai in June 2006, there are now twenty-five partners located in eleven cities throughout China. Additionally, in 2010 IHG established partnerships in America and Russia, with plans to continue expanding the program worldwide.

Each IHG Academy offers a range of certificates and diplomas that combine theoretical sessions, lectures by IHG executives, and internships at IHG's hotels. The Academies train more than 5,000 students per year, and since June 2008, more than 800 students have graduated from the program; sixty-seven have become permanent IHG employees after their internships. A monitoring system to track each student's placement, progress, and career path in our hotels is currently being established.

At the same time, the company wants to build on the success of its "3+2" pilot program, set up in Chongqing in 2007 specifically to tackle industry retention rates. According to the Chinese Education and Tourism Bureau, issues such as long working hours mean that 50 percent of hotel management students don't work in the hotel industry once they have graduated. Under the program, twenty-four students attended lessons two days a week and spent the rest of the week doing hands-on training in a hotel. While many hotel management courses in other parts of the world are operated this way, it was an industry first for China. All twenty-four students completed the course in 2009. All are still working in the industry, fourteen of them in full-time jobs with IHG. According to the dean of Chongqing University, "There has never been such a high percentage of students who want to carry on working at the hotel after their internships. IHG has achieved something unique here." IHG plans to work with more partner schools to expand this program in the coming years.

Conclusion

For IHG, corporate responsibility is an important value that plays a key role in helping the company shape the way it manages costs and revenue. It also builds a competitive advantage. Being responsible reduces costs, especially energy costs, and shows guests that IHG is acting on issues that concern them, such as the environment and supporting the communities in which IHG operates.

At a more profound level, the company asks itself: what is the role of hotels in society? Answering this question is the driving force behind IHG's approach to corporate responsibility, underpinning its deep commitment to a future where its hotels are more intelligent in the way they conduct business and more sustainable. IHG believes this way of thinking will become increasingly important as the company looks for more ways to meet the challenges of climate change and other complex environmental and social issues in a world where the parameters are constantly changing. But while it has an eye on the big picture, IHG also recognizes that, given its scale, small incremental changes across all its hotels can have a large impact.

In particular, IHG is aware that there is often a tension between tourism, the environment, and local communities, and that this tension has been aggravated by the global economic downturn. IHG's response is to draw on the innovation and collaboration principles it applies to all areas of its business. The company sees the environmental and social challenges it faces as opportunities to work alongside partners to develop better ways to design, build, and run hotels.

Ultimately, IHG's approach to corporate responsibility is based on a firm belief that travel and tourism should be operated responsibly, and that the long-term benefits of taking this approach far outweigh the costs.

The company's online corporate responsibility report (www.ihg.com/respon-sibility) gives more details about the areas touched on in this chapter. It includes recent performance data against targets, IHG's priorities for the coming year, and its Global Reporting Initiative (GRI) scorecard. To meet the company's aim to make its reporting more dynamic, certain elements of the site are updated quarterly.

Endnotes

1. International Tourism Partnership website at www.tourismpartnership.org.

2. World Travel and Tourism Council press releases: www.wttc.org/eng/Tourism_News/Press_Releases/Press_Releases_2009/WTTC_Confirms_Increasing_Importance_of_Travel_and_Tourism_to_Trinidad_and_Tobago/ ; and www.wttc.org/eng/Tourism_News/Press_Releases/Press_Releases_2010/ Recovery_stronger_than_expected,_but_likely_to_slow_down_in_2011/.

Sustainable Development Strategies and Best Practices: The Taj Group of Hotels

By Vasant Ayyappan and Foram Nagori

Vasant Ayyappan *is Director–Corporate Sustainability for the Indian Hotels Company Limited in Mumbai, India, which runs the Taj Group of hotels. He is responsible for providing overall direction to the company's mandate of sustainable growth related to social dimensions and environmental protection. In his thirty-two years of work experience, Mr. Ayyappan has held various management positions in the hotel industry in the areas of business excellence; quality management; results orientation, customer focus, and leadership; management by fact; and people development. He has also been involved in the Premium division of Taj hotels. Mr. Ayyappan is a Graduate in Science with a post-graduate degree in Marketing Management from the University of Mumbai.*

Foram Nagori *is Manager–Corporate Sustainability for Indian Hotels Company Limited. She has been working with the Taj Group for over three years and has been instrumental in shaping corporate social responsibility practices in the company, especially in the area of community engagement and development. Prior to this role, Ms. Nagori was associated with Tata Institute of Social Sciences and Sir Dorabji Tata Trust's project in partnership with Ladakh Autonomous Hill Development Council for facilitating grassroots planning and entrepreneurship development in the Leh district in India. Ms. Nagori is a graduate from H. R. College of Commerce and Economics in Mumbai, with a specialization in Travel and Tourism Management. She is also an alumnus of the School of Social Work at Tata Institute of Social Sciences, Mumbai.*

THE INDIAN HOTELS COMPANY LIMITED, owning company of Taj Hotels Resorts and Palaces, operates in the luxury, upper-upscale, upscale, and value segments of the market. The inventory of Taj Group in 2009–2010 stands at a total of 103 hotels in locales ranging from palaces and beaches to cities and more—both in India and international locations. Incorporated by the founder of the Tata Group, Jamsetji N. Tata, the company opened its first property, The Taj Mahal Palace, Bombay, in 1903. For more than 100 years, the Taj has acquainted guests with the living heritage of India and legendary Taj warmth whilst upholding the Tata way of doing business with trust, transparency, and commitment to human values. In addition to its core hotel business, the Taj Group has associated business ventures that include hospitality education, spa, and on-flight catering services.

The Taj business vision is to "embrace talent and harness expertise to leverage the standards of excellence in the art of hospitality to grow our international presence, increase domestic dominance, and create value for all stakeholders." The Tata Code of Conduct is a statement of values that serves as a guideline for the Taj Group's business dealings with its stakeholders. The code urges all companies to "find ways to enhance human, social, and natural capital as complementing financial growth of the enterprise with explicit goals and processes to sustain the effort." This value statement is embedded across all of the Group's companies. (The Tata Code of Conduct can be accessed at: http://tata.com/aboutus/articles/inside.aspx?artid=NyGNnLHkaAc.)

The Tata Group consists of more than ninety companies operating in seven different business sectors, and employing employs more than 350,000 workers across its various areas of operations. One of the attributes common to every Tata enterprise is the time, effort, and resources each of them devotes to the wide spectrum of initiatives that come under the canopy of community development. By a rough estimate, the Tata group as a whole, through its trusts and companies, spends about 30 percent of its net profit after tax (NPAT) on social-development programs.

The Tata culture in this critical segment of the overall corporate sustainability matrix—which includes working for the benefit of the communities in which it operates, helping to build the country's capabilities in science and technology, and showing support for art and sport — springs from an ingrained sense of giving back to society. The Tata founders bequeathed most of their personal wealth to the many trusts they created for the greater good of India and its people. Today, the Tata trusts control 65.8 percent of the shares of Tata Sons, the holding Tata company.

The primary purpose of this chapter is to share the ethos of Taj's sustainability mission, strategies, programs, and initiatives, and to highlight the importance of this spirit for global hospitality enterprises. The "Taj way" can be particularly instructive for companies that operate upscale service enterprises in emerging parts of the world, as it illustrates the benefits of a socially responsible approach to doing business. Key benefits received are not only in the form of ROI (return on investment) but also in a new form of ROE: return on engagement!

Drivers of Sustainability at the Taj

The Taj spirit of giving back to the community is a legacy that has been carried forward from the time of the company's founder, Jamsetji Tata, who believed that communities are truly empowered when companies work together with them to enhance their potential and self-reliance.

Being a part of the service industry, Taj has the unique scope and opportunity to develop raw, potential job candidates from various socio-economic backgrounds into skilled workers who are employable by the hospitality industry. The majority of the company's community projects are focused on the core competencies of food production, kitchen management, housekeeping, customer service, and spas.

The theme for community initiatives is "Building Sustainable Livelihoods," especially for youth and women from less-privileged socio-economic backgrounds. This is primarily being done through custom-made vocational courses in hospitality. The focus is on curriculum development and support for training room setups that train workers for housekeeping, kitchen stewarding, and food production positions; and facilitating on-the-job training and exposure visits at Taj hotels nationwide.

At Taj, promoting the spirit of volunteerism is a major driving force in the company's sustainable development efforts. We believe that volunteering for a societal cause is an enriching experience and allows the human values and self worth of individuals and work teams to flourish. Taj encourages the merging of the "business being" and the "human being," and facilitates spaces for a holistic being to flourish in the workplace.

The preservation and regeneration of the environment is an intrinsic part of the Taj culture. Our commitment to the environmental cause is manifested through our hotels' energy-saving practices and projects to preserve, restore, and enrich their surroundings.

Inducing sensitivity and awareness with respect to the use of natural resources is our priority. The "Green SENSE" initiative at Taj is one example of encouraging responsible behavior amongst employees, with weekly tips on how even the smallest actions can make a difference. Initiatives like the "War on Waste" program that utilizes *kaizen* methodologies (*kaizen* is the Japanese system for continuous improvement of all business processes at all organizational levels, with the end goal of eliminating resource waste) helps hotels reduce consumption of natural resources and promote recycling and reuse. The Tata Code of Conduct also encourages companies to exercise voluntary caution over and above legislative requirements in the way they use natural resources and impact the environment.

Taj's commitment to the environment is in the area of reducing the impact of daily operations on critical natural resources. Therefore, Taj's focus has been on energy management, fresh and waste water management, and solid waste management.

Approaches and Strategies for Sustainable Development

Taj has a strong belief that no company is separate from the environment and communities that sustain it. As a major company with its primary operating base in an emerging economy, we have an intrinsic orientation toward societal consciousness and corporate responsibility, and we are passionate in our commitment to the less privileged members of society. We continuously review and update our corporate responsibility approach and processes, and make a conscious endeavor to align and integrate our efforts to address contemporary societal needs and challenges. Our sustainable strategy is derived from the Tata Corporate Sustainability Charter and our core business strengths, which are outlined in Exhibits 1 and 2.

The company activates its commitment to corporate social responsibility through a financial contribution ranging from $10 million to $15 million. Most of

Exhibit 1 Tata Corporate Sustainability Charter

1. Create sustainable livelihoods:
    *   Build bridges between the organized job market and rural/less-educated/less-exposed youth seeking long-term livelihood options.
    *   Enable marginalized sections like the differently abled, Scheduled Castes, and Scheduled Tribes to gain access to training and employment in the hospitality industry.

2. Preserve and revive indigenous arts, crafts, and culture:
    *   Actively promote indigenous product development and support local vendors.
    *   Facilitate venue and marketing support for local artisans and craftspeople.
    *   Support income-generation projects run by small-scale entrepreneurs, self-help groups, and NGOs.

3. Share our business core competencies:
    *   Private-public partnerships will address entrenched social challenges like child malnutrition, human trafficking, etc.

the projects and initiatives supported by these funds also involve employee volunteering and knowledge-sharing. This year, the Taj Group recorded a total of 59,179 volunteer hours with 5,307 employees participating. This effort benefitted 139,916 people, largely with a long-term impact that economically empowered the target communities.

Developing Human and Social Capital

A people-intensive business like hospitality relies on the strength and quality of its human resource talent. As part of its efforts to attract and develop talent for the hospitality industry in general, Taj has successfully launched two programs: the Taj-Pratham Hospitality Knowledge Centre, and partnerships with industrial and training institutes in rural/interior regions.

Taj-Pratham Hospitality Knowledge Centre. The Hospitality Knowledge Centre was born of the Taj Group's desire to help meet the growing challenge of youth unemployment and under-employment. We partnered with Pratham (which literally means "first"), a pan-India non-governmental organization (NGO) dedicated to the cause of educating the underprivileged. The Centre provides hospitality-operations training for dropouts and other less-privileged job aspirants from rural areas in the key hospitality areas of food production, housekeeping, and food and beverage services.

To implement the project, Taj engaged a cross-functional team that included faculty from Taj's premier training institute IHM, an operations team from one of the Taj hotels, and support and direction from the Taj corporate office, as well as management and local resource persons from Pratham.

Exhibit 2   Taj Core Business Strengths

Taj Core Competencies	Support for Community Development
Food Production	Provide vocational training and certification of less-advantaged target groups; support income-generation projects
Kitchen Management	Improve efficiency of kitchen processes in voluntary organizations, charitable homes, and other developmental organizations
Housekeeping	Provide training to identified groups from poor neighborhoods/targeted communities; maintenance and upkeep of residential facilities maintained by voluntary organizations/charity homes
Personality Development and Grooming	Provide standard input as a part of any "building livelihoods" project as well as stand-alone input that can be provided through volunteering for youth development and other initiatives in partnership with identified NGOs
Spas	Personal hygiene training for adolescent girls and women, promoting self-employment through beautician courses/workshops
Sourcing and Supply Chain	Source and/or co-develop room amenities, stationery and office-use items, artifacts, indigenous/green packaging, etc.

The program was successfully implemented, and about seventy village youth have been trained since the launch of the project in August 2009, with a 100-percent placement ratio for all candidates interested in a hospitality job after completing the program. The process, however, had several challenges that should be considered by hotels planning to implement collaborative partnerships. These primarily involved issues associated with coordination, role definitions, and continuity in volunteering efforts in order to ensure timely progress of various project components.

One of our key insights from this initiative was that patience and communication are key ingredients for success in terms of implementing multi-disciplinary and multiple partners' work processes. It was also interesting to note that several hotel associates from similar rural backgrounds were very enthusiastic about volunteering to help with the program. They served as our champions, trainers, and cheerleaders in helping to demystify for village youth the entire process of training for and securing work opportunities.

Partnership with Industrial Training Institutes in Rural/Interior Regions. India is a country with more than one billion people; more than a quarter of the population remains under the poverty line with little or no access to quality education or training. Although many of the nation's youth are able and willing, they simply lack opportunity and accessibility to the organized sector. For an enlightened company, this population represents a valuable and under-utilized resource.

In keeping with our overall theme of building sustainable livelihoods, since 2007 we have been crafting partnerships with multiple rural technical institutes in order to reach out to youth from less-privileged socio-economic backgrounds. Our core objective is to promote skill development in the relatively marginalized areas of India. Our aim is to reach out to all major regions around our properties in India and provide youth who are less privileged and/or school drop-outs with better access to our skill-building projects. Our primary role in such partnerships is to facilitate market-relevant curriculums and appropriate infrastructure development in terms of training rooms, hands-on trainings, on-the-job exposure, faculty development, guest lectures, and mentoring support for these interior institutions.

The two key insights from this initiative were (1) the need to have a long-term income-generation plan embedded in the project design itself in order to ensure sustainability, and (2) the need to create standardized model curriculums and other operational specifications. Having both of these elements in place would allow for ease of replication as new partnerships are launched. Keeping these lessons in mind, new skill-training initiatives have included a revenue generation program that markets products prepared by the trainees. Revenue from the sale of these products will offset some training expenses, and the program provides real-life market exposure to the trainees.

Sustainable Practices in Supply Chain and Vendor Initiatives

Working in partnership with the linen supplier to our spas, Taj supports less-privileged women by involving them in garment designing and basic stitching, thereby enhancing their skills and empowering them to be self-reliant. Various initiatives conducted in collaboration with NGOs include education and training for physically challenged girls; training in tailoring for destitute women; and a support group for helpless women suffering from post–communal riot trauma. These socially enlightened supplier partnerships extend to a laundry service partnership managed by the NGO Arz, which works toward the economic rehabilitation of victims of commercial sexual exploitation.

The creation of this laundry service partnership involved a high degree of patient, consistent, and unconditional support and training from our team of community service volunteers. They conducted training sessions for women who had basic laundry skills but little knowledge of how to run a business. As the venture was managed by a social foundation, one initial hurdle involved instilling a business mindset and helping them see the importance of a profit motive in any business enterprise. After a series of training sessions in basic communication, team building, customer relations, time management, and quality cleaning procedures, these women have been able to offer high-quality laundry services with operational efficiencies at market rates not only to the Taj, but also to a host of other clients. One of our major gains through this process was a reconfirmation of our belief in the power of an unconditional investment in a meaningful cause. Initiatives like these, when carried out on a continued basis over a period of time, have the power to transform lives and overcome significant social challenges.

Taj Safaris: Combining Conservation and Recreation Is Good Business

Taj Safaris was designed with a distinct sustainability ethos at the core of its business model. Keeping in mind that in today's world being close to nature can be an exquisite and rare experience, we designed a sustainable wildlife safari model in a joint venture with Cigen and &Beyond (previously known as CC Africa). This model promotes biodiversity planning and conservation, while contributing to the economic and social development of the areas in which the wilderness lodges are located. In keeping with social and conservation principles, business processes are designed in a way that engages local and neighborhood communities in delivering this differentiated, close-to-nature experience to our guests. Currently, the Taj has five lodges in Rajasthan and Madhya Pradesh, the heart of India's forest landscape.

Guests visiting our lodges are encouraged to play a part in making a difference, no matter how small. The Baghvan Pench Jungle Lodge team at Pench National Park has come up with creative ways for guests to participate in our social development initiatives, like encouraging them to make intellectual and financial contributions to local schools in the vicinity of the lodge that we support for educating less-privileged children.

Another laudable initiative by Taj Safari has been the promotion of sustainable methods of honey harvesting by the Banjara Tolah Lodge at Kanha National Park. Our associate teams conduct a series of honey-harvesting training sessions for the neighboring villages to teach them scientific ways for gathering honey that is more productive for them and less harmful to nature.

Finally, many Taj hotels source their daily produce and dry goods from local women's self-help groups and volunteer organizations. To cite one example, Taj gives more than $215,000 worth of business per year to aid associations that work for the benefit of family and friends of less-privileged cancer patients who are taking care of patients for long durations, rendering it impossible for them to pursue regular employment options.

Sustainable Practices for Addressing Large-Scale Social Challenges

Leveraging our core competence in food preparation, we have pledged our support to the cause of removing child malnutrition in India. We have been working alongside the government's Integrated Child Development Services (ICDS) Scheme to supplement the nutrition being offered by the government to children aged 0–6 years. Government functionaries were making do with repetitive dishes because of tight budgets and a lack of time and training. When Taj was invited to revise the menu, we were presented with a unique challenge: to make a quality, tasteful, nutritious, hygienic meal for about two cents per person per day! Taj speciality cuisines' chefs took on the challenge of preparing recipes that met the daily dietary requirements of 300 kilocalories of energy and 8 grams of protein. Additionally, in facilitating the implementation of these tasty, nutritious recipes, the locally available ingredients and local palate were kept in mind. More than forty recipes were developed within this tight framework, making it simple for functionaries to adopt these recipes in their daily cooking habits. This represented a real innovation by the Taj staff members, requiring them to think outside the box of their normal work duties. Following a "train-the-trainers" approach, this program has been handed down to 12,000 self-help-group workers and mothers' groups in the villages by a group of ninety women who were trained directly by trainers from the Taj-ICDS-Bhavishya Alliance network. The training encompasses an understanding of the various uses of local ingredients, nutritional basics, cash flow management, and basic cooking hygiene—all possible at a low cost.

This project has been successful in increasing the variety of food served from two dishes to six dishes per week, as well as in increasing the attendance of children in the village day-care centers by 13 percent. This inspired a change in the government policy to incorporate these recipes and training modules as a part of their regular service-delivery scheme. The food leftovers were reduced from 37 percent to almost nil, as a result of improved palatability.

Our focus, with respect to this initiative, was to develop a successful public-private partnership model that was easily replicable and addressed a significant social cause. Each project partner brought its key strengths to the project: food preparation knowledge, expertise, and innovation from the Taj; the mandate, public reach, and human resource networks from the government; and the facilitation and project integration support from the Bhavishya Alliance.

Sustainable Practices in Promoting Indigenous Art, Crafts, and Culture

Sustainability initiatives may also support the preservation of the cultural heritage of communities and regions. Taj hotels located near culturally rich and diverse places proactively engage with cultural troupes and local artisans to help them showcase their local art, crafts, and traditions. More than twelve of our hotels provide a venue, selling space, or slots for indigenous arts and crafts shows from various regions of India.

The contribution also extends to assisting traditional artisan and craft communities, such as the weaver community, by giving individuals within them the marketing, technical, and business expertise they need to revive and reposition their products to appeal to a contemporary market. The company helped jump start this market by purchasing staff uniforms from the weaver community, thereby providing the weavers with a base for their products. More than forty weavers and their families in nearby villages are supported through this project. Villagers are also provided with basic support like solar lighting, health and hygiene, nutritional support for children and women, and drinking water facilities to enable a better quality of life.

Environmental Awareness and Renewal at Taj Hotels (EARTH)

The Environmental Awareness and Renewal at Taj Hotels (EARTH) program was launched in 2008 and is a unique initiative commissioned to help preserve the environment (see Exhibit 3). It identifies three key focus areas for the Taj with respect to its actions on environmental stewardship:

1. Energy efficiency
2. Water management
3. Waste management

The company benchmarks its sustainability practices through Green Globe certification, an international recognition for environmental excellence in the hospitality and tourism industry. Based on Green Globe's assessments and audits across our hotels, covering parameters like energy management, water management, waste management, and management of social and cultural issues, in the first year sixty-six of our hotels achieved Green Globe certification, with ten hotels achieving a "Silver" status in their first attempt and the rest getting accredited with "Bronze" certification. Twenty-eight of our hotels are ISO 14001 certified, and we plan to have all hotels certified by the end of the year 2012. Conscious effort is being made to ensure that our new builds are LEED-compliant. Increasingly our hotels are investing in renewable sources of energy like solar energy, electricity from hydro-power plants, and biogas to replace traditional non-renewable fuels.

We have been steadily improving the energy efficiency of our operations each year by implementing energy-efficiency projects. Several of our hotels participated in the Strategic Programme Fund, which is a low-carbon, high-growth program sponsored by the U.K. Foreign & Commonwealth Office that focuses on energy and cost savings through low-cost and no-cost operational and retrofit measures (see Exhibit 4). In 2008, Taj launched the "Go CFL" program to replace all back-of-the-house lighting with compact fluorescent lighting (CFL) to reduce power consumption. This was done for all our hotels across the globe. We also conducted a series of road shows to encourage employees to use energy-efficiency solutions in their homes.

In another move to promote energy efficiency, beginning in 2008 Ginger Hotels began to install solar panels as water-heating systems; now more than 90 percent of Ginger Hotels has these panels. More than half of Ginger Hotels' guests are corporate professionals who generally are supportive of sustainability practices and appreciate this initiative. Energy savings should offset the initial investment in just a few years. According to Prabhat Pani, the chief operating officer of Ginger Hotels, another value-added element of this energy-saving initiative has been in reinforcing the brand's image of "Smart Basics" and efficient service.

Water reuse is a sustainability measure undertaken in our operations. From 2008 to 2009 we reused 36 percent of the total water procured from various sources. This has helped us in significantly reducing our water footprint. Many hotels that we operate are zero-discharge hotels that recycle/reuse all wastewater either in their processes and/or in landscaping. We ensure that all wastewater discharge is adequately treated and tested prior to release in the municipal drainage system.

Sound waste management practices are one of the key objectives for the Taj Group. We are taking strong initiatives across operations to enhance reduction, recycling, and reusability in our various processes. About 9 percent of the kitchen waste and 28 percent of the horticulture waste generated by our hotels is composted

Exhibit 3   Environmental Awareness and Renewal at Taj Hotels (EARTH)

earth

Vision

The Taj Group of Hotels commits itself to the overall
improvement of the ecological environment,
which we are all a part of.

We recognize that we are not owners but
caretakers of the planet and owe it to our children
and future generations of humankind.

It is our endeavor not only to conserve and protect
but also to renew and regenerate the
environment in which we live and operate.

Our commitment encompasses all actions related to
our products, services, associates, partners,
vendors and communities.

We will partner and engage with our environment through

earth

Environmental **A**wareness and **R**enewal at **T**aj **H**otels.
For us earth is not a program, nor a process;
it is a way of life.

Exhibit 4   Low-Cost and No-Cost Energy-Efficiency Retrofit Programs

- Monitoring sub-meters through a central software system allowing for improved coordination
- Use of heat-recovery chillers to help provide the heat required to produce hot water
- Use of occupancy sensors installed in guest restrooms to help control energy usage (lights, ceiling fans)
- Key card system for guestrooms to minimize electricity waste
- Use of variable frequency drives in pumps
- Aggressive coil maintenance—i.e., filters and air-conditioning coils cleaned monthly, allowing for improved system performance
- Efficient lighting—i.e., CFLs and LED lighting installed in hotel rooms
- Digital thermostats for better management of temperatures within the hotel

Source: Vivanta by Taj—Connemara, Chennai.

and used as manure. We are also in the process of implementing technologies for the conversion of organic waste into bio fuels. This will not only reduce our waste generation, it will supplement our nonrenewable energy sources.

A highlight of our waste management efforts is our high recycling percentage (95.5 percent) of the metal scrap generated at our operational locations. We have taken effective measures to responsibly dispose of "e-waste" (electronic waste such as computers and televisions) generated by our operations by partnering with an authorized e-waste recycler to collect and recycle all of our electronic waste. Printer and toner cartridge recycling has been established with Hewlett-Packard's HP Planet Partners Rewards.

Conclusion

In these times of carbon trading and the many companies that seek merely the bottom-line benefits of environmental initiatives, Taj continues to believe in social responsibility and sensitivity toward stakeholders and the natural environment for an age-old, noble reason: The good of society and the good of the company are still as intrinsically linked as they were when the company began! Taj continues to believe in human values and strong, relationship-based business foundations.

11

Best Practices in Sustainable Development: The Accor Group

By Sophie Flak

*Since early 2010, **Sophie Flak** has been a member of the executive committee at Accor, a hotel management company based in the French city of Courcouronnes. Ms. Flak serves as Executive Vice President for business transformation, innovation, technologies, and sustainable development. She is a graduate of the Institut d'Etudes Politiques in Strasbourg and EM Lyon. After beginning her career at Unilever International Paris, she joined Accenture in 1998. There, she became a partner in charge of innovation and sustainable development strategies. At Accor, she oversees change management programs to help the company transform its businesses, particularly in the shift to management and franchise contracts. Ms. Flak is also in charge of information systems and integrating new technologies, while working to strengthen Accor's position as a leader in innovation and sustainable development.*

ACCOR IS ONE OF THE WORLD'S leading hotel companies, and the market leader in Europe. It maintains a presence in ninety countries, with 4,100 hotels and almost 500,000 rooms. Accor's broad portfolio of hotel brands (Sofitel, Pullman, MGallery, Novotel, Suite Novotel, Mercure, Adagio, ibis, all seasons, Etap Hotel, Formule 1, hotelF1, and Motel 6) and related activities (Thalassa sea & spa and the Lenôtre chain of gastronomy establishments) provide an array of experiences and prices, from luxury to budget. (See Exhibit 1 for a graphical representation of Accor's brand portfolio.) Accor has 150,000 employees worldwide, and offers clients and partners nearly forty-five years of expertise in hospitality management.

Sustainable Development at Accor

Accor believes that growth and development should represent opportunities not only for the company but also for the company's employees, customers, host countries, and the environment. To confirm this commitment, in 2003 Accor signed the United Nations Global Compact, which encourages businesses to develop policies

Exhibit 1 Accor Hotel Brands

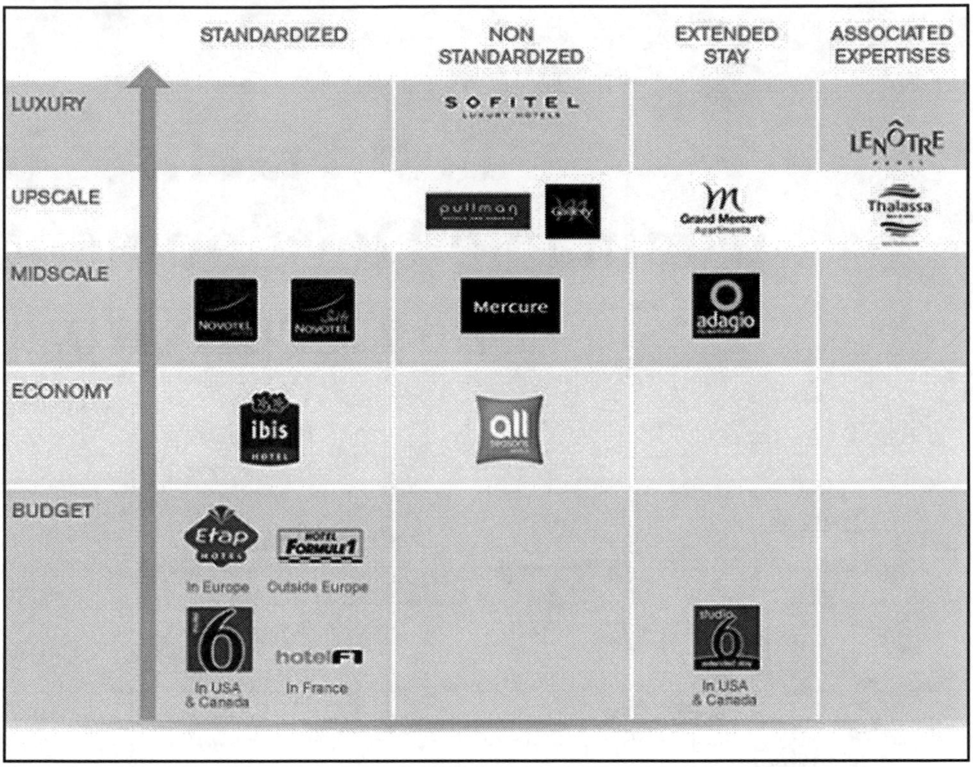

that promote sustainability and social responsibility. Accor is convinced that conducting business responsibly not only helps the planet and its inhabitants; it also positively contributes to the company's social, economic, and commercial performance. Accor makes its business a catalyst that contributes to the social and economic growth of countries, regions, and cities by enhancing those communities' wealth, heritage, and culture. Over the last few years, the Accor Group's commitments have mobilized its 150,000 employees, millions of customers, and thousands of suppliers and partners in 100 countries behind one goal: to protect the planet and the well-being of its inhabitants. By harmonizing its interests with those of the local and global community, Accor ensures the sustainability of its future.

This corporate harmonization is made possible by the empathetic and caring involvement general managers at Accor hotels have with issues in their communities. For example, the Group's commitment to fighting epidemics and child sex tourism came from the involvement of hotel managers. Sustainable development clearly means making positive impacts on destinations where Accor hotels are located.

From a managerial point of view, a strong business case exists for sustainable development. Accor has a great opportunity to organize collective projects within its hotel teams by both showing concern for sustainable development and allowing hotel management to motivate team members (consequently boosting the quality of products and services those team members offer) In addition, Accor can optimize its financial performance through resource management initiatives related to energy and water conservation and waste reduction.

From the customer's point of view, the ultimate goal of sustainable development is to boost humanity's well-being. Ensuring the quality of our environment, health, water, and food are essential means of improving the quality of services Accor provides to guests who have entrusted the company with their comfort and safety.

Sustainable Development Programs and Initiatives

Accor has a dedicated organization and strategy to ensure that sustainable development is firmly entrenched within the company. In 1994, the Group created an Environment department, and in 1998 released the Accor Hotels Environment Charter, the first environmental management tool in the industry. (The charter, a sixty-five-action tool that guides hoteliers' environmental action plans, appears in Exhibit 2.) In 2002, Accor broadened its action scope by creating a Sustainable Development department, which handles social and environmental issues.

Managing and Monitoring Sustainable Development Programs. Since 2002, Accor has adopted a steering dashboard, published in its annual report, that shows the progress Accor made that year toward targets addressing the company's responsibility to its stakeholders (i.e., shareholders, clients, employees, suppliers, the environment, and local communities). An extract from Accor's 2009 steering dashboard appears in Exhibit 3. In 2006, Accor set objectives to be reached by the end of 2010 that guided the company's sustainability actions. Each department takes part in implementing sustainable development and is responsible for meeting its own targets. Thus, sustainable development is a collaboration between the Sustainable Development department and each department within the Group (e.g., operational departments worldwide—Group Procurement, Financial Communication, Quality, Risk Management, Safety, Human Resources, Design and Technical, International Marketing, etc.).

Earth Guest. To organize, systematize, and implement its sustainable development programs, the Accor Group launched Earth Guest in 2006. The program maintains eight priorities, with one motto: "As guests of the Earth, we welcome the world." As noted by Accor's chairman and chief executive officer, Gilles Pélisson, "this sentence, much more than a slogan, expresses the very core of the Accor philosophy, based on hospitality and a respect for diverse cultures." (See Exhibit 4 for more information about Earth Guest, including its list of eight priorities.) Accor plans to integrate Earth Guest priorities into each stage of its hotels' lifecycles, and encourage involvement among the company's stakeholders. For an overview of this approach to sustainability, visit Accor's Sustainable Development website at www.accor.com/en/sustainable-development.html.

Planning for Development and Green Construction. At the stage of hotel development and construction, sustainability guidelines have been issued and integrated into brand standards. Accor has promoted renewable energy since 1998. By

Exhibit 2   Accor Hotels Environment Charter

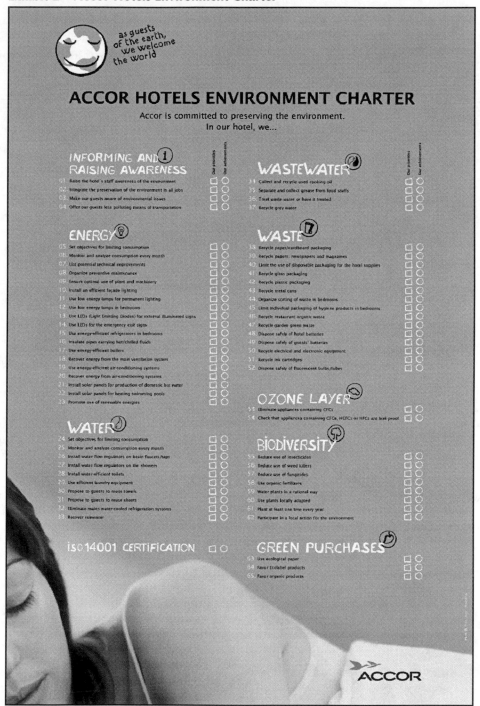

Exhibit 3   Extract from Accor's 2009 Sustainable Development Dashboard

Accor's sustainable development dashboard contains forty-seven indicators and objectives, and is published each year in the Accor Annual Report.

Stakeholders	Objectives	Accor performance indicators	2009 results and highlights	Commitments made in 2006 for year-end 2010
SHAREHOLDERS	Ensure the transparency of financial and strategic information about the company provided to financial markets.	Regular information tailored to each category of shareholder/specifier: number of people met. A working group on individual shareholder relations comprised of 15 members of the Shareholders Club.	Meetings were held with 840 representatives of 404 financial institutions, and 22 roadshows were organized in Europe, the United States, and Canada. Accor also took part in seven investor conferences during the year, in France and the United States. Contact with over 550 individual shareholders through meetings, tours and trade shows and with 600 shareholders at the Annual Meeting. Two meetings with the working group on shareholder relations.	Deepen relationships with individual and institutional shareholders through more instructive content and greater responsiveness.
CUSTOMERS	Guarantee superior service.	Number of ISO 9001-certified hotels.	714 Ibis hotels certified, 83% of the network.	Certification for all Ibis hotels in Europe, Morocco, and Brazil, and deployment in new countries.
	Promote good health through wholesome, balanced diets.	Number of restaurants participating in a healthy, balanced nutrition program.	Ibis has deployed the Nutritional Balance program in France and Spain. Novotel: Fitness & Balance program introduced in France, Italy, the United Kingdom, and Australia; Balance option in children's menus deployed in 35 countries.	Continue to deploy a balanced nutrition offering in new countries and new hotel brands.
EMPLOYEES	Improve employee training programs.	Number of days of training. Training budget as a % of total payroll.	2009: 327,974 days; 2008: 336,382 days; 2009 training rate: 2.4%.	One training session per person per year.
	Ensure employee health and safety.	HIV/AIDS prevention training program.	Distribution of the ACT-HIV approach and implementation of national action plans in 25 countries. Accor teams in 21 countries took part in World AIDS Day.	Distribute the ACT-HIV DVD in all hotels to help combat HIV/AIDS.

Exhibit 4   Earth Guest Priorities

Accor's Earth Guest program
- One motto: *"As guests of the Earth, we welcome the world."*
- Eight priorities, divided into two projects: social responsibility and environmental stewardship

EGO project

 Local development
Support host communities through employment, purchases, and long-term partnerships.

 Child protection
Train employees and inform customers about the fight against child sex tourism.

 Fight against epidemics
Deploy preventive measures and combat major epidemics, in particular AIDS and malaria.

 Balanced food
Encourage customers to improve their eating habits, with a special focus on obesity.

ECO project

 Energy
Promote renewable energy sources and equip hotels with efficient energy systems.

 Water
Equip hotel faucets with flow regulators, monitor and recover wastewater, and raise customer awareness.

 Waste
Recycle more and better, and limit the amounts of waste produced.

 Biodiversity
Create partnerships with specialized associations to build awareness and protect endangered species.

the end of 2009, ninety-nine Accor hotels had solar panels that produced hot water for domestic use. In France, this project was supported by ADEME, the French Environment and Energy Management Agency. The following are examples of other innovative technologies in Accor hotels:

- In 2004, the ibis Porte de Clichy was the first European hotel equipped with photovoltaic panels.

- In 2005, the Novotel Paris Montparnasse was the pilot hotel for High Quality Environmental (HQE) certification from the Association pour la Haute Qualité Environnementale (ASSOHQE).

- The new Etap Hotel Toulouse Airport is three times more energy efficient than heating regulations require, and uses an innovative geothermal system.

- The future Suitehotel Issy-les-Moulineaux is one of the first hotels certified to HQE standards for service sector buildings.

- In 2010, Motel 6's property in Northlake, Texas, became the first economy hotel in the United States to attain Leadership in Energy and Environmental Design (LEED) certification from the U.S. Green Building Council. It was also the first of Accor's hotels to earn this distinction.

In terms of room design, Accor's standardized brands maintain sustainable development criteria. Novotel and ibis rooms use only timber certified by the Forest Stewardship Council (FSC) or the Programme for the Endorsement of Forest Certification (PEFC). This ensures that the hotels' timber does not come from primary forests, whose razing can destroy wildlife habitats and affect biodiversity. In addition, during the creation of new Etap Hotel rooms, designers paid special attention to environmental preservation by including water-saving toilets, low-consumption light bulbs, occupancy sensors, waterflow regulators on taps, and materials that are more easily recycled than traditional materials.

Accor has also developed sustainable products that are available in some of the company's hotels. In 2008, two lines of eco-designed bathroom products were developed. The "I care, ibis cares" line includes soap dispensers 100 percent recyclable, and products certified to European Union (EU) Ecolabel standards. Ecolabel also certified cleansing products in Novotel's "N" line, while the organic certification organization ECOCERT certified the line's cosmetics.

Mobilizing Employees. By increasing their awareness and acquiring new on-the-job practices, Accor employees have played a pioneering role in expressing the company's commitment to sustainable development. A few examples of employee involvement in sustainable initiatives are discussed in the following paragraphs.

Prevention of child exploitation. Since 2002, with southeast Asia as its pioneer area, Accor has trained staff on the prevention of child sex tourism. It sets the principles for an active policy against this practice by collaborating with ECPAT, an international non-governmental organization (NGO) that works to end child prostitution, child pornography, and the trafficking of children for sexual purposes. Accor made its commitment official by signing the "Code of Conduct for the Protection of Children from Sexual Exploitation in Travel and Tourism," created by the World Trade Organization (WTO) and ECPAT. Since 2002, thousands of Accor employees around the world—13,000 in 2009 alone—have been trained to detect suspicious behaviors and have learned how to react to them.

Prevention of HIV/AIDS. Accor's commitment to fighting HIV and AIDS started in 2002, in Sub-Saharan Africa, with a comprehensive program that involved distributing condoms, providing training and information about prevention to employees, and financing treatments and medicines. For World AIDS Day 2008, Accor and Club Méditerranée organized a voluntary screening program for their 800 employees in Senegal. Local professional organizations have duplicated this action, screening several thousand employees in 2010.

Accor has gone international in its commitment to fighting HIV and AIDS by joining the Global Business Coalition on HIV/AIDS, Tuberculosis and Malaria (GBC), and by creating the GBC's Hotel/Travel/Tourism dialogue, which includes fifteen tourism companies. In 2007, Accor also established an initiative, ACT-HIV (now available in twenty-five countries), that focuses on hotel and service managers. The initiative explains, in six steps, how managers and their employees can fight the disease in their communities.

Environmental awareness. In the Accor Group's 4,000 hotels, staff members have learned simple ways to save water and energy, and to sort waste. Hotel managers implement environmental measures by applying the Accor Hotels Environment Charter (mentioned earlier in the chapter). By 2009, 86 percent of Accor hotels—97 percent of owned and leased hotels, and 65 percent of franchised hotels—had implemented the charter. What follows are some of the most significant results achieved through the end of 2009 because of action plans guided by the charter:

- Between 2006 and 2009, Accor's energy consumption per available room decreased by 7.8 percent in owned and leased hotels.

- Seventy-nine percent of hotels are equipped with energy-efficient lamps for permanent lighting.

- Between 2006 and 2009, Accor's water consumption per rented room decreased by 4 percent in owned and leased hotels.

- Eighty-nine percent of owned and leased hotels are equipped with flow regulators on showers and taps.

- Fifty-one percent of owned and leased hotels recycle paper, cardboard, and glass.

- Eighty-six percent of owned and leased hotels safely dispose of batteries and fluorescent tubes and bulbs.

- More than 850 hotels serve organic products.

- Seventy-seven percent of hotels took part in a local environmental action or planted a tree in 2009.

Accor looks to third-party certifications to improve its performance. Since 2004, the ibis hotel chain has been involved in ISO 14001 accreditation from the International Organization for Standardization. Today, 286 of its hotels in seventeen countries are certified per the standard, which focuses on environmental management practices. Other Accor brands are involved in ISO 14001 certification as well. Nine of Thalassa sea & spa's sites in France have received the certification, while Lenôtre's three-star restaurant, Le Pré Catelan, meets ISO 14001 standards. Meanwhile, some Accor properties are pursuing other certifications. In 2007, Novotel engaged its network of hotels in the Green Globe certification program, which deals with sustainable management and operations. By early 2010, fifty-three Novotel sites had been certified through Green Globe. Accor's brands and businesses are increasingly integrating sustainable development concerns into their products and services, to the point that over 10 percent of Accor hotels have now received an environmental certification.

Mobilizing Supply Chain Partners. Accor Group spends billions for products every year. Consequently, the company has significant leverage over its 2,800 suppliers throughout the world. In recent years, Accor has worked closely with these suppliers to involve them in the company's corporate responsibility projects. In 2003, Accor launched the Sustainable Procurement Charter, in which the Group's various purchasing departments committed to requesting information from suppliers on their social and environmental policies. Today, Accor applies the charter for all international purchases, as well as for national purchases in eleven countries.

Promoting Guest Awareness and Well-Being. Accor promotes sustainable development and the well-being of its guests through customer engagement offers and programs. For example, Accor hotels serve fair trade products in seventeen countries. Accor hotels in regions vulnerable to child sex tourism promote ECPAT campaigns to boost guest awareness of this problem. Other examples of Accor's efforts to promote sustainable development and healthy habits among its guests follow.

Fighting epidemics. Accor conducts several initiatives that raise awareness and encourage guests to take part in the global fight against disease:

- In 2007, in partnership with Air France, Accor produced two videos entitled "Going on a Trip?" These videos showed travelers ways they could prevent the spread of HIV, AIDS, and malaria.

- In early 2010, Accor signed a partnership agreement to collaborate on two initiatives with Institut Pasteur, a non-profit organization that works to prevent and treat disease. Accor guests can convert points from A|Club—the company's loyalty program—into donations for Institut Pasteur. In addition, Accor and Institut Pasteur collaborated on a health information and prevention website for travelers, pasteurtravel.com. Experts at Institut Pasteur provide the site's content, which keeps travelers up to date on preventive treatments, mandatory and suggested vaccinations, and the inherent risks of traveling to certain destinations.

- In March 2010, Accor was a partner in the launch of MASSIVEGOOD, a global campaign against AIDS and malaria. Accor encourages customer donations to the campaign through banners on its hotel reservation websites.

Healthy eating. The ibis hotel chain has deployed Edenred's Nutritional Balance program in France and Spain, while Novotel introduced the Fitness & Balance program in France, Italy, the United Kingdom, and Australia. A balanced option in children's menus is deployed in Accor properties in thirty-five countries.

Earth Guest Discovery. In 2008, for its corporate customers, Accor developed Earth Guest Discovery, a travel program in which guests take part in team-building activities that promote respect for the planet and its inhabitants. Through Earth Guest Discovery, guests participate in programs that expose them to the diversity of local cultures and economies, the huge variety of native species, and the beauty of the surrounding landscape. For example, participants in the Earth Guest Discovery program through the Mercure Chamonix Centre in France climb the Mer de Glace glacier, while participants in the Sofitel El Gezirah Cairo program in Egypt visit an archaeological site in the desert. (See Exhibit 5 for sample itineraries of two additional Earth Guest Discovery programs.) Earth

Exhibit 5   Earth Guest Discovery Examples

"We combine our hotel expertise and our commitment to sustainable development to offer original and friendly Incentive Programmes. With the Accor Hospitality expertise and its partners uniting through the Earth Guest Discovery label, you can now carry out team-building activities while respecting the planet and its inhabitants, discover the diversity of different cultures and local economies, and discover the beauty and wide variety of the surrounding nature. Convert to an out-of-this-world experience with sustainable development principles."

Earth Guest Discovery at Sofitel Agadir, Morocco
"Along the Argan Oil Route"
Programme Schedule

Day 1: Arrival
Evening arrival at the Sofitel Agadir

Day 2: Meeting
Meeting day
Departure towards Tiznit region
Traditional welcome in village at the heart of the Argan region
Dinner in the village and Berber party

Day 3: Activities
Cultural and athletic hike
Visit of an Argan cooperative
Traditional lunch in Berber village with local people
Festive farewell with association members
Participants' departure

Earth Guest Discovery at Sofitel Lisbon Liberdade
"Lisbon in Tune with Preserving the Local Traditions"
Programme Schedule

Day 1: Arrival
Evening arrival at Sofitel Lisbon

Day 2: Meeting
Study day; conference with an expert specialized in "slow food"
Dinner at the hotel

Day 3: Activities
Departure towards the Arrabida Massifs
Guided tour of the local craftsmen and local produce
Gastronomic lunch at Setubal
Discovering the flora and fauna of the natural park Arrabida by donkey
Guided tour of the mills situated in the mountains where the Biosani company
    produces organic bread
Participants' departure

Guest Discovery is available in ten hotels within the Accor Group; this number is likely to grow in the future.

Plant for the Planet. Accor's Plant for the Planet project is another method the company uses to promote guest awareness of sustainability issues. By encouraging guests to embrace practices that are not only more environmentally friendly, but also more cost-effective, Accor hopes to finance the planting of three million trees by 2012. To do so, Accor encourages guests to use towels for more than one night. The money the company saves by not laundering those towels goes toward its tree planting initiative. In April 2010, Accor announced that a significant threshold had been reached: 1,000 hotels involved and one million trees financed. Exhibit 6 includes more information on Plant for the Planet, including details about two reforestation initiatives in which Accor is taking part.

Mobilizing Accor's Expert Partners. Accor has developed several partnerships to make its sustainability actions more relevant and efficient. Forming relationships with the right partners has been an essential means of reinforcing the effectiveness and significance of the company's actions. For example, to encourage local economic development, Accor and Agrisud, an organization that promotes entrepreneurship in poverty-stricken areas, have worked together in Cambodia since 2004 to support family-run truck farms. Accor's Sofitel Royal Angkor hotel, in the Siem Reap region, purchases 10 percent of the fruit and vegetables these farms produce. This partnership recently extended to Phnom Penh with the opening of a Sofitel hotel there. The initiative has led to many positive outcomes, including the creation of 120 fully operating agricultural micro-businesses involving 750 people, and an increase in family incomes of 250 percent. In addition, to fight child sex tourism and epidemics, Accor relied on expert NGO partners to provide appropriate training and prevention sessions for its employees.

To promote biodiversity, Accor and its brands have formed several partnerships:

- In affiliation with the International Union for Conservation of Nature (IUCN), Accor produced a guide to biodiversity protection for hotel professionals. Entitled *Biodiversity: My Hotel in Action*, the guide presents actions hotels can take to promote biodiversity in food services, hotel interiors, lawns and gardens, care and spa products, souvenir shops, and, more generally, the tourist destination in which the hotel is located. To ensure the guide met hotel operators' expectations, a working group representing various Accor brands, regions, and support services was created and consulted during the preparation process.

- In France, Etap Hotel and the Bird Protection League (LPO) have worked together for four years to raise awareness of biodiversity among customers through a variety of communication media, and by involving employees in awareness visits and initiatives.

- Partnering with the Slow Food Association, which promotes awareness of the ways food is produced, sold, and eaten, Mercure hotels in Italy offer customers local culinary delights, and raise guests' awareness of the importance of the terroir and its cultural and natural diversity.

Exhibit 6   Plant for the Planet

Plant for the Planet: a flagship project mobilizing guests and employees

In 2008, Accor launched a towel reuse program that gives genuine value to an eco-friendly gesture made by its guests. The Group's hotels encourage customers staying more than one night to reuse their bath towels, raising their awareness with the formula **"5 towels reused = 1 tree planted."** Accor has pledged to invest half of the savings on laundry costs to support seven reforestation programs around the world. Developed by seven NGO partners, the programs are designed to provide the local populations with socio-economic as well as environmental benefits.

For this project, Accor has partnered with the United Nations Environment Programme (UNEP) through its support of the Plant for the Planet: Billion Tree Campaign.

In two years, thanks to the involvement of **1,000 hotels,** Accor has financed the planting of **one million trees** in seven forest areas.

Focus on two projects

In Brazil, in partnership with the NGO Nordesta, Accor is reforesting degraded areas along one of the headwaters of the São Francisco River, the second-largest river in Brazil. More than 30 kilometers of trees are being planted between the Serra da Canastra nature park and the village of Vargem Bonita in the state of Minas Gerais. At the same time, the effort is promoting ecotourism and beekeeping activities to ensure that forest preservation brings concrete benefits to the local population. The ultimate goal is to safeguard the headwaters of the São Francisco River, which flows through many towns for more than 3,000 kilometers.

In Senegal, in partnership with the NGO SOS Sahel International France, Accor is supporting the group of producers that is reforesting the Niayes area along the Atlantic coast, between Dakar and Saint-Louis, in the Louga and Thiès regions. This strip of land is approximately 182 kilometers long and 200 to 500 meters wide. The Niayes area is a strategic food-growing region for Senegal because two-thirds of the vegetables consumed in the country are grown there. This region is threatened by desertification; 80,000 hectares of forest disappear each year in Senegal. In the Niayes area, the agricultural basins are progressively losing their only barrier against the encroachment of sand.

Key Insights and Outcomes of Sustainability Programs and Initiatives

Implementing a sustainable development strategy implies a shift from usual business practices, and a prioritization of efforts. It requires a commitment of time and involvement from all levels within an organization. At Accor Group, we've learned that the successful implementation of a sustainable development strategy within an organization requires three elements:

1. Support from top management, and a shared organizational vision

2. A structured program with priorities, action plans, indicators, and objectives

3. Innovative ideas and practices

Top Management Support and Shared Organizational Vision. The success of Accor's sustainable development practices stems from the support they received from top management, and their alignment with the organization's vision of corporate social responsibility. Experience has shown that this shared approach won the support of managers at the unit level, and was welcomed globally by Accor employees. The company's employees have a strong need for commitment, values, and a meaningful job; sustainable development has been a key element to fulfill this need.

Earth Guest Day is Accor employees' action day for sustainable development. Employees from sixty-nine countries participated in the first Earth Guest Day in 2007. Since then, employees in almost eighty countries have taken part in the annual event, organizing actions that promote local development, health, and environmental preservation. In 2010, employees planted thousands of trees all over the world. In South America, they promoted healthy eating habits by offering organic products to Accor guests throughout the continent. In France, Pullman hotels launched a partnership to promote biodiversity by, among other things, donating money to a research program that studies bees. In the United States, Accor hotels have started an initiative to become part of the Amber Alert process, encouraging team members to remain observant and make themselves aware of information that might help law enforcement officials recover missing children.

Structured Program with Priorities, Action Plans, Indicators, and Objectives. It is important to maintain viligance in looking for ways the company can practice social responsibility. However, it is impossible to tackle all topics at the same time. Therefore, clearly defining priority topics with precise objectives, including performance measures and deadlines for implementation, is essential. Accor did this in 2006 when it set objectives for the end of 2010. Each of these objectives required measurable indicators of performance to gauge actual results. For example, Accor set the ambitious goal of reducing its energy consumption per room by 10 percent between 2006 and 2010. The company relied on the following actions to attain this goal:

• Speeding the installation of energy-efficient lamps and flow regulators

• Systematically analyzing consumption rates on a monthly basis

• Developing energy diagnoses based on experience acquired in France and the United States

• Developing action plans per country

Accor could then follow up on the results through the Accor Hotels Environment Charter, which had been designed as a day-to-day management tool.

Innovative Ideas and Practices. Sustainable development is a great lever for innovation. Consider all the changes that can be integrated into products and services by making them more sustainable: new processes, new materials, new functions, etc. To cite one example, Accor relied on innovation when it designed the Plant for the Planet program mentioned earlier in the chapter. The company found an innovative way to convert a gesture made by its guests—reusing towels—into a meaningful action—planting three million trees. Accor's innovative project consisted of:

- Gaining guests' support by promising to invest the savings created by towel reuse into a worldwide reforestation initiative.

- Training and motivating housekeeping teams, which involved creating a video for room attendants that described the importance of reforestation, explained the program, and provided suggestions for new housekeeping habits to be developed with regard to bath towels.

- Creating a win-win system in which 50 percent of the savings stayed with the hotel, to finance training and incentives, and 50 percent went to seven reforestation projects throughout the world.

Conclusion

Accor's sustainability efforts are being recognized. In 2009, Accor won the Condé Nast Traveler's World Savers Award in the Health Initiatives category for its anti-AIDS policy, and the Tomorrow's Value Rating from Two Tomorrows, which designated Accor as a sustainability leader among the world's ten largest hotel groups. In May 2010, Accor received a Tourism for Tomorrow Award in the Global Tourism Business Award category from the World Travel & Tourism Council. Accor is proud of these recognitions, as they acknowledge the deep commitment Accor has made to sustainable development throughout the world. The company has progressively involved all its departments and its business stakeholders: hotel managers and employees, technical teams, providers, procurement teams, marketing departments, and customers.

However, sustainable development is a process of continuous change, and Accor knows there is still room for improvement. The company believes the hospitality industry is in a privileged position to have a positive impact on the world by inspiring new behaviors among its guests, thereby contributing to the well-being of future generations.

Sustainable Development Strategies at Las Vegas Sands: Vision, Journey, and Future Outlook

By Nicholas Rumanes and A. J. Singh

Nicholas G. Rumanes is the Vice President of Corporate Development for Las Vegas Sands Corporation. His responsibilities include development and portfolio management of the company's integrated resorts. Mr. Rumanes is also responsible for founding and operating the Sands Eco 360° Global Sustainable Development program. He played a key role in the development of The Palazzo, the first property on the Las Vegas Strip to receive LEED Gold EB (Existing Buildings) certification. The Venetian, the Sands Expo and Convention Center, and The Palazzo make up the largest LEED building in the world.

Prior to joining Las Vegas Sands, Mr. Rumanes was a director for Tishman Hotel & Realty, where he was responsible for the design and development of the company's hospitality and residential projects.

Mr. Rumanes is also a sought-after speaker for his expertise in sustainable development and a visiting professor of construction management at the Pratt Institute in New York City. In addition, Mr. Rumanes co-authored with A. J. Singh Chapter 19 of Hotel Asset Management: Principles & Practices.[1]

Mr. Rumanes earned a Master of Science degree in Architecture and Urban Design at Columbia University and a Bachelor of Architecture degree at Southern California Institute of Architecture.

A. J. Singh, Ph.D., is an Associate Professor in The School of Hospitality Business at Michigan State University and focuses on international lodging, finance, and real estate. Dr. Singh was jointly responsible for the establishment of The Hospitality Business Real Estate and Development Specialization at Michigan State University. He has more than fifteen years of hospitality business experience in various management positions in the United States and India. He has worked for Oberoi Hotels, Stouffer Hotels, and Hyatt Hotels. In 1999, he taught financial management at Centre International de Glion in Switzerland. He has also conducted many real estate market and feasibility studies while working as a consultant for Laventhol & Horwath.

Dr. Singh earned his undergraduate degree from the University of Delhi in India, his M.S. from Purdue University in Hotel Restaurant and Institutional

Management, and his Ph.D. in Park, Recreation, and Tourism from Michigan State University. He is an active member of the Hospitality Asset Managers Association; the Council on Hotel, Restaurant, and Institutional Education; the Association of Hospitality Financial Management Educators; the International Society of Hospitality Consultants; and the Urban Land Institute. The National Institute of Standards and Technology appointed him to the 2006 Board of Examiners for the Malcolm Baldrige National Quality Award. He received the Richard Lewis Award for Quality and Innovation in 2006. He currently conducts two study-abroad programs to India, Dubai, Thailand, Hong Kong, Macau, and Southern China.

Research Support: **Neil Naran** *holds a Bachelor of Arts in Finance from Michigan State University's Eli Broad College of Business. Through his study at Michigan State University, Neil held an active role in* The *School of Hospitality Business at Michigan State University, where he participated in numerous supporting projects such as case evaluation led by Jones Lang LaSalle Hotels, was Assistant to Dr. A. J. Singh, and held an executive position within the Real Estate Investment Club. He has held temporary roles in numerous hospitality firms such as Tarsadia Hotels, Jones Lang LaSalle Hotels, and Hilton Hotels & Resorts. Prior to Neil's corporate experience, he had more than ten years of hospitality operational experience in various roles for hotels such as Hampton, Comfort Suites, Homewood Suites, Best Western, and Knights Inn.*

MAJOR HOTEL CHAINS are large consumers of resources such as power and water. Today, many of them are seeking eco-friendly and energy-efficient methods of construction and operation. In part this is a response to governmental pressures. For example, many municipalities are requiring "green" processes in new construction projects when granting entitlements and construction permits. Many state controllers, who invest substantial amounts of state pension funds in real estate, have written to the Securities and Exchange Commission (SEC) requesting that the SEC make it mandatory that public companies disclose their percentage of real estate owned that is in compliance with eco-friendly standards. Greener buildings not only reduce operating costs, but also attract customers who wish to patronize them. With a steady increase in the number of hotels adopting piecemeal or comprehensive sustainable practices, the awareness of the benefits of green development is on the rise within the industry. For sustainable development practices to become truly sustainable and pervasive, however, hotel owners and developers must be convinced that "going green" adds value to properties. Through a case study approach, this chapter will outline the strategic implementation of sustainable practices at the largest hotel and casino building complex in the world. The initial results at Las Vegas Sands positively support a business case for incorporating sustainable development practices.

The Las Vegas Sands Corporation (LVS) is the leading global developer of destination properties (integrated resorts) that feature premium accommodations, world-class gaming and entertainment, convention and exhibition facilities, celebrity chef restaurants, and many other amenities. The Venetian and The Palazzo, five-diamond luxury resorts on the Las Vegas Strip, are among the company's properties in the United States. The iconic Marina Bay Sands in Singapore is the most recent addition to the company's portfolio. The company also owns a collection of properties in Macao through its majority-owned subsidiary Sands China Ltd., including The Venetian Macao, the Four Seasons Hotel Macao, and the Four

Seasons–branded serviced apartments at its Cotai Strip development, as well as the Sands Macao on the Macao peninsula. The company is currently constructing a 6,400-room complex at the Cotai Strip, which will feature the signature hotel brands.

Drivers for Implementing Sustainable Development Practices at Las Vegas Sands

While most hotel owners and operators are aware of the magnitude of the carbon footprint large hotels and casinos leave on the environment, many still do not consciously consider it when developing and operating these buildings. At Las Vegas Sands, the journey to sustainability started with a simple question: "Do green hotels add value to the property?" Despite a limited number of hotel case studies and research on the topic, a statement by company president Michael Leven at a press conference a few years ago clearly shows an understanding of the trend and a broader vision to help other businesses adopt these practices: "We are responding to the green demand from our clients, guests, employees, and local communities. But we not only strive for our properties to be sustainability leaders, we also share our processes and experiences with other businesses and governments."

Las Vegas Sands' journey in sustainability started with the construction of The Palazzo in 2007, an 8-million-square-foot integrated resort with 50 stories; 3,066 rooms; and gaming, retail, entertainment, and restaurant facilities. Developed on sustainable principles, it was the first property on the Las Vegas Strip to be awarded with a Leadership in Energy and Environmental Design (LEED) for New Construction Silver certification from the U.S. Green Building Council. The property introduced several innovative design features to improve building efficiency, which reduced both development and operating costs for the company.[2] This early success gave the company the confidence to take the project further with a more comprehensive vision.

In March 2010 LVS formalized its sustainable business practice with the launch of the Sands Eco 360° Global Sustainable Development program. The program launch was highlighted by the announcement that The Venetian and the Sands Expo and Convention Center in Las Vegas achieved LEED for Existing Buildings Gold certification. The combined LEED-certified properties of The Venetian, the Sands Expo and Convention Center, and The Palazzo compose the largest LEED building in the world, with a total square footage of over 17 million.

LVS created the Sands Eco 360° Global Sustainable Development program because, quite simply, it was the right thing to do. It benefits the company's guests, staff or "team" members, and surrounding communities while providing value to its shareholders and future generations. It is an environmentally and socially responsible endeavor, as many of Las Vegas Sands' properties are in geographic areas where there are limited natural resources, such as in the desert of Las Vegas and on the islands of Asia. Sands Eco 360° is a broad, comprehensive way for the company to respect and protect the local environments, natural resources, climate, and communities where it operates. Sustainability has become a cornerstone of Las Vegas Sands' business philosophy; the company is committed to being the

The Palazzo was the first property on the Las Vegas Strip to receive LEED Silver NC (New Construction) certification from the U.S. Green Building Council.

preeminent sustainable development corporation in the world, and the Sands Eco 360° program was developed to bring this commitment to life.

Las Vegas Sands' initial results prove that "green business is good business." The company estimates that for every $1 invested in the program, LVS saves $4.

Together, The Palazzo, The Venetian, and the Sands Expo and Convention Center make up the largest LEED building in the world.

The company's continued development of sustainable projects has helped answer the growing market demand for green facilities on the part of meeting and convention businesses. Furthermore, other stakeholders, such as individual guests, local governments, investors, communities, and team members, find LVS's sustainability initiatives to be an attractive part of its business model.

As the company grows internationally in China and Singapore, it is leveraging lessons learned at its U.S. properties to benefit these destinations. Given the size and scale of LVS's global operations, it is expected that these policies and practices will have downstream, upstream, and lateral impacts across the supply chain and on related stakeholders. As others adopt these practices, LVS hopes to ultimately leave a legacy of a more responsible, cleaner, and safer world for future generations.

Introducing Sustainable Development within an Organization

The concept, definition, and philosophy of sustainable development were first coined in the 1987 *Brundtland Report*. It stated that sustainable development is

Exhibit 1   Las Vegas Sands' Eco 360° Mission Statement

Las Vegas Sands Corporation is committed to protecting the environment and to being the preeminent sustainable resort development corporation in the world. To achieve these goals, we will continue to develop and implement environmental practices for our existing resorts, and all future developments, that protect our natural resources, offer our team members a safe and healthy work environment, and enhance the resort experience of our guests and the quality of life in the communities in which we operate.

"development that meets the needs of the present without compromising the ability of future generations to meet their own needs."[3] This concept has been adopted and accepted by many major corporations that have developed a value system to suit their corporate sustainability missions. At Las Vegas Sands, this new value system was shaped by John Elkington's "triple bottom line" paradigm, and "People, Planet, and Profit" became the three pillars of sustainability supporting the Sands Eco 360° program. The first pillar, "People," represents LVS's commitment to maintaining a safe and healthy environment for all company guests and team members, and to improving the quality of life in the communities in which the company operates. The second pillar, "Planet," represents the company's commitment to sustainable development to minimize its ecological impact, while the third pillar, "Profit," incentivizes innovative operations through lifecycle cost benefits.

The launch of the Sands Eco 360° Global Sustainable Development program provided LVS the opportunity to apply its values to business practices and influence standards for industry sustainable practices as the company expands globally. The first step in launching the Sands Eco 360° program was to formally define the company's sustainability goals and develop a mission statement (see Exhibit 1). Guided by the mission statement, the program has gained significant accomplishments throughout various areas of the company's development and operations. The Sands Eco 360° program has influenced every department in the organization, from the heavy duty areas such as construction to the daily operations areas such as procurement and purchasing. Sands Eco 360° is a formalization of all of LVS's best practices, technologies, and methodologies in the area of sustainability across all properties rolled into a single integrated program with a shared vision, mission, and goals. The Sands Eco 360° Global Sustainable Development program builds and expands on the successes of the company's best-in-class and award-winning sustainability initiatives at its Las Vegas properties, and is now being implemented at all LVS properties around the globe.

Communication: From Idea to a Shared Value System

After the creation of Sands Eco 360°, the next challenge that confronted the LVS management team was not just the formal implementation of the program, but effectively communicating it to, and truly getting a "buy in" from, the entire organization. New programs and initiatives in most corporations are often well-conceptualized but meet an early demise because the organization's stakeholders do not believe in the programs. LVS, however, had a few things going that ensured that Sands Eco 360° would move forward. The initial success of sustainable practices at The Palazzo had already shown management and staff that sustainability can produce positive results. Furthermore, it established an important fact that had concerned many up to that point: a five-star and five-diamond property can be green and not lose its luxury quality. In working toward the Palazzo's LEED certification, many departments within the company were engaged and involved, ranging from construction to government relations. The management team also had the commitment of top management and the board of directors, which was critical.

Using The Palazzo's detailed analysis and metrics in energy efficiencies and operational efficiencies, LVS communicated the performance measures and lessons learned in Las Vegas to all of the properties in its portfolio. These global sustainable development efforts were approved by the company's president and board and, almost overnight, a good idea became a global initiative.

As the awareness of the LVS sustainability programs permeates through the system and a shared value system takes hold in the organization, team members will most likely extend these practices into their daily lives outside of work. Team members are educated on company sustainability efforts and home sustainability tips through communication channels such as daily and bi-weekly company newsletters and back-of-house display windows. The launch of the Sands Eco 360° program has also made team members much more aware of the company's sustainability efforts. For example, at the Sands Eco 360° Team Member Education Event in early 2010, 54,000 compact fluorescent lightbulbs were distributed to 9,000 Las Vegas team members to encourage environmental practices in their homes. The extension of sustainable behavior to their personal lives makes team members champions and ambassadors of the company's sustainable development initiatives, and extends technologies and benefits to their homes and communities.

Other channels through which Sands Eco 360° initiatives are made known to the public include the following:

- A brochure about LVS's Las Vegas facilities is made available to all guests and visitors. The brochure highlights the sustainable features of these properties that guests can discover as they explore the resort. An electronic version of the brochure can be viewed on the company website. Internally this brochure serves as a template for each property to communicate its unique sustainable efforts in its regions.

- A corporate sustainable development website communicates the efforts the company is making in the areas of water conservation, energy conservation, waste management, indoor environmental quality, sustainable purchasing, sustainable operations, and social responsibility. The corporate website, www.lasvegassands.com, was launched on March 17, 2010, along with Sands Eco 360°.

- Property "green tours" are provided to guests, vendors, media, and investors upon request.

Sustainability has become a shared value from those within LVS's top management down to every single company team member, and it has become an important element of the company's global development and operations strategy. A recent statement by LVS's president Michael Leven shows this commitment: "The launch of Sands Eco 360° demonstrates commitment to sustainable development and operations. Clearly there are important business advantages to operating in a sustainable manner, but when sound business practices are married with sustainable efforts that benefit the environment and our communities, the impact is immense." As these initiatives become more pervasive and ingrained within the day-to-day operations of the organization, and sustainability measures show positive outcomes for all stakeholders involved, top management support for sustainability will more and more be seen as a given.

Implementing Sustainable Development at Las Vegas Sands: Cooperative Effort

The successful implementation of sustainable development strategies is a result of the cooperative efforts of various organizational stakeholders, including top executives, a sustainable development steering team, operational departments, individual team members, suppliers, business partners, and the community. In each sustainable development project, the LVS's steering team works closely with advisors, internal department leaders, and vendors to create strategies to deal directly with the issues of greatest concern regarding environmental stewardship and sustainability. The strategies and policies for new construction, building operation, and maintenance are then implemented in each department with constant monitoring and documentation of improvement by a joint effort of management, team members, and external partners.

In the following sections we will outline how LVS's departments, consultants, suppliers, investors, and communities cooperate in and benefit from the company's sustainability efforts.

Departments

Design and Construction Departments. The design and construction departments are the company's first ambassadors of the program. With goals established to build green buildings, the corporate sustainable development standards are incorporated into the design process and implemented through construction.

Facilities Department. The facilities department was a vital part of launching Eco 360°. It introduced low environmental–impact methods with respect to the building systems maintenance, exterior building cleaning, and paint and sealants, as well as snow removal policies. The department also replaced traditional pest management methods with integrated pest management practices, and introduced a new recycling procedure that increased LVS's recycling rate from 9 percent to 55 percent, making LVS the largest property recycler in Las Vegas.

Purchasing Department. For a company such as Las Vegas Sands that makes purchases in the amount of over $500 million annually, sustainable purchasing policies have a ripple effect through the entire purchasing supply chain. As LVS implemented sustainable purchasing policies to meet LEED requirements, it began to see the vendor market change and meet company needs almost instantly. Although it is counter-intuitive, the hotel industry's down cycle in 2008 and 2009 actually provided an impetus for sustainable purchasing at LVS. The suppliers that were quick to adapt to sustainable products gained a competitive advantage and often earned the company's business. It is expected that the company's sustainable purchasing practices will continue to grow as LVS expands globally, therefore providing further incentives for suppliers to "go green."

Housekeeping Department. When operating a multi-billion dollar sustainable integrated resort, a cleaner, greener facility applies to all services, including housekeeping and room maintenance. The implementation of a low environmental–impact cleaning policy helps reduce guest exposure to potentially hazardous contaminants. The LVS housekeeping department's introduction of an Eco-Linen program invites hotel guests to become sustainable partners by choosing when to replenish linens and towels. This program has achieved startling environmental success through the estimated reduction of 11 million gallons of water, 600,000 kWh of electricity, and 170,000 gallons of detergent used to wash linens and towels by outside linen service providers. (See Exhibit 2 for a detailed summary of LVS's Eco-Linen and Recycling and Waste Management programs.)

Horticulture Department. The horticulture department within LVS takes quick action whenever it identifies opportunities for sustainable practices. This department innovatively created programs that save large amounts of water through replacing natural grass with artificial turf and installing subsurface drip irrigation and central irrigation control systems. The horticulture department also purchases recycled mulch for landscaping from a local organic vendor and buys products from a company that donates a portion of its profits to polar bear habitat conservation.

Sales Department. In the United States and abroad, meetings and conventions are LVS's core business. Heightened awareness of climate change is encouraging corporations to make their events greener and reduce their carbon footprint, which also allows companies to save money while promoting their businesses. Companies such as Autodesk and Ernst & Young are raising the bar by tracking carbon generation with the objective of having their meetings become carbon-neutral. Even large conventions such as the U.S. Green Building Council's GreenBuild International Conference and Expo and both the Democratic and Republican national conventions have gone carbon-neutral.

With the increasing demand for green meetings and conventions, the LVS sales department has incorporated sustainable features into e-proposals and other sales collateral to introduce sustainable initiatives to corporate meeting planners. In addition, the corporate sustainable development department and the sales department work closely together to answer environmental questionnaires requested by meeting planners and help calculate carbon footprints for specific

Exhibit 2 Las Vegas Sands' Operational Improvement Projects Summary

Operational Improvement Projects Summary

Name	Overview	Annual Incremental Project Expenses	Annual Ongoing Economic Benefit	Payback Period (years)	Environmental and Social Benefits
Eco-Linen Program	• Multiple-night resort guests choose when to replenish linens and towels. • Reduces detergent, water and electricity used to wash linens and towels.	$29,000	$1,500,000	0.02	• Electricity savings of 600,000 kWh annually • Water savings of over 11 million gallons per year • Significantly less chemicals and natural gas used • Fuel savings from lower transportation requirements • Promotes sustainability awareness among guests and team members
Recycling and Waste Management	• Recycle over 40 tons per day of glass, plastics, metals, cardboard, paper and food • Program implemented through extensive staff education, upstream separation of waste by staff, an on-site recycling center, and a final step of off-site recycling	$30,000 - $45,000 depending on occupancy	$36,000	Within 3 years	• Increased recycling by over 9,400 tons per year, including more than 55% of solid waste and more than 75% of food waste • Reduced greenhouse gas emissions of 3,777 metric tons of Carbon annually • Less landfill waste • Sets example for employees and other organizations in Las Vegas • Reduces traffic in loading dock • Decreases vehicle emissions and fuel consumption

meetings and conventions. During the planning process, the sales department and the catering department also make every effort to accommodate clients' special requests, such as organic foods and wines, and to utilize a paperless program and products with recycled content when possible.

Advertising and Marketing Departments. The development of collateral materials and the strategic placement of advertisements are an important part of implementing and promoting sustainable development programs. In this regard, the role of the advertising and marketing departments is to consistently communicate the vision, mission, and branding of the Sands Eco 360° program both internally and externally in order to ensure its effective adoption.

Consultants

The successful adoption and execution of sustainability programs at LVS required a third-party, independent advisor that understood the complexities and challenges of implementing sustainable development in such large-scale properties. Because of this, LVS hired Ernst & Young, led by Katherine Hammack, to advise the company on the LEED program requirements. Ernst & Young acted as an advisor for environmentally sensitive and sustainable practices, helping to reduce the company's carbon footprint, improve business performance, and employ energy-saving technologies with long-term cost savings.

Suppliers

LVS offered workshops to prospective and existing vendor partners on the company's rigorous sustainability requirements to become an approved vendor. This ensured that LVS worked with vendor partners who could support the company's sustainability goals. As a result of the size and scope of The Palazzo development, the project design team collaborated with third-party manufacturers and co-developed lighting solutions that decreased power consumption while not reducing the quality of color rendition or lumen output. It is important to note that when mega-developers such as LVS initiate purchase orders of over 500,000 lamps per property per year, each property serves as a market maker. The Palazzo's collaborative ventures with lighting manufacturers and vendors provided the critical mass needed to make it cost-effective for these manufacturers and vendors to produce these new products. By leading the way and creating a market for these innovative lighting products, The Palazzo has helped the industry at large.

Through its cooperation with LVS in recycling efforts, LVS's waste management partner Republic Services, Inc., has been able to pioneer innovative solutions for resort recycling. As the result of those efforts, Republic Services will be investing in a new $10 million material-recovering facility, which will employ between fifty and sixty people to accommodate increasing demand for recycling from companies such as LVS.

In addition, Toto is LVS's preferred vendor on toilet and urinal equipment. The firm's tailored solution for LVS involves urinal flush valves that use a fuzzy logic control microprocessor to automatically provide a variable flow rate that ranges from 0.5 to 1 gallon, depending on the frequency of the hands-free toilet's use. A frequently used urinal flushes with a half gallon of water and a less frequently used fixture will flush with a gallon (to decrease the potential for salt deposits forming in pipes). The Toto urinals with fuzzy logic technology are used in public areas of The Palazzo, and fixtures in The Venetian and the Sands Expo and Convention Center are being converted to them. Toto waterless urinals are available in back-of-the-house areas, and high-performance, 1.28-gallon-per-flush Toto toilets are featured in the guest suites at The Palazzo.

Investors

Las Vegas Sands' sustainable efforts and results are also communicated to investors through its corporate website, collateral materials, investor meetings, and property tours. It is LVS's belief that investors favor companies that display a high level of corporate social responsibility as part of their overall business strategy. The Sands Eco 360° program on sustainable development, along with its program to promote responsible gaming, conveys a positive corporate image of the company.

Communities

The Sands Eco 360° program also includes a give-back philosophy that extends its reach beyond LVS properties. This includes partnering with local community organizations for green job training and creation, providing education materials on going green, and creating internal programs to help LVS team members carry out the green message and implement green measures outside of work.

LVS's primary philanthropic initiatives are pursued through the non-profit Sands Foundation, LVS's charitable arm. The Sands Foundation's mission is to support charitable organizations and endeavors that concentrate on assisting youth, promoting health, and expanding educational opportunities within local communities. The Sands Foundation also supports causes that empower minority communities and improve underprivileged areas, as well as other valuable charitable and philanthropic activities. Sands Foundation charitable gifts are a combination of LVS contributions and voluntary team member donations. In addition to millions of dollars in charitable giving, LVS and its various properties also participate with team members, their spouses, children, and community members in programs and activities that encourage, educate, and enrich the lives of our neighbors.

The Value in Creating Sustainable Development Practices

An important propellant of the continued implementation of LVS's initial sustainable development practices was The Palazzo's receipt of the LEED Silver certification in 2008. As discussed previously, LEED is an internationally recognized green building certification system that provides third-party verification that a building was designed and built using strategies aimed at improving performance across all the metrics that matter most: energy savings, water efficiency, CO_2 emissions reduction, improved indoor environmental quality, and stewardship of resources and sensitivity to their impacts. The process of applying for LEED certification at

The Palazzo allowed the organization to systematically examine all aspects of a sustainably designed and operated building. This initial achievement provided a remarkable learning opportunity for the hotel development and operating teams to create a high-performance building. LVS has now expanded upon this commitment, achieving LEED Gold certification for Existing Buildings for The Venetian and the Sands Expo and Convention Center. In this section of the chapter we will share specific sustainable development practices implemented across LVS's Las Vegas campus, which includes The Palazzo, The Venetian, and the Sands Expo and Convention Center.

Water Conservation. Today, issues related to water conservation are similar to the issues related to carbon waste. Water is becoming the new carbon, with issues of water management and mismanagement gaining wider attention across business sectors and the public.[4] To address these problems, LVS has introduced innovations to minimize water consumption without compromising the overall guest experience, such as the following:

- Natural grass areas have been replaced with artificial turf. Plants and trees are irrigated with subsurface drip systems that distribute water directly to the plant root to avoid wasteful evaporation.

- A central irrigation control system was installed to monitor outdoor air temperature, relative humidity, wind, solar intensity, rainfall, and soil moisture content to ensure plant and tree health is maintained without excess irrigation.

Innovative cooling tower technology saves more than 50 million gallons of potable water per year.

- Water-efficient fixtures such as showerheads, toilets, and lavatory faucets were installed in guestrooms, and yield more than 20 percent water savings over standard fixtures.

- The installation of a rooftop cooling system for the chilled water supply, spearheaded by Executive Director of Engineering John Hess, saves 50 million gallons of water a year.

- A nano filtration system that pumps more than 80,000 gallons of water daily from the bottom level of The Palazzo parking garage was installed (without the system, the water would go into the city storm drain). The captured water from the pump is filtered and injected with liquid fertilizer and delivered directly to landscaping areas throughout the property.

In addition, water savings do not always occur at the spigot. For example, increasing lighting efficiency and insulation reduces the energy load for lighting as well as heating and cooling. As water is an integral element in a cooling system, it results in a significant reduction in water use. Together with other water-saving initiatives, LVS properties have reduced campus consumption by more than 97 million gallons of water annually, enough to supply the water needs of more than 870 average American households.

Energy Conservation. LVS's energy-efficiency systems save 73 million kWh annually against the LEED baseline performance, which is enough to power more than 6,500 average American households or a small city like Boulder City, Nevada. As summarized in Exhibit 3, LVS was able to minimize energy usage and optimize energy conservation, and is projecting a positive return on these investments. The innovative practices incorporated at the LVS properties include the following:

- Energy-efficient lightbulbs such as light-emitting diode (LED) lightbulbs are utilized to optimize energy and provide a high level of aesthetic ambience in the suites and public areas.

- Sensors are installed in guestrooms to adjust the temperature automatically according to guest occupancy.

- A sophisticated building automation system has been implemented throughout the entire hotel, which monitors and optimizes heating, cooling, ventilation, and lighting levels to constantly provide optimal indoor conditions while utilizing energy efficiency.

- Two large atria skylights, located in The Palazzo's lobby and entrance areas, are utilized to introduce the abundance of natural light.

- A solar-thermal system (the largest in the United States) is mounted on the roof to provide hot water for swimming pools, spas, and a portion of domestic hot water.

- Solar photovoltaic panels, which are installed atop team member parking garages, generate 116 kW (DC) peak output of electricity to power garage lights and elevators.

Exhibit 3 Las Vegas Sands' Capital Expenditure Projects Summary

Capital Expenditure Projects Summary

Name	Overview	Total Investment Costs	Total Economic Benefits	Payback Period (years)	Net Present Value [1,2]	Environmental and Social Benefits
Energy Efficient Lighting (3 years)	• LED and CFL lamps replaced traditional incandescents and halogens. • Cost savings from lower energy usage, longer life, and reduced heat load that impacts air conditioning costs.	$1.1 million	$6.6 million	0.5	$4,444,600	• Saves water and greenhouse gases at power stations • Reduced demand for power distribution networks • Improves air quality by reducing demand from coal burning plants • Energy-efficient lighting practices are taught to 25,000 employees for their households
Cooling Tower Upgrades (20 years)	• Reduced volume of makeup water	$259,000	$5.3 million	1.18	$2,137,300	• Saves over 50,000,000 gallons of water per year • Water savings impact overall community resources
"Solar Farm" Pool/Spa/Domestic Hot Water Heating System (39 years)	• 364 panels on 18,200 square feet generate 3,900,000 BTU/hour that heat swimming pools, spa, and domestic hot water.	$3.6 million	$21.3 million	5.2	$691,800	• Less natural gas combustion and greenhouse gases • Lower energy usage results in fewer natural resources consumed • Economic solar harvest solution sets precedent for community use of renewable energy • Federal tax credit available for non-pool use
Advanced In-suite Controls (39 years)	• "Master" light switches and occupancy sensors reduce energy load when rooms are not occupied.	$3.7 million	$5.5 million	6.9	$3,365,300	• Saves water, natural gas, and electricity • Promotes sustainability awareness among guests and employees
Solar Photovoltaic Panels (25 years)	• 680 panels with peak output of 116 kW on parking garage roof	$646,000	$688,000	22.5	($317,390)	• Saves electricity and corresponding water • Less greenhouse gases are generated with renewable energy • Sets precedent for community use of renewable energy • Reduces long-term need to generate fossil-fuel based power • Federal tax credit available

Las Vegas Sands Corp. is the only Strip property that uses solar photovoltaic panels on top of parking garages. These panels turn the sun's power into electricity and generate 116kW of direct current.

Waste Management. The solid waste management program at LVS recycles over 15,000 tons a year, or 55 percent of the company's solid waste stream, including items such as glass, plastics, aluminum, cardboard, and paper. In addition to making a positive environmental impact, the waste management program provides economic benefits to the company; for example, more than 75 percent of food waste from the property level is either re-used as animal feed at a local farm or composted. Additionally, a full 100 percent of used batteries are diverted from landfills, and more than 75 percent of the waste from renovation projects is recycled and reused. During the construction of The Palazzo, some 70 percent of waste materials were recycled, diverting nearly 42,000 tons from the local landfill.

Indoor Environmental Quality. Indoor air can contain a number of potentially harmful chemicals and biological agents, including carbon dioxide, volatile organic compounds (VOC), molds, and various allergens. To maintain a clean and high-quality atmosphere, indoor air quality is constantly monitored at LVS properties to ensure a pleasurable guest experience. To adhere to LEED requirements, the hotels use paints, coatings, adhesives, sealants, and cleaning products with low VOC content. Additionally, hotel carpeting meets the testing and product requirements of The Carpet and Rug Institute's Green Label Plus program. In maintaining a clean and high-quality atmosphere, these steps help reduce the overall quantity of indoor contaminants and improve the quality of the indoor environment.

Employees at Las Vegas Sands Corp. sort refuse into dry and wet categories, separating food waste from recyclable products. Wet (food) waste is sent to a Nevada farm to be used as animal feed or compost. Las Vegas Sands' properties in Las Vegas recycle 55 percent of solid waste and more than 75 percent of food waste.

Sustainable Purchasing. Las Vegas Sands' commitment to sustainable purchasing policies leads to the use of environmentally friendly products. For example, during construction of The Palazzo, the steel used throughout the property averaged more than 95 percent recycled content, while the concrete contained 26 percent recycled content, including fly ash from coal-burning power plants. Efforts were made to procure materials from within a 500-mile radius of the construction site to minimize the negative environmental effects of transporting those materials. In addition, the abundant amounts of office paper, office equipment, furniture, and building materials consumed by the hotels' back-of-house offices incorporate recycled and salvaged material, rapidly renewable materials, or local materials (for example, 25 percent of the hotel's office paper comes from post-consumer recycled content). Other products, such as cleaning products, disposable janitorial products, and trash bags, are supplied from recycled content. A summary of the company's purchasing practices and their related benefits are outlined in Exhibit 4.

Sustainable Operations. LVS has committed to reducing the amount of paper used throughout the property by transitioning to paperless data management systems. This transition includes a wide range of initiatives spanning team member communications, human resources, accounting, and general office functions. The

Exhibit 4   Las Vegas Sands' Eco 360° Sustainable Purchasing Summary

Products	LEED Criteria	Environmental, Health, and Social Benefits
Office paper Office equipment Furniture Furnishings Building materials	Any one of the following: • Contains at least 70 percent salvaged material from outside organizations or through an internal organization reuse program • Contains at least 10 percent post-consumer or 20 percent post-industrial material • Contains at least 50 percent rapidly renewable materials • Contains 100 percent Forest Stewardship Council–certified wood • Contains at least 50 percent materials extracted and processed within 500 miles of project	• Reduces the amount of virgin materials • Lowers solid waste volumes and landfill space requirements • Responsible forestry maintains the function and biodiversity of the forest • Local/regional materials reduce environmental impacts and transportation costs • Reduces manufacturing-related environmental and health burdens • Local/regional materials support the local economy
Adhesives/sealants Paints/coatings Carpets/cushions Composite panels Agrifiber products	Reduced volatile organic compound (VOC) levels that meet one of the following: • South Coast Air Quality Management District Rule 1168 • Green Seal 11 • Green Label Plus Carpet Testing Program • No added urea-formaldehyde resins	• Low-emitting materials have fewer compounds that generate smog, air pollution, and ground level ozone • Low-emitting materials prevent air quality degradation and provide a better indoor environment for occupants
Cleaning materials Cleaning products	Reduced volatile organic compound (VOC) emission levels that meet Green Seal 37 or the California Code of Regulations	• Green Seal–certified cleaning products are tested for toxicity to aquatic life, biodegradability, eutrophication, and air quality degradation • Reduced exposure to VOCs improves occupant productivity and decreases workplace health issues
Disposable janitorial products Trash bags	Recycled content levels that meet the U.S. EPA's Comprehensive Procurement Guidelines	• Reduces environmental impact of raw material extraction • Diverts materials away from landfills Reduces water and air pollution associated with waste disposal • Establishes and maintains a market for plastic recycling
Cleaning equipment	Various	• Minimizes waste production, energy use, noise pollution, and indoor air degradation • Extends life of carpets, floors, and building materials, thereby preventing environmental effects of replacement • Improves indoor environmental quality for building occupants
Lightbulbs	Weighted average mercury content of less than 100 picograms	• Reduces risk of elevated mercury levels contaminating the environment • Reduces risk of health hazards caused by handling and disposing of mercury-containing products

program increases labor efficiencies, realizes cost savings, and substantially benefits the environment.

As mentioned earlier in the chapter, LVS invites multiple-night resort guests to be sustainable partners by participating in LVS's Eco-Linen program. The low initial cost of implementing an Eco-Linen program and the immediate returns gained from it results in substantial savings for the hotel. In addition, the laundry service provider for LVS has implemented new technologies to achieve 72-percent water-use reduction versus a traditional laundry operation. The laundry service provider uses detergents that carry the EPA's DfE (Design for the Environment) certification and non-perchloroethylene dry-cleaning solvents.

Transportation. To encourage the use of alternative transportation, preferred parking spaces are provided for guests and team members who carpool or drive low-emission and fuel-efficient, hybrid, or alternative fuel vehicles. Complimentary valet parking for bicycles is provided at the hotel. Additionally, the hotel has close access to a variety of public transportation options.

Commitment to Social Responsibilities. It is important for organizations to contribute to their communities through various programs and initiatives. For example, LVS supports the Opportunity Village, a local not-for-profit organization that serves intellectually disabled individuals by providing them with vocational training, employment, and social recreation services that aim to enrich their lives. LVS has partnered with Opportunity Village's linen and terry (i.e., towels and sheets) recycling program. Opportunity Village receives clean, worn-out fabrics and converts them to usable cleaning cloths. This joint venture between Opportunity Village and LVS produces a significant improvement in local underprivileged communities; for example, by employing more than thirty people within the program, 200,000 pieces of cleaning cloths were produced in a recent five-month period, diverting more than 90,000 pounds of discarded linen/terry from landfills in the local communities.

Additionally, the Sands Expo and Convention Center partners with the Las Vegas Rescue Mission by donating remaining packaged food products at the end of trade shows to help feed the less fortunate who rely on the Las Vegas Rescue Mission for meals. Other contributions include the donation of used electronic products to the Blind Center of Nevada and shredded office paper to the Nevada Society for the Prevention of Cruelty to Animals for use as animal bedding.

Future Plans. The success LVS has achieved in Las Vegas is the beginning of a new chapter in the company's global sustainable initiatives, and all future LVS developments will comply with current Sands Eco 360° principles and standards. These standards will provide a foundation for future development while leaving room to raise the bar in other countries. Overall, LVS has a company-wide goal to reduce utility consumption by 25 percent, which includes gas, electricity, and water. This goal already has been achieved by its Las Vegas properties.

In reference to its global properties, LVS's new Marina Bay Sands development in Singapore is working to achieve the platinum level of the Building and Construction Authority's Green Mark, which is the local equivalent of the U.S. Green Building Council's LEED certification. In working toward this certification,

LVS invested $25 million in an Intelligent Building Management System, a new system that allows automated controls over lighting, heating, and water supplies for the entire resort. In addition, various energy and water conservation initiatives are being implemented at the Sands Macao Hotel and the Venetian Macao Resort Hotel. The company has also implemented an Environmental and Energy Conservation Awareness Program to educate all team members in minimizing energy consumption. Energy-saving tips and reminders are frequently circulated to all team members. Sands Eco 360° principles and standards will also be applied to new development projects at the Cotai Strip with world-renowned hotel brands.

Conclusion

In this chapter we have seen how Las Vegas Sands Corporation's sustainable practices benefit both the environment and the company's bottom line. The company's strong commitment to creating and improving new programs are examples of how it is becoming one of the industry's preeminent leaders in sustainability. In practice and through education, LVS is committed to being as much a leader in sustainable corporate practices as it is in hospitality. This is the company's promise to guests and to those who will inherit our planet.

The lessons we have learned from LVS's sustainable development practices are substantial. Financially the case for sustainability has been confirmed because the company has been able to integrate sound business strategies and sustainable practices. "Going green" does cost more money initially in many cases; however, for every $1 that is invested into Sands Eco 360°, the company saves $4. In addition, we learned that innovation played an important role in LVS's sustainable practices due to the large size and uniqueness of our properties; Las Vegas Sands worked with consultants and vendors to develop new solutions, technologies, and products. Sustainability is not a new concept, but to a lot of people it is still something to get used to that requires an open mind; therefore, education and communication are vital. As an industry leader in sustainability, LVS is committed to reducing its impact on the environment, and understands that the comfort and satisfaction of its guests, team members, and community neighbors are keys to the company's success. Las Vegas Sands' legacy must be one of a more responsible, cleaner, and safer world for future generations.

Endnotes

1. Greg Denton, Lori E. Raleigh, and A. J. Singh, eds. *Hotel Asset Management: Principles & Practices*, Second Edition (Lansing, Mich.: American Hotel & Lodging Educational Institute, 2009).

2. Nicholas Rumanes and A. J. Singh, "Lessons from the World's Largest LEED-Certified Hotel: The Palazzo," in *Hotel Asset Management: Principles & Practices*, Second Edition (Lansing, Mich: American Hotel & Lodging Educational Institute, 2009).

3. United Nations, World Commission on Environment and Development, *Brundtland Report*, United Nations General Assembly A/42/427 (June 1987).

4. Leslie Guevarra, "Water-Saving Strategies to Make Every Drop Count," *Greenbiz.com* (March 25, 2010).

13

High-Performance Hospitality: Sustainable Hotel Case Studies

By Michele Diener, Amisha Parekh, and Jaclyn Pitera

Michele Diener *strives to combine the often-distinct worlds of environmental sustainability and business administration. Ms. Diener is the Director of Sustainability Strategies for MGM Resorts International, responsible for the development of environmentally sustainable initiatives and operations programs across the entire MGM Resorts portfolio of hotels, which comprises nearly 50,000 rooms and 40,000 employees. Prior to MGM Resorts, Ms. Diener worked for Sustainable Conservation, a nonprofit organization focused on private-sector collaboration to improve environmental quality. While at Sustainable Conservation, Ms. Diener studied environmentally sustainable hotels in California. As a continuation of her research, Ms. Diener co-authored eight case studies with an emphasis on hotel design, construction, and operations in North America. The resulting book,* High Performance Hospitality: Sustainable Hotel Case Studies *was published by the American Hotel and Lodging Educational Foundation and serves as an industry resource for hotel developers, owners, and operators.*

Ms. Diener began her career as a Strategic Planning Associate for Toyota Motor Sales, U.S.A., Inc. At Toyota, she created and led "Process Green," an initiative integrating environmentally sensitive building design within Toyota's 10-million-square-foot U.S. real estate portfolio. Ms. Diener authored the article "A Sustainable Approach to Corporate Real Estate" and was recognized for Process Green with the CoreNet Global's Innovator's Award in 2003.

Ms. Diener is a LEED-Accredited Professional and has worked on five LEED-certified projects, including office, industrial, university, and mixed-use developments. She graduated from the 11th Southern California Leadership class facilitated by Coro, a non-profit educational institute, in 2001. Ms. Diener was also an ecotourism volunteer in Peru with ProWorld. She earned a Master of Business Administration degree and a Master of Science degree in Natural Resources from the University of Michigan and a Bachelor of Science degree in Design and Environmental Analysis from Cornell University.

Amisha Parekh works with Deloitte's Strategy & Operations practice, specializing in Climate Change & Sustainability. She has developed corporate sustainability strategies for large multi-national enterprises, designed and managed the implementation of sustainability initiatives, and evaluated the market potential for new green business opportunities. Ms. Parekh has also led the development of Deloitte's methodology for green retail remodels and strategies for marketing to green-minded consumers. Outside of Deloitte, Ms. Parekh has worked with Walmart's Sustainability Strategy group and in brand management at Procter & Gamble.

Ms. Parekh holds a Master of Business Administration degree and a Master of Science degree in Environmental Policy and Behavior from the University of Michigan. While at the University of Michigan, Ms. Parekh co-authored the book High Performance Hospitality: Sustainable Hotel Case Studies, *in which she made the business case for green hotel construction and operations.*

Jaclyn Pitera is an independent sustainable business consultant currently contracting with GreenOrder and AltaTerra Research. Ms. Pitera has advised firms in developing their sustainability strategy and implementation plans, particularly regarding carbon footprint mitigation, energy efficiency, green building, sustainable material sourcing, employee behavior change, and marketing and communications, generating for client firms documented cost-savings and competitive differentiation. She has also advised start-up companies in the green building and energy-efficiency industries, providing strategy development, industry and market analysis, and product lifecycle analysis.

Prior to GreenOrder and AltaTerra, Ms. Pitera was a sustainable business consultant for Williams-Sonoma; Business for Social Responsibility; H&M; Cummins; and The JBG Companies, a real estate developer in the Washington, D.C., area.

Ms. Pitera holds a Master of Business Administration degree, a Master of Science degree in Sustainable Systems, and a Bachelor of Science degree in Biology from the University of Michigan. While at the University of Michigan, Ms. Pitera co-authored the book High Performance Hospitality: Sustainable Hotel Case Studies, *in which she made the business case for green hotel construction and operations. Ms. Pitera is also a LEED-Accredited Professional.*

THIS CHAPTER consists of an excerpt from a report published in *High Performance Hospitality: Sustainable Hotel Case Studies* by the American Hotel and Lodging Educational Foundation. All of the key findings are provided in this text, while the detailed analysis and in-depth case studies of eight North American hotels can be found in *High Performance Hospitality*.

This report is a starting point to help interested parties learn more about environmentally friendly construction and operations for hotels. While each individual case study in this report may not be directly applicable to all new hotel projects, the key lessons learned in each case are widely applicable. One objective of the report is to evoke serious thought and discussion regarding the advantages and disadvantages of sustainability within the hotel industry. We hope that such discussions will lead to more environmentally friendly hotel construction and renovation projects and business operations practices in the future.

The hotels featured in the report were selected because their cases successfully demonstrate high-performance construction and/or operations. Additionally, the cases show that high-performance sustainable development can be both practical and achievable. The report can be a tool for the hotel developer or owner who is designing and building a hotel from the ground up, just as it can be a tool for the hotel manager who is operating an existing hotel.

To summarize, the report contained herein can be used to learn why some practitioners have created sustainable hotels, understand how sustainable hotels achieve success, and gain insight into what features and practices are feasible. It is not a comprehensive report on all sustainable hotels, nor does it assess whether hospitality or tourism is or can be sustainable. The report does, however, assume that hotels will continue to be built, renovated, and operated.

Given the size and operational demands of the hospitality industry with roughly 50,000 properties in the United States alone, the industry's collective environmental impact is enormous. Rising energy costs in the United States have propelled both large and small hotel developers, owners, and management companies to consider energy-efficiency and resource-conservation initiatives to help reduce operational expenses. Some hotels, for example, have implemented small measures such as towel and linen reuse programs and compact fluorescent lighting retrofits. A vast number of opportunities for expanding sustainability efforts, however, still exist across the entire hotel industry.

What Is a High-Performance Hotel?

Since the beginning of this century, the high-performance real estate development movement in North America has gained significant national attention and momentum, originally with institutional and commercial development, and now with hospitality. Membership in the United States Green Building Council (USGBC), an American non-profit organization committed to expanding sustainable building practices, has grown dramatically. Its Leadership in Energy and Environmental Design (LEED) rating system has been adopted nationally and internationally as the de facto high-performance building standard.

The terms and phrases *high performance, sustainable, environmentally friendly,* and *green* are used interchangeably throughout this report and, when applied to hotel development, define projects of any scale integrating environmental and social goals with financial considerations. Analogous to these terms is the triple bottom line, focusing on "economic prosperity, environmental quality, and social justice,"[1] along with the "3 P's" (people, planet, and profits) and the "3 E's" (equity, ecology, and economy).

What constitutes a green hotel is not defined consistently across the hotel industry. For some, a green hotel is one that incorporates building structure efficiencies, such as a well-insulated building envelope and a reflective roof. Others consider a hotel to be green if it has incorporated energy- and water-efficient fixtures, such as compact fluorescent light bulbs (CFLs) and low-flow toilets. And there are still others in the hotel industry who consider a green hotel to be one that has implemented operational environmental services, such as a towel and linen reuse program. This report uses the designation *high performance* to describe hotels that have implemented green features in building design and construction, in the hotel's operations, or in both.

Three key hospitality stakeholder groups can influence the existence of high-performance hotels in the market. The first set of stakeholders includes developers, owners, and managers of hotel properties. We refer to this group by the designation "property oversight" throughout the report. The second group consists of large corporations, government agencies, and travel management companies that set business contracts. The third group comprises individual travelers who make decisions regarding leisure and personal business travel. These latter hotel guests, like the corporate and government customers, may travel for business, but the assumption is that they have less negotiating power in the decision-making process because they are not initiating business contracts. The property oversight group directly influences high-performance hotel existence by choosing to construct and/or operate a hotel sustainably and to sell its product to consumers; corporate and government clients influence the existence of high-performance hotels if their organizational policies dictate that they select only environmentally friendly vendors; individual travelers who care about environmental features increase the prevalence of high-performance hotels.

Perceived Barriers

Four main barriers to high-performance hotel design, construction, and operations emerged through literature reviews and industry-expert interviews at the beginning of the project. These perceived barriers helped to shape the structure of the project research and served as the starting point of our data analysis. The perceived barriers are:

1. *Business case:* Lack of financial drivers to build and operate high-performance hotels; perception that green costs more.

2. *Consumers:* Lack of demand; perception that green features will harm guest satisfaction.

3. *Property oversight:* Difficulty of implementing procedural changes if the developer, owner, and manager are distinct entities; each entity has different financial drivers.

4. *Hotel characteristics:* Location, climate, size, and brand are variables that limit and restrict successful high-performance hotel design, construction, and operations.

Research Goals and Methodology

The goal of this report is two-fold. The first objective is to understand the business case for high-performance construction and operations while validating or invalidating perceived barriers to high-performance hotels. The second objective of this report is to disseminate information on best practices in high-performance building design, construction, and operations across the North American hospitality industry. We accomplish these objectives by presenting reliable data about environmentally sustainable hotel practices and the associated stakeholder costs and benefits.

Exhibit 1   Location of High-Performance Case Study Hotels

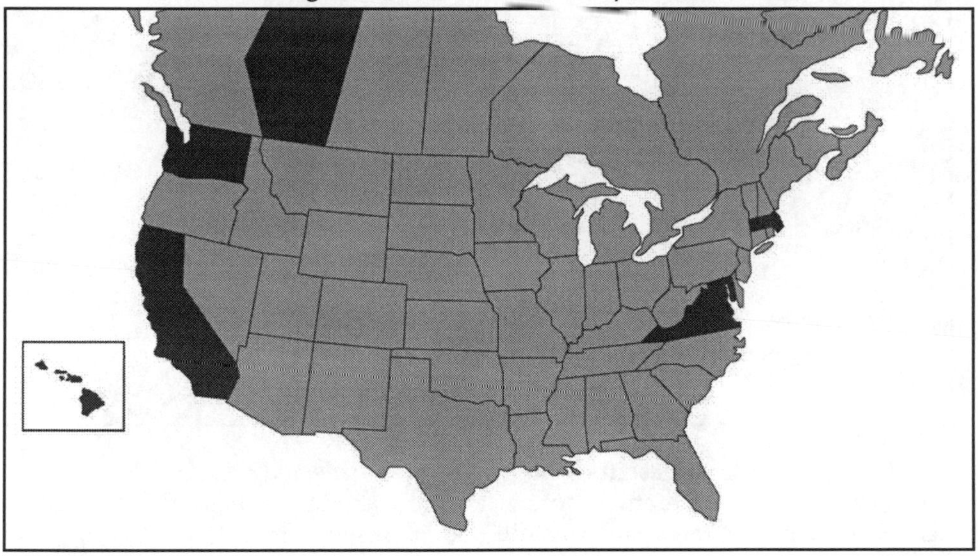

The research for this report was conducted between the summer of 2006 and the summer of 2007. It involved interviewing nine hotel organizations across the United States and Canada, as illustrated by the shaded regions in Exhibit 1.

Hotel Selection Criteria

The research team developed both quantitative and qualitative hotel selection criteria. Initially, the team conducted an extensive review of the existing literature (academic publications, news articles, and business magazines) and interviewed industry professionals and experts to develop a comprehensive list of hotels representing successful high-performance design, construction, and operations. The hotels were then categorized as mid-rate facilities, conference centers, and luxury hotels. These were further broken down into branded properties (e.g., Marriott, Hilton) or independent properties (e.g., Orchard Garden, Mauna Lani), as well as big or small and rural or urban hotels.

The final selection criteria were based on a hotel's level of commitment to environmentally sustainable practices. Under design and construction, these practices were classified as site development, energy consumption, water consumption, materials and resources, indoor air quality, and other innovations. Under hotel operations, practices were classified as front-of-house marketing, community outreach, and guest amenities, and as back-of-house utility consumption, indoor air quality, janitorial/maintenance, measures/instruments, and staff training and compensation. For hotel building design and construction, the LEED rating system was used as a base to measure the extent of high-performance practices achieved. For hotel operations, the combination of a variety of hotel certifications was used as the base. In addition, both construction and operations were measured against the research team's industry knowledge.

Exhibit 2   High-Performance Hotel Case Studies

Mid-Rate Hotels	• Orchard Garden Hotel, San Francisco, California • Comfort Inn & Suites Logan International Airport, Revere, Massachusetts
Conference Centers	• The Inn and Conference Center, University of Maryland University College, Adelphi, Maryland • Airlie Center, Warrenton, Virginia • Hilton Vancouver Washington, Vancouver, Washington
Luxury Hotels	• The Mauna Lani Bay, Kohala Coast, Hawaii • The Fairmont Banff Springs, Alberta, Canada • The Ritz-Carlton, San Francisco, California

Using the criteria described above, the team selected nine hotels—two mid-rate hotels, three conference centers, and four luxury hotels—that are located across the United States and Canada and represent small, large, branded, and independent hotels. One property prefers to remain anonymous, so we present eight detailed case studies (listed in Exhibit 2), while aggregate data and statements include the ninth property.

The case study matrix in Exhibit 3 further describes the diverse aspects of each hotel beyond its assigned category, and includes data on high-performance features, stakeholder advantages, when it "went green," high-performance implementation leadership, and whether or not the hotel achieved LEED or Green Seal certification.

Data Collection

We collected our case study data through on-site, in-person interviews of hotel management teams. These teams always included the general manager and often the directors of the engineering, housekeeping, food and beverage, and sales/marketing departments; front desk personnel; and the hotel owner. We also interviewed members of the project team, including the hotel contractor and the architect, whenever possible.

Key Findings

The project research produced the following significant results:

1. *Business case:* Each hotel pursued high-performance design and construction and/or operations with different objectives, but these were always supported by a strong financial rationale.

2. *Consumers:* Most of the high-performance hotels benefited from increased media attention but only some hotels could link it to increased consumer demand. On the other hand, high-performance hotels did not find that high-performance features compromised the guest experience.

Exhibit 3 Case Study Matrix

Case Study Matrix

		MID RATE		CONVENTION CENTER			LUXURY		
		San Francisco, CA	Revere, MA	Adelphi, MD	Airlie, Virginia	Vancouver, WA	Kohala Coast, HI	Banff, Alberta, CANADA	San Francisco, CA
Key Topics	Site – Brownfield Redevelopment		●						
	Site – Historic Landmark Preservation				●			●	●
	Site – Stormwater Management			●		●			
	Materials and Resources	●	●	●		●			
	Waste Management	●	●		●	●		●	●
	Energy Efficiency	●	●	●		●	●		●
	Water Efficiency	●	●	●	●		●		
	Indoor Environmental Quality	●	●	●	●	●		●	●
Advantages of Green Development	Lower Operating Costs	●	●	●	●	●	●	●	●
	Less Negative Environmental Impact	●	●	●	●	●	●	●	●
	Product Differentiation	●			●	●			
	Education	●	●		●	●	●	●	●
Initial Implementation Phase	Design Phase	●	●	●		●			
	Construction Phase	●	●	●		●			
	Operations	●	●		●	●	●	●	●
Certification	LEED	●		●		●			
	Green Seal – Certified and Pending	●			●	●			
High Performance Champion	Developer		●			●			
	Owner		●	●	●		●		
	Management Company	●	●					●	●
Rating	Two Diamond		●	●					
	Three Diamond	●			●	●			
	Four Diamond						●	●	
	Five Diamond								●
Location	Urban	●				●			●
	Rural				●		●	●	
	Suburban		●	●					
Size	1–300 Rooms	●	●	●	●	●			
	301–600 Rooms						●		●
	601–900 Rooms							●	

3. *Property oversight:* High-performance success was independent of the hotel's oversight structure. The research found that members of the property oversight team collaborated to achieve success for sustainable hotel projects.

4. *Hotel characteristics:* Each hotel among the case study samples had implemented different, yet successful, high-performance programs, regardless of location, climate, size, and brand.

The research also indicates that all of the case study hotels have been successful in implementing high-performance design and construction and/or operations.

High-Performance Hotel Best Practices

As aforementioned, all of the hotels interviewed successfully implemented high-performance design and construction and/or operations, but did so in diverse ways. This section presents the green features that were most commonly implemented across the case studies, as well as those features that were innovative. The green features are construction elements or operational practices that are classified according to site, energy efficiency, water efficiency, materials and resources, waste management, and indoor environmental quality. In addition to construction and operations components, we also reviewed the high-performance educational practices at each hotel.

The research team assessed whether the construction, operations, and educational components were common or distinct occurrences, and whether the complexity and cost of implementation was low, medium, or high. We also evaluated guest perceptions of these components. Our assessments were based on the research results as well as on interviews with industry experts.

In Exhibit 4, complexity is displayed from low to high in the columns and financial cost is displayed from low to high in the rows. The exhibit's key reveals the third dimension, guest response to green features. Exhibit 4 shows that most of the hotel's green features produced either a neutral or a positive guest response.

Common Construction and Operations Features

The most common green features incorporated by the case study hotels are generally low to medium in cost and complexity. Today, many of these practices are common across the hotel industry. They make good business sense and are not too complex or difficult to implement.

Site. A hotel's site location is unique, so trends are less apparent for this feature. Hotel transportation, however, is one site-related activity that has potential for industry-wide incorporation. Forty-four percent of the studied hotels are accessible to public transportation, and the same percentage use environmentally friendly on-site vehicles. Another common site-related practice is minimizing the heat island impact through installation of a reflective roof and/or reflective pedestrian hardscapes.

Energy Efficiency. Among the studied hotels, the most common energy-efficient feature is compact fluorescent lighting (CFL). All the case hotels utilize compact fluorescents, and CFLs have been accepted as cost-effective for the hotel industry. Other prevalent energy-efficient features, utilized by two-thirds of the case

Exhibit 4 Cost, Complexity, and Guest Perception of Common High-Performance Construction and Operations Features

COST	COMPLEXITY — LOW	COMPLEXITY — MEDIUM	COMPLEXITY — HIGH
LOW	**SITE** Public Transportation Accessible Minimize Heat Island Impact—Roof & Hardscapes **MATERIALS & RESOURCES** Fly Ash in Concrete FSC Certified Wood EPP Paper Products Minimize Water Bottles On Site **WASTE MANAGEMENT** Back-of-house Recycling **ENERGY EFFICIENCY** Occupancy Sensors **WATER EFFICIENCY** Low-Flow Hardware Linen and Towel Reuse Program Washable Drapery and Linen **INDOOR ENVIRONMENTAL QUALITY** Low VOC Adhesives Low VOC Paint Operable Windows CO_2 Sensors *Smoke-Free Environment* **EDUCATION** In-House Guests Prospective Customers Local Community Members Staff/Employees	**SITE** Minimize Construction Site Disturbance Minimize Light Pollution **MATERIALS & RESOURCES** Locally Extracted Materials Locally Manufactured Materials Recycled Content for Construction Natural and Rapidly Renewable Chlorine-Free Pool Cleaning Process **WASTE MANAGEMENT** Guest Room Recycling Common/Public Area Recycling On-Site Composting **WATER EFFICIENCY** Washing—Environmentally Friendly Drycleaning—Environmentally Friendly Irrigation—Environmentally Friendly Drought Tolerant/Indigenous Plantings Brackish Water **INDOOR ENVIRONMENTAL QUALITY** Green Cleaning Supplies HCFC/CFC Free/No Ozone Depleting Substances **EDUCATION** Shareholders/Investors/Owners Government/Regulators	
MEDIUM	**ENERGY EFFICIENCY** Low e (energy-efficient) Glazing (windows) Compact· Fluorescent Light Bulbs Energy Star Equipment **WATER EFFICIENCY** Dual-Flush Toilets	**SITE** Alternative Fuel House Vehicles **ENERGY EFFICIENCY** Commissioning Energy Recovery Units Hydronic HVAC LED Light Bulbs **INDOOR ENVIRONMENTAL QUALITY** Daylighting Natural Ventilation	**SITE** Storm Water Treatment Restored Native Vegetation Wildlife Protection **WATER EFFICIENCY** Recirculated Water
HIGH	Guest Room Key Cards	**SITE** Underground Parking	**SITE** Urban Infill Development Historic Site Preservation Brownfield **ENERGY EFFICIENCY** On-Site Cogeneration Photovoltaic Solar Panels **WATER EFFICIENCY** On-Site Sewage Treatment

Key:

Neutral-Positive Guest Perception	Neutral-Negative Guest Perception	Negative Guest Perception	*Mixed Guest Opinion*

study hotels, include occupancy sensors, hydronic heating and cooling systems, and low-emittance windows that reflect radiant heat, thus lowering the total heat flow through the window. All of these features have the potential to become mainstream hotel practice. Occupancy sensors, however, have produced some negative guest responses, and are more controversial for luxury hotels where guests expect their rooms to be at a certain temperature when entered. ENERGY STAR equipment and light-emitting diode (LED) lighting are common in more than half of the hotels studied.

Water Efficiency. Water-efficient irrigation is common in the hotel industry and was found at all of the hotels included in this study. Drought-tolerant landscaping, in combination with efficient irrigation, improves overall water efficiency. Two-thirds of the studied hotels use this kind of landscaping. Two-thirds of the hotels also offer linen and towel reuse programs. Water-efficient low-flow bathroom fixtures are a cost-saving technology implemented at two-thirds of the hotels, even though some guests view low-flowing water as less than luxurious.

Materials and Resources. Currently, materials and resources are not the strongest environmental focus in the hotel industry. The most prevalent trend is the use of recycled content materials for office paper, brochures, toilet paper, and other paper products. For the future, the industry seems to be moving toward locally extracted and manufactured materials and an on-site ban of bottled water.

Waste Management. Waste management is an area on which hotel management groups have focused for a long time. All of the hotels in this study perform back-of-house recycling and use old linens and towels as rags—common industry practices that have proven to be cost-effective. Many of the case hotels are now adding food composting and public area recycling to their waste management programs. These are cost-effective practices and can facilitate the achievement of Green Seal certification.

Indoor Environmental Quality. In the arena of indoor environmental quality, certain programs already exist, including smoke-free environments, heating and cooling equipment that is free of ozone-depleting substances (now required by regulation for new construction), and programmable thermostats. The no-smoking policy trend is seen across other building types. At hotels, the guest response is mixed on this issue. Programmable thermostats have become a hotel industry norm and are now classified as environmentally friendly. Seventy-eight percent of the studied hotels have operable windows, which is not a common feature in the hotel industry. The use of low–volatile organic compound (VOC) paints and adhesives in building construction and renovation, as well as green cleaning supplies, is increasingly common and will most likely become the industry standard.

Innovative Construction and Operations Features

As just mentioned, most of the hotels interviewed have incorporated high-performance features that require low financial investment and are fairly simple to implement. Each of the hotels, however, also has implemented fairly expensive and complex features. Several hotels have used creative financing techniques or have retrofitted existing systems to meet their objectives. For example, one case study hotel wanted to implement a key card system to control guestroom lighting and electricity consumption. The cost of the key card system went beyond the hotel's budget, so the management decided to install a simple circuit breaker in each guestroom. This in-house system is not as sophisticated as the advanced technology option, but it meets the hotel's goal of reducing energy consumption and expense. Many of the other more complex and expensive green features, such as co-generation plants and photovoltaic solar systems, have been implemented with creative financing techniques. These include partnering either with suppliers or with a local bank to reduce initial capital investment. Exhibit 5 describes some of the innovations implemented by the nine hotels and the rationale behind the decisions.

High-Performance Hotel Education

The most common educational trend across all hotel categories is educating the hotel's employees regarding green construction design and/or green operational practices (see Exhibit 6). The second most prevalent educational trend is that of engaging local community members in a hotel's environmental efforts. Over half of the studied hotels have a staff green team for researching and implementing environmental initiatives. These green teams consistently have been volunteer efforts and have proven to increase staff morale. We predict that green teams will become standard for hotels pursuing sustainability goals.

Business Case

Each of the nine hotels had a strong business case for constructing and operating a high-performance hotel. This section highlights the key financial drivers for considering high-performance features, the market response, and how each stakeholder group benefited from implementing high-performance features.

Drivers for Constructing and Operating Sustainable Hotels

The drivers for pursuing sustainable hotel design, construction, and operations are diverse. In addition, the timing of feature implementation is different for those hotels ranking higher in the sustainable-design-and-construction spectrum when compared to those ranking higher in sustainable operations. Lastly, among the hotels studied, the person leading the green charge varies from owner to architect to governor (see Exhibit 7). The findings in terms of operations and construction include the following:

- *Operations.* Many of the hotels studied did not decide to pursue sustainability goals until the hotels already were in operation. This is possibly due to the fact that these hotels were operating before the beginning of the twenty-first century, at a time when high-performance construction was not yet a part of the industry's mainstream agenda.

- *Construction.* Hotels pursuing more substantial environmentally sustainable construction goals initiated the process during the facility's original construction, in contrast to hotels that primarily were undergoing renovations. A key

Exhibit 5   Rationale for Innovative High-Performance Construction and Operations Features

Green Feature	How Did They Make It Work?
Site	
Urban Infill Development	• The project received the construction permit allowing the developer to begin work immediately, which reduced the overall project time.
Historic Site Preservation	• The hotel's historic site was key to the guest experience and a significant reason guests selected the hotel.
Brownfield	• The project obtained the land at a low market cost, which reduced the total project cost. • The selected brownfield site required minimal cleanup. • The project made use of an Alternate Use License and purchased insurance against any liability claims. • The hotel has not received any negative feedback from guests.
Underground Parking	• The parking area is also used as an exhibition hall for large conventions.
Stormwater Treatment	• The new construction shared a retention pond with an existing building on-site. • The project installed stormwater retention tanks on-site, which also counted as LEED credits.
Restored Native Vegetation	• Drought-tolerant native vegetation requires minimal maintenance, and thereby reduces overall operational costs.
Wildlife Protection	• Wildlife on-site became a tourist attraction and may help increase occupancy rates. • Improved relations with environmental groups may preempt resistance to further development.
Energy Efficiency	
On-Site Cogeneration	• Leveraged federal and state tax rebates. • Leveraged subsidies offered by local utilities. • Captured excess heat, generated by heating and cooling air or water, and reduced overall energy consumption.
Photovoltaic Solar Panels	• Leveraged federal and state tax rebates. • Leveraged subsidies offered by local utilities.
Water Efficiency	
Recirculated Water	• Reduced potable water consumption and the associated sewage fees.
On-Site Sewage Treatment	• Used reclaimed water for landscape irrigation instead of using potable water. • Used reclaimed water to control construction dust. • May allow the developer to continue expansion by not exceeding the usage cap on county water and sewage systems.

Exhibit 6 Audiences for High-Performance Hotel Education Among Hotel Types

EDUCATION	TOTAL	HOTEL CATEGORY		
		Mid-Rate	Conference Center	Luxury/Resort
Staff/Employees	89%	100%	67%	100%
Local Community Members	78%	100%	67%	75%
In-House Guests	67%	100%	67%	50%
Shareholders/Investors/Owners	56%	100%	67%	25%
Prospective Customers	56%	50%	67%	50%
Government/Regulators	56%	50%	33%	75%

finding from this analysis is that all the hotels pursuing green construction have indicated market differentiation and/or public relations value as a leading financial driver for achieving sustainability.

The University of Maryland Inn and Conference Center by Marriott is an exception to the findings about green construction. The hotel was built sustainably as a result of a government mandate. In 2001, at the time of the project's design, the cost premium for a LEED building was 15 percent because of the lack of product options. The State of Maryland mandated the decision to pursue LEED certification during the design phase of the project.

In the State of Washington, the Hilton Vancouver Washington pursued LEED certification with a 0.29 percent premium because it would allow the hotel to achieve market differentiation. At San Francisco's Orchard Garden Hotel, the general manager led the agenda and pursued high performance at a premium of 0.17 percent, primarily to gain market differentiation. This finding is consistent with an overall industry trend that appears to require high-performance construction to achieve differentiation in the marketplace. High-performance operations traditionally have been the hotel industry's focus if any high-performance practices are implemented. As a result, high-performance operations are viewed as more common and less innovative than high-performance design and construction.

Market Response

The consumer response from the case study hotels indicates that high-performance features do not compromise the guest experience. Six out of the nine studied hotels have received free media attention for their high-performance activities. Over half of the hotels have begun to receive inquiries from individual guests and corporate clients regarding efforts to reduce the hotel's environmental footprint. This public attention reduces marketing costs for some hotels, but it is hard to translate those savings into increased occupancy rates. In general, hotel managers still believe that guests will choose a hotel for its location, price, amenities, and special features.

Exhibit 7   Drivers for High-Performance Hotel Design and Construction

		FINANCIAL DRIVERS	OTHER DRIVERS	TIMING	WHO LEAD THE CHARGE
MID RATE	San Francisco, CA	Market differentiation	Owner – Healthy building passion	When GM was already working with contractors, first learned about LEED. Had owner's passion prior.	General manager with aid of general contractor
	Revere, MA	Long-term business commitment	Family values	During construction design phase	One of the owners
CONFERENCE CENTER	Adelphi, MD	Government mandate	NA	During conceptual design	Governor of Maryland
	Warrenton, VA	Market differentiation	Mission alignment	During hotel operation	Hotel executive team
	Vancouver, WA	Market differentiation	City revitalization	During construction design phase (GC on board)	Architects (and developer on board)
LUXURY/RESORT	Kohala Coast, HI	Reducing expenses	Owner philosophy	During hotel operation	The president of Tokyu Corporation of Japan
	Banff, Alberta	Brand standards	Park regulations	During hotel operation	Fairmont corporate leadership
	San Francisco, CA	Reducing expenses	Local expectations	During hotel operation	Engineering department

Convention hotels, however, are noticing an increase in occupancy rates and customer interest related to high-performance activities (see Exhibit 8).

Stakeholder Advantages

Property oversight, hotel category, size, location, climate, and whether the hotel was branded or independent did not negatively affect the success of the hotel case studies. The developer, owner, and manager make up the hotel property oversight. The research team found that the property oversight structure was irrelevant to the overall success of a high-performance strategy and that the property oversight structure varies greatly among hotels (as seen in Exhibit 9).

Exhibit 8   Consumer Response to High-Performance Hotel Design and Construction Activities

	Mid-Rate	Convention	Luxury
Did the hotel receive free media attention for high-performance activities?	100%	67%	50%
Are guests inquiring about high-performance activities?	100%	67%	50%
Are corporate or government customers inquiring about high-performance activities?	50%	67%	50%
Can the hotel attribute high-performance activities to higher occupancy rates?	0%	67%	0%

Exhibit 9   Number of Hotels with Similar Property Oversight Structure

	Number of Hotels
Developer, Owner, and Manager are all different entities	4
Developer, Owner, and Manager are the same entity	3
Developer, Owner are the same entity (Manager is different entity)	2

An important finding of the property oversight structure analysis is that, regardless of the type of structure, the nine studied hotels have been successful because they had a collaborative property oversight group and a collaborative project team (including the architect and contractor). The hotels stated that this was an essential component of their success and was more cost-effective in the long run than conventional isolated practices. In the cases of the Orchard Garden Hotel and the Inn and Conference Center at the University of Maryland University College, for example, the owner depends on the management company to implement environmentally sustainable operational practices and to realize additional cost-savings in excess of what is produced by high-performance construction. The Hilton Vancouver Washington is an example of a public/private partnership where distinct entities (FaulknerUSA, the City of Vancouver, and Hilton Worldwide) worked together to revitalize the local community and the environment.

Additionally, independent versus branded is not a key criterion in determining the success of environmentally sustainable projects, nor is a mid-rate, conference center, or luxury category. All nine hotels, covering the entire criteria spectrum, have implemented successful environmentally sustainable initiatives, regardless of these differences.

This section digs deeper into the financial drivers of each hotel case study by looking at the advantages to each property oversight stakeholder (that is, the developer and owner/manager), as well as by examining the effect sustainability measures have on employees.

The Developer's Advantages. Developers derive multiple benefits from high-performance construction. Green construction practices can be implemented at minimal additional cost, which allows developers to create a differentiated product and potentially earn a higher profit when they sell the property. This scenario is evident both when the developer and owner are the same entity and when they are not; however, the benefit is greater for hotels pursuing a high level of sustainable construction.

A second advantage for developers derives from choosing a location with a beautiful natural site. Industry trends indicate that consumers still care most about a hotel's location and price. This trend is evident at the Airlie Center, where the property oversight is performed by a single entity, and at The Mauna Lani Bay, where the property oversight is performed by multiple entities.

A few among the nine hotels were unique in their developer advantages. The developer of the Hilton Vancouver Washington, for example, benefited by obtaining LEED-project experience, while the developers of The Ritz-Carlton, San Francisco, benefited from building on a historic site in a premier location that created a highly attractive consumer product.

The Owner/Manager's Advantages. If the hotel manager and owner are the same entity, or if the manager is paid a fee based on profit, then the most common high-performance benefit is reduced cost. Managers whose pay is based on revenue are more likely to focus on methods that boost sales, such as public relations and an enhanced guest experience. Typical cost savings occur for utilities, public relations, and/or employee productivity. Utility cost savings are the only quantifiable measure, but this data is difficult to collect from hotels. The public relations and employee measures also defy quantification and are based mainly on qualitative data.

Utility cost savings originate in a wide variety of efficient technologies and resource conservation practices. Implemented energy and water programs achieve the largest savings.

Hotel owners and management companies achieve public relations savings when they differentiate their hotels by marketing their green features. This is the case with the Orchard Garden Hotel, Comfort Inn & Suites Logan International Airport, The Inn and Conference Center at the University of Maryland University College, the Hilton Vancouver Washington, The Mauna Lani Bay, and The Ritz-Carlton, San Francisco.

Sustainability Effect on Employees. Employee-related savings result from decreased staff turnover, increased productivity, and increased morale. The research also revealed that green cleaning products improve employee productivity and that green teams or other staff environmental programs boost employee morale and reduce turnover.

Lessons Learned

Exhibit 10 highlights the lessons learned by property oversight or project teams while they were implementing environmentally sustainable design, construction,

Exhibit 10   Highlights of Strategic and Practical Lessons Learned by High-Performance Hotels

Strategic	Lesson Learned	Example
Team Management	• If pursuing environmentally sensitive design and construction (and/or a LEED-certified building), hire the general contractor early in the process; it may appear to cost more, but it saves money during the project and over the life of the building. • Hire an experienced LEED-Accredited Professional to facilitate the LEED-certified building process and paperwork. • Leverage external experts to keep abreast of trends. • Establish performance-based contracts with building system providers and third-party consultants to guarantee operational savings. • Establish solid relationships with local utility and municipal representatives and create symbiotic public/private partnerships that may reduce permit approval time and potentially create tax incentives and rebate programs. • Seek out other groups and companies to collaborate in sharing new knowledge and celebrating successes. • Provide guests with information explaining how they can support the hotel's environmental initiatives. • Consider incentive programs that make employees partners in developing a hotel's sustainability initiative.	A mid-rate hotel depended on its architect and general contractor teams for guidance and leadership throughout the project. A luxury hotel hired an external consultant via a performance-based contract to perform an energy audit.
Communication	• Keep senior management informed, but realize that managers focus on payback; they are not technology experts. Encourage management to make decisions using lifecycle evaluations. Senior management should champion environmentally sustainable programs through consistent messages, especially if the effort is not led by senior management. • Continually inspire the staff to suggest innovative green initiatives. Employee awareness is the "lowest hanging fruit." • Explain to employees how energy savings benefit hotel operations as well as lower the cost of running their homes. Employees take the lessons learned at work and apply them at home.	A conference center hotel initially took time to educate its general manager to facilitate the processing of all future lifecycle analysis proposals.
Project Management	• If pursuing a LEED-certified building, make the commitment early so you can track construction and demolition waste hauling. Do not wait until the end of the project to calculate recycling rates for LEED certification. • Consider multi-phase projects; it may be cost-effective to implement programs in steps rather than all at once.	A luxury hotel had more than five phases to install photovoltaic solar panels that now generate more than half a megawatt of energy from the sun's radiation.

(continued)

Exhibit 10 *(continued)*

Strategic	Lesson Learned	Example
Procurement	• Study new technology and consider a trial-and-error strategy. Work with prototypes and investigate new products. No product is as good or bad as it initially appears. Similarly, what worked yesterday may not work tomorrow, so be aware of the products and trends that are in the pipeline. • Leverage the research of Green Seal and other third-party experts when evaluating alternative products to minimize internal time and resources allocated for similar activities. • Leverage parent company and/or corporate resources and buying power to improve the hotel's return on investment by taking advantage of bulk purchases and economies of scale.	Employees at a conference hotel took home and tested a number of low-flow shower heads before selecting a product.
General Strategy	• Challenge conventional wisdom. • When evaluating new initiatives, consider opportunities that reduce expenses and/or have the potential to increase revenues. Energy conservation is more than reducing expenses if it also generates more business. • Never lose sight of the core business. Even if the philosophy is green, ensure that all programs and initiatives are appropriate for the hotel and its locale. • It does not have to cost more to build an environmentally sustainable LEED-certified building.	At the time of a conference hotel's proposal for a new building, it cost approximately 15 percent more to build green, but now it is getting closer to nothing (i.e., currently 2–5 percent).

Practical	• Lesson Learned	Example
Marketing and Consumer Response	• Leverage consumer databases to gauge sustainability preferences to develop relevant customer-facing programs. • Start learning about LEED early and then educate the staff; help everyone respond appropriately to guests' questions. • Help consumers see that green operations do not equal poor aesthetics or compromised services. • It is critical to train front desk staff and prepare them with responses to guest questions and concerns related to the on-site green programs. • Some people take advantage of green claims and use them solely as a marketing tool and not as a way to do business. This discredits the efforts of others. One way to mitigate this is to educate people. • Continue to be a showpiece; work to educate guests and staff and to promote green awareness for the industry.	A luxury hotel is putting together an environmental response "cheat sheet" to communicate a consistent message to guests.

Exhibit 10 *(continued)*

Practical	Lesson Learned	Example
Operations	• Understand your building systems! • Plan solar collection from photovoltaic solar panels in the design phase of a new or renovation project. The financial impact of retrofits as well as legacy building systems may prohibit modification. • Twenty percent of the achieved energy savings come from implementing a good preventive maintenance program.	A conference hotel is pursuing Green Seal certification to validate its ongoing operations and preventive maintenance program.
Materials, and Resources and Waste Management	• Water-based wood stains should be tested for use in high-traffic areas. • There are now aesthetically and environmentally preferred products on the market, so aesthetics can drive environmental decisions in a positive direction.	A luxury hotel has changed its room standard from vinyl wall-covering to low-VOC paint.
Measuring Performance	• If you can't measure it, you can't improve it. • Benchmark and learn from the industry leaders who have paved the way. • Best practices can be replicated at other properties, so sharing information is key. • Before considering any project, understand the purpose (environmental and economic benefits) and the associated financial implications. Generic case studies and comparison data without exact numbers are acceptable. Since every hotel situation is different, rough orders of magnitude should suffice. Use the framework and overlay your own business conditions to make the business case based on your locale. • Periodically audit supply chain and business partner practices to make sure these partners are acting on their commitments.	A mid-rate hotel shares its best green practices with other properties in the brand portfolio. A conference hotel followed its recyclables hauler only to find the materials were being sent to the landfill.

and operations programs at the eight case study hotels. This is not meant to be a thorough "how-to" guide of high-performance practices. The lessons are either strategic or practical in nature and include examples from the individual hotels. The strategic advice falls under team management, communication, project management, general strategy, and procurement, while the practical advice includes marketing and consumer response, operations, materials and resources, waste management, and performance measurement. (For more information on measuring performance, see Appendix B.)

Opportunities for Industry Improvement

Exhibit 11 summarizes some of the gaps that currently exist in environmentally sustainable design, construction, and operations as indicated anecdotally by the

Exhibit 11   Opportunities for Industry Improvement by Business Area

Business Area	Need
Management	• Provide a service or a framework to help hotels evaluate and prioritize projects using the following criteria: financial impact (initial cost and cost over the expected life), environmental impact, consumer impact. • Create a de facto green hotel certification program—a single point of reference for the industry—and reduce the cost of the certification process.
Materials, and Resources and Waste Management	• Improve the recycling infrastructure throughout North America and identify uses for recyclable materials. • Find someone who can recycle telephone books. • Provide carpeting style options that are durable and conservative; sustainable options seem to be limited in design and are primarily edgy and modern. • Improve the durability of rapidly renewable flooring products. • Improve the options for recycled content toilet paper and other paper products. • Design bulk shower amenity dispensers for high-end luxury properties.
Energy	• Create special nightlights and CFL bulbs that are difficult to remove from guestrooms. • Create more cost-effective light bulbs.
Indoor Environmental Quality	• Create organic weed killers that perform as well as the traditional chemical products.

nine studied hotels. We believe these deficiencies regarding management, materials and resources, waste management, energy, and indoor environmental quality represent opportunities that can move the hospitality industry toward more environmentally sustainable practices, and that an entrepreneurial supplier will have a sympathetic audience.

Conclusion

The hospitality industry is the third largest retail industry (after automobiles and food) in the United States, generating annual revenues of $133 billion in 2006 and spending $3.7 billion in energy to do it. The hospitality industry is not immune to the demands of the green market shift, nor is it denied the opportunities to be gained by embracing that shift. As the report excerpt shows, there are financial benefits in green buildings, both in construction and operations. If you are a hotel operator, owner, or developer, and you do not recognize the benefits of going green, you are leaving money on the table. Your customers are beginning to ask for it; your workers will have more allegiance to you if you do it; and, finally, your competitors will steal your market share if they do it before you do.

For more detailed analysis and eight complete case studies, please see *High Performance Hospitality*.

 # Endnote

1. John Elkington, *Cannibals with Forks: The Triple Bottom Line of 21st Century Business* (Gabriola Island, British Columbia: New Society Publishers, 1998).

Appendix A:

Advantages of High-Performance Hotel Design, Construction, and Operations

A myriad of advantages exist for hotel industry stakeholders if hotels are designed, constructed, and operated sustainably. Opportunities still exist if one is implemented without the other, but the advantages are maximized if design/construction and operations work in tandem. For example, if a hotel's management performs a lighting retrofit by replacing all of the incandescent bulbs with compact fluorescents, the facility will realize a considerable cost savings. However, if that same hotel management performs the retrofit after the developer has constructed the building with a tight envelope, efficient heating and cooling, occupancy sensors, and maximized daylighting, the overall savings will be compounded. (See Figure 1 for a summary of the prevailing financial, environmental, and social advantages of high-performance hotel design, construction, and operation.)

A hotel realizes more value when environmental considerations are integrated into the design and construction process as early as possible. With integrated design, buildings perform better during their initial operation, and this performance continues over the life of the facility. This is the result of utilizing a "whole building" design approach. For integrated design to occur, however, it is critical to include input from hotel managers and owners during the design process. In addition, all property oversight stakeholders (developers, owners, and managers) must continue to communicate throughout the life of the project.

As of January 2008, there is broad consensus on the environmental and social benefits of high-performance buildings. Additionally, a consensus also is emerging on the financial benefits of green buildings. Published studies emphasize that the capital costs for these buildings range from significantly less to slightly more than those of comparable buildings, with green buildings carrying an average premium of 2 percent.[1]

According to Davis Langdon, a green-building scholar, many projects now are achieving LEED certification within budget and within the same cost range as non-LEED projects. Even though construction costs have increased sharply, projects continue to pursue LEED certification.[2]

High-performance practices generally make economic sense if their evaluated costs are based on lifecycle cost analysis. This requires a long-term mindset, and it is not the most common method of cost analysis in the industry. Most hospitality decision-makers still favor a short-term analysis that looks only at payback or initial cost.

---

[1] Greg Kats, "The Cost and Financial Benefits of Green Buildings: A Report to California's Sustainable Building Task Force" (developed for the Sustainable Building Task Force, a group of over forty California state government agencies, October 2003).

[2] Davis Langdon, "Cost of Green Revisited: Reexamining the Feasibility and Cost Impact of Sustainable Design in the Light of Increased Market Adoption" (July 2007).

Figure 1   Financial, Environmental, and Social High-Performance Hotel Advantages

	HIGH PERFORMANCE ADVANTAGES
Financial	• Reduced capital costs of hotel construction and equipment by reducing the size of heating and cooling system needed, stormwater capacity needed, and by reusing infrastructure and materials.
	• Reduced operating costs of hotel buildings and landscapes through energy and water efficiency measures, lower maintenance requirements, less waste produced, and having a "systems thinking" approach.
	• Market differentiation can create a competitive advantage that saves marketing dollars through free press, and increases guest occupancy rates.
	• Reduced liabilities and risks can be realized by building a healthier building that is ahead of regulation.
	• Improved health and higher productivity of workers can result from a more pleasant work environment, which leads to lower employee costs.
	• Municipal-based financial incentives such as fast-track permits, increased FAR, or tax incentives for sustainable construction and/or operations can be obtained.
	• In some markets, buyers will pay a premium to own or invest in a hotel that is built and/or constructed sustainably.
Environmental	• Lower energy and resource use, and fewer vehicle miles traveled, reduce overall CO_2 and greenhouse gas emissions.
	• Redevelopment of existing land (infill development) reduces the demand on greenfields and takes advantage of current transportation and stormwater infrastructures.
	• Sustainable construction methods can reduce the amount of material in landfills and minimize site disturbance.
	• The demand on natural resources can be reduced by selecting materials and products that have recycled content, are recyclable, and/or are rapidly renewable.
	• Natural stormwater filtration techniques improve stormwater quality and the flow of natural hydrology systems.
Social	• Sustainable hotel design, construction and operations can benefit the community through economic revitalization and by retaining business locally.
	• Sustainable hotel design, construction, and operations can benefit staff and guests through improved comfort, health, and productivity.

The misconception that high-performance buildings cost significantly more than traditional buildings is a result of the learning curve with regard to sustainable design and technologies, and an imprecise definition of high-performance buildings that regards green features as add-ons to the construction budget instead of essential components of the project.

Overall, it makes financial business sense to build and manage hotels with environmental considerations in mind. This fact is consistently evident in the hotel case studies presented in this report. What varies are the means by which developers, owners, and management companies achieve cost-effective projects, and the advantages they choose to target.

Financial Advantages

Financial Advantage #1. Properties can reduce the capital costs of hotel construction and equipment by reducing the size of required heating and cooling systems and stormwater capacity, and by reusing infrastructure and materials.

- Reducing the required size of a building's heating and cooling systems can be achieved with an energy-efficient building envelope.

- Employing natural stormwater retention and/or filtration can reduce the need for more expensive tanks and systems.

- Adapting an existing building or reusing building materials for a project can reduce up-front costs by minimizing the amount of new construction materials and reducing the amount of waste sent to the landfill.

- By creating an integrated planning and design team, and by utilizing whole-systems thinking, overall capital construction costs can be reduced.

- Minimizing impervious surfaces reduces the required amount of stormwater infrastructure and the use of traditional paving materials.

- Recycling construction waste can minimize expenses because most landfill fees are higher than recycling charges, and leftover construction materials can be reused or resold.

Financial Advantage #2. Hotels can reduce the operating costs of buildings and landscapes through energy and water efficiency measures, lower maintenance requirements, less waste, and a "systems-thinking" approach.

Energy efficiency:

- Any actions taken to make the hotel building envelope tighter will result in energy savings. This includes installing a reflective or vegetative roof, well-insulated walls, and low-emittance windows.

- Using occupancy sensors and installing compact fluorescent light bulbs all improve energy efficiency.

- Utilizing energy recovery units and carbon dioxide (CO_2) sensors creates energy savings by reducing demand on the heating and cooling systems.

- Installing energy-efficient equipment, such as heating and cooling systems, ENERGY STAR equipment, and LED (light-emitting diode) exit signs reduces energy consumption.

- Energy-efficient lighting can save 20–75 percent in lighting energy use, potentially saving the industry $133–$777 million.

Water efficiency:

- Planting native, drought-tolerant landscaping minimizes irrigation and potable water consumption.

- High-efficiency water fixtures can cut water consumption levels. These fixtures include sink aerators, low-flow showerheads and toilets, dual-flush toilets, and waterless urinals.

- Recirculated water from showers, sinks, and fountains can be used for landscaping irrigation or flushing toilets.

- Water-efficient fixtures can reduce water and sewer bills by 25–30 percent.

Lower maintenance requirements:

- More efficient systems last longer and require less maintenance.

- Commissioning building systems, which is the process of ensuring that a building's systems are designed, installed, and tested to perform according to the design intent and operational needs, ensures a more accurate and relevant performance.

- Some flooring material (e.g., wool carpeting) made from highly renewable resources is durable, long lasting, and requires minimal maintenance beyond cleaning.

- Natural ventilation, heating, and/or cooling causes less wear on building heating, cooling, and ventilation (HVAC) systems, which results in lower energy demand and equipment maintenance.

- Reduced operating waste can save money if the cost of recycling or composting is less than landfill waste fees.

- By creating an integrated planning and design team, and by utilizing "whole-systems" thinking, operating costs can be reduced.

Financial Advantage #3. Market differentiation can create a competitive advantage that saves marketing dollars through free publicity and increases guest occupancy rates.

Free publicity:

- According to the Rocky Mountain Institute, the Rosewood Inn of the Anasazi in New Mexico received free and unsolicited coverage from major publications such as *Food & Wine, National Geographic Traveler,* and *Travel + Leisure* magazines. This led to a 20-percent increase in business from guests and travel agencies (based on the Rosewood Inn's projections).

Product differentiation:

- According to Cornell University, 58 percent of travelers indicate they would be willing to pay more for an allergen-free guestroom.[3]

Financial Advantage #4. Properties can reduce liabilities and risks by building healthier buildings that are ahead of regulation.

- Better ventilation and the use of non-toxic substances result in improved indoor air quality. This allows the hotel to mitigate liability and the risk of litigation from sick building syndrome. According to the Environmental Protection Agency (EPA), sick buildings are one of the top five environmental threats to human health.[4]

[3.] "Green Buildings and the Bottom Line" (fourth in a series of annual reports on the Green Building Movement by *Building Design + Construction,* November 2006), pp. 24–25.

[4.] U.S. Environmental Protection Agency, "Indoor Air Facts No. 4 (revised) Sick Building Syndrome," accessed November 2007, http://www.epa.gov/iaq/pubs/sbs.html.

- Lower-risk buildings decrease insurance costs. Fireman's Fund Insurance Company, for example, now offers lower rates for LEED-certified buildings.[5]

- Sustainable hotel design, construction, and operations can help a hotel stay ahead of potential future resource or systems regulations. This is less costly than post-enactment compliance.

- Resource efficiency will be more important in the future when resources become even more scarce and costly.

Financial Advantage #5. A more pleasant and healthier work environment can result in the improved health and higher productivity of workers, and lead to lower employee costs.

- Workers are more comfortable in environmentally friendly surroundings, such as those produced by improved indoor ventilation, individualized temperature control, increased use of daylighting, a commitment to the use of low (or no) volatile organic compounds (VOCs), and green cleaning supplies. Studies indicate that employees are more productive and have higher morale in these environments.

- Staff who have healthier indoor environments experience less sick time.

Financial Advantage #6. Financial incentives for implementing high-performance practices are available through government and local utility programs.[6]

- Municipalities promote green-building and renewable-energy practices with a variety of incentive programs. These include: fast-track site plan permits; grants for LEED-certified projects or for projects built to LEED standards; low-interest loans; tax credits and fee reductions for different LEED certification levels; recognition programs; free training; and density bonuses.

- Under the Energy Policy Act of 2005, commercial building owners and developers can obtain tax breaks for energy-conservation measures.

Financial Advantage #7. In some markets, buyers will pay a premium to own or invest in a hotel that is built and/or constructed sustainably, a phenomenon that is seen across other property types.

---

5. Fireman's Fund, "Fireman's Fund First to Introduce Green Building Coverage," press release, October 12, 2006, www.firemansfund.com/Documents/NewsReleaseGreenInsurance 1006.pdf.

6. Online sources: (1) Federal and State Incentives for Renewable Resources and Building Efficiency. Visit DSIRE for a current list at http://www.dsireusa.org/. Click on your chosen state or on the "Federal Incentives" icon. (2) Government LEED Incentives. For a current list, go to www.usgbc.org/DisplayPage.aspx?CMSPageID=1780. See "LEED Initiatives in Governments and Schools." (3) Tax Deductions for Commercial Buildings (from the Energy Policy Act of 2005). For information on tax deductions from Energy Star, go to ENERGY STAR Brochure for Commercial Tax Deductions at www.energystar.gov/index. cfm?c= products.pr_tax_credits. (4) Information on tax deductions from the United States Green Building Council. For current information, go to www.usgbc.org/DisplayPage. aspx?CMSPageID =1780; see Energy Policy Act of 2005 analysis.

Environmental Advantages

Environmental Advantage #1. Lower energy and resource use and fewer vehicle miles traveled, as a result of access to public transportation and locally sourced materials, reduce overall CO_2 and greenhouse gas emissions.

Environmental Advantage #2. Redevelopment of existing land (infill development) reduces the demand on greenfields and takes advantage of current transportation and stormwater infrastructures.

Environmental Advantage #3. Sustainable construction methods can reduce the amount of material in landfills and minimize site disturbance.

Environmental Advantage #4. The demand on natural resources can be reduced by selecting materials and products that have recycled content, are recyclable, and/or are rapidly renewable.

Environmental Advantage #5. Natural stormwater filtration techniques improve water quality and the flow of natural hydrology systems.

Social Advantages

Social Advantage #1. Sustainable hotel design, construction, and operations can benefit the community through economic revitalization and by retaining local business.

- Hotel infill development prevents resources from leaving communities and economically revitalizes the area.
- Utilizing locally manufactured and extracted materials minimizes vehicle emissions, reduces transportation energy consumption and dependence on foreign oil, and retains financial profits within the community.

Social Advantage #2. Sustainable hotel design, construction, and operations can benefit staff and guests through improved comfort, health, and productivity.

- Improved indoor ventilation and individual temperature control, increased use of daylighting, and a commitment to the use of low (or no) volatile organic compounds and green cleaning supplies can result in the improved health, productivity, and morale of workers, as well as an enhanced guest experience.

Social Advantage #3. Sustainable hotel design, construction, and operations increases environmental awareness and encourages stakeholders to change their lifestyles.

- Hotel press releases, interior signage, and guided tours educate hotel guests, staff, and other stakeholders. The knowledge these individuals gain about a hotel's environmentally friendly practices can be applied to their personal, at-home lifestyles.
- Hotel developers, architects, contractors, management companies, owners, and other partners can share innovative practices with other portfolio facilities for implementation in future development and operations.

This report specifically emphasizes the financial advantages of high-performance hotel design, construction, and operation. Our intent is to focus on the very real business opportunities that exist, without diminishing the importance of the environmental and social benefits that are realized as well.

Appendix B:

Metrics and Key Performance Indicators

Measuring the performance of a hotel's operations is one of the key best practices identified by the case study hotels, especially those that have green teams. Measuring performance means that the hotel establishes a baseline measurement to determine how well or how poorly it is performing on a daily, weekly, monthly, and/or annual basis. The hotel determines progress by comparing its own performance to the baseline measurements, by benchmarking against other hotels in its portfolio, and/ or benchmarking against an appropriate "comp set" – a comparative set of competitor hotels typically compiled by a third party. In addition to determining a baseline measurement, a hotel also may set targets and goals to motivate the management and operations team.

The following list offers suggestions for measuring a hotel's progress toward environmentally sustainable operations:

1. Use the audit/criteria checklist from one of the hotel certification programs, even if there is no intent to apply for certification.

2. Hire a third-party consultant to assist with implementing an environmental operations reporting process.

3. Leverage third-party business partners to create usage reports (e.g., request summary reports from the waste hauler). Prepare a sample report to show the business partner what kind of information is being sought.

4. Leverage third-party business partners to perform annual energy audits.

5. Participate in a third-party survey, such as Smith Travel Research or Gallup, to benchmark against a hotel comp set.

6. Benchmark results with other hotels in the portfolio.

7. Regularly conduct room checks (once a month) specifically to evaluate environmentally sustainable attributes. Check whether the lights and the HVAC are turned off, all bulbs are compact fluorescent, and the environmental brochure is still in the room. One common approach is to check two rooms per floor, each at a different end of the floor.

8. Check utility meters daily for leaks and/or other problems. This includes gas, electric, water, and sewage.

9. Regularly (once a month) review and summarize utility bills—for energy, water, sewage, gas, and waste. Discuss energy consumption trends at staff meetings.

10. Implement an energy-management system that is tied to the building systems and automatically generates monthly usage reports.

11. Implement an environmental management system to track all resource consumption, including water and energy resources.

12. Create a balanced scorecard by establishing baseline measurements and goals. Regularly monitor progress and adjust goals as needed. Incorporate relevant environmental feedback from guest satisfaction surveys.

14

Creating a Culture of Sustainability at the Doubletree Portland

By Michael Luehrs and Steve Faulstick

Michael Luehrs *was the General Manager of two hotels in the Northwestern United States before serving as the Director of Operations for the Doubletree Portland. While there he worked to integrate sustainable practices into day-to-day hotel operations and helped reposition the hotel as one of the leading green hotels in the United States. During his tenure the Doubletree Portland won several environmental awards, including the State of Oregon Sustainability Award.*

In 2007 Mr. Luehrs joined MCI Group, a global association, communication, and event management company. As the Group's Sustainability Services Manager, he helped found MCI Sustainability Services, a consulting firm with a focus on strategic sustainable development for the events industry. Within MCI, Mr. Luehrs assists associations, corporations, municipalities, and convention and visitors bureaus to develop internal sustainability systems and a culture of commitment to sustainable business practices. He promotes sustainable practices within the MCI organization as well as to MCI's clients.

Mr. Luehrs co-authored the Copenhagen Sustainable Meetings Protocol, *a practical and strategic guide to implementing sustainable development in organizations and destinations. He also represents the Green Meeting Industry Council on the working group to create an international standard (ISO) for sustainable event management systems. Mr. Luehrs has sat on the IMEX Green Awards judging panel and participated in the Summit on Climate Change, the European Wind Energy Conference and Exhibition (EWEC), and World Water Week. Mr. Luehrs has nineteen years of industry experience in staff education, sustainable business development, and management of sound environmental operational plans.*

Steve Faulstick *is the General Manager of the Doubletree Hotel in Portland, Oregon. The Doubletree Portland features 477 guestrooms complemented by 49,000 square feet of meeting space. In 2006, the hotel became Oregon's first Green Seal Certified Hotel. Since then, the property has become an industry leader in sustainability, receiving local, state, and national recognition for its efforts. For example, the hotel received AH&LA's "Good Earthkeeping" award for its leadership in sustainability.*

Mr. Faulstick's hospitality career spans more than twenty years, including positions with Hilton, Red Lion, and Doubletree Hotels in Medford,

Oregon; San Jose and San Diego, California; and Scottsdale, Arizona, before he arrived at the Double-tree Portland in 1999.

Mr. Faulstick is also an active board member with Tri-County Lodging, the Lloyd Transportation Management Association, Travel Portland, The Natural Step, the Green Meetings Industry Council, and the Oregon Lodging & Restaurant Association.

THE DOUBLETREE PORTLAND is a 477-room hotel in downtown Portland, Oregon. It is just four blocks from the city's convention center, and is positioned to be a primary player in the city's convention business. The hotel has 49,000 square feet of meeting space, including a 9,000-square-foot executive meeting center. Its amenities include two full-service restaurants, a coffee bar, an outdoor pool, and its own parking structure. It employs 250 people. This chapter will describe the journey to sustainability at the Doubletree Portland. Owners and management companies planning comprehensive programs to create their own green hospitality products and services will benefit from the lessons we learned while converting this formerly traditional hotel into one based on sustainable principles. For us, the economic, social, and environmental benefits surpassed the effort required to modify our organizational business practices in order to achieve a more responsible hotel.

Transformative Leadership: The Starting Point for a Culture of Sustainability

For every leader, the potential exists that spirited innovation will fall victim to ineffective risk avoidance. Business traditionally rewards conservative models and secure approaches. Yet real reward and achievement are often the results of visionary leadership unafraid to push for constant improvement and educated risk. While traditional business models and processes can provide structure and security for day-to-day operations, leaders should not yield their roles as innovators and bar-setters. Leaders should spark new ideas and challenge norms that can ossify innovation or silence creative ideas. While many hotels might have respectable energy management programs, only inspired, informed, optimistic leadership can create a successful culture of sustainability.

Great companies like Patagonia, carpet manufacturer Interface, and even Walmart credit inspired leadership with shaping their cultures of sustainability. It comes as no surprise, then, that the key component of the Doubletree Portland's sustainability initiative—and the development of the culture that made it possible—was transformative, inspired leadership. "Dare to be great!" has become a rallying cry for the Doubletree Portland team, a phrase that invites new thinking and encourages thoughtful risk-taking. "Dare to be great!" is an example of a culture-building phrase that must be supported over time by passionate leaders humble enough to realize that innovation and improvement do not occur in the executive office, but in the minds of individual department members who are trusted and encouraged to contribute ideas.

Sustainable business practices and the development of a culture of sustainability require that leaders invest more than tacit approval of the concept. Property leaders who do not embrace sustainability as critical to their business strategies will see their sustainability initiatives fail. Property leadership is the spark and heart of the sustainability culture. Leaders who do not embrace sustainability as integral to business success—who do not dare to be great—face challenges in achieving their full potentials and in acquiring the power that would have awaited them had they built cultures of sustainability.

In recent years, the movement towards sustainability, or corporate social responsibility (CSR), defined as the need for businesses to take responsibility for their impacts on internal and external communities of stakeholders, has fueled growth in initiatives like the Carbon Disclosure Project (CDP), in which organizations divulge their climate change strategies and greenhouse gas emissions as a means of informing policymakers and other interested parties; the Global Reporting Initiative (GRI), in which organizations provide information about their performances in the economic, environmental, and social arenas; and the United Nations Global Compact, a set of principles for businesses interested in following humane practices in the areas of human rights, labor, the environment, and anti-corruption. Today every Fortune 500 company is expected to communicate its responsible actions and complete an annual report outlining its performance on sustainability objectives. Still, as conversations with employees of these companies often reflect, the businesses fail to ignite vibrant cultures of sustainability.

Sustainability is often seen as an add-on. A business might invest in a vice president of responsible business, place him or her in a dark corner, and feel it has fulfilled its sustainability obligations. Another business might proclaim itself "green" or "carbon neutral" with no plans to improve its performance or reduce its negative impact. In some cases, marketing teams and savvy managers put "green" messages into print and do something to reduce utility costs, yet each initiative is ad hoc and independent of a larger attempt to unify the company's sustainability efforts. Without an integrated approach, the effort to create a lasting, sustainable business culture will not develop in a viable way, and will not deliver the desired result over the long term. Message tone, direction, and passion are energies only a business's leadership team can control. Consultants can provide resources, and work groups can identify improvements, but without transformative leadership, optimal progress will be limited. Leadership must be engaged for sustainability plans to themselves be sustainable.

Defining Sustainability at the Doubletree Portland —————

Sustainability advocate John Elkington coined the term "triple bottom line" as the foundation of his theory that businesses succeed only when they balance and serve the needs of people, planet, and profit. Businesses that focus exclusively on profit may prosper in the short term, but will fail over time. Similarly, owners who do not create positive atmospheres for employees and who do not support their communities may find their businesses unsustainable. At the Doubletree Portland we strive to integrate the philosophy and practice of the triple bottom line—people, planet, and profit—into our operational model.

Most hotel owners grasp the idea that reducing energy use will reduce utility costs. More complicated is the concept that paying fair wages and serving employees' needs will yield greater productivity and loyalty, thereby increasing revenues and reducing costs. With a triple-bottom-line business strategy, these ideas are interdependent. A healthy business reaps its best profits when it enriches internal and external communities.

Sustainability is the starting point of the Doubletree Portland's business philosophy, rather than an added feature. The business of sustainable companies is to care for people—an understanding inextricably linked to the value, cleanliness, and social equity the companies' services provide. Sustainability seeks the same ends, and provides a robust and intuitive framework through which to improve service delivery.

Buzzwords or external consultants did not influence the Doubletree Portland's attachment to sustainability. Its growth and evolution occurred organically, and continues as the result of small victories that inspire the hotel to continually improve its practices. For example, when the Doubletree Portland's business systems reduce waste, the hotel is more profitable and can reduce operating costs, thereby delivering value to guests and investors/owners. The hotel's pursuit of a cleaner environment has led to improved waste-sorting solutions, while its concern for employees' and guests' health inspired the use of non-toxic chemicals and paints. Step by step, the hotel pursues improvements to its sustainable business plan, with the understanding that the plan does not represent a cost, but a savings, and added security for the business's future.

Using the definition, "A sustainable corporation is one that creates profit for its shareholders, while protecting the environment and improving the lives of those with whom it interacts," sustainable business leader Andrew Savitz helped clarify sustainability's purpose.[1] Sustainability is not just a novelty or an attempt to appeal to a niche market; it is a new way of doing business that is responsible—and not just to the bottom line.

Aligning a Sustainable Philosophy with the Demand for Sustainability from Stakeholders: A Perfect Storm ——————

The creation and implementation of sustainable lodging products and services at the Doubletree Portland could not have come at a better time. For the past few years, more and more of the market has demanded hotels that put sustainability on their agendas. Based on our experience, the convention, leisure, and corporate traveler is increasingly conscious of hotel operators that maintain sustainability ethics and programs. What follows are examples of ways stakeholders have encouraged sustainability policies, both at the Doubletree Portland and in the travel industry at large.

Guests

The combination of consumer interest, new sustainability products and materials, and sustainability standards development has created a strong business demand for sustainable practices. Requests for proposal (RFPs) from meeting planners now routinely require that venue providers outline their sustainability policies and commitments. We witnessed this in 2002 when the Doubletree Portland began receiving RFPs from large groups and conventions that asked about the hotel's green practices. This trend is expected to continue. With that in mind, industry associations—the Green Meeting Industry Council chief among them—provide resources that event planners and hotel owners can use to integrate sustainable practices into their events.

Other movements, such as the Lifestyles of Health and Sustainability (LOHAS) market segment, with its demand for organic food and sustainable products, provide evidence of the market's changing nature. These movements have influenced a new generation of leisure travelers—individuals who keep ethics in mind when making travel decisions. The LOHAS market segment is demographically broad, and influential due to its significant buying power. The travel industry in general, and our hotel in particular, have felt its influence through the exponential growth in both eco-tourism (i.e., tourism that preserves the environment, respects local cultures, and educates the traveler) and third-party programs that certify environmentally friendly hotels.

A final guest segment—highly influential because of the volume of business it generates—is the government. Led by initiatives within the Environmental Protection Agency (EPA), government travelers established sustainability requirements that have become game changers for the hotel and travel industry. For example, the Convention Industry Council's Environmentally Sustainable Meeting Standards, released in 2010 in conjunction with ASTM International and the council's Accepted Practices Exchange (APEX), outline expectations industry suppliers must meet before winning government business.

Employees

Numerous studies underscore the importance employees place on working for companies with robust, responsible business plans. Businesses with engaged cultures and socially responsible practices (such as fair wages and community giving campaigns) see reduced turnover costs because they retain employees. Engaged employees are more productive than unengaged employees, and earn higher scores on customer surveys. This, in turn, creates workplaces that are more attractive to potential employees, reducing both hiring costs and, over time, costs associated with grievances.

The Community

Communities invested in sustainability support sustainable businesses. The Portland community has been chief among them. In 2008, *SustainLane* magazine named Portland the United States' most sustainable city. Before that, Portland was among the first cities in the nation to create an office of sustainable development. Portland leaders also signed the United Nations' Kyoto Protocol, an international agreement to reduce greenhouse gas emissions. It is no surprise, then, that the Portland community rewarded the Doubletree Portland for its efforts to promote sustainability. Positive media attention and referral business demonstrated that the Doubletree Portland's community investment can—and did—lead to significant returns.

The Public

Anyone who has passed a newsstand in the last few years has likely seen head-lines and articles about sustainability. The topic is broad, but public interest in it is intense. This situation creates both opportunities and risks for businesses. Sustainability leaders receive increased exposure in the form of interviews, articles, and case studies. Such attention might place performance pressure on sustainable businesses, but it also underscores the fact that innovative practices and a sincere commitment to sustainability can lead to free advertising. In 2007, the Doubletree Portland estimated that the value of the free media coverage of the hotel's sustain-able practices equaled over $200,000. The awareness that sustainability, especially in hotels, was newsworthy provided affirmation that the philosophy was not just a fad, but a viable way of doing business.

Owners/Shareholders

By creating a business case for sustainability, the Doubletree Portland dispelled the myth that green businesses cost more than non-green businesses. Lower util-ity costs, increased employee morale, a favorable public image, and guest demand were powerful motivators to convince our ownership stakeholder group that sustainable practices offered definite benefits.

Putting the Doubletree Portland's Sustainability Initiative into Action

Creating a Green Team

Some of a sustainability plan's most influential stakeholders are its practitioners— the department members on the front lines of business operations. The Doubletree Portland invited staff members to form a "Green Team" that would collaborate on the sustainability initiative. The object was not only to communicate the initiative's intentions, but to seek representatives' participation, perspectives, and ideas for improvement. By forming a Green Team, the Doubletree Portland also took a step toward complying with Type 1 eco-labels like the Green Seal environmental standard, and meeting the APEX/ASTM Environmentally Sustainable Meeting Standards mentioned earlier in the chapter.

Yet like many businesses with good intentions and little experience in building sustainability programs, the Doubletree Portland struggled to find its way. A bewildering array of ideas and initiatives confronted team members, creating confusion. New participants joined the Green Team, but questioned whether they could sustain the interest and energy shown by initial members. A clumsy, passion-over-strategy approach yielded the team's first achievement: frustration.

In part, this was because the Doubletree Portland's sustainability program required Green Team members to pass along information about their initiatives to department managers, who would promote the initiatives to fellow manag-ers during monthly meetings. Each manager would then pass along what he or she learned to staff members in his or her department. What we found, however, was that many department managers did not solicit ideas for meeting topics from employees. Because managers did not seek their input, Green Team members felt uninvolved, and their interest in the initiative waned. At the same time, because the sustainability initiative did not have a structured framework to identify goals, Green Team members felt as though they had no concrete ideas to share.

Slowly, and only after sacrificing time and goodwill, the team found its legs, along with increasing levels of effectiveness. Since its initial efforts, the Green Team has changed its approach. With clear goals, a confirmed speaking slot at every department meeting, and a focus on specific projects, team members feel relevant and respected. Representatives come from every operational and administrative area, and have expanded their focus to include not only environmental stewardship, but also social responsibility. The Green Team meets monthly and distributes a quarterly newsletter, creating a visibility that not only gives the team added prestige, but demonstrates leadership's engagement with the sustainability initiative. Despite the challenges the Doubletree Portland faced in creating and nurturing its Green Team, the effort has helped establish a culture of sustainability within the hotel.

Based on its experience, the Doubletree Portland learned that a focused action team that integrates sustainable processes into daily operations is vital to advancing sustainability initiatives. Most businesses will encounter challenges in adding yet another committee meeting to an already crowded workweek. Yet creativity and leadership support will promote a green team's development. Green team development should include the following criteria:

- An achievable number of clear goals
- Cross-department representation, with a mix of senior and junior employees
- An energetic and organized chairperson
- Smaller project teams that focus on specific tasks, thereby boosting the energy at committee meetings and increasing the likelihood that goals are met

Engaging the Brand Partner

The Doubletree Portland's owner/management company has a franchise agreement with Hilton Hotels. A hotel with a franchise affiliation gains access to the national brand's reservation and marketing muscle, in exchange for giving up a degree of operational control over the facility. The brand maintains ultimate control over a set of characteristics—known as brand standards—that define its image. This presents a need for ongoing dialogue between both the hotel and the franchisor to ensure each enjoys the benefits of brand integrity.

Doubletree Portland's property management team initiated the hotel's commitment to a sustainable business model. In doing so, the team worked with Hilton Hotels to eliminate potential deviations from brand standards. Sustainable innovations made business sense at the local level, but Hilton Hotels' key interest was in maintaining a consistent brand standard for all its properties. For example, Doubletree Portland initially encountered resistance from its parent company, Doubletree Corporation, when the latter's management denied requests from Doubletree Portland to use attractive bulk soap dispensers in hotel bathrooms. Doubletree Corporation said dispensers would compromise the brand's standard in-room amenity package. Yet replacing small bottles of soap and shampoo with bulk dispensers could save fifteen cents per room night, not to mention the environmental benefits. Eventually, Doubletree Corporation approved Portland's proposed addition of bulk dispensers to a select number of rooms.

As this and other sustainability initiatives at Doubletree Portland achieved positive results, Doubletree Corporation committed itself to sustainability principles. The company proposed to Hilton Hotels that all flagged Doubletree hotels seek third-party certification through the Green Seal standard. Doubletree Corporation encountered its own stumbling block when Hilton representatives said they would pursue a more modest approach to green practices at the corporate level, and required that Doubletree Corporation shelve its certification plan. Yet as dialogue over initiatives at the Doubletree Portland continued, national awareness of sustainable tourism grew. Doubletree began new talks with Hilton Hotels that focused on helping the brand develop a sustainability goal for the rest of its properties. By understanding the perspectives of corporate brand managers, and by sharing examples of products and solutions that met the sustainability and customer service agendas of brand standards, Doubletree found a middle ground that worked for both parties. The Doubletree Portland served as a test site for the previously mentioned soap dispensers, and for locally produced, high-quality amenities and coffee. Results were integrated into sustainability initiatives for corporate desks at both Hilton and Doubletree offices. Although a franchise hotel, the Doubletree Portland found a flexible relationship model that benefitted both franchisor and franchisee.

Engaging Internal Stakeholders

Without stakeholder engagement, a business operates in a vacuum. The business sets goals and creates products without a fundamental understanding of what its user groups value most. Businesses guided exclusively from the board room often make decisions based on past successes, rather than on stakeholder feedback. This approach compromises a business's ability to respond nimbly to market demand. Instead of anticipating demand, such organizations can become reactive, and will remain a step behind their competitors. If a business's purpose is to bring value to *stake*holders (not just *share*holders), this approach is not effective or—with respect to the business's long-term life and health—sustainable. Stakeholder engagement gives leaders perspective. By creating a strategic approach to understanding its stakeholders and their needs, a business can anticipate how to serve them with the products and services it offers.

The examples mentioned in previous sections shed light on the barriers hotels can face when they integrate responsible practices into their business models. In many cases, as with Doubletree, senior leaders see potential benefits, but more pressing issues prevent them from obtaining consensus. The delays are not because leaders want to deter savings or other benefits; instead, their hotels' business models have not evolved to the point where they can integrate sustainability into business plans or require sustainability input from properties as part of the properties' reporting metrics.

Support from internal stakeholders can create a favorable environment for implementation of a sustainability plan. The most effective way to reach internal

Exhibit 1 Sustainability Engagement Model

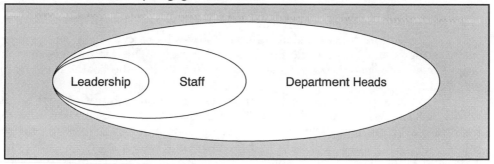

stakeholders, both at the Doubletree Portland and at hotels with whom the hotel works, could be described as a "top down, bottom up" approach. According to this philosophy, because stakeholder engagement is key to a company's business plan, the senior leadership team should initiate any sustainability plan. This team should articulate demand for sustainable practices, educate stakeholders about sustainability principles, and describe the potential business benefits those principles will create. (See Exhibit 1 for a rendering of the sustainability engagement model.)

The first stakeholder group to engage the sustainability plan should be the senior leadership team. A half-day sustainability training session followed by a half-day strategy session can gather ideas that will shape the stakeholder engagement plan's direction. This session's tone and energy will inform and influence the business's culture of sustainability. To ensure the engagement strategy becomes an integrated part of the planning process, leaders should block appropriate spaces on budgets, goals, and calendars to gain desired outcomes. Leaders should also identify measurements that support the strategy workshop's vision and goals, and consider these factors when creating goals for the executive team.

By matching the language of sustainability to the language used by various hotel departments (i.e., by sharing definitions and clarifying shared benefits), the Doubletree Portland's sustainability team achieved unity and support for its initiative from on-site leadership. For example, the hotel's property engineering team wanted to reduce utility expenses, as water use, electricity use, and waste hauling costs served as measures of the team's performance. Engineering team members did not connect with the term "sustainable business practice" until they discovered that the hotel's sustainability plan could add leverage to their goal of replacing outdated equipment with more efficient units. Projects that team members had requested for years were now approved because they aligned with the hotel's sustainability initiative. As a result, the engineering team became one of the initiative's most active proponents. Indeed, the team had already used sustainable practices for years without realizing it.

Middle managers might prove a more challenging group to bring on board. Modern hotels often require middle managers to wear many hats. They direct their energies to deliver the measurements their businesses value most. When middle managers understand that sustainable business objectives will be measured and valued, they, too, will deliver impressive results.

Line-level employees often understand and embrace sustainable practices immediately. If businesses take strategic approaches toward providing information, tools, and resources to their employees, often the employees will become the most vigilant protectors of sustainability initiatives like recycling systems, energy savings plans, and responsible purchasing programs. This fact underscores the importance of engaged, transformative leadership; when the goal is clear, teams respond.

Many large businesses have programs that promote cultures of quality customer service. The spirit and intentions of these programs often align with the fundamental principles of sustainable development, and can be used to promote sustainability initiatives and train staff members in their deployment. Caring, fair play, and efficiency are tenets common to most quality service programs. Doubletree's Caring, Attentive, Responsive, and Empowered (CARE) program, a core brand strategy that underscores the hotel's commitment to total service quality, was an ideal framework for promoting sustainability because for years CARE had been the heartbeat of the hotel's culture.

In addition to the CARE program, the leadership team at the Doubletree Portland created an associated service- and culture-building program, PPFE. The Positive, Productive, Fresh, and Enthusiastic program distilled four main drivers of a healthy CARE program into a campaign that enhanced the drivers' presence throughout the property. Internal communications reinforced the PPFE initiative, and it became a brand in and of itself. The initiative was simple, optimistic, and maintained leadership support; employees at every level embraced the concept. The Doubletree CARE program, combined with the Doubletree Portland's PPFE movement, informed and improved our sustainability efforts by providing a ready culture and a structure on which to build. In the process, the CARE program and the PPFE initiative were strengthened and became better integrated into the property's norms and culture.

After sustainability training began, light bulbs went on in the minds of frontline staff. As employees understood the implications of the Doubletree Portland's sustainability processes, they developed a deeper commitment to monitoring their actions in light of the hotel's sustainability initiative. For example, kitchen crew members embraced the chef's Fresh, Local, Organic, Seasonal, and Sustainable (FLOSS) policies; the concept of using locally grown food was not only sustainable, it made sense from a culinary perspective. Some employees initially resisted the hotel's sustainability efforts, but an invigorated bottom line won over these stragglers. Declining energy bills, as well as waste hauling costs that were half their pre-sustainability levels, dispelled concerns from employees, owners, and brand managers alike. Sustainability was no longer simply "nice to have," but a business philosophy that provided a new return on investment (ROI). (More detailed information about the hotel's sustainability programs appears later in the chapter.)

Based on the Doubletree Portland's experiences in stakeholder engagement, we can offer a few insights for hotels seeking to optimize the results of their sustainable business plans. First, these hotels should consider their existing cultural frameworks and work within them as much as possible. They should thoughtfully evaluate the principles on which they have based their sustainability plans, and find commonality with the triple bottom line principles of people, planet, and profit. Businesses should consider both the ways new sustainability plans would support and enhance their companies' existing cultures, and the aspects of existing service program frameworks that resonate most with those cultures; those aspects might become pillars upon which the sustainability plan can be built. At a minimum, as much as possible of the same language used to educate and inspire teams in the past should be applied when creating a sustainability plan, to speed understanding, acceptance, and, eventually, integration.

External Resources: Building a Network of Champions

A network of influential local voices guided and supported the Doubletree Portland's sustainability initiative. The Portland Office of Sustainable Development was an important initial resource. With tools, templates, and guidance, the office helped the Doubletree Portland create a responsible purchasing plan and environmental compliance policy. Both required simple, concrete commitments to purchase items made from recycled-content materials and to establish a robust recycling program for employee areas. Because of these and other initiatives, the Doubletree Portland met the criteria to become a BlueWorks Business—which at the time was a small but respected group of businesses recognized as sustainability leaders by the City of Portland. This distinction proved transformative, as it provided an early "win" for the Doubletree Portland's sustainability initiative and created positive momentum for additional efforts.

Building on its relationship with the Portland Office of Sustainable Development, the Doubletree Portland became the city's first large hotel to join the Portland Composts! program, which turns scrap food from participating businesses into compost that gardeners can buy at local home improvement stores. The Portland Composts! team helped the Doubletree Portland set up its composting program and provided follow-up support. The Portland Office of Sustainable Development, along with Metro (the regional government for the Portland metropolitan area), obtained access to a facility where they tested the composting program. The project received a great deal of press, leading to word-of-mouth referrals that sparked the interest of high-placed journalists, including reporters from the *Wall Street Journal* and Alaska Airlines' in-flight magazine—both important publications for the Doubletree Portland's feeder markets.

Jennifer Erickson of Metro helped create Portland Composts! and became a vocal advocate for the Doubletree Portland after she saw firsthand the culinary team's enthusiasm for its composting initiative. As part of the Doubletree Portland's community outreach efforts, groups were given back-of-house tours of the hotel's waste management program. Erickson joined a tour with a group of visiting mayors. As the chef described the hotel's involvement in Portland Composts! Erickson noted that a line cook, not assigned to the tour, jumped in to finish the chef's thoughts, then shared his own views about the program's effectiveness. That level of engagement, Erickson later shared, was unique among her experiences with hundreds of businesses in the composting program. Erickson would later coordinate Portland's Fork It Over! project—in which Portland culinary businesses donate unused food to area homeless shelters and safe houses—and personally handled the Doubletree Portland's transition to this initiative.

Emboldened by the attention and positive operational results these programs achieved, the Doubletree Portland sought additional support from municipal offices, including the Portland Water Commission. The commission sponsored a program to help businesses map and reduce their water consumption. Each participating business received a free on-site evaluation conducted by the program head. The resulting two-page document offered consultation and support services. Eager to test the effects of a new toilet flow restrictor, the water commission team conducted a trial at the Doubletree Portland. When team members found that the flow diverter, a thirty-five-cent plastic device, saved more than two gallons per flush without compromising power, they immediately ordered 500 units and gave them to the hotel at no cost.

The Doubletree Portland also sought guidance from Energy Trust of Oregon, a public/private partnership that funds capital investments that reduce energy use. (Many municipalities and state governments sponsor similar programs.) The Doubletree Portland contacted Energy Trust to ask whether the organization could help the hotel buy low-energy light bulbs. This contact launched a powerhouse of support from Energy Trust representative Lyn Schmidt, who in 2008 was the Oregon Restaurant & Lodging Association's Industry Partner of the Year. Schmidt was instrumental in revolutionizing the Doubletree Portland's energy savings plan, not simply by offering information and recommendations for improvements, but by showcasing the Doubletree Portland in a number of well-placed advertisements and news stories. Schmidt, like representatives of the Portland Office of Sustainable Development and the Portland Water Commission, became an influential advocate for the hotel. The Doubletree Portland was saving money, reducing emissions, and gaining statewide prominence as a leader in sustainable business practices.

Impressed with the Doubletree Portland's efforts to incorporate sustainability into its day-to-day operations, representatives at the Portland Office of Sustainable Development encouraged the hotel to apply for a BEST Award, which honors businesses whose practices demonstrate interest in social equity, economic growth, and respect for the environment. The BEST Award application process was rigorous; an independent judging panel of fifteen sustainability experts from various business sectors scrutinized each application. The Doubletree Portland, small by big-city standards, competed for the 2007 award with both global shoemaker Nike and the region's largest and most successful fast-dining corporation. The hotel emerged a winner in the Large Company category, demonstrating the community's awareness of—and appreciation for—the Doubletree Portland's success at promoting responsible business practices.

Programs, Initiatives, and Results of Sustainable Operations at the Doubletree Portland

One of a business's responsibilities is to increase its economic value by investing in profitable initiatives. This is as true for sustainable businesses as it is for non-sustainable businesses. When choosing projects, businesses must carefully consider ROI, as many programs are expensive and offer marginal benefits. Yet rather than using ROI analyses to eliminate eco-efficiency initiatives, sustainable businesses should use them to identify green projects that make the most business sense. As we learned from our sustainability journey at Doubletree Portland, initiatives to reduce waste, lower energy costs, and efficiently operate resources proved economically feasible, in part because they received state incentives and grants. In addition, state-provided educational resources, as well as guidance on energy savings from Energy Trust of Oregon, helped us navigate the sustainability learning curve while reducing utility and waste costs.

Not to be lost in the profit discussion is the potential for reduced expenses related to employees. A work environment with toxin-free cleaning products, no-smoking guestrooms, and clean air commitments can decrease sick days and workers compensation claims. In addition, because employees want to work for responsible organizations, sustainability programs can reduce costs associated with employee dissatisfaction and turnover.

What follows are descriptions of the Doubletree Portland's key sustainability initiatives, each of which maintained an economic basis (profit), while focusing on social commitments (people) and environmental impacts (planet).

Waste Reduction Programs

Trash in waste bins represents both money paid and money to be recovered. Almost every community in the United States recycles plastic, aluminum, steel, cardboard, and office copy paper, and does so at costs lower than what they would have paid to send these products to a landfill. Since 2006, the Doubletree Portland has reduced its waste haul costs by 35 percent through recycling, composting, and staff training.

Reuse Before You Recycle. To avoid unnecessary waste, the Doubletree Portland seeks suppliers that reuse shipping containers and pallets. Doubletree Portland engaged its supplier partners on this issue by creating clear expectations for them to align themselves with the hotel's sustainability policy for key suppliers (i.e., they must take back their shipping containers). In another reuse initiative, the Doubletree Portland reupholstered and reconditioned its dining room chairs for less money than it would have cost to replace them with new furniture. This also reduced the costs associated with removing materials from the property. The hotel also donates unused, safe food and still serviceable furniture and light fixtures to area shelters.

Recycle at the Source. Guest access to recycling bins in guestrooms and public spaces raised awareness of the hotel's sustainability initiative; it also improved recycling rates. Costly bins were not necessary. Instead, we affixed appropriate signage to existing trash containers, converting them into waste stations that met brand standards.

Hotels with employee cafeterias can use these common spaces to showcase waste minimization efforts. Initiatives like buying reusable dishware and mugs, creating composting and recycling stations, and providing bulk condiments can elevate team awareness and engagement. At the Doubletree Portland, experienced staff took pride in showing new team members how to separate waste. By making sustainable actions easy, the hotel ensured that team members integrated these practices into their jobs, thereby supporting the larger cost savings initiative.

Avoid Waste, Avoid Cost. Hotels purchase many items that generate piles of packaging. Businesses can reduce disposal costs by looking upstream in their purchasing cycles to identify items they can buy and serve in bulk. For example, the Doubletree Portland reduced its breakfast packaging by switching to a local provider that offered five-grain cereal in fifty-pound bags. Not only did this lower food costs, it reduced packaging, which meant employees spent less time opening wrappers and fetching product from pantry shelves, and there was less packaging to add to the waste stream. The hotel extended its bulk service to other items, like sugar, jam, butter, and condiments, each of which reaped cost savings and reduced waste.

A composting program can also reduce operational costs associated with waste. The Doubletree Portland's composting initiative removes an average of fourteen tons of waste from the waste stream every month. The initiative did not increase net costs beyond the initial $1,500 spent to retrofit the hotel's compactor so that it could handle food waste. (The hotel recovered this money through a regional grant that supported the composting initiative.) Savings realized from an effective composting program can fund other eco-efficiencies, which themselves can help a hotel save money.

Beyond food disposal, the Doubletree Portland reduced its waste costs by forming lease agreements with providers of large electronic office equipment systems. As part of the lease agreements, these suppliers agreed to take back the equipment at the end of its service life. See Exhibits 2 and 3 for more information on the Doubletree Portland's waste reduction initiatives.

Landfills. In Portland as in most communities, the municipal government faces increasing costs from landfill waste. Because of this, the city's waste management infrastructure provides incentives and reduced costs for businesses that recycle and compost. The Doubletree Portland has benefited from this initiative, as, through its composting and recycling efforts, it diverts more than 50 percent of its waste from the landfill. In addition to reaping an economic benefit from decreased landfill use, the Doubletree Portland is helping reduce methane emissions. Methane is a greenhouse gas twenty-three times more detrimental to the environment than carbon dioxide. When one ton of organic material decomposes in a landfill, it emits 123 pounds of methane. The Doubletree Portland's composting program is the hotel's direct response to climate instability, and demonstrates its belief that businesses must take action against it.

Water Management Programs

Efficient Water-Reducing Fixtures. Hotels can save money on water by employing a phased approach in which they first install sink and shower flow restrictors, then incorporate dual-flush toilets. The Doubletree Portland replaced its showerheads and installed flow restrictors, which reduced water use by 14 percent per occupied room, with no negative effect on guest service scores. These capital investments typically have ROIs of less than two years, making them a cost-effective means of

Exhibit 2   Waste Minimization at the Doubletree Portland

Doubletree Case Study: Waste Minimization

In 2005, as part of an effort to meet criteria for Type 1 eco-certification through Green Seal, the Doubletree Portland increased its focus on an already active waste minimization and landfill diversion strategy. Four recycling stations, complete with customized signage, were added to public spaces. Staff sustainability training and Green Team activation was initiated. Hotel participation in the Portland Composts! program added great momentum to the waste minimization effort. After nine months, the recycling rate had increased to **30 percent,** creating a 59-percent diversion rate (i.e., waste diverted from the landfill), with monthly averages of fourteen tons of organic waste collected for conversion to compost, and seventy-five gallons of used cooking oil converted to biofuel.

Exhibit 3   Waste Diversion at the Doubletree Portland

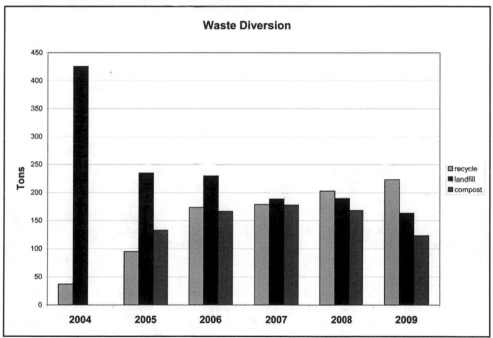

reducing a property's water consumption. The Doubletree Portland also implemented a "No Leaks" initiative, which involved an exhaustive effort to repair running toilets, replace aging systems, and reduce demand for water consumption throughout the facility. Municipal resources provided ideas and hands-on consultation, reducing costs further. Before-and-after measurements helped track costs and improvements.

Landscaping. The Doubletree Portland redesigned its entryway to showcase local plants. The concept—known as naturescaping—requires that gardeners use vegetation from local environments rather than vegetation from other regions. Because native plants have adapted to indigenous climates, they require less water and fertilizer—and resist insects and diseases better—than non-native plants. The Doubletree Portland also discontinued its automatic watering system and installed a drip irrigation system that uses less water. The benefits these initiatives offered were threefold: the entryway maintained a more colorful appearance, the hotel reduced its water consumption, and maintenance costs diminished.

Team Training. As part of their daily activities, kitchen and housekeeping operations consumed large amounts of water. With that in mind, the Doubletree Portland initiated a plan to reduce water use in these areas. Daily meetings offered water saving tips and gave prizes to employees who provided new ideas for water conservation. Representatives from the property's engineering department provided guidance and measurement updates. This intra-departmental approach was a key to raising awareness and creating a sustainable culture that reduced operational water consumption and cost.

Energy Management Programs

Efficient Lighting. Energy Trust of Oregon supported initiatives that reduced energy use at the Doubletree Portland. The Shut Down program was a simple but effective initiative that encouraged employees to switch off energy when it was not in use. The plan's operators set goals and took measurements. By sharing the results during daily meetings and employee rallies, hotel leadership created a participative culture in which each staff member served as an energy monitor. The Shut Down program helped the Doubletree Portland understand that operational practices can save as much money as many infrastructure investments.

Like many hotels, the Doubletree Portland has also saved money by using compact fluorescent bulbs instead of traditional incandescent bulbs. In the future, the hotel will likely replace its compact fluorescent bulbs with next-generation light-emitting diodes (LEDs) to achieve even more savings. Hotel teams are taking a look even at small bulbs that are on twenty-four hours a day, like those in exit signs and stairway lighting. Similarly, ballasts for fluorescent tubes must be replaced with electronic units to further reduce energy consumption.

Old equipment can increase costs through inefficiency and an increased need for repairs. The Doubletree Portland created a strategic plan to replace outdated kitchen equipment with higher-performance, more-efficient models. Energy Trust of Oregon identified equipment that qualified for rebates under its energy saving program, and, thanks to this information, the Doubletree Portland earned more than $15,000 in rebates over a two-year period. Many states offer similar programs that provide incentives for companies to replace inefficient equipment. Hotels should identify potential upgrades and research grants available for businesses that maintain integrated approaches to reducing their consumption of resources.

Social Engagement to Positively Affect Internal and External Communities

As mentioned previously, the broadest definition of CSR is the need for businesses to take responsibility for their impacts on internal and external communities of stakeholders. These stakeholders include employees, communities, consumers, vendors, and the environment. The Doubletree Portland has implemented several programs that solidify its status as a responsible business.

Responsible Supply Chain Management. Often, the drive to increase bottom-line profits results in a nearsighted approach to vendor selection. Businesses typically choose vendors based on price, service, and quality, yet sustainable businesses have another responsibility—to "green" their supply chains by ensuring that suppliers' values are consistent with their own. Green businesses have a responsibility to learn not only how production and shipping practices affect the environment, but also whether the goods they buy are manufactured in ways that ensure fair labor practices and social equity.

Purchasing Policy. A responsible purchasing policy clarifies a property's definition of "sustainable" while making expectations clear for suppliers. Purchasing policies should align with principles from established, well-regarded initiatives like The Natural Step, One Planet Living, or the United Nations Global Compact. (The Doubletree Portland adopted principles from The Natural Step, a non-profit sustainability advisory and research organization.) With additional guidance from Green Seal and Portland's Office of Sustainable Development, the Doubletree Portland developed a comprehensive responsible purchasing policy that inspired more suppliers than it alienated. For the most part, providers were eager to align with the policy, and offered recommendations for products that would support the Doubletree Portland's sustainability initiative.

At first, this was not the case with all suppliers. For example, a global provider of cleaning chemicals indicated it did not carry non-toxic products. Later, when staff from the Doubletree Portland provided samples of the company's promotional material that listed non-toxic cleaners, the supplier said that until a critical mass of customers would purchase these items, the supplier would not be able to stock them. Only after the Doubletree Portland reached out to other hotels did the company stock these supplies. The provider has since noted the products' popularity. What started as an attempt by the Doubletree Portland to purchase green products for its sustainability initiative became a catalyst for the creation of another resource local businesses can use to obtain non-toxic cleaning supplies.

Doubletree Portland staff members revised other purchasing decisions based on their new sustainability plan. The hotel's coffee program had become a liability because it based purchasing decisions on lowest prices, without considering aspects like human rights or fair wages associated with the coffee's production. Because the hotel had staked out a position on sustainability, it now had to "walk the talk." To that end, the Doubletree Portland joined forces with Portland Roasting, a local coffee company committed to sustainability principles. By working with a provider that verified the sustainability of its supply chain and its commitment to the people working along that chain, the Doubletree Portland demonstrated its own commitment to sustainable principles.

Another important aspect of sustainable purchasing policies is the emphasis they place on investment in local economies. If individual hotels can overcome corporate buying restrictions, they can promote local products while giving guests tastes of regional hospitality. In addition to bringing on Portland Roasting as its coffee supplier, the Doubletree Portland invested in high-quality local jam, ice cream, produce, fish, beer, and even liquor. Because many competing hotels offer few, if any, regional choices, the Doubletree Portland has created a market advantage based on unique fare that exposes local cuisine and products to guests, many of whom do not mind paying more for a better product. Food costs—an indicator of a hotel's profitability—have not increased substantially and, in some cases, actually went down as a result of the hotel's effort to promote local products. Meanwhile, the Doubletree Portland strengthened the local economy by directing over $1 million to regional suppliers.

Employee-Centric Work Environment. Businesses with employee-centric work environments reap many benefits. Younger generations seek employers that maintain responsible business practices and offer healthy work environments. Businesses that find ways to boost employee benefits, morale, compensation, and energy can strengthen their teams and deliver value, both for themselves and their communities. As the Doubletree Portland implemented its sustainability initiatives, staff morale improved and loyalty increased. Employees saw that the Doubletree Portland did more than promote itself as an "employer of choice"—it backed that claim with responsible business decisions. Instead of jumping to the next job that offered a minimal wage increase, employees remained part of the Doubletree team.

Like many hotels, the Doubletree Portland conducts employee opinion surveys that uncover concerns and seek ideas for improvement. For the four years the Doubletree Portland has actively pursued its sustainability initiative, its ranking by employees has been among the top tier of 240 participating Doubletree hotels. Likewise, the hotel's retention statistics during these years show that employee turnover was less than half the industry average of 55 percent. These findings underscore the fact that green tactics need not come at the expense of employee morale but, rather, can enhance team performance and engagement. The effect was so apparent that in 2009 *Oregon Business* magazine named the Doubletree Portland one of the "100 Best Green Companies to Work For in Oregon" (the company ranked third on the list).

Additional insight into the Doubletree Portland's culture of sustainability comes from a collection of initiatives that reveal the level of commitment among the hotel's employees. In 2009, during a difficult economic time both at work and at home, Doubletree Portland employees initiated an employee pantry for hardest-hit team members. The concept was simple: *For each according to their need.* Manned by a small volunteer team, the pantry offered canned goods, pasta, beans, rice, condiments, and other staples to co-workers who needed them. Likewise, employees reaped benefits from the Better Living Fair, a volunteer-organized event that gave staff members information about how they could live more affordably and healthily. The Green Team also initiated an effort to clean Portland city parks and neighborhoods that resulted in over eighty volunteer hours of work by employees.

Sustainable Transportation Solutions. Through its involvement with a regional program focused on clean transportation solutions, the Doubletree Portland learned about an initiative in which companies offer employees reduced-price annual passes on MAX, the local public transportation system. This program costs the hotel $30,000 annually, but a holistic review of accounts shows that reduced costs from employee turnover and missed shifts results in a positive budget variance. The Doubletree Portland also participates in the Metro public transportation initiative, saving 75,625 gallons of gasoline and eliminating 690 tons of carbon dioxide emissions.

In 2008, the hotel replaced its aging shuttle bus with a fuel-efficient bus that burns biodiesel. Local suppliers provide the biodiesel, which is made from fossil fuel diesel and used cooking oil (some of which comes from the Doubletree Portland's own kitchen). In 2009, the new van's operating costs were equal to what Doubletree Portland spent the previous year on its old van.

Environmental Impact of the Doubletree Portland's Sustainable Policies and Programs

A hotel significantly affects its community and the environment. Mass consumption of energy and water, waste production, chemical and compound use, and large carbon footprints all make an impact, both locally and globally. At the Doubletree Portland, the sustainable practices and programs discussed in this chapter minimized the hotel's negative effect on the environment. Summaries of some of those practices follow:

- *Solid waste reduction.* Effective, aggressive recycling programs reduced the hotel's demand for natural resources and diminished the environmental impacts associated with their extraction.

- *Responsible purchasing program.* The Doubletree Portland's purchasing policy has reduced the environmental impact associated with transportation by as much as 20 percent over 2005 averages. The hotel's partnership with vendors that reuse packaging has also resulted in eco-efficiency.

- *Non-toxic chemicals.* The Doubletree Portland switched 95 percent of its chemicals, paints, and adhesives to non-toxic products. This effort not only protects local water tables, where damaging chemicals eventually end up, but also demonstrated concern for the health of employees who apply these products. The hotel's policy to purchase certified non-toxic chemicals is a key aspect of its commitment to environmental stewardship.

- *Responsible renovation.* As part of the hotel's public space renovation project, it collaborated with local reuse and recycling initiatives to donate building materials, diverting more than 80 percent of its project waste. In addition, use of environmentally friendly products and practices led to savings, primarily because the hotel's project waste did not end up in landfills.

- *Energy efficiency and water reduction.* The Doubletree Portland measured its carbon footprint and used this measurement to establish initiatives that reduce energy use. Since 2005, the Doubletree Portland has invested over $38,000 in renewable energy, cleaner fuels, and an efficient electricity infrastructure. The hotel has also reduced its carbon dioxide emissions by 900 tons annually. Through water-saving initiatives like low-flow toilets and flow restrictors in sinks and showerheads, the Doubletree Portland has reduced its wastewater costs by sixty-one cents per occupied room since 2005. This has led to a reduced need for fresh water and a reduction in the amount of energy needed to move and heat water used on-site.

- *Carbon calculator.* The Doubletree Portland is working to reduce carbon dioxide emissions in its everyday operations. The hotel discontinued its airport shuttle in favor of the door-to-door MAX light rail that runs to and from Portland International Airport. Car sharing is available nearby, and so is a biodiesel shuttle for in-town transportation. The hotel also encourages guests to offset their personal carbon dioxide emissions. By using a carbon calculator, accessed through the Doubletree Portland's website (www.doubletreegreen.com), guests can determine the amount of carbon dioxide their travels create, then learn the dollar amount needed to offset those emissions.

Lessons Learned: Focus on the Sustainability Journey, Not the Destination

With its monthly and quarterly budget reviews, weekly forecasts, and minute-to-minute revenue management, the hotel industry is known for focusing on short-term goals. From this thinking developed a business culture that does not typically value long-term initiatives, such as those required by meaningful, well-integrated sustainability plans. Hotel leaders risk over-emphasizing short-term gains and failing to reap the benefits that follow holistic, long-term views of their hotels' health and needs. Instead of tactical, reactionary thinking, sustainability (and the development of a culture of sustainability) requires forward-looking, process-oriented thinking. Managers who create sustainable business frameworks that prompt thoughtful questions while rewarding innovations and ongoing improvements will enjoy incremental—and sometimes quite significant—returns, especially if those returns are measured from a triple-bottom-line viewpoint.

The Doubletree Portland, having initiated a number of sustainable business practices—and having experienced many benefits and rewards from its efforts—has evolved to the point where it understands that sustainability is a journey, not a destination. Successes achieved and lessons learned generate energy and passion that help the Doubletree Portland pursue new sustainability initiatives. The hotel sets and reevaluates its sustainability goals in light of industry innovations and system results.

Yet, while creating a business that embraces sustainability is truly a journey, sustainability plans map out essential destinations along that journey. Just as the keys to a sustainable culture are trust and investment in management and employee groups, the key to successful sustainability plans is the realization that they represent targets to aim at along the journey. Though some of those targets may never be reached, their pursuit produces measurable results on the journey to sustainability.

 Endnote ————————————————————————————

1. Andrew W. Savitz, *The Triple Bottom Line* (San Francisco: Jossey-Bass, 2006).

Part IV

Operating Perspectives

Planning and Delivering Sustainable Meetings and Events

By Tamara Kennedy-Hill and Emily Lustig

Tamara Kennedy-Hill is the Executive Director of the Green Meeting Industry Council (GMIC). She has more than ten years' experience in the hospitality and meetings industry. Ms. Kennedy-Hill has been a champion for green meetings for over six years, speaking at various industry events and serving as active member and program chair for GMIC prior to her role as Executive Director. She holds a Bachelor of Science degree in Communication, with an emphasis on training and development, and a professional certificate in conflict resolution and mediation from Marylhurst University.

GMIC is a nonprofit, membership-based organization that strives to encourage the global meetings, incentives, conventions/conferences, and exhibitions/events (MICE) industry to adopt sustainable best practices. As a member of the Convention Industry Council (CIC), GMIC is working through CIC's Accepted Practices Exchange (APEX) to develop green standards for all sectors of the industry. The mission of GMIC is to transform the global meetings industry through sustainability.

Emily Lustig is a recent graduate of The School of Hospitality Business at Michigan State University. She earned a Bachelor of Arts degree in Hospitality Business, with a specialization in real estate and development. Ms. Lustig is involved with various organizations, including the Real Estate Investment Club and the American Hotel & Lodging Association. In July 2010 she joined Marriott International's Management Development Program as the Assistant Rooms Manager at the Renaissance New York Times Square Hotel.

IN THIS CHAPTER, WE WILL EXPLORE green meeting trends, drivers, challenges, benefits, certifications, standards, and implementation tools from the perspective of the meeting planner versus that of the hotel or conference center. The Green Meeting Industry Council (GMIC)—a nonprofit that advocates for international green meeting standards and research—reports that green meetings have become an area of growing interest in the meetings and hospitality industry, in North America mostly since 2005.

According to a 2008 Meetings Market Trends survey, "nearly 38 percent of respondents said they have either planned a green meeting or expect to plan a green meeting during the next year (42 percent, association; 36.6 percent, corporate; 35 percent, independent)," *Meetings South* reported in January 2008.[1] While for a number of years there were many meeting organizers planning and making decisions that involved environmental considerations, the widespread reporting, case studies, and surveys related to planning green meetings have only recently become common topics in the meetings industry. According to a 2008 focus group survey on the greening of business tourism by IMEX, a worldwide exhibition for incentive travel, meetings and events, 79 percent of buyers—those who purchase meetings, events, and convention services—would likely avoid destinations/venues known to have a poor environmental record. This is a gain of thirteen percentage points since 2006.[2]

The growing demand for sustainable meetings, the increasing awareness of the impact of lodging venues on the environment, and the more frequent calls for organic and locally grown food make it imperative for hotels to accommodate meetings by creating sustainable venues that take into account environmental and social factors. We believe hotels that make the effort to plan and deliver sustainable meetings will enjoy a competitive advantage.

Driving Forces for Green Meetings

In addition to the increase in consumer demand, other driving forces for the increased conversation and support within the hospitality industry for sustainable meetings and sustainable hotels are societal pressures that include the following:

1. Corporate social responsibility (CSR)

2. Growing awareness and acceptance of climate change

3. Global reporting initiatives

4. Renewable energy use

5. An increase in green construction

6. Legislation and infrastructure that supports sustainability

7. Increases in oil prices

Furthermore, companies that participate in the Carbon Disclosure Project (CDP) are now adding elements to "green" their supply chains to mitigate their "Scope 3" impacts. The CDP defines Scope 3 impacts as "a category of indirect emissions that arise as a consequence of an organization's activities, but from GHG [greenhouse gas] sources that are owned or controlled by others." More specifically, CDP Scope 3 emissions include those from business travel, distribution and logistics, the use and disposal of a company's products, and supply chains.[3] Member companies of the CDP (including major Fortune 500 companies) are beginning to request that their suppliers report their environmental impacts. Suppliers that want to do business with these public companies are recognizing the necessity to track, measure, and manage their emissions.

The type of event and its purpose will be the main drivers behind the decision-making process that meeting planners go through. Meeting planners still must balance the elements of budget, price for value in vendor selection, and appeal of destination/venue for delegates. However, while "being green" typically is not the chief priority in the decision-making process of a meeting planner, it is increasing in importance due to the market-driven and related societal factors just listed.

Overview of Sustainable Meetings and Events

What Is a Sustainable or "Green" Meeting?

The Green Meeting Industry Council defines a green or sustainable meeting as a meeting that incorporates environmental considerations throughout all stages of the event planning process in order to minimize the negative impact to the environment and contribute positively to host communities.[4] Thus, a green meeting involves a strategic process of balancing economic benefits to an organization with its environmental and social impacts. This drive toward sustainability reflects recent widespread societal understanding of, and interest in achieving, the "triple bottom line"—people, profit, and planet—throughout all human activities, especially business. A related concept is full-cost accounting (FCA) or true-cost accounting (TCA).

There are at least nine critical areas involved in planning and executing a green/sustainable event:

- Destination selection
- Meeting venues
- Accommodations
- Food and beverage
- Transportation
- Exhibitions
- On-site office
- Marketing and communication
- Audio/visual

The hospitality (accommodations) sector is just one of many critical elements to the success of a meeting or event. For the purpose of this chapter, we will narrow the focus of green/sustainable meetings to the aspects of a large event that interface with the hospitality industry, or to meetings that are self-contained in a hotel. While it will be important to understand the external factors that are involved in the full meeting planning process, they will only be mentioned contextually.

Green Meeting Myths and Truths

There are many myths regarding green meetings that challenge meeting planners when they are thinking about "greening" their events.[5] This portion of the chapter will present these myths and dispel them by offering the truth behind the misconceptions. According to MeetGreen® (the founders of GMIC), there are five main myths about green meetings:

1. Green meetings are too expensive.
2. If it cannot be 100-percent "green," then why bother?
3. Greening requires too much effort.
4. Only "environmental types" are making efforts to go green.
5. Individuals are powerless to change their workplaces and communities.

The first statement implies that it costs too much to conduct an eco-friendly event. In fact, most environmental practices can help reduce costs, not increase them, at little to no cost to the provider. An example of a green initiative that saves money and has minimal costs is to offer a "USB key" to conference attendees for quick, easy access to all supporting conference documents. Also called a USB flash drive (or thumb drive, as it is about the size of a thumb), this digital storage device plugs into a computer's USB port and uses rewritable flash memory to store and transport information quickly and easily. USB keys can be bought in bulk to lower their cost, and they allow the conference provider to save money on paper and copies, and benefit the environment by saving trees and ink. Also, unlike paper copies, flash drives can be repurposed by attendees, making them a valuable giveaway.

Many event organizers have found that, starting with simple tactics—eliminating water bottles, for example—they are able to show measurable cost-savings to their organizations' leadership. The cost-saving tactic in this example has environmental benefits as well and can demonstrate that green meeting practices don't necessarily add costs to an event.

Most meeting planners believe that it is a waste of their efforts to "go green" unless they are able to green every aspect of their event (Myth 2). However, every sustainable act, whether big or small, can potentially have a huge impact. Meeting planners must recognize that in the beginning it may appear daunting to create a sustainable event, especially if there is no integrated action plan or internal policy to support green practices. The meeting planner will need to identify what is important to his or her organization or event, and then narrow the focus to a few sustainability areas to track and measure. Thus, GMIC recommends first identifying a few measurable goals that are aligned with the overall objectives of the event or organization. These could include cost savings, environmental impact reduction, supplier engagement, public relations benefits, community value, and so forth. This will begin the process of narrowing the scope of what to measure before developing a comprehensive program. Meeting planners can counter resistance to green meetings by tracking and recording their successes from previous years. This will help them benchmark results, set new targets each year to promote continuous improvement, and eventually achieve complete integration of green practices into the meeting planning process.

The third myth is that sustainable practices require too much effort. On the contrary, meeting planners who implement a green "filter" in every aspect of the planning process find that they are able to strategically and systematically implement change over time without excessive effort. Many green initiatives do not require much additional work for meeting planners, but it will require them to look differently at how they plan events. For example, before sending out a request for proposal (RFP) to select a hotel, a meeting organizer could add "green" questions to the RFP to use as additional criteria in evaluating a site (see Appendix A at the end of the chapter for examples of these types of questions). Over time, the green practices would become standard operating procedures in the meeting management cycle.

As for the fourth myth, "environmental types" are certainly not the only people interested in sustainability. Many Fortune 500 companies and major hotel chains are participating in environmental benchmarking programs. (Appendix B is a case study from Oracle that highlights the importance of green meetings for that Fortune 500 company.) Furthermore, major hotel companies such as Marriott, IHG, Accor, Kimpton, and many others are pursuing environmentally friendly initiatives. Green meetings are becoming a major trend in today's society, and many organizations are looking at sustainability as an important factor before choosing to book a meeting with a specific vendor.

The final myth states that individuals cannot contribute to sustainable change in their workplaces or communities; like all of the other myths, this also is not true. There are countless sustainability success stories that began with one individual who made a difference in his or her organization. In addition, a major component of many green meetings includes empowerment of the individual attendees. An example of this empowerment is allowing all attendees the option to partake in a carbon-offset donation program to reduce the environmental footprint of the conference or meeting.

The Benefits of Green Meetings

After having developed core background knowledge of green meetings, it is important to recognize the benefits of sustainable events and the pending standards transforming the marketplace. In this section we will focus on the economic, ecological, and social benefits of green meetings from the perspective of meeting planners and hotels, as well as the driving business pressure for sustainable meeting standards and certifications.

Economic Benefits

The underlying and primary driver of sustainable practices is the resulting economic benefits. The benefits of sustainability practices may especially be seen with events and meetings, since these typically generate a great deal of waste. Economic benefits include decreased costs in garbage removal, because recycling materials costs less than removing waste. Decreased energy costs to run meeting facilities are a direct economic benefit when using energy-efficient systems and appliances. Additional economic benefits come from a reduction in staffing and paper by providing online registration, and reduced paper/copy expenses by allowing alternative methods for accessing event documents, such as USB flash drives. (See Exhibit 1 for a list of typical economic and environmental savings for green meetings.)

Exhibit 1   Economic and Environmental Savings for Green Meetings

Green Practice	Scope	Economic Savings	Environmental Savings
Reducing handouts	1,300-attendee conference, 2 days	$2,000	488 lbs wood 617 gal water 1 million BTUs energy 149 lbs emissions 79 lbs solid waste (Neenah Paper)
Reusing 45 percent of banners	40,000-attendee conference, 5 days	$89,250	12,750 sq.ft. of vinyl banner material kept from landfill
Reducing daily shuttles by 11 buses	40,000-attendee conference, 5 days	$60,000	486,420 lbs CO2 (Carbonfund.org)
Not using individual water bottles	1,200-attendee conference, 5 days	$48,000	19,000 liters water 1,181 kg CO2 216 kg oil 23,840 megajoules energy
Replacing 3.5 gal per flush toilets with 1.6 gal per flush	296-room hotel	Thousands of $ per year	307,914 gal water per year
Towel and sheet reuse program	150-room hotel	Thousands of $ per year	6,000 gal of water, 40 gal of detergent per month (Sustainable Lodging)
Green power	23,000-attendee conference, 3 days	No additional cost	500,000 kWh of Green-e certified wind renewable energy credits sourced and 200,000 kWh of Green-e certified biomass and wind-generated renewable energy credits
Switching to fluorescent lights	1,365 hotel rooms and lobby areas	$51,000 per year	Efficient lighting uses about 75 percent less energy and lasts 10 times longer (National Geographic Traveler, 2004, EnergyStar.gov)
China and linen service	5,000-attendee conference, 5 days	No additional cost	125,000 plates, 175,000 napkins, 150,000 cups or glasses, and 180,000 cans or bottles

Meeting planners can save large amounts of money by selecting venues or hotel accommodations that value sustainable development. For example, choosing to team up with organizations that offer linen reuse programs, in-room energy-saving strategies, paperless registration and billing opportunities, and extensive recycling can produce significant savings.

From a food and beverage perspective, meeting planners can choose to purchase locally grown and seasonal food. This can offer economic advantages because planners will not have to pay transportation fees for long-distance shipping. Another potential source of savings would be to purchase eco-friendly products, because not all eco-friendly products are more expensive. For example, one caterer found that purchasing biodegradable utensils actually cost less than regular plastic utensils. In this example, the caterer's economic savings amounted to $2,700 by just switching to eco-friendly dining products.[6] (See Appendix C for a case study on how the DoubleTree Hotel in Portland, Oregon, saved money with green/sustainable meetings.)

Ecological Benefits

Many meeting planners view the main benefit of sustainable meetings as an economic benefit to their firms; however, many of the same actions that increase savings can also simultaneously reduce the adverse environmental impact of the meetings. An Environmental Protection Agency (EPA) study found that an average conference attendee generates more than 80 pounds of waste and emits more than 1,400 pounds of greenhouse gases in three days.[7] To put these numbers into perspective, the amount of emissions released during these three days by one person would equal the same amount of greenhouse gases produced by a typical driver driving a car for a whole month.

Exhibit 2 outlines various sustainable meeting practices that can help reduce a meeting's ecological impact; it also illustrates the direct economic benefits associated with those efforts. One of the practices discussed in Exhibit 1 demonstrates the direct benefit of switching from bottled water to drinks served in pitchers. Meeting planners can go one step further by monitoring not only the amount of plastic being used, but also the amount of drinking water served. When banquet servers fill water glasses only at the attendees' request, hundreds of gallons of water can be saved. In addition, this demonstrates a higher level of perceived service because the conference delegates are confident that their water glasses have not been sitting out all day.

When choosing accommodations for their events, meeting planners should recognize the importance that these organizations place on eco-friendly practices. For example, if the venue offers low-flush toilets and energy-efficient hand dryers instead of paper towels, the environment will be less damaged by the meeting. Most planners recognize that environmental impacts at conferences and meetings are inevitable, and therefore need to be offset with carbon-offset programs. These programs commonly invest in projects such as renewable energy, tree planting, and other energy-efficiency projects. Top industry leaders can promote carbon-offset programs at green meetings by being the first to donate money to help fund these projects.

Social Benefits

Social benefits of green meetings have not been researched as much as economic and ecological benefits, yet they represent major benefits. MeetGreen identified voluntary social responsibility as having three degrees[8]:

Exhibit 2   Environmental and Economic Benefits of Green Meeting Practices

Sustainable Meeting Practice	Ways to Implement Practice	Economic Benefit	Environmental Benefit
Switching from bottled water to water that is served in a pitcher	May provide water pitchers (potential sponsorship opportunity)	Direct Benefit: Replacing bottled water with pitcher water at a 3 day, 1,100-person conference can save over $40,000 and more than 8,000 plastic bottles	Reduces the amount of plastic in landfills; not pre-filling water glasses can save hundreds of gallons of drinking water for an event serving 2,200 guests
Reusing lanyards	Offer collection boxes at the conclusion of the event to reuse for following years	Meeting organizers do not have to purchase new lanyards	Reduces the amount of garbage in landfills
Reusing Signage	Do not print dates on the signs so you can reuse them for following conferences	Will not have to spend money on copies or re-prints of large or small signs	Less paper and ink is used
Selecting lodging accommodations within walking distance to the event	Carefully assess various lodging options near the conference site; be sure to evaluate hotel options by assessing their green initiatives	Event organizers may not have to pay for shuttles; attendees may not need to rent a car or pay for cabs	Less carbon emissions being released into the atmosphere; attendees will get more exercise and can see the local area
Serving condiments in bulk containers	Refrain from using individually wrapped or bottled items	Can offer up to 50 percent in savings	Less plastic and waste is being produced
Providing online exhibitor kits, online registration, and reducing speaker handouts	Advertise online registration (may offer a discounted entry fee for attendees who participate); offer speaker handouts on a USB drive that attendees may take home after the conclusion of the event	Reduces costs on staffing, printing/copies, mailings, and postage	Reduces paper and ink usage
Implement a recycling program (can be as extensive as you wish)	Place recycling bins in accessible areas, such as near garbage cans; offer labeled bins so attendees can pre-sort the materials	Recycling costs less than garbage removal in most states in the U.S.	Materials that can be recycled are not wasted or put in the landfill
Apply for certification and green initiative award recognition	Research the basic qualifications for the various certifications such as LEED and Green Seal	Direct benefit: the Doubletree Hotel in Portland, Oregon, calculated over $500,000 in increased convention business after becoming Green Seal certified	Specific standards are implemented for best practices and strategies across various industries

Source: Amy Spatrisano and Nancy J. Wilson, *Simple Steps to Green Meetings and Events: The Professional's Guide to Saving Money and the Earth* (Brisbane, Australia: Self-Published, 2007).

1. *Feel good, look good.* Donations and volunteer projects fall under this degree. The social benefits of these programs can be measured in the number of media exposures/opportunities and their financial value.

2. *Responsible action in planning.* Social responsibility can be applied to the planning process by reassigning how a company typically does business. For example, buying fair trade items sends the message to conference delegates that you care about where the products came from and how they are made. Planners can utilize Fairtrade Labeling Organizations International (FLO) as a source to find fair trade items (www.fairtrade.net/home.html). Purchasing local products can be sustainable because they require less transportation, thus costing less energy and creating fewer greenhouse gas emissions. Meeting planners can reap the benefits of this socially responsible act by paying less, due to lower shipping and transportation costs. Use of local labor can help give back to the communities where the meetings are hosted.

3. *Advocacy for responsibility.* Meeting planners have the power to negotiate socially responsible practices and add them to their contracts with hotels and other suppliers. Planners who keep social responsibility in mind when choosing a destination may book their meetings in locales that are recovering from natural disasters (i.e., New Orleans after Hurricane Katrina) or avoid certain destinations that support poor human rights.

As just mentioned, the social benefits of green meetings have not been explored and measured as much as the other benefits; however, by practicing the three degrees of social responsibility, meeting planners will witness benefits that frequently return to their businesses in terms of goodwill and customer loyalty.

Green/Sustainability Standards and Certifications

Currently the meetings market is confused as to how to clearly define, evaluate, and measure a green/sustainable event. Thus, for the past three years a global effort has been mounted to develop sustainable meeting standards. These standards come from two sources: (1) the BSI Group (formerly British Standards Institution) sustainability standards for meetings (BS 8901)[9] in the United Kingdom, and (2) ASTM International (ASTM)[10] standards in the United States. The International Organization for Standardization (ISO) is also developing a standard based on the BSI Group standard.

British and ISO Standards

The BSI Group's British Standard BS 8901 is a specification for a sustainable event management system, with guidance for its use. It employs an environmental management systems approach to sustainable events in order to improve sustainable performance, reduce carbon emissions and other environmental impacts, as well as improve social impacts. BS 8901 was developed by a BSI Group committee comprised of events industry experts; BSI has responsibility for its review and integrity. BS 8901 is similar to ISO 14001, the standard for environmental management developed by the ISO, but was designed specifically for meeting professionals.

The BS 8901 standard defines the process for engaging stakeholders, establishing objectives, identifying performance metrics, and evaluating the success of a sustainability action plan for an organizer of an event.[11]

The ISO defines ISO 14001 as "a management tool enabling an organization of any size or type to:

- Identify and control the environmental impact of its activities, products, or services, and to

- Improve its environmental performance continually, and to

- Implement a systematic approach to setting environmental objectives and targets, to achieving these, and to demonstrating that they have been achieved."[12]

At the time of this writing, BS 8901 is in the process of becoming an ISO standard (ISO 20121). ISO 20121 will expand the focus of sustainable event management beyond ecological and economic considerations to address issues of inclusivity, stewardship, integrity, and transparency. ISO has big ambitions for the new standard, now being developed by a new ISO project committee, ISO/PC 250, "Sustainability in Event Management," as noted on its website:

> Fiona Pelham, Chair of ISO/PC 250, explains, "The future standard will provide a framework which event planners, venues, and other members of the event supply chain can use to implement, maintain, and improve sustainability within their way of working."
>
> The standard (ISO 20121) will take a management systems approach requiring identification of key sustainability issues like venue selection, operating procedures, supply chain management, procurement, communications, transport, and others.
>
> "The future ISO standard will make a great difference to the event industry," says Ms. Pelham. "Just imagine the change in thinking that could follow as the international event industry starts to systematically address their negative social, economic, and environmental impacts."[13]

U.S. Standards

In 2008, the Convention Industry Council's APEX (Accepted Practices Exchange, the division of CIC that focuses on creating industry best practices and guidelines), the GMIC, and the United States Environmental Protection Agency wanted to develop standards based on performance metrics for green meetings. This would be a checklist approach to green meetings, based on the nine industry sectors involved from the start to the finish of the meeting experience.

ASTM International (formerly the American Society of Testing and Materials) develops standards for all major industries, both domestically and internationally. Because of its voluntary consensus-building process and designation as an American National Standards Institute–certified (ANSI) standards body, ASTM was the EPA's choice to develop green meeting standards.

At the same time that the EPA contacted ASTM, CIC's APEX began to address green meetings standards for the meeting industry. The question of whether it is possible for industry and government to collaborate on the standards development process was raised. GMIC encouraged APEX and ASTM to work collaboratively in creating green meeting standards. The intention of bringing these two parties together was to avoid duplication of efforts with the standards-building process and ensure that industry and government goals would align.

APEX/ASTM Environmentally Sustainable Meeting Standards will apply to a wide spectrum of users, including meeting organizers, government procurement specialists, and green suppliers (hotels, venues, and meeting service providers). For suppliers already performing at exceptional levels, the standards have levels built in to recognize excellence in performance. For meeting organizers who want to know how to plan a green meeting, these standards will present clear guidelines.

The goal is for these standards to indicate varying levels of "greenness" of an event or supplier but still have a minimum environmental requirement across all sectors of a meeting in order to be called a "green event." The standards will also include a guide that will provide references and best practices, and a how-to guide for those that need assistance or clarification on what they can do to achieve the performance metrics and/or increase their performance level. The accommodations sector of the standard is a critical component of this standards development process for green meetings and events.

The APEX/ASTM green meetings standards are a checklist approach that provides environmental metrics and policies as well as some social targets across the nine meeting sectors. These standards include levels of performance for both the meeting organizer and the contracted supplier in order to ascertain whether a meeting or event is considered "green." The purpose of the APEX/ASTM standards is to focus on the operational performance of a supplier relating to a particular event during a specified period (rather than the built infrastructure or ongoing operations that other standards address, such as LEED or Green Seal).

The APEX/ASTM and BS8901 (or ISO 20121) standards complement each other. BS8901 aids an event organizer in developing an internal environmental management system approach to tracking goals and engaging stakeholders for continuous performance improvement. However, this environmental management system standard does not identify performance-based metric targets across a supply chain for tracking sustainability comparisons. Since the BS8901 (or ISO 20121) and APEX/ASTM standards complement each other, an organizer ideally would use both in concert in creating a sustainable event, but would have the choice of using the standards separately depending upon his or her goals.

Implementation of Green Meetings and Events

As discussed earlier in the chapter, one of the myths about green meetings is that they are too difficult. This section of the chapter will combat that myth by offering various approaches toward offering green meetings.

GMIC outlines six steps for meeting planners and companies for starting a green initiative program[14]:

1. *Create a plan.* The management system approach allows you to identify and achieve objectives. Your firm can evaluate what you want the key performance

indicators to be. This first step can also help you recognize how you want to monitor your accomplishments and successes.

2. *Engage internal stakeholders in supporting your plan.* The plan that you established in step one should be implemented and reflected in the mission and vision of your organization.

3. *Engage vendors in supporting your plan.* Negotiate with current vendors to find out whether they can offer cost-neutral or cost-saving pricing. Be sure to include in the RFP process that the vendors should report to you regarding data needed to track green success. Typically, firms use their first year as a benchmark for subsequent years.

4. *Track your performance.* This step is of utmost importance because we must make sure that we can evaluate how we are performing. After each event, make sure that accurate reporting is taking place, so that you can learn from past experience to ensure better success for the future.

5. *Communicate the results, celebrate the successes.* Always be sure to recognize your contributions and your successes. Continuous improvement is always the long-term goal for green meetings/events, but you must also recognize your current achievements. A great way to do this is to quantify your results by measuring, for example, the amount of money or number of trees that you saved.

6. *Be innovative and have fun.* As a meeting planner, you must genuinely enjoy what you are doing. Additionally, the goal of meeting organizers is to create memorable experiences for attendees; use creative methods to allow delegates to appreciate the local environment. An example of something you could do, if weather permitted, would be to have a networking session outside instead of indoors; attendees would be able to get some fresh air while also being able to experience the local environment. In the end, your attendees will appreciate all of the steps you are taking to minimize the environmental effects of the meeting.

In addition to the six steps outlined above, there are many other actions (outlined in the 2004 Convention Industry Council's Green Meeting Report[15]) that event suppliers and organizers can do to implement sustainable concepts in their meeting strategies. (See Exhibit 3 for ten sustainable initiatives that meeting organizers can take.) Event suppliers fall into sectors, each with its own opportunities to help make meetings sustainable. It may help to organize these opportunities by sector; these include convention and visitors bureaus/destination management companies, accommodations (lodging), event venues, transportation suppliers, and food and beverage providers.

Convention and Visitors Bureaus/Destination Management Companies

Convention/visitors bureaus and destination management companies can compile a great deal of useful information on sustainability for meeting organizers. They can consistently monitor the city's various venues, hotels, transportation providers, event suppliers, and local government departments to recognize any

Exhibit 3   Top Ten Sustainable Initiatives for Meeting Organizers

1. **Put it in writing.** Develop an environmental policy or statement for your meeting and get buy-in for it. Include this statement in your communications with delegates, vendors, speakers, and sponsors.

2. **Use paperless technology.** Consider digital alternatives to mass mailings. E-mail your banquet orders. Review and set up room layouts online. Where paper must be used, use post-consumer recycled content and print on both sides.

3. **Meet close.** If possible, select meeting destinations that reduce the overall travel distance required by attendees. Select venues and accommodations that are within walking distance of one another. This is the best way to reduce greenhouse gas emissions.

4. **Reduce, Reuse, Recycle:** *Reduce* the amount of giveaways, paper, and other materials you provide to delegates. *Reuse:* Where you must produce items like conference bags or gifts, design them in a way so that delegates are encouraged to reuse them. Also, consider this approach with your signage; you can often produce quality signage that can be reused as long as you don't put dates on it, and/or provide removable items to change out per event. *Recycle:* At a minimum, ensure that materials such as plastics, paper, metals, and glass are recyclable, and ensure that they *are* recycled.

5. **Bulk up.** Contract with your food and beverage supplier to provide condiments in bulk whenever possible. Contrary to what your caterer might say, this does not contravene health guidelines in the case of many foods.

6. **Lighten your stay.** Select accommodation providers that have environmental policies and practices, such as a linen and towel reuse program. If possible, consider hotels that use energy-efficient lights and water-conserving plumbing fixtures.

7. **Eat green.** Inquire after and, if possible, ensure a minimum presence of local organics on the menu at your meeting. Provide a vegetarian option.

8. **Buy green.** Ensure that all vendors are aware of your environmental preferences and reward those that meet your green requirements with your contracts.

9. **Save energy.** Turn off lights and equipment when closing offices, or when meeting rooms are not in use. Ensure energy-saving features on office equipment are enabled, and look for Energy Star–certified products, if available.

10. **Spread the word.** Tell people of your green efforts (especially your attendees!). Your experience teaches others and provides great promotional benefits for your organization and its meetings.

Source: BlueGreen Meetings; www.bluegreenmeetings.org/HostsAndPlanners/10EasyTips. htm.

environmental efforts being done by those organizations. After gathering this information, these companies can compile the data and make reports that meeting planners can access to find the best possible locations, providers, and modes of transportation to support a green meeting or event. In addition to making this information available, CVBs and DMCs can assist meeting planners in selecting suppliers and hotels or venues. GMIC strongly recommends that these organizations organize maps of readily accessible walking trails and local parks; they should suggest off-site events and tours that encourage event delegates to enjoy and experience the natural surroundings of the host city with minimal environmental impact.

Accommodations

Many businesses within the accommodations sector of the meeting industry are establishing environmental strategies and policies in their operations. These policies should be communicated to all employees, suppliers, and guests. Many times, third-party auditors can determine and recognize areas of sustainable improvement within a lodging business.

One strategy that lodging businesses should be employing is an energy management program. As discussed earlier in the chapter, it is also imperative that the lodging sector implement linen reuse and on-site recycling programs. A practice GMIC strongly recommends for the lodging industry is to offer amenities such as shampoo, conditioner, and lotion in bulk containers to reduce the amount of plastic from individual packaging headed for landfills. Alternatively, lodging facilities can donate used soap products to Clean the World, a charity that distributes disinfected, recycled soap to people in impoverished areas to reduce the spread of deadly diseases. Diseases that are largely preventable by hand washing, such as acute respiratory infection and diarrheal disease, kill over five million people a year—most of them children.

Hotels can also install energy-efficient compact fluorescent lighting (CFL) as well as water-saving showerheads, toilets, and sinks throughout their properties. Some hotels offer even greater environmental initiatives by wiring the facility so that guestroom keys activate the electricity in the room.

Event Venues

Event venues can participate in many of the same green practices discussed in the accommodations section above. This sector should implement purchasing policies that favor eco-friendly suppliers. Event venues can contract with private companies if the local government will not collect recyclables. Installing programmable thermostats and motion sensors for lighting can greatly reduce energy used for meetings.

Transportation Suppliers

Transportation suppliers should recycle used oil, vehicle batteries, tires, and other transportation materials. They can ensure that shuttles are only running during peak travel periods to reduce unnecessary fuel waste, and that air conditioners are used minimally. Drivers can be instructed in fuel-efficient driving techniques, such as avoiding fast starts at stoplights, keeping to speeds of about fifty-five miles per hour on highways, using braking techniques that save wear on brakes, and turning off engines instead of idling. In addition, this sector has the power to strongly promote fuel-efficient vehicles such as hybrids.

Food and Beverage Providers

Providing locally grown and seasonal food is extremely important when implementing green initiatives for meetings and events. Another important sustainable practice is to give back to the local community; by purchasing locally, a "green" meeting supports the host city's economy. These local food providers can also give back to the community by donating any unused food to a local soup kitchen. Even minor alterations to meeting planning can yield positive results, such as having event attendees sign up for meals to cut food waste.

Endnotes

1. "2008 Meetings Market Trends Survey," *MeetingsFocus.com,* retrieved May 14, 2010, www.meetingsfocus.com/Magazines/ArticleDetails/tabid/136/ArticleID/9722/Default.aspx.

2. "Global Warming and Business Tourism," IMEX 2008 survey, IMEX survey summary; www.imex-frankfurt.com/documents/September2008GlobalWarmingandBusiness-Tourism.pdf.

3. "2010 Chain Report," Carbon Disclosure Project, www.cdproject.net/CDPResults/CDP-Supply-Chain-Report_2010.pdf.

4. "Green Meetings," *Convention Industry Council* website, retrieved May 14, 2010; www.conventionindustry.org/StandardsPractices/GreenMeetings.aspx.

5. This section is based on material from Amy Spatrisano and Nancy J. Wilson, *Simple Steps to Green Meetings and Events: The Professional's Guide to Saving Money and the Earth* (Brisbane, Australia: Self-Published, 2007).

6. Ibid.

7. "The Economy and the Environment: One Solution for Two Meeting and Event Industry Issues," MeetGreen, 2008; http://greenmeetings.travelportland.com/whyPortland/caseStudies/Sources/Meeting_Strategies_Worldwide_Economy_and_Environment.pdf.

8. Shawna McKinley, "What Is Social Responsibility for Meetings?" *Issues Brief, Meet-Green, March 2010,* retrieved June 20, 2010; www.meetgreen.com/files/articles/SR_Issues_Brief_ 032010.pdf.

9. "BS 8901: Specification for a Sustainability Management System for Events," BSI: Standards, Training, Testing, Assessment & Certification, retrieved December 13, 2010; http://shop.bsigroup.com/en/ProductDetail/?pid=000000000030196056.

10. ASTM International website, retrieved June 5, 2010; www.astm.org/index.shtml.

11. "BS 8901: Specification for a Sustainability Management System for Events."

12. "ISO 14000 essentials," International Organization for Standardization, www.iso.org/iso/iso_14000_essentials.

13. "ISO to Develop Sustainable Event Standard in Run-Up to 2012 Olympics," ISO website, retrieved December 13, 2011; www.iso.org/iso/pressrelease.htm?refid=Ref1281.

14. Green Meeting Industry Council website, www.greenmeetings.info.

15. "Green Meetings Report," Convention Industry Council, 2004 self-published, retrieved December 13, 2010; www.conventionindustry.org/StandardsPractices/GreenMeetings/GreenMeetingTaskForceReport.aspx.

Chapter Appendix A:

Sample Hotel Contract/RFP Greening Document

Sleeping Rooms	Yes – an existing standard already	Yes – can implement for this program	No – this is not possible (please describe why)
Hotel has a property-wide linen and towel re-use program. Please explain: • How this is communicated to the staff • How it is communicated to guests			
Hotel will donate unused portions of shampoo/conditioner/ shower gel/lotion to a local charity			
Hotel will provide recycling in all guestrooms			
Hotel has water conservation fixtures in hotel guestrooms			
Hotel has programmable thermostats with motion detectors used to control HVAC in guestrooms			
Function Space			
Hotel will provide clearly marked recycling containers in meeting room areas			
Hotel will provide a recycling program to include paper, plastic, glass, aluminum cans, and cardboard at no cost to the Group			
Hotel turns off lights and heat/air conditioning when meeting rooms are not in use			
Food and Beverage			
Hotel agrees to a minimum of 15 percent of local, seasonal, and/or organic ingredients for all banquet functions at standard banquet pricing			
Hotel will provide condiments in serving containers and not individual packets for all food functions			
Hotel will not use disposable service ware unless specifically requested by Group			
Any disposable service ware that is used will be recyclable or compostable and will be disposed of in an environmentally responsible manner			
Hotel will use cloth napkins and silverware in lieu of paper and plastic for all food functions			
Hotel has a program in place to donate food to local shelters and/or food banks. Please describe.			
If the facility does NOT have a food donation program, Hotel will agree to work with the Group to provide food donations, at not cost to the Group			
For food waste that is not able to be donated, hotel will compost			

Sleeping Rooms	Yes – an existing standard already	Yes – can implement for this program	No – this is not possible (please describe why)
Misc.			
Hotel will provide guests with paperless check-in and check-out			
Hotel will use non-toxic cleaning products in guestrooms and public facilities (prefer products with MSDS rating of 1 or lower)			
Hotel has energy-efficient lighting throughout the property			
Hotel to provide any documentation of environmental initiatives that have been undertaken, or a green meetings program already In place			

Source: Green Meeting Industry Council.

Chapter Appendix B:

Case Study: Oracle OpenWorld 2009

Oracle OpenWorld is the world's largest information technology event dedicated to helping enterprises understand how to harness the power of information. Oracle OpenWorld was hosted from October 12–16, 2009, in San Francisco, California, and was dedicated to ensuring that the event would support "Oracle's environmental brand and policy, and build a position of leadership by improving the overall attendee experience and Oracle brand experience through sustainable ideas and practices" (Oracle OpenWorld Green Team Vision). Oracle's strategy is to operate its facilities and run its business in a way that diminishes any undesirable effects on the environment. Three objectives that Oracle OpenWorld 2009 focused on included:

1. Measure and reduce environmental impacts from Oracle OpenWorld in the areas of energy, water, and waste.

2. Measure economic costs and savings of sustainable event practices in order to substantiate the business case for this program.

3. Improve stakeholder engagement in sustainability.

The planners of Oracle OpenWorld 2009 measured their successes by hiring MeetGreen® to conduct an audit of their on-site practices. MeetGreen® created an event calculator that met and exceeded the Environmental Protection Agency's purchasing policies and the Convention Industry Council's Green Meeting Guidelines. The calculator tracked progress in the following areas: destination selection, meeting venue selection, accommodation selection, transportation, food and beverage, exhibit production, communications and marketing, and on-site office. The main source of improvements were destination selection, which increased 85 percent from 2007 to 2009; accommodation selection, which increased 68 percent from 2007 to 2009; and communications and marketing, which rose 35 percent from 2007 to 2009. Some other highlights included the following:

- Used 32 fewer shuttles than during the previous year's event, which resulted in a 30-percent decrease in usage, reduced emissions by 18,000 pounds of carbon dioxide, and cut fuel use by 800 gallons.

- Provided an online procedure for organizing information on sustainable hotel operations, improving the publication of best hotel practices.

- Made sure that fifty-two percent of signage used during the conference was from recyclable substrates; 10 percent of signage used was from renewable substrates.

- Executed a volunteer tree-planting community service event to tie into Global Volunteer Day.

Source: "Sustainable Meetings Report," MeetGreen, prepared for Oracle Event Marketing for Oracle OpenWorld 2009, retrieved December 13, 2010, www.oracle.com/us/javaonedevelop/043365.pdf.

Chapter Appendix C:

Case Study: The Doubletree Hotel, Portland, Oregon

The Doubletree Hotel Lloyd Center has implemented a comprehensive Environmental Purchasing Policy, and the property is certified by both Green Seal and Energy Star. Some of the hotel's other achievements include the following:

- Reduced overall waste disposal by 67 percent since 1996.

- Redirected 126 tons of waste from landfills and saved $10,000 in six months.

- Reduced total energy consumption by 32 percent.

- Reduced water usage by 15 percent.

- Saved 9,500 gallons of gasoline per year with employee mass transit subsidies.

- Purchased 65 percent of food products from within a 500-mile region.

Add those savings to an increase in revenue. "We have booked approximately $4 million worth of business due to green/sustainable practices," said Jenny Baird, director of sales and green meeting specialist for the hotel.

Source: "Hospitable. Sustainable. Responsible." Website of Doubletree Hotel Portland, retrieved December 13, 2010; www.doubletreegreen.com.

Appendix D:

Sustainable Success: Marriott International

Interview with Richard Green,
Vice President, Association Sales and Industry Relations

Q: What do you consider Marriott's greatest success or benefit since converting its meeting practices to comply with sustainable goals?

A: Marriott believes strongly in the training, development, and education of our associates. Our Green Meetings Certification Program has been a great success story in that many of our event and sales associates have become more aware of the impact meetings have on the environment. Besides the green meetings brand standard Marriott and Renaissance Hotels are required to adhere to, individual hotels have made efforts to exceed the standard by offering sustainable menu items and use of linen-less buffet/meeting tables, and providing recycling bins in meeting spaces.

Q: What is Marriott International's goal for sustainable savings from meetings and events?

A: Our goal has been to keep the green meetings program cost-neutral. In fact, we are investing in equipment that reduces the use of energy, such as linen-less meeting and buffet tables. Our products and services do not increase costs to the consumer and do not affect the overall meetings/events experience. The green meetings program is about minimizing harm to the environment.

Q: Marriott International partnered with the Amazonas Sustainable Foundation and various other organizations to expand their Spirit to Preserve Program by helping to protect the Juma rainforest in Brazil. How did Marriott choose these partners, and how is this program integrated into Marriott's green meetings?

A: In 2007, Marriott partnered with Conservation International, a global environmental organization, to map the company's carbon footprint and develop its Spirit to Preserve environmental strategy. A major part of that strategy is to address climate change through the protection of the rainforest. We have made a $2 million commitment to the Amazonas Sustainable Foundation, and selected them as the NGO [non-governmental organization] partner to help protect the 1.4 million-acre Juma Reserve in the state of Amazonas, Brazil. Two initiatives—the "Spirit to Preserve the Rainforest" meetings promotion, and the "Green Your Marriott Hotel Stay for $1/Day" program—are helping to raise funds for Juma through group and individual contributions. [For more information, visit marriott.com/spirittopreserve.]

Q: Marriott International currently has over 3,000 sales and event associates who are certified green planners. What are the criteria for these certifications, and is Marriott mandating that its sales teams hold these qualifications?

A: To achieve certification, a sales and an event manager must score 90 percent on the internal Marriott certification website. The certification is divided up into three key areas: operations, planning/sales, and general terms used in the industry. Because of the interest in our companies green initiatives, we have also certified chefs, restaurant associates, and hotel operations associates.

Q: In regards to purchasing policy, has Marriott made an effort to purchase goods locally?

A: We do encourage hotels to purchase products locally as long as they meet high quality standards.

Q: How has Marriott marketed its green meetings to potential clientele? Are consumers actively seeking out companies that comply with green standards?

A: We have heard from our sales managers that more companies are asking for information on what our hotels are doing regarding green meetings and/or green initiatives in general. As a brand standard, all North American Marriott hotels are required to include on their individual hotel website a fact sheet of the green initiatives the hotel offers.

Q: What does Marriott consider the most important factor that clients are looking for in a green meeting or event?

A: Offering recycling programs, sustainable foods, linen-less tables, and web-based menus. Calculating the carbon footprint of a meeting.

Chapter Appendix E:

Green Meeting Pioneers: Kimpton Hotels and Restaurants

Interview with Steve Pinetti,
Senior Vice President of Sales and Marketing

Q: Kimpton's Green Meeting initiatives include implementing twelve simple eco-friendly practices nationwide. Can you please describe the most difficult action to implement, and how you have countered those challenges?

A: There are three areas that we find are difficult to implement long-term:

1. "Eliminate plastic or wood stir sticks for coffee stations by using only reusable teaspoons." We started with teaspoons, but as soon as they ran low, the staff kept reverting back to straws and stir sticks. The fix was to gain support and momentum from the entire team (catering managers, banquet managers, and hourly staff as enforcers of the standard) and explain *why* we are doing it. Then we purchased more teaspoons.

2. "A recycled paper container will be placed in each meeting room." To help the housemen, we placed it on the BEO as a standard setup item so the housemen do not forget it, and placed it on the meeting room checklist for when the conference/catering manager checks the room prior to the guests' arrival.

3. Believe it or not, trying to find the right recycling bins for the meeting rooms that work both aesthetically and functionally is a major challenge.

Q: Kimpton currently offers green meeting options at every one of its operating hotels. What do you consider to be Kimpton's greatest success or benefit since converting its meeting practices to comply with sustainable goals?

A: We have reduced the amount of waste and paper from banquets; and we have had great comments from our guests (social and corporate), which have led to referrals and new business. It has also resulted in continuing to help drive the point home for our employees that we are committed to our EarthCare practices on every level of our operation.

Q: Many people believe in the common misconception that "going green" will reduce customer satisfaction. When working with Kimpton's various guest and clients, what are the typical reactions when they are notified of the green initiatives?

A: The exact opposite for green meetings; the guests are thrilled and really appreciate that we are making decisions that help the environment. It is an educational process on our part. When we promote the green meeting concept, we point out what we are doing and why; and more importantly that we can add to a meeting's success versus creating a negative perception.

Q: Has Kimpton acquired new business because of sustainable meeting practices? If so, approximately how much new business has been added?

A: Yes, we estimate that approximately ten percent of our new meeting business is a result of those bookings, based on the shared value of wanting to do something to support green efforts. We know that approximately eighteen percent of our individual guests choose Kimpton Hotels due to our overall EarthCare program and practices.

Q: How has Kimpton marketed its green meetings to potential clientele?

A: We have collateral in an electronic form that we e-mail our clients; information on our complete programs are on local hotel websites and on the Kimpton website; also many managers (all departments, not just sales) have information on their [e-mail] signature lines indicating awards or certifications that they are proud to share. Additionally, we search the local *Business Times* for "green-orientated" organizations that we currently do not do business with, that seemingly would align with our program.

Q: What do you consider Kimpton's most creative sustainable solution when dealing with green meetings? What was the reaction of the meeting attendees?

A: The most creative initiative was creating our signature EarthCare meeting; within the EarthCare concept is incorporated all of our green meeting elements. The attendees loved the elements and it enhances the meeting. We have more sustainable solutions to come.

Q: Do you offer any client incentives to conduct their meetings in a green manner? If so, what do these incentives include, and have they proven successful in securing meeting business?

A: We have found that an actual incentive is not that necessary. The simple fact that we are paying attention to the negative impact a meeting can have, and that we are doing something to offset that impact is, in most cases, enough. There are planners who do want to see more, and in this regard we are working on a carbon offset program.

Q: What does Kimpton consider the most important factor that clients are looking for in a green meeting or event? How did Kimpton identify this main demand generator?

A: In promoting our green meetings program, the clients to which this program was important told us that they wanted to see us incorporate products and practices that resulted in the reduction of waste, reducing the amount of paper (saving trees), and going to recycled paper options whenever possible.

16

A Guide to Measuring Sustainability

By Eric Ricaurte

*A graduate of Cornell University's School of Hotel Administration and an M.S. in Tourism Management candidate at New York University, **Eric Ricaurte** has eleven years of experience in tourism and sustainable development work within hospitality. He began his career managing a rainforest lodge and tour operation in Costa Rica and winning a student research finalist award in 2001 for his paper titled "Carbon Sequestration, Credit Trading and Offsetting, and Their Relation to Travel and Tourism." Since then, Mr. Ricaurte has consulted for hotel properties; hotel companies; hospitality vendors; tourism operators, attractions, and complexes; and tourism boards and tourism clusters over the past six years.*

Mr. Ricaurte's current consulting practice, Greenview LLC, based in New York City, helps hotels and hotel companies produce sustainability reports and address related issues of metrics and measurement. He is actively involved as a speaker, organizer, and writer in the topic of sustainability measurement within the hotel industry. He has also worked as a tourism consultant since 2005, specializing in the development, implementation, and optimization of small and mid-scale tourism attractions, activities, and accommodations in Latin America, with an emphasis on authentic natural and cultural heritage. Mr. Ricaurte has also worked on other diverse projects, including facilitating tourism cluster and regional development initiatives in Brazil. Prior to consulting, he managed operations and served on committees for the privately operated nature parks in the Mexican Caribbean, after managing lodges in Costa Rica and working in resorts in Spain, Brazil, and the United States.

Mr. Ricaurte also provides services through the partner and affiliate organizations of EnviRelation, La Paz Group, and Cayuga Hospitality Advisors. With EnviRelation, he produced the first hotel property report on sustainability for the Global Reporting Initiative in 2008 and the first hotel adaptation of the Global Sustainable Tourism Criteria in 2009.

SUSTAINABLE DEVELOPMENT CAN BE CONSIDERED a journey traveled by humanity since the dawn of civilization, with considerable evolution in its concepts and methods since its most noteworthy and concise conceptualization in "Our Common Future," the groundbreaking 1987 report by the United Nations' World Commission on Environment and Development (also known as the Brundtland Commission).[1] The oft-quoted report defines sustainable development as that which "meets the needs of the present without compromising the ability of future generations to meet their own needs."[2] Measurement of sustainability is one of the key achievements and requirements of this journey.

The concept of sustainability, refined by John Elkingington to encompass the "triple bottom line" (a phrase he coined in 1998), is supported by three essential pillars: people, planet, and profit. This concept has been further refined, developed, and codified over recent years. More recently, the idea of "natural capital"[3] was introduced to the business world. The concepts of sustainable development and natural capital have evolved into the concept of ecosystem services, which are processes and measurable benefits that people and business obtain from ecosystems.[4] Carbon is now traded on markets, and non-financial performance indicators are becoming more commonplace in many areas of the world. The societal interdependence with the natural environment is more easily grasped and understood when it is translated into measurable indicators related to our activities in both the personal and business realms; this kind of measurement is essential to justify the value of sustainable development, at least from a business perspective.

As in other industries, the lodging industry has suffered from the lack of a common definition of sustainability, varying impacts on multiple stakeholders associated with a project, and the complexity of the process of integrating sustainability into business activities. Yet, as frameworks and standards for sustainability have emerged, related measurements are increasingly required. Clients increasingly utilize these kinds of measurements when making business decisions, and hotel companies are now incorporating sustainability executives into their organization charts. Introducing a formal sustainability measurement system at the property level is now an initiative that hoteliers cannot overlook.

The first step to measuring sustainability is to understand what sustainability means and why it should be measured; the answers to these questions ultimately depend on the property's stakeholders. Measuring sustainability requires asking the following questions:

- Why measure sustainability?
- Who are the property's stakeholders?
- What do they consider important to measure?
- What does the property's management consider important to measure?
- What current issues are most urgent at a regional, national, and global level, which must be addressed regardless of their weights with stakeholders?

Performing this exercise will aid greatly in understanding each hotel's journey toward sustainability. The answers to these questions will also shed light on two key equations in measuring sustainability:

$$Sustainability = People + Planet + Profit$$

and

$$Green \neq Sustainable$$

After the question "Why measure?" follows the question "What do we measure?" Many current frameworks today help take the guesswork out of what to measure. Certification programs such as LEED, Green Seal, and Green Key specifically outline necessary items to be measured, and the metrics that correspond to those items, as part of their certification. The Environmental Protection Agency's Portfolio Manager (an online, secure, interactive energy management tool) offers a benchmarking system and a platform for tracking utilities performance and consumption. Guidelines and criteria such as AH&LA's Green Guidelines and the Global Sustainable Tourism Criteria (GSTC) offer standards, practices, and practical as well as theoretical insight as to the most salient sustainability issues. Reporting frameworks such as the Carbon Disclosure Project (CDP) and the Global Reporting Initiative (GRI) offer a wealth of perspective on approaching sustainability issues, disclosing performance and strategy, and measuring performance.

However, certification programs are in the business of certification, not measurement. Criteria and guidelines in certification programs indicate specific measurement items, but do not contain requirements that all actions within the criteria or guidelines should be collectively tracked and monitored over time. Reporting frameworks imply continual tracking, but are either very broad or very specific, and do not speak to the specific needs of hotel operations. No single sustainability performance measurement system specifically designed for hotel operations is broadly accepted or adopted by hotel companies and recognized by guests.

This chapter will discuss the three pillars of sustainability: environmental, social, and economic. It will examine how sustainability performance is measured and tracked in hotel operations, providing solutions that will enable operations staff to tackle the task of measurement independently.

Measuring the Environmental Pillar of Sustainability

In the environmental category of sustainability, measurement begins by examining the hotel's related policies, programs, procedures, and drivers, which fall under the umbrella of processes. Processes are the building blocks affecting the hotel's consumption. Using this framework, environmental sustainability measurement can be divided into three main categories:

1. Processes
2. Consumption
3. Impacts

Each category, and the items within each category, will have their own set of metrics and performance indicators, as outlined in the following three sections.

Measuring Processes

Processes—the activities of operating a hotel—are the key to ensuring long-term sustainability performance. "There's no point in building an efficient hotel if nobody knows how to run it efficiently," David Jerome, senior vice president of corporate responsibility at InterContinental Hotels Group, said to me. Process evaluation begins with measuring a property's existing policies and programs. Within each policy and program are various procedures and drivers. Measuring these reveals the performance metrics associated with carrying out the policies and programs in time-specific and ongoing bases. These metrics are expressed in integer values and percentages.

As part of its energy efficiency policy, a property may have a program to phase out all its incandescent light bulbs, replacing them with compact fluorescent bulbs as necessary. Existence of the program can be tracked, and the percentage of bulbs converted to CFLs tracked as well, to monitor progress. Common examples and quantification of sustainability policies and programs are outlined in Exhibit 1.

Though processes are the fundamental building blocks for measurement, they ultimately represent the means to an end of mitigating impacts. We will address the measurement of processes in the next two sections.

Measuring Consumption

Although processes appear more commonly in current sustainability measurement initiatives, consumption is the most understood and quantifiable category, with the most data readily available at a property level. The three main components of consumption measured in hotel operations are energy, waste, and water.

Energy. The five most common sources of energy usage consist of electricity, natural gas, steam, fuel oil, and liquid propane gas. While units of measurement differ for each, the figures should be normalized and tracked over time. "Normalizing" means transforming data into comparable units so that it can be compared with other data measured on a different scale. The amounts of energy or energy-producing substances measured may be units of space (per unit of square footage or per occupied room), consumption of energy (British Thermal Units, or BTUs), or standardized data from utility providers (cycles). It is necessary to normalize this data in order to allow "apples to apples" comparisons. Converting energy measures into the standard of BTUs is preferable, because BTU is an internationally recognized measure of energy consumed (see Exhibit 2).

Electricity. Electricity is measured in consumption of kilowatt hours, or kWh. Data from a utility provider can be obtained through invoices and consumption history reports. If a property generates electricity on-site through a generator or renewable energy source such as solar panels or wind turbines, then the amount of electricity in kWh should be quantified in each source and tracked separately within the general category of electricity. In the case of electricity generation from fuel burning, the amount of fuel burned should be tracked.

Other fuels. Fuel consumption may be invoiced in values such as cubic feet, gallons, pounds, or Therms. Converting, or normalizing, all tracked energy consumption to BTUs will help enable portfolio comparisons. It is important to obtain specific data from equipment and fuel sources, which will help in quantifying carbon as well as making decisions. For example, the efficiency of the boiler should be noted, and the type of fuel oil used (#1 through #6).

Waste. Two key data factors are paramount for tracking waste measurement: category and weight. Waste must be tracked consistently by each available waste category as it is disposed. This allows for monitoring the progress that specific operational or purchasing actions have on the waste stream, and to identify reductions and diversion rates accurately. In many cases, landfilled and diverted waste (that which is recycled, composted, or destined for third-party reuse) is not invoiced in tonnage, nor are data furnished in weight. Not only does this inhibit

Exhibit 1 **Common Examples of Sustainability Process Measurement**

Policies and Programs	Procedures and Drivers	Value
Existence of a recycling program		Yes/No
	Number of waste items recyclable	Number
	Number of recycling bins	Number
Existence of a green committee		Yes/No
	Number of green committee meetings	Number
	Number of ideas generated/researched/implemented	Number
Linen/towel reuse program		Yes/No
	Percentage of guests who participate in the program	Percentage
Sustainability training policy		Yes/No
	Number of employees receiving training	Number
	Number of hours per employee of sustainability training	Number
Sustainable purchasing policy		Yes/No
	Percentage of items purchased that adhere to policy standards	Percentage
	Number of times policy was revised	Number
	Number of vendors in compliance with policy	Number
	Percentage of vendors in compliance with policy	Percentage
Vendor no-idling policy in loading docks		Yes/No
Energy efficiency and renewable energy policy		Yes/No
	Percentage of energy derived from renewable sources	Percentage
	Installation of occupancy sensors, digital thermostats, low-flow bathroom equipment	Yes/No
	Percentage installation of occupancy sensors, digital thermostats, low-flow bathroom equipment	Percentage
	Installation of energy-efficient lighting	Yes/No
	Percentage installation of energy-efficient lighting	Percentage
Monitoring Policy		Yes/No
	Monitoring of energy, waste, and water	Yes/No

Source: American Hotel & Lodging Association website.

proper measurement of efficiency initiatives, but waste reduction or diversion efforts will not translate into cost savings. Waste should be documented in the metric of weight whenever possible.

Waste categorization. The EPA's Waste Reduction Model tool (WARM), which quantifies the lifecycle impacts of reduction and diversion, groups thirty-four different waste categories, including mixed waste categories. (This tool can

Exhibit 2   Energy Conversion Metrics

Energy Source	Conversion to BTUs	Conversion from BTUs
Electricity	3412 BTUs per kWh	.000293083kWh per BTU
Natural Gas	100,000 BTUs per Therm	.00001Therm per BTU
	1031BTUs per Cubic Foot	0.000969932 Cubic Foot per BTU
Liquid Propane	95,500 BTUs per gallon	1.04712E-05 Gallon per BTU
Fuel Oil	138,700 BTUs per gallon	7.20981E-06 Gallon per BTU
Steam	1,000 BTUs per pound of steam	.001 pounds per BTU

Source: U.S. Department of the Interior Buildings and Facilities Energy Management and Water Conservation Plan, Attachment 2, BTU Conversion Table, www.doi.gov/pam/eneratt2.html.

be found at www.epa.gov/climatechange/wycd/waste /calculators/Warm_home. html.) Most common categories of routinely disposed waste in hotel operations include the following:

- Aluminum cans
- Steel cans
- Glass
- Food scraps
- Corrugated cardboard

    Similar waste items are grouped into mixed categories:

- Mixed office paper
- Mixed plastics
- Mixed (commingled) recyclables
- Mixed organics

    Some recycling programs, termed single-stream recycling programs, allow for commingling among all diverted categories.

    Non-routine waste categories in hotel operations include the following:

- Computers
- Phone books
- Carpet
- Batteries

    Waste that is not separated or diverted is grouped into a category based on its end grouping, called Municipal Solid Waste (MSW).

    Measuring waste weights. Waste should be measured and tracked in tonnage. In order to obtain weights from waste data, the following options exist, in order of precision:

1. Obtain weights from monthly invoices or by contacting the hauler for the data.

2. Weigh each waste container at its moment of disposal or loading into aggregate containers.

3. Perform a volume-to-weight conversion based on the average densities of waste per type; this can be done if waste data cannot be obtained in weight from the supplier, nor physically measured routinely at the property. An explanation of this conversion can be found in Appendix A.

Waste stream composition. Measuring the composition of the waste stream (volume and percentage of each type of waste) can provide meaningful insight into opportunities for reducing and diverting waste. Given the grouping of diverted waste and the commonly low diversion rates, however, it is difficult to measure the composition of the waste stream on a continuous basis. The solution is a periodic analysis of the ratio of each individual type of waste within the waste stream. This is done through waste auditing, or physical inspection of waste, colloquially referred to as "dumpster diving." This can be performed for non-diverted waste as well as mixed or commingled recyclables. Waste auditing also enables internal benchmark references for performing volume-to-weight conversions.

Tracking waste. Waste is tracked in weight and per category, as just noted. Consistently measured waste categories mean more precise tracking, and allow for goal-setting. Routinely disposed waste such as plastics, glass, paper, and food scraps are effectively tracked on a monthly basis. Non-routine waste such as batteries, computers, and phone books can be tracked annually, then averaged over monthly periods, allowing for smoothing based on factors such as occupancy or seasonality.

Monthly and yearly performance indicators for waste consumption include:

- Aggregate waste in tonnage per waste category
- Percentage composition of waste categories within the commingled waste stream
- Categorized waste weight per cover
- Categorized waste weight per occupied room

While these indicators will help hotel managers understand the relationship between the waste stream and the operation, two important performance indicators are keys to understanding a hotel's overall performance of waste management: the diversion rate and the variation of waste consumption, referred to as waste reduction.

Diversion rate. The diversion rate of waste is the percentage of the waste stream that is diverted from a landfill:

$$\sum Diverted\ Waste\ +\ \sum Undiverted\ Waste\ =\ Total\ Waste$$
$$\sum Diverted\ Waste\ +\ Total\ Waste\ =\ Diversion\ Rate$$

For example, suppose that a hotel's monthly waste tonnage is the following:

- 2.5 tons of corrugated cardboard

- 3 tons of food scraps

- 7 tons of commingled recyclables

- 15 tons of landfilled trash waste

Therefore:

$$2.5 + 3 + 7 = 12.5 \text{ tons of diverted waste}$$

$$12.5 + 15 = 27.5 \text{ tons of total waste}$$

$$12.5 / 27.5 = 45.5\% \text{ diversion rate}$$

Waste reduction. The waste reduction rate is the percentage of total waste and waste per category that has been reduced, in aggregate and normalized figures, between two periods:

$$\left[\sum \textit{Waste Period 1} - \sum \textit{Waste Period 2} \right] \div \sum \textit{Waste Period 2} = \textit{Waste Variation}$$

When this value is negative, it results in waste reduction. An overarching measurable and trackable waste goal is to reduce the tonnage of non-diverted waste. This can be achieved by a combined function of increasing waste reduction (reducing the total amount of waste generated whether diverted or not) and increasing the overall diversion rate.

Continuing with the same hotel example, let's assume that for the following month, the waste tonnage figures were:

- 4 tons of food scraps

- 8 tons of commingled recyclables

- 10 tons of landfilled trash waste

$$\text{Total waste} = 25 \text{ tons}$$

$$(25 - 27.5) \div 27.5 = 9.1 \text{ percent total waste reduction}$$

Although the diverted waste increased, the diversion rate increased to 60 percent. Non-diverted waste was reduced by 33 percent. These figures do not take into account occupancy levels, or number of covers, or events, so normalizing them will help evaluate performance.

Water. Water consumption is the simplest to measure, with a few considerations:

- Measure water withdrawal, adjusting for any cooling tower deductions that reduce the overall consumption figures from any utility invoices.

- Measure water in gallons, converting from cubic feet when necessary.

- In operations that use bottled water, add this consumption to total water consumption.

Specified Consumption. Departments or units within a hotel's operation may have their consumption measured specifically in addition to the total consumption. The most common example of this is linen and towel laundry, either within a facility or outsourced. This enables tracking the benefits of towel and linen reuse programs, for example by routinely measuring the total weight of linen and measuring the heat, water, and electricity usage from washing and drying. This can be performed through sub-metering or logging consumption within the specific laundry facility. If sub-metering is not available, then calculations can be performed based on tallying the number of uses of each machine, then multiplying each by the energy and water used during each use.

Ongoing consumables. Reductions and alternative sourcing of many products consumed within a property's operation may be measured separately, since they will not be reflected accurately in the hotel's waste stream. Common types of ongoing consumables measurement may include:

- Cleaning supplies
- Guestroom amenities
- Food and beverage Ingredients
- Packaging
- Office paper
- Disposable flatware and utensils

Sustainability-related labels or characteristics of products, and their significance, vary widely. These depend on the context of the supply category as analyzed through lifecycle management in the following section. Examples include:

- Organic
- Local (sourced within the community or within a given geographic boundary)
- Biodegradable
- Non-toxic
- Cage free or free range
- Fair trade
- Recycled content
- FSC certified
- Energy efficient
- No or low VOCs

Three steps are important in evaluating sustainability labeling. First, it is important to understand and document the definition and significance of the label provided. Recycled content, for example, may be post-consumer or pre-consumer, and the term "organic" may have varying meanings, depending on the product. Labels for non-toxic cleaning supplies vary as well. Some products may carry Green Seal certification; some may not carry certified labeling, but may be free of certain chemicals or compounds, such as phosphates. By understanding these variances, hotels can source products that fall within the same category for measurement.

Second, the unit of measurement must be consistent and transparent in order to determine the percentage of supplies that fall within a measured category. No standard exists for unit of measurement, but common metrics are volume, weight, and dollar value. In the case of cleaning supplies, the percentage of total liquid volume in gallons is the denominator:

$$\Sigma non-toxicVgallons \div Total\ Gallons = \%\ non\text{-}toxicgallons$$

If a hotel uses a percentage measurement of Green Seal–certified liquid cleaning product, the data for a period can be calculated as follows:

- 300 gallons of Green Seal products

- 500 gallons of non-Green Seal products

$$300 + 500 = 800$$

$$300 \div 800 = 37.5\%\ \text{of liquid cleaning supply volume is Green Seal certified}$$

Liquid cleaning supplies inevitably vary in their container size. All volumes should be converted to gallons in order to arrive at the total volume of cleaning supplies. Purchase orders, invoices, and internal tally sheets can all be used to verify amounts used; they can also provide crosschecks for accuracy when compared.

Third, measurement of supplies used should be defined, and supplies used should be consistently measured, either when consumed or when purchased. How this is done will depend on the availability and feasibility for collecting data, given available information and controls. Understanding, defining, and consistently measuring supply purchases within the same measurement criteria will enable consistent tracking.

Goal-setting for goods within specific measurement criteria may also vary. Whereas an appropriate goal for durable goods is the percentage of durable goods that fall within the criteria, a target can be developed for reducing the volume of cleaning supplies that do not fall within the criteria, rather than increasing the percentage of non-toxic cleaning supplies used in order to address and monitor consumption at the same time.

Measuring Environmental Impacts

All processes and their related resource consumption in hotel operations have some form of environmental impact. These impacts are often the least understood, and measuring them and the environmental benefits from different choices in sourcing can be difficult and imprecise. But as technology, data collection and processing techniques, and awareness of environmental issues and impacts converge, we are better able to understand and track the specific sources of negative anthropogenic (related to human activity) environmental impacts throughout the entire lifecycle of a product or service. Furthermore, certain impacts may now be quantified across industries.

Common anthropogenic impact categories and associated endpoints (indications of the impacts) include:[5]

- *Climate change*—polar melt, soil moisture loss, longer seasons, forest loss/change, and change in wind and ocean patterns.

- *Stratospheric ozone depletion*—increased ultraviolet radiation.

- *Acidification*—building corrosion, water body acidification, vegetation effects, and soil effects.

- *Eutrophication*—nutrients (phosphorous and nitrogen) enter water bodies, such as lakes, estuaries and slow-moving streams, causing excessive plant growth and oxygen depletion.

- *Photochemical smog*—decreased visibility, eye irritation, respiratory tract and lung irritation, and vegetation damage.

- *Terrestrial toxicity*—decreased production and biodiversity, and decreased wildlife for hunting or viewing.

- *Aquatic toxicity*—decreased aquatic plant and insect production and biodiversity, and decreased commercial or recreational fishing.

- *Human health*—increased morbidity and mortality.

- *Resource depletion*—decreased resources for future generations.

- *Land use*—loss of terrestrial habitat for wildlife and decreased landfill space.

- *Water use*—loss of available water from groundwater and surface water sources.

Quantitative impact indicators are made possible when characterized conversion factors exist. Two examples are illustrated in Exhibit 3. As you can see, climate change is only one negative anthropogenic impact, and hotel operations have negative impacts in addition to climate change.

Quantifying Impacts. As a primary step to measurement of environmental impacts, consumption from ongoing consumable goods, durable goods, and utilities can be quantitatively linked to their impacts. To quantify environmental impacts from consumption, the following steps can be taken:

1. Identify, itemize, and measure all of the operational consumption (waste, energy, water, or consumable goods) within the scope of measurement and appropriate methodology.

2. Determine the characterization factors for each unit of operational consumption.

3. Quantify the itemized consumption's impact by multiplying the units of consumption during the period by the characterization factor.

4. Sum the itemized values to arrive at the aggregate impact value.

5. Normalize the impact value.

Exhibit 3   Anthropogenic Impact Measures

Impact	Source	Conversion Unit	Example
Climate Change	Greenhouse gases	Global warming potential (GWP), based on the ratio of the warming caused by a substance to the warming caused by a similar mass of carbon dioxide*	1 gallon of gasoline burned = 19.4 lbs. of CO_2e released into atmosphere
Stratospheric Ozone Depletion	Ozone depleting substances	Ozone depletion potential (ODP), based on the ratio of the ozone impact of 1 unit of chemical substance mass compared to the same unit of mass of CFC-11 (ODP Tons)#	50 pounds of CFC-12 (fugitive emissions from a chiller) released into atmosphere = .2268 ODP Tons@

* U.S. Environmental Protection Agency, "Ozone Depletion Glossary," 2010; www.epa.gov/ozone/defns.html.

\# Millennium Development Goals Indicators, "Goal 7: Ensure Environmental Sustainability"; http://unstats.un.org/unsd/mdg/Metadata.aspx?IndicatorId=0&SeriesId=753.

@ U.S. Environmental Protection Agency, "Ozone Layer Depletion—Science," 2010; www.epa.gov/ozone/science/ods/classone.html.

An example in Appendix B shows how a sample hotel would quantify its carbon footprint from direct emissions sources. Once these impacts have been quantified, they may be tracked and compared over time or across a company portfolio. Part of these calculations can also be obtained and tracked via tools such as the EPA's Portfolio Manager by entering consumption data.

Benchmarking such impacts in hotel operations is difficult for two reasons. The first is a lack of standardized industry metrics. In the case of specific properties, data from minor sources such as refrigerants or fuel from restaurant propane tanks or lawn mowers may not have been considered. Nuances in hotel operations also cause calculations to vary. For example, hotels that outsource their linen and towel laundry services will have substantially less energy use and Scope 1 and 2 emissions; however, the environmental impacts of those services still exist. Definitions of facility amenities included in calculations also vary among hotels.

Second, the largest source of greenhouse gas (GHG) emissions in hotel operations is electricity usage. Emissions factors for electricity usage vary widely from region to region, depending on the source of fuel used, such as nuclear power or coal.

As measuring carbon footprints becomes more commonplace, this measurement will be utilized as a lens to evaluate operational performance. As more and more clients request per-room-night carbon footprint data, carbon footprint metrics will become more prevalent and agreed upon. (See Exhibit 4 for an explanation of a carbon footprint measurement tool.)

Other Impacts. Measurement of other impacts is becoming more widespread. One clear example of this is in addressing the issue of water scarcity, where water footprint research is advancing the capability of companies to calculate the water footprints of their products, services, and businesses. Data are becoming available, and in the near future water footprinting could be just as common as carbon footprinting.

Exhibit 4   Carbon Footprint Measurement Tool

Through EnviRelation and Greenview, we have developed a guideline that hotel properties may use for comparing the carbon footprints of hotel operations on a per-occupied-room basis. This methodology uses the metric of greenhouse gas emissions per occupied room (GEPOR), which accounts for all greenhouse gas emissions linked with all available guest experiences within the lodging operation. The calculation totals the carbon footprint of a night's stay in order to quantify emissions resulting from the following operational sources:

- Burning of fuels directly on-site for heating or cooking
- Fuel usage for on-site electricity generation (whether primary or backup)
- Fuel usage for property-operated vehicles (shuttles, vans, boats)
- Fugitive emissions derived from replacement of coolant from refrigeration equipment or chillers
- Corresponding emissions produced from electricity generation, as purchased from a utility provider
- Corresponding emissions from steam or heat generation, as purchased from a utility provider
- Emissions from the fuel usage from the transportation of employee commutes to and from work, regardless of their mode of transportation
- Emissions from fuel usage resulting from air travel of property-level employees
- Emissions from the generation and disposal of solid waste

Emissions from the energy and transportation fuel consumed from linen and towel laundry are integrated, regardless of the organization that financially controls the laundry facilities. Also, function space and outlets such as restaurants, gift shops, fitness centers, and spas are included within these criteria.

GEPOR metrics are produced in annual, monthly, and quarterly figures, and can be compared across properties, segments, and portfolios. Direct versus indirect emissions can be separated, and function space can be separated for evaluation.

Day-to-day purchasing decisions can be affected when weighing impacts. For example, when faced with a choice, is it better for a property to use 100-percent post-consumer recycled paper, FSC certified paper, non-tree paper, or chlorine-free paper? Questions about these and other indirect impacts are not easily answered; they can be tackled by the property's green team. In order to analyze these issues, a framework of lifecycle assessments can be applied by hotels.

Lifecycle assessment (LCA) is defined as "a tool to assess the potential environmental impacts of products, systems, or services at all stages in their lifecycle."[6] LCA methodology seeks to identify and quantify environmental impacts through data collection, analysis, and interpretation. A product's life cycle is divided into four stages:

- Raw materials acquisition
- Manufacturing

Exhibit 5   Impact Analysis for Paper Reduction Options in a Hotel

| Action | Life Cycle Stage | | | |
	Raw Materials	Manufacturing	Use	Waste
Paperless	Reduced consumption of paper and ink raw materials	Reduced papermaking process inputs Reduced transportation inputs/outputs	Less printer maintenance Less need for capacity to store/use	Reduced waste
50% Reduced Printed Content	Reduced consumption of paper and ink raw materials	Reduced papermaking process inputs Reduced transportation inputs/outputs	Less printer maintenance Less need for capacity to store/use	Reduced waste
Locally Sourced Paper	No	Reduced transportation (and energy for transportation)	No	No
Recycled Content	Reduced papermaking resource material inputs	Reduced pulp (in this scope)	No	No
Certified Paper	Sustainable resource use	Sustainable papermaking process	No	No
Organic Ink	Less unsustainable resource use	(?)	(Is the efficiency the same?)	Less toxic material in waste stream
Recycling Paper Waste	Reduced resource extraction	(increased process inputs)	No	Reduced landfill waste
Recycling Ink Cartridges	Reduced cartridge materials	Reduced manufacturing inputs	No	Reduced landfill size and associated emissions/deposits
Offsetting via Tree Planting	No	No	No	No

(continued next page)

- Use/reuse/maintenance

- Recycle/waste management

The responsibility for performing a lifecycle assessment ultimately falls on the product's manufacturer, not its user. But from a hotel's perspective, a simplified approach is to map all the potential environmental initiatives and integrate this information into an overall cost/benefit analysis. This approach can be quantitative or qualitative, as data are available. Mapping will list all practices or products, and compare their impacts over their lifecycles. Their impacts can then be weighed and compared with their potential costs. Exhibit 5 illustrates the possible initiatives available to a hotel when addressing paper use within its sustainability program.

The blank cells in Exhibit 5 and those with a question mark represent areas where the hotel's green team is unsure about the environmental impacts, and may choose to investigate further as part of its action plan. These tables can be further developed to include specific quantifiable impacts and changes in costs based on hotel data. For example, going paperless in departments versus a target to reduce

Exhibit 5 *(continued)*

Action	Life Cycle Impacts				Associated Costs
	Climate Change	**Water Use**	**Resource Depletion**	**Land Use**	
Paperless	Lower Emissions	Less water consumption	Less resource use	Less landfilling	Lower costs
50% Reduced Printed Content	Lower emissions	Less water consumption	Less resource use	Less landfilling	Lower costs
Locally Sourced Paper	Lower emissions	Less water consumption			Increased costs
Recycled Content	Lower emissions	Potentially increased	Less resource use	Less landfilling	Increased costs
Certified Paper	Lower emissions (when reducing deforestation and degradation)	Fewer threats	Less resource use		Increased costs
Organic Ink	Less fossil fuel used	?	Less resource use	?	Increased costs
Recycling Paper Waste	Lower emissions	?	Less resource use	Less landfilling	No change
Recycling Ink Cartridges	Lower emissions	?	Less resource use	Less landfilling	Lower costs
Offsetting via Tree Planting	More carbon sequestration	?	(reducing global depletion)	?	Increased costs

paper by 50 percent will have the same effects, but to different degrees. Boundaries may also be set for specific criteria (i.e., "local" meaning manufactured within the state versus within the county). This LCM application, however, is not an equation for deriving the specific return, but rather a springboard for discussion and exploration of impacts. The exploration will help hotel green teams understand the operation's relationship to, and impact on, the environment. Although the environmental impacts may not be characterized and quantifiable, the consumption may be measured, and better-informed decisions can be made once the impacts and benefits are understood.

Measuring the Social Pillar of Sustainability

The measurement of the social dimension of sustainability within hotel operations is not as clearly defined, because of less standardization in performance measurement, and diverse, location-specific attributes of hotels. Although less structured in measurement, the people-intensive nature of the business makes social sustainability a vital component of sustainable development for hotels.

The Global Reporting Initiative closely follows the triple bottom line approach for its overall framework. It divides social aspects into four categories of performance indicators:[7]

- Labor practices
- Human rights
- Society
- Product responsibility

Labor Practices

Labor practices involve aspects of staffing, training, and compensation. Possible measurements include:

- Hours of training and professional development
- Diversity or local hiring percentages
- Salary ratios and comparisons of minimum wage and gender
- Employee health and safety, including wellness initiatives
- Employee satisfaction

Human Rights

The human rights category involves aspects of the rights of communities and groups, with potential indicators that include:

- Policies against discrimination
- Policies against child labor
- Policies against sexual exploitation
- Policies allowing freedom of association

Society

The society category includes the property's interaction with local governments and society's influence on policy. Potential indicators include anti-corruption policies and procedures.

Product Responsibility

Product responsibility involves aspects of health and safety attributes of products; in the case of hotels, hotel products include guestrooms, food and beverage products, facility amenities, guest satisfaction, and responsible product marketing and communication efforts. More information on the performance indicators for this category put forth by the Global Reporting Initiative can be found at www.globalreporting.org.

While the GRI performance indicators address key issues at corporate levels, they do not address the context of local communities within hotel operations. The Global Sustainable Tourism Criteria (GSTC) offer guidelines for tourism-related businesses, including hotels. These criteria offer several measurement possibilities for impacts on local communities, including the following:

- Employment of local residents

- Local sourcing of supplies and hiring of local vendors

- Operational impact on local energy, water, and sanitation

- Incorporated elements of local heritage into operations and design

- Contributions to local heritage

- Use of native plant species

- Interactions with wildlife

- Support of local biodiversity conservation

More information on the performance indicators put forth by the GSTC for this category can be found at www.sustainabletourismcriteria.org.

Social performance by no means limits itself to these frameworks; it will depend on the context of the property within the community. Social performance measurement often overlaps among these categories, and between the other two sustainability pillars of the environment and economics. For example, employee commuting initiatives that encourage the use of public transportation, walking, and bicycling involve the environmental benefits of reduced pollution and GHG emissions; and social benefits such as increased employee health from exercise and lower stress from reduced traffic congestion. These benefits can be analyzed against impacts on operational costs.

As with environmental sustainability metrics, social performance metrics can be developed beyond yes/no checklists. Examples of initiatives and performance measurement include the following:

- Number and value of partnerships with local organizations

- Metrics of employee wellness, including exercise programs, health indicators, smoking and obesity program performance

- Number of community service volunteer hours through employee programs

Measuring the Economic Pillar of Sustainability ──────

On a basic level, economic metrics of sustainability represent the financial effects of programs, policies, processes, and consumption. When analyzed against environmental and social performance indicators, economic metrics can provide insight into program effectiveness. On a deeper level, economic sustainability can include the economic impacts of hotel operations generated within the community.

Waste diversion and reduction programs can be tracked alongside the cost of waste to identify correlations. Monthly and yearly financial performance indicators for waste include:

- Categorized waste weight per revenue dollar

- Categorized waste hauling costs as a percentage of total costs

- Categorized waste hauling costs as a percentage of revenue

The cost of linen and towel laundry can be compared to linen-reuse-program participation rates. Moreover, tracking consumption is a valuable tool for identifying billing errors. Economic values can also be derived from in-kind sustainability actions. Just as public relations and marketing departments or agencies take into account the equitable dollar value of unpaid advertising, so can a hotel that donates its used linens or toiletries. In some cases, this can even become a charitable, tax-deductible donation.

The number of volunteer hours by staff can also be translated to an in-kind contribution, derived from equivalent hourly pay rates. An example of this can be seen at Marriott, which tracks the total number of employee volunteer hours each year. Results in 2009 totaled 320,987 hours during company-sponsored events. Multiplying this figure by an average wage of $20.25/hour, Marriott estimated the company's financial contribution to volunteerism at $6.5 million.[8]

The Practice of Measurement

In practice, measurement requires effective management. Tracking should be just as consistent as the data in question. Three steps to measuring sustainability can be followed to ensure its effectiveness: track, analyze and interpret, and communicate performance.

Track Performance

Whether the ultimate goal of a hotel is to obtain certification or to communicate positive environmental and social performance to stakeholders, the first step begins with tracking. Financial performance is tracked in straightforward terms, and the process of tracking performance is just as straightforward with sustainability indicators as with financial indicators: this year's results, last year's results, this year's budget, next year's budget, and the rolling twelve-month average, all broken down month-by-month in total, per-room, and percentage change figures.

Sustainability measurement often falls short by only qualitatively describing the company or property's initiatives at the present, without providing comparisons from previous years, and by omitting quantitatively formatted information that can be analyzed. In order to track performance in meaningful ways, the key step is to identify the team members responsible for collecting each piece of data. This must be clearly mapped out and communicated within the property, given the range of data that will come from many sources. Next, all indicators should be compiled and consolidated in the same place, which can range from a simple spreadsheet to an interfaced database. Designating a team member to be responsible for consolidating the information and producing any reports greatly facilitates this process.

Aside from the Excel spreadsheets and models developed internally, several tools exist to help track performance. The EPA Portfolio Manager is an online tool to track energy consumption. AH&LA members can access a hotel-specific program called GreenQuest through the American Hotel & Lodging Association's website.

Hotel companies are beginning to roll out tools to submit data and track performance. In 2009, InterContinental Hotels Group launched the Green Engage online software system to help hotels measure, manage, and report their energy, waste, and water consumption. In 2010 Hilton Hotels announced the Lightstay sustainability measurement system, which is designed to analyze and reduce the company's environmental impact throughout its portfolio.[9] These programs and platforms may not cover all initiatives within the scope of sustainability. Consolidation via spreadsheet may cover needs at a property level, but serious sustainability measurement with analytical capabilities for larger portfolios will require a more comprehensive platform, for which independent software solutions exist, some highly sophisticated and customizable. For example, SAS offers sustainability management software, a platform capable of integrating all possible data relating to sustainability and producing forecasts based on its business intelligence platforms.

Analyze and Interpret Performance

Theodore Levitt, an author and the former editor of the *Harvard Business Review*, said, "Data do not yield information except with the intervention of the mind. Information does not yield meaning except with the intervention of imagination."[10] This is true of sustainability data as well. All sustainability data and performance metrics must be analyzed and evaluated with the same scrutiny as financial and operational performance data. Just as a manager will identify and seek explanations for significant drops in RevPAR, he or she should also do so with spikes in energy consumption per room or any "no" checks on sustainability projects previously targeted for completion. Comparisons from two similar periods, and analysis of correlations between indicators such as laundry utility costs and guest participation in linen and towel reuse programs can offer interesting insights.

Finally, a broad analysis of a property's overall sustainability platform can be undertaken once all performance indicators are consolidated. This allows a hotel to evaluate its sustainability program and performance by returning to the initial questions and meanings from stakeholders, operations, and the sustainability context.

Communicate Performance

The final measurement step is to communicate the property's sustainability performance. This can be done in several forms, such as guestroom pamphlets, hotel website information, electronic and printed sustainability reports, and press releases.

Reporting sustainability performance is a powerful communication tool that offers a distinct advantage over certification in the context of communicating sustainability efforts. Whereas certification operates under the premise that the certification criteria determine a level of sustainability performance, and that the certification body judges and verifies that performance, disclosing sustainability performance publicly or even to limited stakeholder groups places the judgment and performance evaluation on the reader. This adds an element of transparency not attainable from certification. When communicating sustainability efforts, transparency is the key to credibility and avoiding implications of greenwashing. This can be achieved through full disclosure of methods, sources, and assumptions.

Communicating about sustainability offers several benefits. Specifically pertaining to measurement, successfully communicating sustainability performance has three practical applications and benefits, in requests for proposals (RFPs), guest engagement, and stakeholder satisfaction.

Requests for Proposals. Regardless of certification or standards adherence, a meeting planner seeking to quantify the impact of a meeting will prefer a venue that is able to provide precise purchasing, energy, water, and waste data in a timely fashion.

Guest Engagement. Effective measurement is a key to getting guests involved in property and company programs, which may range from towel reuse to charitable donations. For example, if a program is operated at the property for guests to make charitable donations, this can be converted into a matching program. First, guests should be made aware of the programs, such as supplies donations, community partnerships, renewable energy, and employee wellness. Next, measurements of these initiatives in per-guestroom metrics can be communicated to encourage guests to match with a donation to one of the programs. In addition, recycling, energy efficiency, and conservation efforts implemented at the hotel can be communicated to guests to facilitate any other changes in guest behavior related to sustainability, such as reusing linens and towels.

Stakeholder Satisfaction. A hotel has several stakeholders other than its guests and clients. Three main stakeholders are the hotel's employees, the community in which it is located, and its ownership.

For its employees, sustainability performance communication can boost employee morale, demonstrate successful results for which they are responsible, and encourage further action. For the local community, sustainability performance that is fully communicated in a timely way can demonstrate the hotel's commitment to the community effectively, transparently, and concisely. And finally, in the same way that financial reports offer insight to an entity's operation, the management, metrics, and achievements of a sustainability program are best communicated to owners and other stakeholders through data, performance indicators, and comparisons. The ability to report on sustainability performance itself demonstrates management competence.

Conclusion

Measuring and reporting sustainability can essentially be seen as an evolutionary development traced from corporate social responsibility (CSR) reporting and utility management that has existed for decades. It did not come out of nowhere, and it certainly will not be the same in ten years. While the prospect of businesses allocating truly equal weights to the three pillars of the triple bottom line remains distant, the current step toward this goal that we can take is to pursue sustainability performance measurement on par with that of financial measurement, and in this sense treat all pillars with equal managerial and analytical attention.

Finally, this chapter is dedicated to the hotel engineer. Facilities engineers have long held much of this valuable knowledge and information (in many cases, in greater detail than the author has provided), and the time has arrived for hotel operators to delve into this knowledge and information in order to satisfy emerging sustainability needs and make strategic decisions. Diverse stakeholders are asking for information that was once buried in obscure places without cross-functional application, and held by staff that did not interact with external clients routinely. Hotels need to react, and those that recognize this need as well as opportunity will be in a position to succeed. Ultimately, the facilities engineer will play an integral part in measuring sustainability; he or she should be engaged to understand the scope and relevance of the data and make important decisions where its interpretation is needed, rather than simply being asked to provide data or fill out forms for others to analyze.

Endnotes

1. "United Nations Report of the World Commission on Environment and Development: Our Common Future," accessed December 20, 2010; www.un-documents.net/wced-ocf.htm.

2. Chapter 2, "Towards Sustainable Development," from the "United Nations Report of the World Commission on Environment and Development: Our Common Future," accessed December 20, 2010; www.un-documents.net/ocf-02.htm.

3. John Elkington, *Cannibals with Forks: The Triple Bottom Line of 21st Century Business* (Oxford: Capstone, 1999).

4. Millennium Ecosystem Assessment, "Millennium Ecosystem Assessment Synthesis Reports," 2006; www.millenniumassessment.org/en/Products.Synthesis.aspx.

5. Scientific Applications International Corporation, "Life Cycle Assessment: Principles and Practice," Ohio: National Risk Management Research Laboratory, Office of Research and Development, U.S. Environmental Protection Agency, 2006.

6. Ibid.

7. The Global Reporting Initiative, "Sustainability Reporting Guidelines Version 3.0," 2006; www.globalreporting.org/ReportingFramework/G3Guidelines/.

8. "Marriott 2009 Corporate Sustainability Report"; www.marriott.com/corporateinfo/social-responsibility/default.mi.

9. Green Lodging News, "Hilton Worldwide Unveils LightStay Sustainability Measurement System," April 19, 2010; www.greenlodgingnews.com/content.aspx?id=4636.

10. Theodore Levitt, "The Globalization of Markets," *Harvard Business Review*, May/June 1983, pp. 92–102.

Appendix A:

Volume-to-Weight Conversion

In order to accurately track amounts of waste diverted from landfills, it is essential to normalize all amounts measured; that is, convert all measures into measures that can be compared on an equal basis. Volume is converted to weight (in this case, measured in tonnage). This conversion is performed in five steps:

1. Identify and calculate the volume (in cubic feet) of each waste receptacle that is pulled by the waste hauler or carted into the building waste stream. The volume in cubic feet of a container can be calculated by multiplying the width by the height by the depth for a rectangular receptacle, or the area by the depth for a cylindrical receptacle. Common examples:

    a. 1-yard bin: 27 cu. ft.
    b. 2-yard bin: 54 cu. ft.
    c. 96-gallon tote: 12.83 cu. ft.
    d. 64-gallon tote: 8.56 cu. ft.

2. In a collaboration among the hotel staff, waste hauler, and carting service (if applicable), the hotel should maintain a tally sheet for each waste disposal event. This sheet should contain a running tally each month of the number of pulls for each container for each type of waste, and a visual estimate of the percentage or fraction of volume occupied by each receptacle. Note that this estimate can sometimes exceed 100 percent; for example, in the case of cardboard, the material can easily be stacked in the bin at 120 percent of capacity.

3. At the end of each month, total the amount of waste hauled. The following is an example sheet for various items:

Date	Cardboard (1-yd bin)		Commingled Recyclables (64-gallon tote)		Waste (4-yard bin)		Food Waste (35 gallon drum)	
	#	Percentage Fill	#	Percentage Fill	#	Percentage Fill	#	Percentage Fill
10/10	1	80%	3	100%/100%/60%	1	80%	4	2@75%, 2@50%
10/12	1	100%	3	100%/100%/20%	1	50%	4	3@75%, 1@100%
10/15	1	120%	5	4@400%, 1@50%	1	110%	6	2@100%, 3@75%, 1@50%
10/18	1	75%	3	100%/100%/75%	1	90%	3	2@75%, 1@25%

4. For each type of waste, determine the density of each item in order to calculate its volume-to-weight percentage. This can be obtained from the following options:

    a. Weighing actual containers or material in the containers
    b. Requesting density estimates from the waste hauler

    c. Using benchmark figures from public waste data from state or federal institutions (EPA)

    d. Using benchmark figures from proprietary sources (LEED certification guidelines, for example)

These factors will vary depending on the state of the waste (loose bulk, compacted, crushed, etc.). Examples of common volume-to-weight average conversion factors include the following:

    a. Uncompacted corrugated cardboard: 100 pounds per cu. yd.

    b. Office paper: 42.35 pounds per 55-gallon drum

    c. Municipal solid waste (uncompacted): 150–300 pounds per cu. yd.

    d. Food waste: 412 pounds per 55-gallon drum

5. Multiply the tallies and their respective percentages by the volume-to-weight factors to arrive at the total estimated weights for each waste category (waste category $= n)$):

$$(ft.^3\, n) \; + \; \frac{Lbs.n}{ft.^3} \; = \; Lbs.n$$

    Note that the factors for mixed or commingled recyclables will vary depending on their composition. Therefore, obtaining density factors will require more data. The most accurate approach is to perform a waste stream audit to determine the composition of the commingled recyclable stream, and then perform a weighted average calculation with each volume-to-weight factor. Here is an example of a commingled glass, bottles, and metal cans calculation:

$$\left(\tfrac{Lbs.}{ft.^3}\, Glass\right) \times \left(\frac{lbs.glass}{lbs.total}\right) + \left(\tfrac{lbs.}{ft.^3}\, Bottles\right) \times \left(\frac{lbs.\, bottles}{lbs.total}\right) + \left(\tfrac{Lbs.}{ft.^3}\, Glass\right)$$

$$\times \left(\frac{lbs.glass}{lbs.total}\right) = \frac{Lbs.\; Commingled\; recyclables}{ft.^3}$$

Appendix B:

Quantification of a Hotel's Carbon Footprint

In order to accurately measure the carbon footprint of a hotel (or any business, entity, building, etc.), it is essential to measure the volume of carbon and other greenhouse gases (GHGs) produced, then convert them to internationally accepted, normalized figures. Metric Tonnes (tons) Carbon Dioxide Equivalent, or $mTCO_2e$, are the internationally accepted reporting standard for CO_2 emissions.

The method for quantifying the amount of fuel spent, or other means by which GHGs are produced, follows in these five steps:

1. Identify, itemize, and measure operational consumption:

    *   12,000 CCF of natural gas burned from the boiler for heating
    *   2,400 gallons of diesel fuel consumed from the airport shuttle
    *   50 gallons of diesel fuel consumed during the operation of the backup generator
    *   40 pounds of refrigerant (in this case R-22) used to refill guestroom air conditioning units (decentralized HVAC, assuming that no equipment was purchased or replaced during the period)
    *   1,700,000 kWh of electricity consumed from the grid

2. Determine characterization factors in order to convert to metric tons:

    *   Natural gas characterization factor of carbon dioxide equivalent (CO_2e) obtained from the World Resources Institute's tool, "GHG Emissions from Fuel Use in Facilities Version 3.0," (2007): .0051781 $mTCO_2e$ per CCF
    *   Diesel fuel characterization factor of CO_2e obtained from the EPA's Emission Facts:[1] 22.2 lbs CO_2e per gallon
    *   R-22 Refrigerant characterization factor of CO_2e obtained from published research:[2] 1,810 lbs CO_2e per pound of refrigerant
    *   Electricity conversion factors of CO_2e obtained from the EPA eGrid (example property located in Ohio):[3] 1537.82 lbs CO_2 per MWh (1.53782 per kWh)

3. Quantify itemized consumption impacts:

Item	Conversion
Natural gas	12,000 CCF $\times$ .0051781 $mTCO_2e$/CCF = 62.14 $mTCO_2e$
Diesel fuel	(2400 + 50) gallons $\times$ 22.2 lbs.CO_2e/gallon = 54390 lbs. CO_2e $\div$ 2205 lbs./metric ton = 24.667 $mTCO_2e$
R-22	40 lbs. $\times$ 1810 lbs. CO_2e/lb = 72400 lbs. CO_2e $\div$ 2205 lbs./metric ton = 32.834 $mTCO_2e$
Electricity	1,700,000 kWh $\times$ 1.53782 lbs./kWh = 2,614,294 lbs. CO_2e $\div$ 2205 lbs./metric ton = 1185.62 $mTCO_2e$

Note: 1 metric ton = 2,205 pounds.

4. Add the itemized impacts:

   $62.14 + 24.667 + 32.834 + 1,185.62 = 1,305.26 \text{ mTCO}_2e$

5. Normalize the impacts in terms of metric tonnage:

   Per Square Foot – the property's built square footage is 181,000 sq. ft.

   $1,305.26 \div 181,000 = 0.007211376 \text{ mTCO}_2e/Ft.2 \times 2,205 \text{ lbs./metric ton} = 15.9$ lbs CO_2e

   Per Occupied Room – the property's occupied room count was 63,875 during the year.

   $1,305.26 \text{ mTCO}_2e \div 63,875 \text{ occupied rooms} = 0.020435 \text{ mTCO}_2e \times 2,205 \text{ lbs./metric ton} = 40.87 \text{ lbs./occupied room}$

---

[1] U.S. Environmental Protection Agency, "Overview: Pollutants and Programs," EPA420-F-05-003, February 2005; www.epa.gov/otaq/climate/420f05003.htm.

[2] J. M. Calm and G. C. Hourahan, "Refrigerant Data Update," Heating/Piping/Air Conditioning Engineering, 79(1): 50–64, January 2007.

[3] U.S. Environmental Protection Agency, eGRID2007 Version 1.1 Year 2005: "GHG Annual Output Emission Rates," http://cfpub.epa.gov/egridweb/ghg.

Sustainable Hotel Operations: An Engineering Perspective

By Art Attaway and Robert Elliott

*After his discharge from the U.S. Army Special Forces in 1977, **Art Attaway** started his career in the hospitality industry as a corporate management trainee for Hyatt Hotels. During his seven years with Hyatt, he worked in New Orleans at the 1,200-room convention hotel attached to the Superdome, and helped open the Hyatt Regency Kansas City (733 rooms), Grand Hyatt New York (1,400 rooms), and Hyatt Regency Savannah (350 rooms), all in executive-level rooms management positions. He finished his Hyatt career at the 600-room Hyatt Regency Phoenix, and subsequently worked for a high-end Stouffer's resort and the premier Ritz-Carlton Buckhead. During these years he worked for a diverse set of owners, from Prudential Properties and Donald Trump to W. B. Johnson and local businessman/owner Merritt Dixon at the riverfront in Savannah, and saw several recessions and booms come and go.*

Leaving operational management to establish a service company for the hospitality industry, Mr. Attaway has spent the last twenty years providing goods and services to the industry, with a focus on renovation and newly opened properties. He has provided FF&E services, general contracting for renovations, granite countertop and natural stone tile supply and installation, and operates a nationwide business that restores natural stone. His newest focus is on the engineering and security departments of hotels, as he thinks these are the areas that have experienced and will continue to see for years to come the greatest changes in hotel operations. Most recently, Mr. Attaway has been assisting in the development of NAHLE—the National Association of Hotel & Lodging Engineers. He counts it a privilege to be asked to contribute to a book on sustainable development for the hospitality industry.

*With more than twenty-five years of combined experience in the commercial building and trade association industries, **Robert Elliott** currently serves as the Executive Director of the National Association of Hotel & Lodging Engineers (NAHLE). He has a Bachelor of Science degree in engineering, specializing in general building construction, from Arizona State University. He is a former Vice President of the American Hotel & Lodging Association, where his duties included acting as a staff liaison for the association's Engineering & Environment Committee. Mr. Elliott authored the internationally acclaimed Y2K Technology Guide for Hotels and co-authored AH&LA's Energy Management Guide. He was project manager for AH&LA's HITIS (Hospitality Industry Technology Integration Standards) four-year program*

that developed seventeen ANSI standards, including Central Reservation Systems and Remote Devices, among others. He recently contributed as editor and author of NAHLE's Hotel Engineering, a study guide for the association's Certified Chief Engineer (CCE) designation. Mr. Elliott is NAHLE's first Certified Chief Engineer. He was also named an honorary Certified Lodging Security Director by AH&LA and was a Certified Building Inspector for BOCA (Building Officials & Code Administrators). Mr. Elliott has also chaired the National Fire Protection Association's Lodging Section, held a general building contractor's license in Arizona, and worked for three years at Marriott's corporate headquarters as Director of Special Projects and Technical Services.

About NAHLE: *Recognizing the ever-present need within the hotel engineering community to receive consistent and ongoing education and training, NAHLE offers an engineering curriculum and specialized training in cooperation with the American Hotel & Lodging Educational Institute (AHLEI). NAHLE's program focuses on providing relevant, up-to-date educational content for the entire range of engineering personnel at a hotel, from line-level employees performing routine maintenance all the way up to the director of engineering managing a large, full-service, high-rise hotel. NAHLE's curriculum is comprehensive and covers subjects organized by building system and/or engineering discipline, such as HVAC, plumbing, electrical, lighting, landscaping, swimming pools, and vertical transport, to name a few. NAHLE certifies that those who successfully complete its program have mastered the educational content required of a hotel's chief engineer. It is NAHLE's educational mission to teach everyone on the hotel engineer's staff more about the environment in which they work, thereby empowering each employee to better deal with the challenges associated with hotel engineering and maintenance. Continuing the education and training of hotel engineers and their maintenance staff maximizes a hotel owner's investment by protecting capital assets and increases guest satisfaction, hotel profitability, and guest and staff safety. NAHLE's CCE program was strategically developed to complement AHLEI's Certified Maintenance Manager (CMM) program and its Certified Engineering Operations Executive (CEOE) program. NAHLE's overall strategic goal is to advance engineering professionalism within the hotel and lodging industry through education and training.*

Authors' Acknowledgments

The authors would like to thank Harry Hobbs of InterContinental Hotels; Ann Hannosh of Starwood Hotels & Resorts; Rick Werber of Host Hotels & Resorts; Paul D'Andrea of Gemstone Hotels & Resorts, LCC; Tim Arwood of Sonesta Hotels; and Todd Isbell of Hilton Hotels.

SUSTAINABLE DEVELOPMENT is a relatively recent phenomenon in the hospitality industry, but has gained momentum during the past five years as designers, architects, suppliers/manufacturers, and operators increase their focus on it. Other factors have boosted demand for sustainable initiatives as well:

- Consumer demand for "green" destinations
- Municipal and state legislation related to low carbon emissions
- Meeting planners who expect hotel operators to be environmentally conscious

Virtually all major hotel companies have responded to the sustainability movement by creating green footprints and communicating those footprints to consumers. This chapter provides case studies from actual hotel operations that demonstrate how green decisions are good for the planet, the guest, and the bottom line.

An Evolution of Sustainable Operating Practices

The American lodging industry has more than four million hotel rooms, but only a fraction of them meet internationally recognized sustainability standards, such as Leadership in Energy and Environmental Design (LEED), Green Seal, or various designations from the International Organization for Standardization (ISO). Given the need and the rising demand for these conversions, green compliance presents an opportunity for the lodging industry. Over the years, individual hotels have taken steps to incorporate environmentally friendly operating practices, albeit driven primarily by cost reduction. These steps included reduced linen consumption, responsible disposal of toxic chemicals and detergents, and replacement of incandescent light bulbs with long-life fluorescent bulbs. Other early money-saving initiatives focused on water use. Hotels that reduced the sizes of their toilet tanks and the water supply capacities of their showerheads and faucets made real impacts on water consumption. The success of these initial programs was measured mainly by their ability to reduce operating costs.

Now, a myriad of products are available to retrofit hotels for sustainability, from lighting fixtures that reduce energy use, to energy management systems that shut down guestrooms' systems (except critical outlets) if rooms are unoccupied. Packaged Terminal Air Conditioners (PTACs), which supply heat and air conditioning to individual guestrooms, are available with radio frequency or motion sensor controls that return units to preset parameters when rooms are unoccupied. Central controls for public areas create maximum guest comfort while reducing energy consumption. These automated systems boost hotels' energy efficiency, as they control not only active use of energy, but also passive consumption created by items that are plugged in but not in use.

As hotels incorporated these initiatives, many saw reductions in their consumption of energy and water—and reductions in their production of waste material—by as much as 30 to 40 percent. In addition to this direct economic benefit, hotels gained the intangible benefit of positive word of mouth. As technology improves and costs per unit go down, we expect that solar panels, heat exchangers, wind turbines, and fuel cells will continue the trend toward lower consumption as they are incorporated in new construction and major renovation projects alike.

Today, a hotel operator's decisions regarding capital expenditures must take environmental ethics into account. As previously mentioned, increasing numbers of guests expect hotels to begin or maintain green initiatives, so operators should implement not only capital projects that save costs and create profits, but those that have no or low increased costs while boosting the property's green standing. For example, in addition to incorporating initiatives that promote energy efficiency and guest health, operators can reduce their properties' carbon footprints by using low–volatile-organic-compound (VOC) paints, adhesives, and pesticides, as well as chemical-free cleaning products. It might not be fiscally responsible to incorporate every new green technology, but any decision that promotes environmental responsibility for guests and the planet while providing a positive return on investment (ROI) is a good decision, both financially and in terms of sustainability.

The Engineer's Role in Green Certification

Hotel companies and individual operators implementing sustainability initiatives will want to measure the results of those initiatives and communicate their efforts to potential guests. With that in mind, several standards and certifications have emerged to measure and validate the environmental friendliness of buildings and businesses. But the increasing number of green certifications and standards has made the landscape confusing to hoteliers. Therefore, the lodging engineer has an important role, to not only navigate myriad certification and other "green" programs, but present criteria that help management decide which certifications to pursue. This section provides a brief overview of three certification programs, and offers an engineer's perspective on factors that can help operators determine which certifications are appropriate for their hotels.

LEED

LEED is an internationally recognized certification that verifies a building was designed and built using technology that reduces energy and water use, curbs carbon dioxide emissions, improves indoor environmental quality, and encourages responsible use of resources. According to the U.S. Green Building Council, LEED gives building owners and operators a framework for identifying and implementing practical, measurable solutions regarding green building design, construction, operation, and maintenance.

From the chief engineer's (CE's) perspective, the decision to pursue LEED certification is largely up to the owner, as the process can require significant capital expenditures. Yet should a hotel work toward LEED certification, the CE will maintain an important role, helping identify and promote expenditures that not only achieve certification, but do so efficiently and economically. In many cases, ROI on LEED projects is less than two years, providing significant long-term savings. Once a hotel recovers its investment in LEED-friendly technologies, its savings fall straight to the bottom line.

Later in the chapter appear case studies from hotels that sought LEED certification, ranging from a two-year-old property with new energy and plumbing systems to a seventy-one-year-old property on the National Register of Historic Places. Each hotel required different degrees of financial investment; for example, much of the newer property's equipment was still under warranty, while the older property required a complete retrofit. Yet in each case, the property's operations team and ownership committed themselves to achieving LEED certification. A CE's technical expertise often makes him or her the "champion" of such projects who ensures efficiency, competitive pricing, and the selection of products that meet LEED standards.

The "LEED for Existing Buildings (EB): Operations & Maintenance (O&M) Rating System" is a tool that ensures existing commercial and institutional structures are operated and maintained in sustainable ways. Of all certifications, LEED

EB: O&M is the most operationally oriented and the most easily obtained by a property's staff. However, LEED EB: O&M requires that the CE—not the building—receive the certification. Studying and passing the LEED EB: O&M exam is the CE's responsibility; yet upon attaining certification, the CE can more easily affect change at the property level.

ENERGY STAR

ENERGY STAR is a joint program of the Environmental Protection Agency (EPA) and the Department of Energy (DOE). By promoting energy-efficient products and practices, ENERGY STAR helps building owners save money and protect the environment. The program involves evaluating buildings' energy performances, setting goals to reduce consumption, tracking savings, and rewarding improvements. More than 130,000 buildings have participated in ENERGY STAR; top-performing buildings (i.e., those that score 75 or higher on the program's Portfolio Manager tool) receive the ENERGY STAR label and recognition on the ENERGY STAR website.

As with LEED certification, ENERGY STAR criteria often require large capital expenditures that operating budgets cannot accommodate. Therefore, a CE's role is to identify the most important changes and solutions, focusing on efficiency, cost competitiveness, and quality. ENERGY STAR might be the easiest certification to attain, as it requires the use of approved products the property will need to buy anyway. The CE can ensure proper selections are made to benefit a hotel's ownership.

Green Seal

Green Seal is a nationally recognized private certification that began in 1989 and took hold in the 1990s. Green Seal published the first edition of its lodging standard in 1999; its fourth edition, published in 2008, offers certification at three levels: Bronze, which recognizes buildings with strong foundations of sustainability; Silver, for buildings that have become leaders in sustainable practices by substantially reducing their environmental impacts; and Gold, which recognizes buildings at the top tier of sustainability leadership. Green Seal's criteria require that buildings minimize waste, reuse or recycle products, conserve energy, manage freshwater and waste water, and safely handle hazardous substances while reducing their use. Green Seal also requires that properties create environmentally sensitive purchasing policies. The certification is consistent with LEED EB: O&M in that it focuses on projects operations staff can accomplish on their own, rather than on projects requiring capital expenditures. An engineer can easily champion requirements to achieve Green Seal certification, and assist various hotel departments in accomplishing their individual sustainability tasks.

Summary

The previously mentioned certification programs and their standards have become marketing tools that set apart certified properties from their competitors. Engineers should take leadership roles in helping their properties achieve certification, as

Exhibit 1   Cost Savings: Room Energy Control System

Cost Installed (160-room hotel)	$59,360
Annual Room Energy Cost	$129,120
Annual Savings	$45,192

their technical expertise can help identify, evaluate, and meet their hotels' sustainability needs. Many sustainability projects not only help the environment, but offer financial incentives, reaping savings for owners. With that in mind, an engineer's responsibilities should include making sustainable options known to upper-level management and ownership.

Engineering Perspectives on Energy-Efficiency Programs

Energy efficiency is a key component of both sustainability certification programs and the case studies mentioned later in the chapter. The following sections provide information on ways engineering teams can incorporate energy efficiency into their hotels' operations.

Room Energy Control Systems

Several systems on the market virtually shut down a room's power consumption when it is unoccupied. These systems use either a key card–controlled thermostat or a motion sensor. With the key card system, a guest or employee enters a room and inserts a card into a thermostat slot; this brings the room's power and outlets to full capacity. When the card is not present, most of the room's power shuts down, except for select units like the heating, ventilating, and air conditioning (HVAC) system (set to pre-determined efficient ranges) and the outlet used for the alarm clock or computer. A motion detector system works the same way, but requires no card, simply the presence of a body in the room. Exhibit 1 illustrates the potential savings a 160-room mid-scale hotel can achieve by installing a room energy control system. The payback is estimated at eighteen months.

PTACs

PTACs are self-contained air conditioning machines—installed through outward-facing walls—that guests control in their rooms. Because the units work independently of each other, they can be turned on only in rooms that need them. PTACs do not require ductwork, and therefore can drastically reduce installation costs and space requirements. The devices are less efficient than central air conditioning systems, but many manufacturers now offer PTAC systems—similar to the previously mentioned room energy control systems—that return energy consumption to pre-set levels when a room is unoccupied.

To understand how these PTAC systems save money, consider that room energy control systems can reduce annual energy consumption costs by 35 percent. With that in mind, as represented in Exhibit 1, a 160-room hotel with an annual per-room energy consumption cost of $807 would spend $129,120 on energy for its rooms every year. If an energy control system saved the hotel 35 percent, the potential savings would be $45,192. According to the EPA, 47 percent of energy expenditures go toward HVAC systems. If 47 percent of the $45,192 energy savings was HVAC-related, the PTAC units could potentially save $21,240. Hotels can save additional money by following advice from the EPA, the DOE, and the National Air Duct Cleaners Association (NADCA), which claim that properly maintaining coils on existing PTAC systems increases their efficiency by 30 percent. These systems should be inspected annually, and condensers, coils, and evaporators cleaned on a regular basis.

Central HVAC Systems

With its potential for cost savings, an efficient HVAC system is a high-value investment. While hoteliers can enhance and upgrade most existing systems, older properties with systems that cannot be upgraded should consider new technology. New systems reduce energy consumption by at least 35 percent. A full-service hotel with 300 rooms would see the following savings:

300 rooms with an annual energy cost of $1,400 per room	= $ 420,000
35-percent reduction and annual savings	= $ 147,000
The life of a system (twenty years) × annual savings	= $2,940,000

Engineering Perspective on Water-Consumption Programs

Water consumption initiatives started in the 1980s, with properties using valves that reduced the amount of water needed in supply. Waterless tanks and flush-control devices on toilets also helped reduce water consumption, in some cases by more than 50 percent. The following section describes an additional way engineering teams can incorporate water conservation efforts into their hotels' operations.

Window Cleaning

New systems facilitate water-fed, detergent-free cleaning of exterior windows for buildings up to five stories tall. Not only do these systems offer ecological benefits (i.e., keeping detergents and other chemicals out of the environment), they also reduce costs. Because the systems require less setup time, they decrease the number of labor hours required to execute them. In addition, they eliminate cleaning product costs, and save money on water by recycling it through the system. Likewise, because detergent residue attracts dust and dirt, water-fed cleaning systems reduce, by up to one-third, the number of times windows need to be cleaned. A 300-room hotel with 800 windows realizes the following savings:

800 windows × $3 per window × four washings per year	= $9,600 annually
800 windows × $1.50 (cost reduction) per window × two washings (frequency reduction) per year	= $2,400 annually

This represents a 75-percent cost savings through the reduced use of water, chemicals, and detergents, creating benefits for both the environment and the hotel's bottom line.

Case Studies: Reengineering Hotel Operations

As we've discussed, the growing interest in sustainability has provided opportunities for lodging engineers to incorporate green initiatives into their properties. Hotel managers have traditionally relied on CEs to efficiently regulate building structures and systems; today they are relying on them to be knowledgeable about sustainable energy, water, and waste management technologies. This section describes projects implemented by leading hotels that highlight the importance of engineers' changing roles as they relate to sustainability. The three case studies cover a range of property sizes and ages, from a two-year-old downtown high-rise property, to a sprawling thirty-year-old resort, to a small, historic downtown property that is seventy-one years old.

Case Study One: InterContinental San Francisco

The InterContinental San Francisco received an ENERGY STAR score of eighty-five, placing it among the top 16 percent of buildings, in terms of energy efficiency, in the United States. What follows is an outline of the process the InterContinental San Francisco followed to meet ENERGY STAR criteria and attain Gold-level status in the LEED EB program.

Overview. What follows is some general information about the InterContinental San Francisco's sustainability initiative:

Project Leader: Harry Hobbs, director of engineering

Project Team: Pacific Gas and Electric Company; LodgingSavers; CB Engineers; City of San Francisco Environment Department; Jubilee Daniels, LEED AP; Regency Lighting; and Western Allied Mechanical

Project Goal: To earn the sixty credits required to become the first LEED EB Gold-level certified luxury hotel, and to achieve an ENERGY STAR score of eighty-three.

Project Motivation and Process: Work with local energy companies to earn rebates and incentives based on measurable efforts to reduce energy consumption.

Energy Savings Program and Initiatives: To implement its energy savings program, the hotel launched several HVAC upgrades:

- Resetting the chilled water and air supply temperatures
- Resetting the condenser water temperature
- Optimizing economizers on the air handlers
- Adding a waterside economizer
- Optimizing in-room thermostats

The hotel's goal was to reduce energy consumption by over 16 percent from the baseline year. The property achieved this goal, and is considering a "guaranteed savings" program from an energy service company that would achieve an additional 36 percent reduction in energy consumption, bringing the total potential reduction to over 50 percent of the baseline. Considering that, at the beginning of this sustainability initiative, the building was only two years old, the project demonstrates that energy use even in buildings designed to the demanding efficiency standards of California's Title 24 can still be dramatically reduced. For example, when the property was built the HVAC system was designed to provide fifty-five-degree air to all public conditioned spaces, then to re-heat the air to a desired comfort setting (typically seventy-two degrees). Anyone who evaluated this system could see how it wasted electricity and natural gas, first by overcooling the air, then by re-heating it to the desired comfort level. Descriptions follow of actions the InterContinental San Francisco undertook to solve this and other energy-related problems.

Resetting Chilled Water and Air Supply Temperatures. The room temperatures noted above are not always needed, and are dynamically reset to provide only the amount of hot or cold air that satisfies comfort settings. The new control system calculates these settings, which are never below forty-two degrees (water) and fifty-five degrees (air), but can be set higher based on room occupancies, outdoor temperatures, and demand in public areas. The settings allow for a four-degree "deadband" of two degrees above or two degrees below a set point. This is all accomplished by computer programs and digital controls pre-set to selected protocols.

Resetting the Condenser Water Temperature. The condenser water temperature was designed to be seventy degrees; however, these chillers operate more efficiently if condenser water is cooler, so the project team increased fan horsepower by 25 percent by using two twenty-horsepower condenser fans over the original fifteen-horsepower condenser fans. The condenser is now capable of achieving sixty-degree water. The $20,000 cost was offset by a $7,000 rebate from the local power company. The result not only improves the chillers' life expectancies, but saves an estimated $5,000 annually, achieving ROI in less than two years.

Optimizing Economizers on Air Handlers. The hotel's outside air dampers, or economizers, take advantage of "free" cool air from the San Francisco climate. On-site calibration of the outside air dampers offered a significant improvement over factory settings, which are often the defaults in a new building. The air system includes a weather station that references outdoor temperatures; this information is used to compare indoor temperatures with valve and damper positions and determine final settings. Optimizing the economizers on the hotel's air handlers was a retro-commissioning exercise that fine-tuned this aspect of system performance.

Adding a Waterside Economizer. Team members added a 310-ton heat exchanger to the central plant, eliminating the use of chillers when ambient temperatures fall below fifty-two degrees wet-bulb. Historically, the weather in San Francisco meets these conditions 1,800 hours per year. This measure has accounted for 8 percent

Exhibit 2   InterContinental San Francisco's Cost Savings: Lighting Equipment

1. **Garage lighting**

    Cost: $40,000

    Rebate: $32,000

    Annual energy savings: $35,000

    ROI: three months

2. **Motion sensors on stairwell emergency evacuation lighting**

    Cost: $45,000

    Rebate: $17,000

    Annual energy savings: $16,000

    ROI: 1.9 years

of the 16 percent energy-consumption savings. Based on this data, the $180,000 waterside economizer will provide ROI in approximately three years.

Optimizing In-Room Thermostats. During the retro-commissioning process, the project team sampled twelve room thermostats and discovered they tracked "between the wall" temperatures, resulting in readings as much as six degrees higher or lower than actual room temperatures. Team members determined that an insulating gasket added between the wall and the thermostat housing would eliminate this variable. The change was difficult to quantify, and did not qualify for a direct rebate, but did reduce guest complaints and decrease energy consumption.

Replacing Lighting Equipment. Engineering teams reaped lighting-related energy savings when they replaced 140 210-watt low-pressure sodium luminaries in the valet parking garage with thirty-eight-watt compact fluorescents. When combined with several smaller fluorescent retro-fits, the project cost $40,000, though a $32,000 incentive offset much of that cost. Related energy savings were $35,000 per year. Another lighting project involved adding motion sensors to all twenty-four-hour evacuation stairs. Teams retro-fitted 260 fixtures at a cost of $45,000, and received an incentive of $17,000 from the city of San Francisco. The project saved $16,000 per year in energy costs (see Exhibit 2).

A number of additional projects can reduce lighting-related energy use in hotels. Old fixtures can be retrofitted with inexpensive inserts, or replaced with cost-efficient fixtures. In parking lots, engineering teams can replace inefficient bulbs with compact fluorescent or light emitting diode (LED) fixtures. Replacement programs can reduce wattage consumption by 50 to 75 percent, with a tenfold increase in lamp life. The InterContinental San Francisco's program reduced annual electrical usage by 300,000 kilowatt hours. In general, these programs pay for themselves within one to three years. They also offer other benefits: because efficient lighting systems emit less carbon than inefficient systems, they help prevent the formation of greenhouse gases; and because they create lighting that

Exhibit 3   Results of Energy-Saving Programs at the InterContinental San Francisco

Energy Category	Current Usage	Proposed Usage	Current Annual Cost	Proposed Annual Cost
Electrical Usage	Six million kilowatt hours	5.1 kilowatt hours	$675,000	$550,000

The property also realized a reduction in the Costs Per Occupied Room (CPOR) for electricity and gas:

Year Over Year Usage, Electricity					
Date	2009	2010	kWh	kWh	Variance
Through May 2010	Days	Days	2009	2010	2009 vs. 2010
	154	151	15,242	12,827	-15.84 percent

Year Over Year Cost Per Kilowatt Hour, Electricity					
Date	2009	2010	kWh	kWh	Variance
Through May 2010	Days	Days	2009	2010	2009 vs. 2010
	154	151	0.103	0.112	8.95 percent

Year Over Year Usage, Gas					
Date	2009	2010	Therm	Therm	Variance
Through May 2010	Days	Days	2009	2010	2009 vs. 2010
	154	151	753	581	-22.85 percent

Year Over Year Cost Per Therm, Gas					
Date	2009	2010	Therm	Therm	Variance
Through May 2010	Days	Days	2009	2010	2009 vs. 2010
	154	151	0.801	0.789	-1.54 percent

looks more natural and has a higher color index, they are considered healthier and more conducive to staff and guest productivity.

Summary. Total annual net savings reaped by the InterContinental San Francisco's energy initiatives were $217,000. Direct savings from the HVAC and lighting upgrades (see Exhibit 3) were supplemented by incentives of $108,000 from LodgingSavers, a rebate program operated by the Pacific Gas and Electric Company, and $17,000 from the city of San Francisco. These rebate programs give energy consumers incentives to make capital investments that lower energy use long-term. Power companies across the country have similar incentive and rebate programs; hotel operators and owners should contact their local power companies for more information. In addition, tax rebates and incentives are available for many energy-saving initiatives. These rebates and incentives change from time to time, so a hotel's accounting firm should review current laws every tax season.

Case Study Two: Sheraton San Diego Hotel & Marina

The Sheraton San Diego Hotel & Marina implemented several energy-reduction and recycling programs to reduce its carbon footprint and provide ROI for its owners.

Overview. What follows is some general information about the Sheraton San Diego's sustainability initiative:

Project Goal: To give travelers a green lodging choice verified by sustainable building certifications like the California Green Lodging Program, Green Seal, and LEED EB. After implementing these programs, the property received Gold certification from Green Seal in 2010.

Project Motivation and Process: Work with local energy companies to earn rebates and incentives based on real and measurable efforts to reduce energy consumption. The program was structured with the help of a third-party engineering consultant.

Energy Savings Program and Initiatives: The Sheraton San Diego Hotel & Marina implemented energy-efficiency programs based on several recommendations, including those from a retro-commissioning study. By implementing these findings, the hotel optimized its HVAC systems for improved indoor air quality and energy savings in public and meeting spaces. Changes made to HVAC systems during retro-commissioning included the following:

- Fixed economizers on air handling units
- Adjusted schedules on air handling units
- Balanced the air handling units
- Adjusted boiler operations
- Replaced outside air temperature sensors

The program initiatives earned $70,000 in energy rebates from the Sheraton San Diego Hotel & Marina's local energy provider. The hotel used this money to offset the capital expenses it incurred in implementing its energy-efficiency program. The rebate, along with energy savings, provided ROI in less than one year.

Other projects undertaken to accomplish the Sheraton San Diego Hotel & Marina's goals are as follows.

Installing Reflective Roofing. Reflective roofing deflects the sun's rays, reducing the amount of heat that enters a building and cutting a hotel's need for cooling equipment. The Sheraton San Diego Hotel & Marina replaced the roofing on its Bay Tower with Sarnafil G410 EnergySmart Roof, an ENERGY STAR–approved, single-ply membrane whose solar reflective index (SRI) of 104 indicates that

Exhibit 4   Recycling Program Results at the Sheraton San Diego Hotel & Marina

Recycled Waste	2008 Pounds	2009 Pounds
CRV* glass	23,440	19,370
Non-CRV glass	10,925	36,287
Metal cans	610	2,314
CRV plastic	2,400	158
Cardboard	97,590	138,856
Paper	—	1,020
TOTAL POUNDS	134,965	198,005

*"CRV" is the California Refund Value, which is the amount recycling centers pay for empty bottles and cans.

it reflects the majority of a building's heat while minimizing cooling loads and energy use. In this case, the hotel's old roof was torn off and the Sarnafil membrane placed where it had been; however, the membrane can also be applied over existing roofing systems.

Utilizing Fuel Cell Technology. Fuel cells are ultra-clean sources of electricity. They require no combustion, as they create energy by combining hydrogen fuel (in this case, natural gas) and oxygen from the air. A private owner and operator of a fuel cell plant sells electricity to the Sheraton San Diego Hotel & Marina under a Power Purchase Agreement, and does so at a discount to the commercial rate published by San Diego Gas & Electric, the local distribution company. The hotel uses six fuel cells that, combined, produce 1.5 megawatts of electricity. Fuel cells generate heat and water as byproducts, so heat exchangers capture waste heat and use it for pool and guestroom water, reducing the hotel's need to purchase natural gas from the utility company. The fuel cells' owner/operator provides regular on-site inspections to monitor maintenance and performance. Because of its fuel cell program, the hotel purchases 10 percent less gas from the local energy provider. ROI on capital expenses that allowed the hotel to capture free waste heat generated by the fuel cells was approximately one-and-a-half years.

Recycling Program. In 2009, the Sheraton San Diego Hotel & Marina recycled 47 percent more waste than it had in 2008. The hotel has recycling bins throughout its back-of-house areas, all public and meeting spaces, and in every guestroom. Material in guestroom bins is co-mingled (i.e., not sorted) and recycled by the local waste hauler. Recycled waste from other areas is single stream, and sorted for pickup by a third-party recycler. Exhibit 4 contains statistics about the Sheraton San Diego Hotel & Marina's recycling program. (Note: This exhibit excludes composted landscaping and food waste, as well as waste taken by the local hauler for recycling.)

    Food waste reduction program. Using a 220-pound-capacity food dehydrator, kitchen staff dehydrate food waste to less than 20 percent of its original weight. The processed material is taken off-site for composting. In addition, the Sheraton

San Diego Hotel & Marina partners with a local food bank to donate leftover prepared food served at on-site events.

Sustainable Landscaping Program. Several initiatives have improved the quality of the hotel's landscaping while employing environmentally friendly practices. All landscaping waste is picked up weekly for composting. The hotel also waters its plants at night, saving water by minimizing its loss to evaporation.

Other Efforts. The hotel's flip charts and office paper are made from 30-percent post-consumer waste (PCW). In addition, its toilet paper is made from 20-percent PCW, while its trashcan liners and facial tissue contain 10-percent PCW. The hotel also uses eco-friendly laundry, housekeeping, and stewarding chemicals, as well as low-VOC paints, adhesives, and sealants. These programs, along with a number of other operational changes, including an environmentally sensitive purchasing policy, helped the Sheraton San Diego Hotel & Marina achieve its sustainability goals.

Case Study Three: Hotel Andaluz

In 1939, Conrad Hilton built this Albuquerque property, designed by Anton F. Korn, and touted as the first air-conditioned building in New Mexico. Its new owner, Gary Goodman, committed $30 million to restoring the 104-room hotel, with $5.2 million dedicated to green energy solutions. The property, which closed for renovation in 2005, reopened in 2009.

Overview. What follows is some general information about the Hotel Andaluz's sustainability initiative:

Project Goal: To operate a fully committed sustainable property and achieve Gold-level LEED certification.

Project Motivation and Process: The property was shut down to complete restoration.

Energy Savings Program and Initiatives:

- Solar panels for hot water – the panels heat 60 percent of domestic hot water annually

- Energy-efficient HVAC system, including chillers and towers

- Energy-efficient windows

- Building Automation System (BAS)

Unfortunately, the property is not old enough to provide ROI information. The hotel also does not maintain estimates as to how much money its sustainability initiatives will save. The hotel's utility numbers are available, however, comparing rates from the time period the newly renovated hotel has been open (October 2009 to June 2010 as of this writing) to rates the hotel experienced before the renovation (averaging numbers from October to June of the previous three years). Some explanation is required to understand these numbers; the following sections provide that explanation.

Exhibit 5   Energy Consumption at the Hotel Andaluz

Hotel	Electricity Use (monthly average)
Former hotel (nine-month average, October through June)	106,953 kilowatt hours
Renovated Hotel Andaluz (nine-month average, October through June)	125,016 kilowatt hours

Hotel	Electricity Costs (monthly average)
Former hotel (nine-month average, October through June)	$8,281.26
Renovated Hotel Andaluz (nine-month average, October through June)	$10,705.36

Electricity Usage. The renovated Hotel Andaluz's electricity usage is higher than it was in the former hotel, because although the hotel's new equipment is more efficient, it experiences greater demand (see Exhibit 5). Ten rooftop air conditioning units and a chiller—a total of 200 tons of refrigeration—were replaced by two chillers that represent 240 tons of refrigeration. The increased refrigeration was necessary because the former chiller did not run during the winter, while the two new chillers operate year-round. Likewise, the former hotel had conventional fans and pumps, while the new hotel's fans and pumps are variable-frequency drives (VFDs); also, the new hotel uses more fans and pumps than the previous hotel did.

The new hotel requires an additional 1,000 amperes of power over the old hotel. Previously, three guestrooms ran off one twenty-ampere circuit; now, each guestroom runs off three twenty-ampere circuits. In addition, Hotel Andaluz has numerous kitchen and housekeeping equipment, as well as additional lighting, which helps accounts for its larger energy consumption.

Gas Usage. The Hotel Andaluz's average gas use is lower than it was before the renovation. The hotel's engineers installed two domestic high-efficiency water boilers and three high-efficiency heating boilers, a 600,000-British Thermal Unit (BTU) ironer, and a solar thermal system designed to heat approximately 60 percent of domestic hot water annually. See Exhibit 6 for the hotel's gas usage statistics.

Water Usage. A comparison between the new and old hotels' water use shows a significant decrease in consumption (see Exhibit 7). The old hotel had three-gallon-per-flush toilets; the renovated hotel has dual-flush toilets that use .08 or 1.6 gallons per flush. The new hotel also has low-flow showerheads. It is significant to note that the old hotel did not run its cooling tower during the winter, while Hotel Andaluz's cooling tower operates year-round.

Other Efforts and Summary. Based on ASHRAE 90.1-2004, the property expects to save 21 percent on its power consumption, leading to an annual savings of $18,067. (Note: Comparisons made in the previous sections were not based on American

Exhibit 6   Gas Consumption at the Hotel Andaluz

Hotel	Gas Use (monthly average)
Former hotel (nine-month average, October through June)	6,334 therms
Renovated Hotel Andaluz (nine-month average, October through June)	6,003 therms

Hotel	Gas Costs (monthly average)
Former hotel (nine-month average, October through June)	data unavailable
Renovated Hotel Andaluz (nine-month average, October through June)	$4,508.03

Exhibit 7   Water Consumption at the Hotel Andaluz

Hotel	Water Use (monthly average)
Former hotel (nine-month average, October through June)	871,482 gallons
Renovated Hotel Andaluz (nine-month average, October through June)	261,052 gallons

Hotel	Water Costs (monthly average)
Former hotel (nine-month average, October through June)	$3,687.94
Renovated Hotel Andaluz (nine-month average, October through June)	$1,772.95

Society of Heating, Refrigerating and Air-Conditioning Engineers [ASHRAE] standards, but on differences between the old hotel's performance and the newly renovated hotel's performance.)

Hotel Andaluz installed a BAS—a central-control room management system that delivers chilled and heated water throughout the hotel—at a cost of $391,460. The hotel also installed energy-efficient windows at a cost of $237,088. The fact that energy-efficient windows should produce long-term savings made them cost-effective and environmentally friendly alternatives to traditional windows.

At $5.2 million, the hotel's green initiatives represent approximately 17 percent of the project's $30 million budget. To draw a comparison with a non-green build would require determining the amount Hotel Andaluz would have spent on traditional (i.e., non-sustainable) systems, then comparing that number with the amount the hotel actually spent on its sustainable systems. In addition, the comparison would require determining the reduction in energy consumption created by the more-efficient equipment, as well as the accompanying cost savings. For example, if a traditional reconstruction project would have cost $4.7 million, Hotel Andaluz's "green" reconstruction project cost $500,000 more than that amount. A person could then analyze, in dollars, the green project's reduced energy consumption costs, and derive ROI from those numbers.

Conclusion

In the coming years, sustainable properties will remain attractive alternatives to traditional development as they create new approaches and products for green construction and promise long-term savings in energy and other costs. A property's operating staff, with its engineer at the lead, will face challenges as it creates greener policies, procedures, and products for guests, staff members, and the environment. As we have seen, many green initiatives have financial benefits and create marketing opportunities for hotels. With those benefits in mind, engineers can take leadership roles in the sustainability movement, wielding significant influence in the hospitality industry for the foreseeable future and beyond.

18

Going Green: The Business Impact of Environmental Awareness on Travel

By Carroll Rheem

As Director of Research for the market research firm PhoCusWright, **Carroll Rheem** *contributes in-depth market reports, survey findings, and analysis for the firm's* Global Edition Research Subscription *and* European Edition Research Subscription, *as well as producing special reports and attending to customized client needs. One of her areas of focus is consumer research; to that end, Ms. Rheem is author of PhoCusWright's* Consumer Travel Report *and* Going Green: The Business Impact of Environmental Awareness on Travel *(from which this chapter was adapted). Ms. Rheem also leverages her experience in hotel distribution for publications like Pho-CusWright's* U.S. Online Travel Overview, *and oversees content for the* European Edition Research Subscription. *Prior to joining the PhoCus-Wright team, Ms. Rheem spent six years at Starwood Hotels & Resorts Worldwide, in positions that included hotel operations, sales, and global online distribution. She holds a Master of Management degree in hospitality from Cornell University and a Bachelor of Arts degree in economics from New York University.*

T HERE IS LITTLE DOUBT that environmental awareness has achieved mainstream status in the United States, as evidenced by the media attention paid to earth-friendly initiatives and the plethora of "green" consumer products available on store shelves. American companies can no longer operate without acknowledging what is perhaps their oldest, but most recently recognized, stakeholder—the environment. As one of the country's largest industries, travel is no exception to this rule.

Unlike many trends shaping the travel industry today (e.g., a slumping economy), the genesis of green consumer products stems from personal values that encourage awareness of a general good, rather than pursuit of technology or financial gain. Understanding the connection consumers make between personal values and travel decisions is critical to helping travel companies confront a changing marketplace.

To determine how mainstream environmental awareness colors consumer behavior and drives change in the travel industry, PhoCusWright launched a multifaceted study, *Going Green: The Business Impact of Environmental Awareness on*

Exhibit 1   Green and Environmentally Friendly Categories

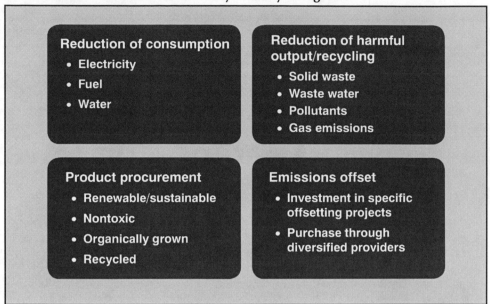

Travel. The study examined consumer values, attitudes, and behaviors, as well as trends among travel suppliers, distributors, and the media. This chapter presents key findings and strategic implications from the report that published the study's results.

The report did not assume that companies should or should not be green-based. Instead, its purpose was to help travel companies understand how green social values affect their business and how they can compete in an evolving marketplace. Though the report focused primarily on the study's consumer responses, it used industry perspectives as a foundation for much of its analysis. The report explored issues like the breadth of the green audience, differences between green travelers and other travelers, business opportunities created by green trends, and effective messaging for green audiences. In the report, the terms "green" and "environmentally friendly" referred to efforts outlined in Exhibit 1.

To understand the effect environmental awareness has on the American travel industry, PhoCusWright conducted comprehensive research into three core components of the marketplace: consumers, suppliers, and influencers (i.e., distribution intermediaries and the media). See Exhibit 2 for information regarding each sample and the techniques used to query respondents. The chapter appendix describes the research methodology.

Defining the Green Lifestyle Audience

To build a context for understanding green travel trends, PhoCusWright created a baseline for consumer adoption of green actions. The firm did this by examining

Exhibit 2   Research Sample

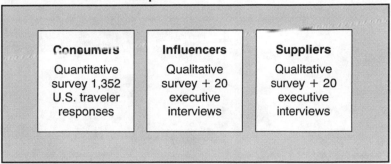

Consumers	Influencers	Suppliers
Quantitative survey 1,352 U.S. traveler responses	Qualitative survey + 20 executive interviews	Qualitative survey + 20 executive interviews

multiple indicators that described behaviors, values, and attitudes toward green trends. This analysis created a comprehensive picture showing how deeply consumers embrace green ideals and how their acceptance of those ideals affects daily purchases.

One of the core characteristics of a green lifestyle is a person's attitude toward energy consumption, which encompasses two resources: fuel and electricity. When asked to self assess their day-to-day activities, American travelers show an extremely strong awareness of—and at least a light level of activity toward—consumption reduction. The report isolated five groups of consumers based on their energy-related self assessments: indifferent, passive, uncommitted, dedicated, and activist (see Exhibit 3). Upon cluster analysis, these groups were found to be consistent throughout other lifestyle factors, like behaviors and values. Therefore, these groupings represent not only a person's attitude toward energy conservation, but also his or her general lifestyle. Within the five groups, responses reflect a relatively normal distribution, with a skew toward the more actively green category.

Participants in the more actively green category respond higher across a range of green behaviors (see Exhibit 4). This consistency indicates that consumers extend their self-described levels of energy commitment to other green lifestyle choices. For all lifestyle groups, lighting-related actions and recycling are the most common practices. Use of hybrid/flexible-fuel vehicles and solar energy are the least common practices. This last finding is consistent with expectations, given that many respondents find hybrid/flexible-fuel vehicles and solar energy inaccessible because of the commitments of time and money they require.

Lifestyle groupings are also relevant when considering personal values and attitudes. Generally, all travelers respond positively to abstract concepts and situations in which being green is free or easy (see Exhibit 5), though differences among lifestyle groups still exist. When situations involve cost or inconvenience, the differences widen dramatically (see Exhibit 6). In the actively green category, 77 percent of respondents choose green options when those options save money, while 62 percent will pay a premium for green options. For the less actively green category, 74 percent of respondents choose green options when those options save money, while only 31 percent will pay a premium for them. The sizable drop-off reveals the extent to which less actively green consumers value environmentally friendly initiatives.

Exhibit 3   Green Lifestyle Scale

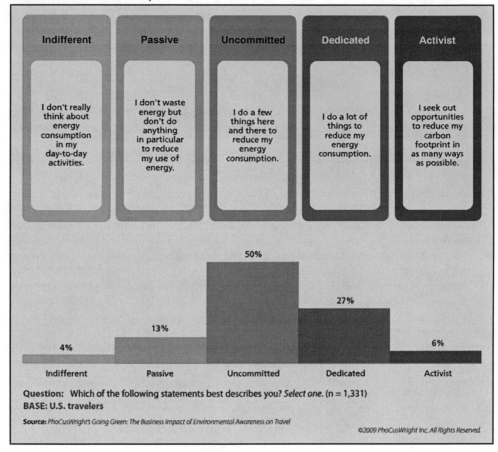

Indifferent	Passive	Uncommitted	Dedicated	Activist
I don't really think about energy consumption in my day-to-day activities.	I don't waste energy but don't do anything in particular to reduce my use of energy.	I do a few things here and there to reduce my energy consumption.	I do a lot of things to reduce my energy consumption.	I seek out opportunities to reduce my carbon footprint in as many ways as possible.

4% Indifferent · 13% Passive · 50% Uncommitted · 27% Dedicated · 6% Activist

Question: Which of the following statements best describes you? *Select one.* (n = 1,331)
BASE: U.S. travelers

Source: *PhoCusWright's Going Green: The Business Impact of Environmental Awareness on Travel*

The contrast between lifestyle categories all but disappears in regard to negative statements about green initiatives, except in the category of global warming (see Exhibit 7). Even among those in the actively green category, a majority believe that companies often label products "green" so that they can charge more for them. A remarkably consistent 57 percent of respondents in both categories (actively green and less actively green) agree with this statement. Meanwhile, 23 percent of respondents from both lifestyle groups indicate they sometimes feel peer pressure to make environmentally friendly choices, implying that social pressure affects different strata of green lifestyle groups somewhat evenly.

Responses to communication-related statements show a strong demand for information about environmentally friendly practices. A critical tangent is that respondents exhibit high levels of skepticism regarding what companies say about their green practices (see Exhibit 8). The actively green category maintains a significantly higher percentage of respondents who would like more information, and also a slightly higher percentage of skeptics. However, American travelers exhibit a consistent level of skepticism overall; 59 percent of actively green respondents

Exhibit 4 Actions Taken Due to Environmental Concern

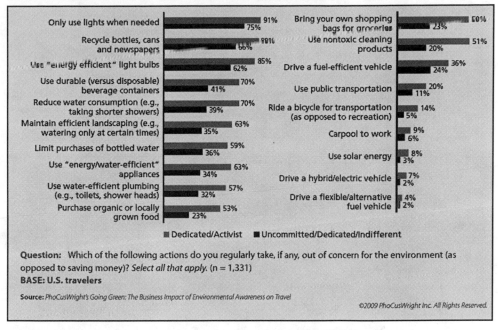

Question: Which of the following actions do you regularly take, if any, out of concern for the environment (as opposed to saving money)? *Select all that apply.* (n = 1,331)
BASE: U.S. travelers

Source: *PhoCusWright's Going Green: The Business Impact of Environmental Awareness on Travel*

©2009 PhoCusWright Inc. All Rights Reserved.

Exhibit 5 General Green Motivators by Lifestyle Category

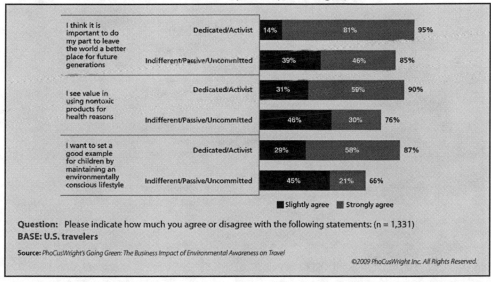

Question: Please indicate how much you agree or disagree with the following statements: (n = 1,331)
BASE: U.S. travelers

Source: *PhoCusWright's Going Green: The Business Impact of Environmental Awareness on Travel*

©2009 PhoCusWright Inc. All Rights Reserved.

are wary of company information, while 54 percent of less actively green respondents are wary of company information. These interlocked trends (demand for more information and skepticism about information) present an obvious challenge for travel companies. They emphasize the need for more fact-based

Exhibit 6 Cost/Saving Green Statements

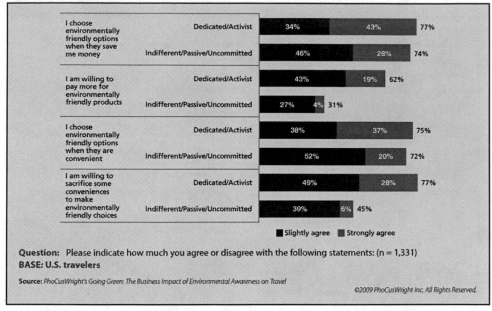

Exhibit 7 Negative Green Statements

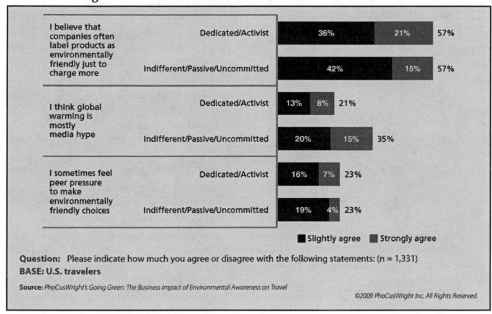

information and better dissemination through a range of channels. Posting information on a website is the ubiquitous first step in any green communication plan, but a website is inherently a "pull" channel that makes consumers seek

Exhibit 8   Communication-Related Green Statements

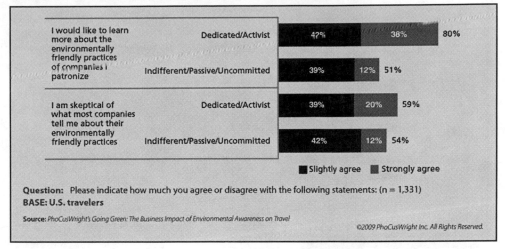

Question: Please indicate how much you agree or disagree with the following statements: (n = 1,331)
BASE: U.S. travelers

Source: *PhoCusWright's Going Green: The Business Impact of Environmental Awareness on Travel*

©2009 PhoCusWright Inc. All Rights Reserved.

Exhibit 9   Impact-Related Green Statements

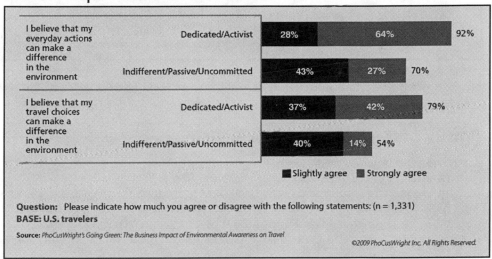

Question: Please indicate how much you agree or disagree with the following statements: (n = 1,331)
BASE: U.S. travelers

Source: *PhoCusWright's Going Green: The Business Impact of Environmental Awareness on Travel*

©2009 PhoCusWright Inc. All Rights Reserved.

information themselves. "Pushing" communication to consumers—through pre- and post-purchase e-mails and in-house/in-flight video channels, for example—is the essential next step in widening information dissemination.

To understand how travel relates to the overall green lifestyle, the survey asked respondents if they believe their everyday actions and travel choices affect the environment (see Exhibit 9). Not surprisingly, the more actively green category showed stronger agreement with both statements, but the drop-off rates between everyday actions and travel choices were similar between categories. This provides evidence that travel choices are often not seen as effective means of helping the

Exhibit 10   Green Travelers

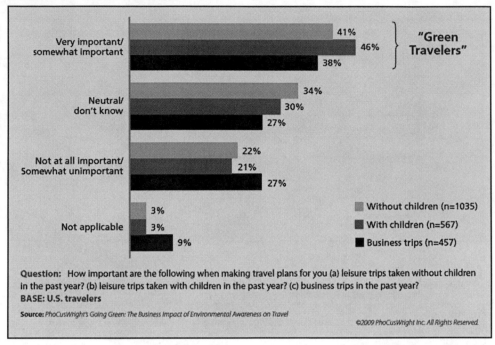

Very important/
somewhat important — 41% / 46% / 38% — **"Green Travelers"**

Neutral/
don't know — 34% / 30% / 27%

Not at all important/
Somewhat unimportant — 22% / 21% / 27%

Not applicable — 3% / 3% / 9%

Legend:
- ▨ Without children (n=1035)
- ■ With children (n=567)
- ■ Business trips (n=457)

Question: How important are the following when making travel plans for you (a) leisure trips taken without children in the past year? (b) leisure trips taken with children in the past year? (c) business trips in the past year?
BASE: U.S. travelers

Source: *PhoCusWright's Going Green: The Business Impact of Environmental Awareness on Travel*

©2009 PhoCusWright Inc. All Rights Reserved.

environment. Despite the drop-off, the majority of respondents (even in the less actively green category) believe their travel choices could affect the environment.

Profile of the Green Traveler

Travelers who have adopted green lifestyles and attitudes do not necessarily apply green values to their travel decisions. Therefore, the report isolated "green travelers" by identifying respondents who consider environmental impacts when planning trips. Overall, about 42 percent of American travelers consider environmental impacts to be somewhat or very important when traveling (see Exhibit 10). Because the nature of a trip or a traveler's companions might affect the importance that a traveler places on environmental impacts, the survey separated travel into three categories: leisure trips with children, leisure trips without children, and business trips. Though frequent business travelers are significantly more likely to be green travelers than infrequent business and leisure-only travelers, a small portion (15 percent) of green business travelers prioritized environmental impacts when traveling for leisure, but not for business. Results also indicated that a slightly higher percentage of respondents are green travelers when taking leisure trips with children than when taking leisure trips without children.

As expectations would suggest, travelers in the more actively green lifestyle category are significantly more likely to be green travelers (see Exhibit 11). Interestingly, a portion (albeit small) of the indifferent and passive groups falls into the green traveler category, suggesting that while the environment is not a significant

Exhibit 11   Green Traveler Penetration of Green Lifestyle Groups

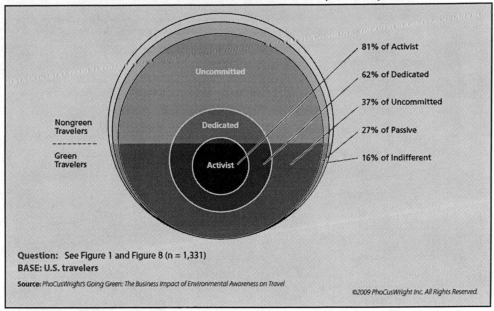

Question: See Figure 1 and Figure 8 (n = 1,331)
BASE: U.S. travelers

Source: *PhoCusWright's Going Green: The Business Impact of Environmental Awareness on Travel*

©2009 PhoCusWright Inc. All Rights Reserved.

everyday consideration for members of these groups, they consider environmental friendliness important when traveling. On the flip side, a small portion of the dedicated and activist groups does not fall into the green traveler category, implying that these respondents do not extend to travel decisions the importance they place on everyday green lifestyles.

Across demographic and travel segments, green travelers exhibit the following characteristics:

- Higher penetration among frequent business travelers (55 percent) than among infrequent business travelers (48 percent) and leisure-only travelers (41 percent)

- Higher penetration among travelers in the $75,000 to $99,999 annual household income (HHI) range (50 percent) than among travelers with HHIs of less than $75,000 (43 percent) and travelers with HHIs of more than $100,000 (45 percent)

- Higher penetration among travelers who typically stay at higher-rated hotels (50 percent for four-star hotels versus 42 percent for budget hotels)

- Higher-than-average penetration among travelers who shop for travel online (50 percent for online travel agency shoppers, 47 percent for supplier website shoppers)

- Even penetration across gender (44 percent for males, 45 percent for females)

Of the environmental qualities associated with travel, distance most often influences green travelers' decisions. This implies that transportation-based

Exhibit 12   Factors Influencing Travel Decisions

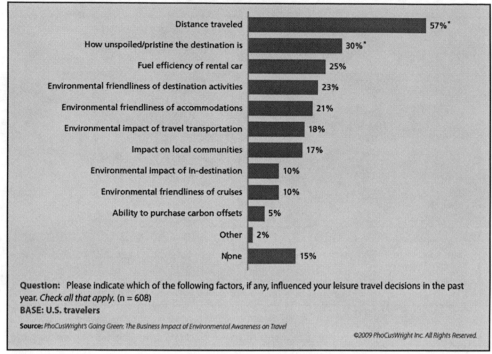

Distance traveled — 57%*
How unspoiled/pristine the destination is — 30%*
Fuel efficiency of rental car — 25%
Environmental friendliness of destination activities — 23%
Environmental friendliness of accommodations — 21%
Environmental impact of travel transportation — 18%
Impact on local communities — 17%
Environmental impact of in-destination — 10%
Environmental friendliness of cruises — 10%
Ability to purchase carbon offsets — 5%
Other — 2%
None — 15%

Question: Please indicate which of the following factors, if any, influenced your leisure travel decisions in the past year. *Check all that apply.* (n = 608)
BASE: U.S. travelers

Source: *PhoCusWright's Going Green: The Business Impact of Environmental Awareness on Travel*

environmental impacts are a common concern among members of the green population (see Exhibit 12). With that in mind, an effective form of green communication could involve distributing information about a destination's accessibility to consumers.

The survey identified barriers to and enablers for green travel by asking consumers which conditions could lead them to make environmentally conscious travel decisions. For both green travelers and non-green travelers, lack of a cost premium was the most common enabler; the percentage of respondents who made this statement was remarkably similar across both groups, given the vast differences in opinion that existed for other conditions (see Exhibit 13). One significant difference surfaced regarding the question of whether environmental standards, ratings, and certifications would influence travelers' decisions. Results indicate that standards are more important to green travelers than to non-green travelers.

Analysis of Key Findings

The Potential for Price Premiums

Most American travelers—and green travelers—see cost as the top barrier to eco-friendly travel. Approximately two-thirds of American travelers cite lack of a cost premium as a condition that could lead them to make more environmentally conscious travel decisions. In addition, almost the same ratio (63 percent) of green

Exhibit 13   Barriers/Enablers for Green Travel

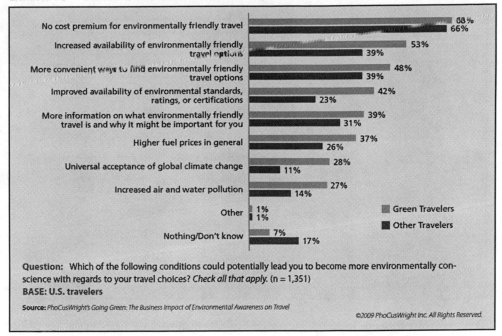

No cost premium for environmentally friendly travel — 68%, 66%

Increased availability of environmentally friendly travel options — 53%, 39%

More convenient ways to find environmentally friendly travel options — 48%, 39%

Improved availability of environmental standards, ratings, or certifications — 42%, 23%

More information on what environmentally friendly travel is and why it might be important for you — 39%, 31%

Higher fuel prices in general — 37%, 26%

Universal acceptance of global climate change — 28%, 11%

Increased air and water pollution — 27%, 14%

Other — 1%, 1%

Nothing/Don't know — 7%, 17%

■ Green Travelers
■ Other Travelers

Question: Which of the following conditions could potentially lead you to become more environmentally conscience with regards to your travel choices? *Check all that apply.* (n = 1,351)
BASE: U.S. travelers

Source: *PhoCusWright's Going Green: The Business Impact of Environmental Awareness on Travel*

©2009 PhoCusWright Inc. All Rights Reserved.

travelers who had trouble finding environmentally friendly travel options cited cost as the reason.

However, upon completing industry interviews, PhoCusWright found that no major travel companies had implemented systematic price premiums for green products. Companies indicated their justifications for green initiatives stemmed from the cost benefits these initiatives provide, rather than from the initiatives' ability to reap revenue. For example, for its new Element Hotels brand, Starwood Hotels & Resorts does not charge premiums based on "greenness," though environmental friendliness is part of the company's core brand concept. By connecting industry trends to consumer points of view, one can see how strongly customers' perceptions about premiums for "everyday" green products affect their expectations for green travel products.

Broad consensus among interviewees across the travel industry, as well as consumers' generally negative reactions to price premiums for green products, seem to indicate that the travel marketplace cannot bear price premiums for green travel products. Yet consumers say differently. When green travelers evaluate their willingness to pay premiums for environmentally friendly travel products, a significant majority (72 percent) say they will pay a price premium (see Exhibit 14). Among the American traveler population at large, 32 percent will pay a premium. On average, just less than half of green travelers indicate they will pay a 1- to 10-percent premium for green travel products. The obvious questions are: Why has the travel industry not been able to build price premiums for green products?

Exhibit 14   Willingness to Pay a Premium for Environmentally Friendly Travel

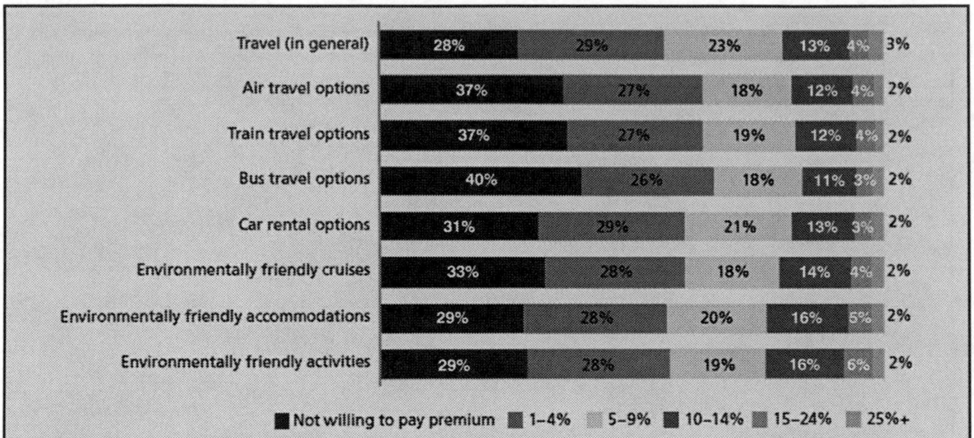

Question: How much of a premium would you be willing to pay for any environmentally friendly travel choices when traveling for leisure? (n = 608)

BASE: U.S. travelers

Source: *PhoCusWright's Going Green: The Business Impact of Environmental Awareness on Travel*

©2009 PhoCusWright Inc. All Rights Reserved.

What would have to happen or change for consumers to actually pay the premiums they indicate they would be willing to pay?

Premium Prerequisite 1: A Common Consumer-Recognized Standard. A consumer's purchasing decision, pared to its most basic level, involves two pieces of information: price and product quality. For a company to charge a higher price for a product, it must give consumers corresponding information about what makes the product better in quality. Without this information, consumers have no basis upon which to adjust their willingness to pay more for the product.

In the context of travel, the target market (green travelers) lacks product-quality information. Only 8 percent of green travelers can very easily or somewhat easily locate green travel choices; more than half have difficulty locating green choices (see Exhibit 15). By definition, green travelers consider environmental impact when planning trips, so a sizable gap exists between the information consumers seek and the information companies provide.

One of the biggest challenges companies face when addressing this gap is the skepticism consumers maintain toward green messaging. Confusion about commonly used terms like "zero-waste" and "carbon neutral" exacerbates the issue. In this set of circumstances, objective third-party information is essentially the only vehicle to address consumer concerns. Unfortunately, no entity has emerged as a consumer-trusted source for information. As seen in Exhibit 16, none of the listed organization types reaches 50-percent approval for being a trusted source of green travel information. Without widely trusted sources of information and a benchmark that lets consumers determine whether a product is green, the pportunity for actualizing any price premium will remain unrealized for major travel companies.

Exhibit 15   Finding Environmentally Friendly Travel Options

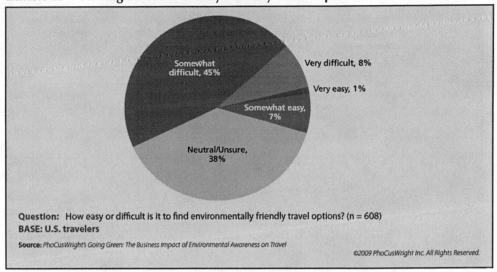

Question: How easy or difficult is it to find environmentally friendly travel options? (n = 608)
BASE: U.S. travelers

Source: *PhoCusWright's Going Green: The Business Impact of Environmental Awareness on Travel*

©2009 PhoCusWright Inc. All Rights Reserved.

Exhibit 16   Environmental Ratings

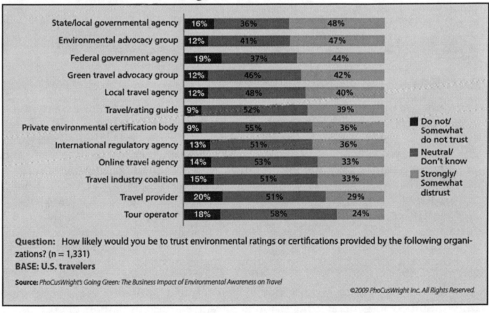

Question: How likely would you be to trust environmental ratings or certifications provided by the following organizations? (n = 1,331)
BASE: U.S. travelers

Source: *PhoCusWright's Going Green: The Business Impact of Environmental Awareness on Travel*

©2009 PhoCusWright Inc. All Rights Reserved.

Premium Prerequisite 2: Incorporation of Green Elements that Go Beyond Consumption Management. Some of the consumer skepticism surrounding green products and their pricing derives from the knowledge that many green initiatives reduce costs. While efforts saving fuel, electricity, and water clearly lessen environmental impact, they also financially benefit the companies that make them. Consumers are

Exhibit 17   Consumer Perceived Value

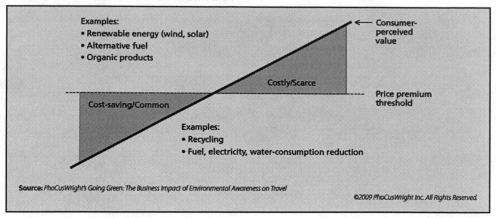

familiar with these types of initiatives, as they take similar actions in their own lives (refer back to Exhibit 4). For this reason, consumers create an informal standard in which they expect travel companies that implement cost-cutting or common green initiatives to do so at no charge to the guest. Consequently, companies that want to build price premiums must surpass the threshold set by consumers' common sense. Hotel linen re-use programs fall into the cost-saving/common category depicted in Exhibit 17. Yet initiatives that require significant financial investments, or that incorporate unusual or scarce products like alternative fuels, create a differentiated product that could elicit price premiums from consumers.

Establishment of a Consumer Standard

Consumers evaluate a rating's quality by comparing their actual experiences to expectations that a given rating sets. The challenge for companies creating green standards is that consumers sometimes have difficulty judging the accuracy of green ratings. Consumers can easily recognize an inaccurate four-star rating for a hotel because they see and interact with the qualities that determine the rating. By contrast, many of the qualities that make a hotel green might not be obvious. For example, consumers cannot see the recycled materials that went into a property's construction or the renewable energy the property uses. Therefore, to determine whether a property is environmentally friendly, consumers must rely almost entirely on a green rating provider. With that in mind, consumer trust is an important aspect of the green rating system, more so than it is with generic quality-rating systems.

Another feature of green rating systems is that providers must be scientifically qualified to generate their ratings. Because green initiatives often measure environmental impact, consumers expect a quantitative approach toward rating assignments. Travelers might trust the American Automobile Association (AAA) to recognize high-quality beds and furnishings in a hotel, but they might not trust AAA to accurately calculate the hotel's carbon footprint.

As seen in Exhibit 16, no single entity has a wide base of consumer trust for its green rating system. Partnerships and coalitions involving multiple organizations, such as the Tourism Sustainability Council (formed by a merger of the Partnership for Global Sustainable Tourism Criteria (GSTC) and the Sustainable Tourism Stewardship Council (STSC)), are a logical step toward creating reliable, accepted green rating standards. Unfortunately, though these entities might help the travel industry build standards for itself, they will not likely capture mainstream consumer mindshare. This brings to light another quality an effective consumer standard must have: a wide distribution network.

Upon reviewing the three characteristics of a widely accepted consumer green standard—a trusted brand, scientific integrity, and a wide distribution network—one can see why consumers have not yet accepted any one standard on the market. Of the travel industry's contenders for developing an accepted green standard, the ratings and travel guide giants seem best suited, as they already have two of the three characteristics (i.e., a trusted brand and wide distribution). To maintain scientific integrity, these companies will likely have to partner with an environmental advocacy group or government agency.

Though development of a consumer green standard will undoubtedly be difficult and time-consuming, its usefulness will be assured. The vast majority of American travelers want to make green choices (refer back to Exhibit 5). An easily accessible, trusted standard will be the source of information travelers need to make those decisions.

Green Communications

Issues surrounding green communications represent the next hurdle for travel companies. Industry survey respondents and interviewees indicate that, throughout the next two years, much of the effort put toward green initiatives will relate to communication. The vast majority of companies have already established goals and implementation plans for communications strategies.

Because consumers maintain a skeptical attitude toward company-supplied green information (refer back to Exhibit 7), communications must incorporate factual, specific information rather than subjective, vague claims. Communication efforts must also present facts in terms relatable to consumers. For example, when discussing the results of its fuel-saving initiative, a company might mention the number of cars it has taken off the road rather than the percentage of emissions its efforts have reduced. Even among green travelers, who are likely more familiar than the average traveler with environmental terms, a majority (54 percent) indicate that confusing terminology deters their efforts to find environmentally friendly travel options.

Effective green communications also give consumers responsibility for achieving positive environmental impacts. For example, instead of merely describing a product's environmental friendliness, a green communications message might describe how, by using the product, consumers actively help the environment. A hotel that states it has saved enough electricity to light Cleveland for a year might be providing interesting information, but its next step should be to explain what that information means to an individual traveler. Messages phrased in ways that transfer the product's benevolence to consumers will likely resonate with the vast majority of American travelers who place importance on green values.

Exhibit 18   Effect of Economic Pressure

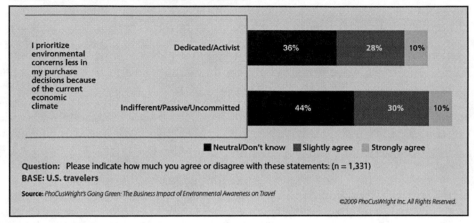

I prioritize environmental concerns less in my purchase decisions because of the current economic climate

Dedicated/Activist   36%   28%   10%

Indifferent/Passive/Uncommitted   44%   30%   10%

■ Neutral/Don't know   ■ Slightly agree   ■ Strongly agree

Question: Please indicate how much you agree or disagree with these statements: (n = 1,331)
BASE: U.S. travelers

Source: *PhoCusWright's Going Green: The Business Impact of Environmental Awareness on Travel*

©2009 PhoCusWright Inc. All Rights Reserved.

The Impact of the Economy

Because efficiency and reduced consumption are basic elements of environmentally friendly initiatives, many green efforts save money, both for the industry and for consumers. Consequently, a tough economy should heighten the priority of green actions that create cost savings.

Yet a common assumption among consumers is that green products cost more money than non-green products. Consumers reveal this attitude in their reactions to economic challenges (see Exhibit 18). Nearly four out of ten respondents indicate that, because of the current economic climate (the survey was fielded in August and September 2008), they give environmental friendliness less priority in their purchasing decisions than they do during more favorable economic times. Given that the economy took a significant turn for the worse in late 2008, it is likely that a portion of the "neutral" group shifted its stance and gave environmental friendliness less priority as well. The green lifestyle category responded in a manner similar to the less actively green category, indicating that economic factors affect even active supporters of green initiatives.

Economic trends will likely decrease the industry's emphasis on green initiatives (with the exception of practices that provide immediate cost savings). Because most major travel companies implemented environmental programs several years ago, many initiatives are already in place. Therefore, with the possible exception of large development projects requiring long-term planning (such as new hotels and airplane technology development), a general lull will stem the progress of green initiatives as travel companies focus on overcoming near-term economic challenges.

What's Next for Green Travel?

The "Hygiene Factor"

Consumers expect that travel companies will maintain a basic level of responsibility to the environment. This green expectation threshold will likely evolve and increase over time, but a natural settling point seems to fall at the consumer "price premium threshold," depicted in Exhibit 14, where a company has exhausted its no-cost opportunities to reduce consumption and now faces initiatives that require financial investment. For most travelers, this base level of greenness is something of a "hygiene factor." That is, if a travel company does not meet the baseline, travelers will be dissatisfied, but if the company exceeds the baseline, travelers will not necessarily express more satisfaction. For example, many corporate travel managers collect information regarding hotels' environmental friendliness as part of the standard request for proposal (RFP) process. The travel managers can easily reject hotels that do not follow environmentally friendly practices, but will not necessarily choose a hotel based on its environmental friendliness alone.

Premiums for Differentiated Green Products

Though it does not represent the majority, a sizable portion of travelers (three out of ten) will pay a premium for differentiated green products. Brands that distinguish their products from the baseline can charge premiums to consumers who find environmental friendliness a source of satisfaction. The challenge for companies seeking premium-paying consumers is that these consumers are skeptical and savvy. Not only must a company ensure its product stays on the cutting edge of green technology, it must also build its communication strategy in a way that draws attention to the product's green aspects without overselling it and potentially alienating wary consumers.

Green Information from Major Travel Rating and Guide Organizations

Sixty-two percent of American travelers believe their travel choices affect the environment. With that in mind, rating and guide companies that do not systematically supply green information ignore a strong consumer need. A large portion of green travelers (42 percent) views standards and rating systems as enablers that help them make green travel choices. The high demand for green information presents an opportunity for organizations like AAA and Mobil to supply this information in their travel guides. While these organizations would not need to generate green information in-house, they could increase their relevance by adding an environmental component to their traditional standards, simultaneously enhancing the new green standards' relevance by giving them the credibility of endorsement by respected transportation organizations.

Conclusion

The travel industry is eager and determined to meet the challenge of "greening" the world of travel. Travel companies and industry associations have launched programs that provide information and share best practices. These efforts, though not the focus of this study, deserve recognition for the progress they will undoubtedly achieve. While findings suggest that mainstream travelers will be most receptive to standards from established players, efforts made by all travel companies, large and small, will help shape the future of green travel.

Appendix:

Research Methods and Sample

Consumers

Through Global Market Insite, Inc. (GMI), PhoCusWright fielded an online consumer survey targeting the general American online traveler population. The survey lasted from August 8, 2008, through September 12, 2008, and required respondents to have taken at least one leisure trip involving an overnight stay in paid accommodations a minimum of seventy-five miles from home during the past year. PhoCusWright received 1,334 qualified responses; the respondent pool can be projected with confidence to the American adult population of online travelers defined above. The error interval for analysis of groups within the respondent population is plus or minus 2.7 percent at the 95-percent confidence level.

In addition to the general American online traveler population, the consumer survey was fielded to research partner Sustainable Travel International's (STI's) consumer database. Eighteen qualified responses were received from this list. Due to the source of these participants, their responses were included in the sample set for certain questions only.

Suppliers and Influencers

In addition to forty executive interviews, PhoCusWright, STI, and the Hospitality Sales and Marketing Association International (HSMAI) Foundation fielded a qualitative survey to industry members from August 14, 2008, through September 26, 2008. Collectively, this effort acquired 134 qualified responses.

Marketing Sustainability: Practical Tips for Hotel Operators

By Robert A. Gilbert

*As President and CEO of the Hospitality Sales & Marketing Association International, **Robert A. Gilbert,** CHME, CHA, has been guiding HSMAI through a dynamic and exciting period of change as the 7,000+ member organization has re-established itself as the definitive hospitality and travel marketing association in the world.*

During Mr. Gilbert's tenure, HSMAI has achieved tremendous success with a number of initiatives. It has re-affirmed its commitment to industry-specific education through HSMAI chapters and the creation of five special interest groups (SIGs) that provide segment-specific programs in the areas of Internet marketing, resort marketing, and revenue management strategy conferences. Mr. Gilbert was also instrumental in the development of HSMAI University and the expansion of HSMAI's Affordable Meetings trade shows into three markets. HSMAI U today produces nearly fifty webinars annually and manages two world-class simulation training programs and three certifications, while Affordable Meetings provides HSMAI members with a direct opportunity to meet potential customers and secure leads for meetings business for their hotels or destinations. Mr. Gilbert has also led the global expansion of HSMAI through the formation of HSMAI Global in 2003, the opening of an Asia-Pacific regional office in Singapore in 2005, and the recent establishment of a new national chapter in the United Arab Emirates.

Mr. Gilbert holds a Bachelor of Science degree from the School of Hotel Administration at Cornell University and has been a member of HSMAI since joining the student chapter at Cornell. He is a frequent guest lecturer at his alma mater. Mr. Gilbert serves on the Board of Directors of the American Hotel & Lodging Association, the Convention Industry Council, and the Travel and Tourism Coalition of the U.S. Travel Association. He also serves on a number of advisory boards of hospitality and hotel management schools.

SALES AND MARKETING PROFESSIONALS have spent decades trying to differentiate individual brands, hotel products, and marketing strategies to attract different types of guests. While many guests from all major market segments (corporate, leisure, groups, etc.) value hotel companies that have a socially responsible corporate culture, the integration and implementation of this culture in sales and marketing strategies is a delicate task.

Before developing sustainability marketing initiatives for a hotel or other lodging company, it is important to recognize that the success of these initiatives

Exhibit 1   U.S. Green Consumer Behavior

Top Three Green Behaviors	2007	2008
Turn off lights when leaving room	85%	88%
Recycle trash/compost	60%	76%
Regulate AC when not at home	67%	75%

Source: Ypartnership.com.

will be a function of the corporate culture and the ability to integrate a "green" philosophy throughout the company. An organization's overall commitment to corporate social responsibility and to the community must come first; environmental practices or operations will then most likely encompass that commitment. Hotels and other travel companies that reflect the social values of the traveler will, over time, gain favor as a travel supplier. This obviously has sales and marketing benefits in driving rate and marketing efficiencies.

This chapter will outline consumer trends and identify six major areas in which a hotel's sustainability practices may be included and leveraged in an effort to attract and retain more customers from any market segment.

General Consumer Trends

While the sustainability trend has evolved and grown globally, there are still many opportunities for green growth. A 2009 U.S. study reported that 78 percent of Americans considered themselves to be "environmentally conscious." The study also showed that the number of consumers who were aware of the term "carbon footprint" had grown from 12 percent to 54 percent between 2007 and 2009. This heightened awareness of the carbon issue, however, has not had much of an impact in the realm of personal travel, as only 3 percent of travelers purchase carbon offsets when booking travel. In addition, recent studies show that only 39 percent of consumers would pay a 5-percent premium to an environmentally responsible supplier.[1] This data suggests that most travelers believe that the additional expenses typically incurred to "go green" should be borne by hoteliers as a cost of doing business.

While there is definitely room for improvement of consumer behavior on the tourism front in terms of sustainability, there has been an increase in the practice of several sustainability behaviors at home, including turning lights off when leaving a room, recycling and composting trash, and regulating the use of air conditioning when not at home. Exhibit 1 shows the increase in the practice of these behaviors in the last two years.

Another general trend among consumers that has had an effect on sustainability is that more and more corporations are implementing "green" standards that influence hotel selection for their employees. According to a 2009 survey done by the National Business Travel Association, 21 percent of corporate travel managers say that environmental practices are important in choosing a travel company; this statistic is up from 16 percent the year before.[2] Questions corporate travelers are asking hotels include: "How much water and energy are you conserving?"

"How much waste are you trimming?" "How often are towels and linens replaced at your hotel?" and "What are you recycling?" However, current surveys of travelers also suggest that a hotel's environmental practices are rarely deal breakers.

In addition to using green criteria to select hotels, many corporations are implementing sustainability measures within their organizations. According to a 2009 survey conducted by MedPanel, LLC, 80 percent of corporate sustainability executives in Fortune 500 companies across North America were planning to maintain or increase levels of sustainability-related spending in 2009, despite tough economic conditions. The survey revealed that cost savings, revenue generation, and brand strength were the most important drivers of environmental and clean technology initiatives. These executives and their companies clearly believe that sustainability is an opportunity to achieve greater competitive advantages and higher efficiencies; their actions also reflect a belief that in the near future sustainability will start to be required by customers and supply chain partners.[3]

If a hotel has identified current or potential key accounts as environmentally conscious or having active sustainability initiatives in place, clearly this is a sales and marketing opportunity to align the hotel's core values with those companies, which should help to secure their business.

Sales and Marketing Practices to Gain "Green" Market Share

Many hotel companies have implemented sustainability practices in their operating equipment and back-of-the-house processes and systems. Many have also implemented sustainability practices in front-of-the-house operations, where guests can see and possibly be influenced by them. In any event, there are numerous ways to promote a hotel's sustainability practices to attract more guests; the most important is just being part of the green conversation. This conversation needs to happen with customers, and it needs to be engaging and encompass all of the sustainable actions taken by the hotel, including those relating to the sales and marketing department.

A hotel's overall sustainability strategy should be included in its annual strategic plan; the marketing and sales tactics to communicate the hotel's sustainability efforts should also be included in the annual plan. Six sample strategies and tactics that can be used to communicate and practice green initiatives include the following:

1. In-house merchandising

2. Reservations and websites

3. Direct sales

4. Advertising and branding

5. Social media

6. Public relations

In-House Merchandising

In-house merchandising was among the first ways hotels communicated their early conservation efforts. In-room signs illustrating the amount of water that can be saved by reusing towels and sheets is one of the most common practices still used by hotels. This type of signage in the guestroom and throughout the hotel portrays an important "green" marketing message to guests.

"Green" messages can be shown on the home screen of the guestroom television, in the guest directory, in elevator signage, on menus in the hotel's restaurants, and in many other places that are visible to guests. If the hotel wants its current guests to know what sustainable actions the hotel is taking and how guests can help, posting messages is one of the easiest ways to let them know. Signage can certainly inform guests that they have the choice to help the environment by reusing towels and sheets, shutting off lights, and taking other measures that promote sustainability. Even if guests choose not to engage in the hotel's sustainability practices, in-house "green" merchandising is important in communicating to hotel guests that the hotel is environmentally conscious.

Reservations and Websites

Consumers with a particular interest in sustainability may ask a hotel's reservations agent or search the hotel's website for a list of the hotel's green practices. Hotels should make sure that the reservations department is trained and all staff can easily articulate the hotel's position on being green and give examples of the hotel's initiatives. A hotel should devote a section of its website to its green initiatives; this section will be of special interest to current and potential guests and corporate travel planners who are looking to identify the hotel's sustainability position and the practices it employs.

Direct Sales

As with the hotel's reservations agents, all sales managers should be trained and be able to articulate the same information regarding the hotel's position on sustainability. If sales managers are asked by current or potential clients about environmental programs and initiatives, for example, they should be able to quickly summarize the hotel's efforts. Language should be included in sales proposals to corporations and other groups that articulates the hotel's position on sustainability and clearly impresses upon these prospective customers what green initiatives the hotel has implemented or is implementing. See Exhibit 2 for examples of what the sales and marketing department itself can do to promote sustainability.

Advertising and Branding

Currently a very small segment of the population selects hotels based solely on their sustainability efforts; thus, it is rarely beneficial to dedicate messages promoting sustainability to this audience only. Rather, all advertising and marketing materials should get the green message out by including any "green" logos or designations earned (LEED certification, for example) to verify the hotel's sustainable practices. These logos or designations should be made part of the standard

Exhibit 2   Sustainability in the Sales and Marketing Department

In addition to communicating the hotel's sustainability initiatives, the sales and marketing department can adopt a number of sustainability practices that, in addition to being environmentally friendly, can save the department and hotel money. Sustainability measures a sales and marketing department can implement include the following:

- Replace printed materials with electronic materials whenever possible. This saves trees, water, and electricity from paper production processes and reduces pollution. Today most customers are comfortable with digital documents such as PDFs, and many even prefer them. This is not only an environmentally responsible practice, but it addresses current customer needs and preferences as well.

- Replace paper forms with online, web-based forms. Many marketing departments still rely on paper forms to initiate new projects, request materials, and approve marketing and sales expenditures. Implementing these forms as web-based entries to database systems reduces the use of paper and streamlines internal workflows.

- When printing is necessary, print the minimum needed and no more. This results in less paper consumption, less waste, and reduces the print budget. A key objective for printing and fulfillment operations should be eliminating wasted materials. Also, mass distribution of new literature ("please send fifty copies to each office") should be replaced with electronic notification.

- Use e-fulfillment. Enable your users to download and/or e-mail marketing assets directly from an online repository. This eliminates the need to transport print materials by truck from a warehouse or fulfillment center and reduces harmful emissions to the environment.

- Stop creating marketing materials that are ineffective. Check with your sales force and ask what is working for them and what is being wasted. Usage reports from your marketing intranet or sales extranet provide the intelligence marketers need about which materials are popular and which are rarely used. If you also give sales managers the ability to rate marketing/sales items, you can determine which materials are most effective for customer purposes. This avoids printing and later throwing out materials that no one wants.

- Eliminate overnight shipments to and from agencies and printers. Instead, send large electronic files via secure web services designed for this purpose.

A web-based marketing portal offers an excellent way for marketers to execute these tactics and help their operations become greener. Web-based marketing portals are designed for marketers who need to deliver more marketing/sales programs, more leads, and more sales tools in the face of reduced headcounts and tight discretionary budgets. With a web-based marketing portal, most, if not all, printed marketing and sales assets can be switched to an electronic format and delivered via the web. A marketing portal helps marketers create and maintain a searchable online repository that promptly communicates mission-critical materials and information to salespeople, sales channels, marketing partners, customers, and others. It helps manage the ever-growing volume of a company's information assets and keeps them current.

(continued)

Exhibit 2 *(continued)*

> Other benefits of a marketing portal, in addition to those that are "green," include the following:
>
> - Reduced costs in managing/distributing marketing assets:
>   - Reduction in time spent on managing, e-mailing, and shipping materials
>   - Increase in accuracy/quality/timeliness of information distributed
>   - Reduction in inquiries for electronic files
> - Increased ability to serve multiple channels:
>   - Increase in number of supported sales executives and sales reps with the same (or less) staff members
>   - Different websites and applications addressed by one system instead of multiple, isolated systems
>   - Reduction in cost of lead processing and/or costs of follow-up
> - Reduced cost of print literature fulfillment and shipping costs:
>   - Reduction in time spent fulfilling print inquiries
>   - Saving in shipping costs, as many more items can be accessed and downloaded electronically

Source: www.chiefmarketer.com/green.

hotel graphics so they are used consistently in all communications. The use of recycled and minimal impact materials, with the appropriate logos, also communicates a commitment to sustainability. Third-party recognition or endorsements are always more credible with consumers versus promotions directly from the hotel, so researching green awards and seeking recognition for sustainability initiatives is another way to position the hotel as "doing the right thing."

Social Media

There are various social media tools that can supplement hotel websites in communicating a hotel's commitment to sustainability. Social media such as Facebook, MySpace, TripAdvisor, and so on allow businesses to engage in online communication with communities of like-minded consumers, and in some cases allow businesses to monitor what consumers are saying about them. *The Travel Marketer's Guide to Social Media and Social Networks: Sales and Marketing in a Web 2.0 World* provides detailed information to hotels on how to integrate social media into their overall sales and marketing strategies, as well as information on monitoring comments or reviews about a hotel or brand and managing current and prospective guest engagement.[4]

Public Relations

A hotel's promotion of its sustainability efforts should be done with tact and caution. Consumers generally do not want to hear what a hotel has to say about its own achievements, but, rather, what others are saying about the hotel. In addition to promoting awards, hotels can leverage public relations to promote unique stories about their sustainability programs. Public relations today often intersects with social media, as it relates to what a hotel can showcase in various online mediums such as YouTube and Facebook. Utilizing these social media tools for public relations purposes should be done in addition to hotel promotion via more traditional media such as travel magazines, newspapers, and electronic newsletters.

The challenge for hotels in promoting their agendas is doing so without "green washing." For example, while a lengthy explanation of the benefits of a hotel's towel recycling program screams of self-promotion, a few statistics on the number of wash loads the hotel does may be of some interest to consumers (e.g., "You think it's tough to do laundry at your house? Try doing 20,000 loads per year!"). Work a percentage or some other quantifiable figure into the conversation that reflects how the hotel's green initiatives have made a positive impact on the environment.

Conclusion

Marketing sustainability requires innovation and creativity. The way in which a guest responds to an eco-tourism resort in Costa Rica is likely to be different from the way that same guest responds to practices implemented in a commercial hotel in New York City. The trends related to our global society and travel consumers will continue to evolve, and hoteliers must stay abreast of the latest research and trends to customize their sales and marketing strategies to their specific customers and target audiences. Furthermore, differentiation of a hotel as an eco-friendly business will become more difficult as more hotels adapt practices and install technology and equipment that will allow them to position themselves as "environmentally friendly." As always, marketers will need to identify and leverage unique attributes and strategies to stay ahead of their competition.

Endnotes

1. Ypartnership.com.

2. National Business Travel Association, August 2009 survey, www.nbta.org.

3. Panel Intelligence, September 2009 survey, www.panelintelligence.com.

4. Cindy Estis Green, *The Travel Marketer's Guide to Social Media and Social Networks: Sales and Marketing in a Web 2.0 World* (McLean, Virginia: HSMAI Foundation, 2007).

20

Understanding and Implementing Carbon-Neutral Policies

By Jeanne Varney and David Mahood

Jeanne Varney, CHA, is a Principal with Olive Hospitality Consulting, where she provides practical sustainability solutions to businesses looking to improve their triple bottom line. Her service specialties include how to start a sustainability program, operational audits, sustainability workshops, green meetings, marketing green, certifications, and more. She has more than twenty years of real estate, operational, and sustainable hospitality experience. Prior to establishing Olive Hospitality Consulting, Ms. Varney was Vice President of Asset Management at Host Hotels & Resorts, administering the full range of ownership responsibilities, including operational and capital expenditure budgeting, ongoing operational reviews, and long-term strategic planning for the properties. Ms. Varney has held positions with Marriott International corporate headquarters, Horwath Landauer Hospitality Consulting, as well as positions with The Ritz-Carlton Hotel Company and Four Seasons Hotels and Resorts.

Ms. Varney is a past international president for NEWH, Inc., and is a founding member of the NEWH Sustainability Committee. She is also a member of the U.S. Green Building Council, the Hotel Asset Managers Association, the Cornell Real Estate Council, and the Cornell Hotel Society. Ms. Varney holds a Master of Business Administration from The George Washington University and a Bachelor of Science in Hotel Administration from Cornell University.

David Mahood, LEED AP, is a Principal of Olive Hospitality Consulting, where he provides consulting services to hospitality, commercial, residential, and other furniture and furniture-related manufacturing operations. His services include sustainability training and workshops, branding and marketing, bringing products to market, operational audits, and other technical services. Mr. Mahood's intricate knowledge of the furniture industry and his keen interest in the preservation of the diversity of the planet led him to the creation of Olive Designs in 1998, an environmentally focused commercial furniture manufacturer committed to a reduced environmental footprint, where he remains a principal today. Through his twenty-plus years of experience in the furniture industry, Mr. Mahood has gained valuable knowledge of the manufacturing operations of both domestic and international suppliers. He has assisted manufacturers in locating sustainable materials, eliminating potential harmful toxic processes, creating simpler, more recyclable designs, and reducing energy use and pre-consumer waste. He has also created a template for transition to sustainable practices for a major importer of hospitality furnishings.

Mr. Mahood is the Vice President of Sustainable Hospitality for NEWH, Inc., and a member of the NEWH Sustainable Hospitality Committee. He is also a founding board member, and chair of the standards committee, of the Sustainable Furnishings Council, an organization noted for its efforts in creating sustainable product and services platforms for the home furnishings industry.

Every organization operating in the twenty-first century has the responsibility to reduce its greenhouse gas (GHG) emissions. Carbon dioxide (CO_2), which makes up a significant proportion of all greenhouse gases, is being released into the earth's atmosphere at an alarming rate. Carbon dioxide emissions have reached about 390 parts per million as of November 2010 (the most recent data available at the time of this writing).[1] A recent study by climate scientists at the U.S. National Aeronautics and Space Administration (NASA) suggests that we have reached a tipping point at which humanity faces unprecedented climatic activity without reduction in CO_2 emissions.[2]

"There is a bright side to this conclusion," wrote Dr. James Hansen of NASA's Goddard Institute of Space Studies, and the lead author of the study. "By following a path that leads to a lower CO_2 amount, we can alleviate a number of problems that had begun to seem inevitable, such as increased storm intensities, expanded desertification, loss of coral reefs, and loss of mountain glaciers that supply fresh water to hundreds of millions of people."[3]

By virtue of its sheer size, the U.S. hotel industry contributes significantly to CO_2 emissions and thus can play a major role in developing and implementing solutions to tackle this challenge. The U.S. lodging industry, consisting of almost 51,000 properties, has combined annual sales of just over $127 billion, based on 2009 figures.[4] As such, hotels are one of the largest sectors of building real estate; their owners and operators can play an important role in reducing CO_2 emissions, contributing greatly to the process of establishing "carbon neutrality" (see Exhibit 1 for a definition of "carbon neutral" and other key terms). Although achieving carbon neutrality may seem daunting, hoteliers can maximize their efforts by focusing on both the real estate aspect as well as the customer aspect of their businesses. While offering "carbon offsets" to guests is a critical step, every lodging property would be well-served financially and socially to reduce its energy consumption through significant internal efficiency upgrades and environmentally sensitive operational practices.

In carbon offsetting schemes, carbon-reducing projects compensate for, or offset, the emissions produced by the carbon offset purchaser. A hotel's carbon emissions are, in theory, reduced by the financial support it gives to projects that reduce carbon emissions in general, such as reforestation or renewable energy projects.

Establishing Carbon Neutrality for Hotel Buildings ———

According to the U.S. Green Building Council, in the United States, buildings account for 39 percent of the nation's total energy use, 38 percent of our carbon dioxide emissions, 40 percent of our consumption of raw materials, 30 percent of our waste output, and 14 percent of our potable water consumption.[5] Because hotels are open for business twenty-four hours a day, 365 days a year, their consumption and emission levels may be even higher. The process of establishing

Exhibit 1   Climate Change Terminology

Carbon Footprint—A cumulative measure of the impact a product, service, activity, company, individual, or other entity has on the environment, in terms of the amount of greenhouse gases produced, and measured in units of carbon dioxide. These impacts usually result from energy consumption, pollution, deforestation, and other sources. Carbon dioxide and other greenhouse gases are also released by natural processes, such as forest fires and volcanoes.

Carbon Neutral—A combination of efficiency improvements (resulting in reduced carbon dioxide emissions) and purchases of carbon offsets that balance 100 percent of a carbon footprint.

Carbon Offsets—A reduction in carbon dioxide emissions by a project (such as rainforest preservation) that is sold to a purchaser to balance the purchaser's own carbon dioxide emissions. The funds generated by the sale of offsets support the development of additional reductions.

Greenhouse Gases (GHGs)—Atmospheric gases that contribute to the greenhouse effect; some of them help sustain life on earth. The main greenhouse gases include carbon dioxide, water vapor, nitrous oxide, ozone, methane, and fluorinated gases such as HFCs and PFCs. Some GHGs are naturally occurring, others are solely created by humans. Increasing concentrations of greenhouse gases in the atmosphere (mostly caused by human activity) are altering the habitat via a process called global warming or climate change.

Renewable Energy—Energy resources, such as wind or solar power, which produce indefinitely without being depleted.

Source: Adapted from the American Hotel & Lodging Association's *Green Glossary* at www.ahla.com/ Green.aspx?id=25018.

carbon neutrality with respect to hotels starts with establishing a baseline or measurement of the environmental impact of all of a hotel's operations and activities, specifically the volume of its carbon emissions, or its "carbon footprint" (see Exhibit 1). The result of this process is the identification of (1) key activities, operations, and systems that contribute significantly to the hotel's emissions; and (2) opportunities to significantly reduce those emissions (see Exhibit 2).

Measuring a Hotel's Carbon Footprint/Energy Rating

In order to neutralize a hotel's carbon footprint, an evaluation of its building systems and baseline measurements must be completed. A free carbon footprint measuring tool is available to all hotels that input their data into Energy Star's Portfolio Manager.[6] Portfolio Manager calculates a building's carbon footprint by measuring both direct emissions (fossil fuels consumed directly on-site) and indirect emissions (fossil fuels consumed off-site in the generation of heat, cooling, or electricity delivered to the building).[7] The initial measurements form the benchmarks against which all improvements will be measured. It is recommended that multiple years of historical data be reviewed for the management team to track average consumption, then benchmark against past performance.

Exhibit 2   Balance of Carbon Neutrality

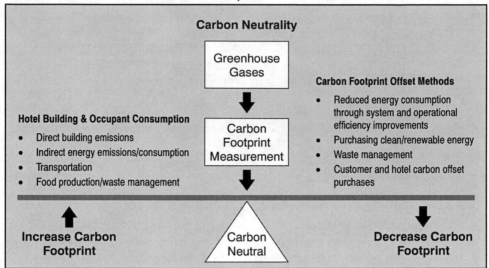

Source: Olive Hospitality Consulting.

Energy and sustainability consultants also have software to accurately record and measure a hotel's carbon footprint. Many of these will measure carbon in terms more specific to hotels, such as greenhouse gases per occupied room, per available room, or per square foot.

Implementing Upgrades to Reduce a Hotel's Carbon Footprint

On the real estate side, there are many ways to reduce a hotel's carbon footprint. In order to prioritize and capture all areas of potential improvement, a building systems and operational audit should be performed that will review the efficiency of equipment and practices currently in place. Once the baseline inventory is taken, the engineering and "green team" at the hotel should review it for areas of potential improvement.

This exercise will produce multiple benefits. First, it will highlight areas within the hotel's building systems that could be replaced or upgraded for greater efficiency. These items, such as low-flow water fixtures, energy management systems, or mechanical equipment upgrades, should be added to the hotel's capital budget plan. Second, it will provide the hotel's engineering staff with smaller projects that can be accomplished at low or no cost. Examples of these projects include waste diversion and installations like energy miser controls on ice and vending machines, motion sensors in lightly used areas, and digital thermostat controls. Third, it will offer areas of improvements for operations, such as training staff in energy and water conservation, consolidating activities in less space (which include closing floors of guestrooms during periods of low occupancy, consolidating staff into fewer offices, and "going dark" in unused spaces), and reducing the use of paper products. Fourth, a review of energy purchasing practices may reveal opportunities for properties to purchase renewable energy at equivalent or lower rates.

Purchasing Carbon Offsets

Once the hotel facility has measured its carbon footprint and implemented energy-efficient capital and operational improvements, the remaining carbon footprint may be offset by the purchase of carbon-offset credits. Carbon offsets come in a wide variety of options described later in the chapter.

Implementing Carbon-Neutral Stays for Hotel Guests

While most hotels are searching for substantial methods of reducing energy requirements through a variety of programs, and many are making significant improvements internally, it has been a challenge for hotels to provide a tangible "green" experience for individual guests. Internal improvements (behind-the-scenes equipment upgrades that reduce energy consumption, for example) are typically neither felt nor seen by guests. It is for that reason that many hotels have concluded that sharing the facility's carbon footprint information is one option that would resonate with guests.

Connecting the Hotel Guest Experience with Carbon Footprint Reduction

Travelers today are becoming more aware of their own carbon footprints. Many environmentally conscious travelers want to be able to assess their carbon footprint for each hotel stay, make adjustments based on the data, and purchase carbon offsets. A small number of hotels have begun to assess how to allow their guests access to this information and make it a part of the guest experience. Each hotel should customize this experience based on its attainable technology and exploit any management company or brand programs already in place.

Innovative programs could be developed to provide discounts or frequent-guest points based on carbon-footprint-offset usage. Implementing a carbon-offset program would clearly be a strong demonstration of the hotel's environmental commitment to individuals, meeting planners, and corporations.

Measuring Carbon Footprints for Guest Travel and Purchasing Carbon Offsets

A hotel could easily partner with a carbon-offset company like Sustainable Travel International to allow each guest to offset a travel experience with little effort. Several options exist for hotels to provide carbon-offset calculators to individual travelers. The most common method in use today is to allow guests to purchase carbon offsets at the time of their reservation, most commonly over the Internet.

To provide options once a guest is on property, each guestroom television could have a channel dedicated to carbon footprint calculations. A simple table could be used to calculate the figures based on a guest's energy usage, with options to offset food and beverage consumption and local fossil fuel–based travel, including air or car travel to and from the hotel. Carbon-offset calculators could be integrated into the front desk check-in kiosks as well.

Exhibit 3   Carbon-Offset Costs and Emissions

Provider	Type of Offset	Cost per Night	CO² Emissions
Travelocity/Go Zero	Hotel Night Stay	$0.25 per night	0.023 metric tons per night
Travelocity/Go Zero	Medium-Haul Flight (280-994 miles)	$1.90 per seat	0.336 metric tons per seat
Marriott International	Hotel Night Stay	$1.00 per night	0.031 metric tons
Sustainable Travel International	Hotel Night Stay	$0.39 per night	0.015 metric tons
Sustainable Travel International	Driving a car 500 miles at 20 miles per gallon	$5.61 per trip	.221 metric tons per trip

Source: Data from corresponding corporate websites.

As depicted in Exhibit 3, there are many carbon-offset calculators available for consumer use for hotel stays. Many providers also offer offset options for car and flight emissions. Each provider has access to different industry or corporate measurement data, therefore the CO_2 emission tonnage varies slightly. The cost per ton of the offset will also vary depending on the type of clean energy purchased.

Carbon-Neutral Meetings

There is a financial payoff for offering green meetings or conference packages. Demand is growing, from corporations and associations in particular, for green events. With companies looking to minimize their carbon footprints throughout their operations, company travel and lodging is heavily scrutinized. Some organizations have shifted to teleconferencing options versus face-to-face conferences to minimize their carbon footprint, while others have sought out hotels and convention centers with green meeting programs. Many organizations require hotels to outline their green hotel practices and green meeting services as a part of the request-for-proposal process. These organizations typically have minimum standards that must be met. These standards are being elevated as consumers become more educated about green options. Hotels and convention centers can enhance their green profile by offering a carbon-neutral meeting package that could include options such as carbon offsets, consolidated transportation options, or locally sourced food offerings.

Carbon-Offset Options

Hotel management teams should view carbon-offset options from two perspectives: (1) using carbon offsets to operate a carbon-neutral hotel business—in other words, purchase offsets to neutralize their building's energy consumption; and (2) providing carbon-offset options to their individual guests and meeting planners. Two types of carbon-offset markets exist. In the compliance market, such as in

Exhibit 4   Lodging Industry Carbon-Offset Programs

Lodging Source	Name of Program	Carbon-Offset Provider
Marriott International	Spirit to Preserve	Amazonas Sustainable Foundation—Juma
Wyndham Hotels & Resorts	Wyndham Green	Native Energy
Kimpton Hotels & Resorts	EarthCare	The Nature Conservancy—Plant a Billion Trees
Travelocity	Go Zero Carbon Offset	The Conservation Fund—Go Zero
Leading Hotels of the World	Leading Green	Sustainable Travel International

Source: Data from corresponding corporate websites.

Europe, companies or other entities buy carbon offsets to comply with governmental regulations that set limits on the volume of carbon dioxide they can emit. In the smaller voluntary markets, offsets are purchased by entities to reduce their carbon-emissions profile.

There are a large number of carbon-offset providers in today's market. Based on a report by the U.S. Government Accountability Office (GAO), over 600 entities develop, market, or sell offsets in the United States.[8] When evaluating potential carbon-offset providers, the following traits should be considered:

- Experience of the provider
- Location of the provider (international, domestic, local)
- Offset project locations (international, domestic, local)
- Project types—energy efficiency, renewable energy, methane capture and destruction, biological sequestration (land use, forestry) and biomass (capture of emissions from other processes)[9]

As consumer demand grows for sustainable practices in the hospitality industry, several reservation systems have integrated the purchase of carbon offsets with the normal guest reservation process. Many travel industry companies have alliances with carbon-offset projects to provide clean-energy offset opportunities for their guests (see Exhibit 4). A more comprehensive listing of the top fifty carbon-offset providers worldwide and guidance on selecting an appropriate provider is located in the report "Getting Carbon Offsets Right: A Business Brief on Engaging Offset Providers,"[10] produced by BSR, a consulting firm on sustainability and social responsibility.

Government Regulations

With government focus on environmental issues increasing, it is critical that the hotel industry take the lead in implementing sustainable business practices in order to set the agenda for how these practices should be implemented and preempt increased regulatory scrutiny and oversight. As traditional energy resources become depleted and more expensive, governmental bodies (local, state, national, and international) continue to increase legislation that affects the production of fuels and energy, the efficiencies of everything from cars to kitchen equipment, and how we dispose of our waste.

Most U.S. businesses are aware of energy-efficient light bulbs and recycling options. The area of greenhouse gas emissions is less well known. Governmental regulations related to greenhouse gas emissions are only in their infancy and few apply directly to the hotel industry. However, many companies have proactively engaged in measuring their carbon footprint and overall energy consumption, and have even participated in cap and trade systems such as the Chicago Carbon Exchange and the Environmental Protection Agency's Acid Rain Program (both described below). These types of programs are used internationally and participation is growing in the United States.

Greenhouse Gas Emissions Reduction Programs

Cap and trade is an environmental policy tool that uses economic incentives to reduce emissions pollutants, with a legally enforceable cap or limit on emissions.[11] The principle of the trades or exchanges is for members to make legally binding commitments to reduce their GHGs in accordance with an emissions reduction schedule. Members who exceed their GHG reduction are allowed to either sell their excess allowances in the market or bank them for future use. If a member does not meet its target, it must purchase offset contracts.

The Chicago Carbon Exchange (CCX) is a U.S. corporation that, until the end of 2010, was the only cap and trade system in North America that dealt with the reduction of all six types of greenhouse gases. The cap in a CCX trade, however, is not government-mandated, but part of a legally binding voluntary contract between the parties involved. The exchange was the first global multi-sector trading system established to reduce GHG emissions. The company announced in November 2010 that it would stop trading as of the end of 2010, although it will still facilitate carbon exchanges. All baseline and emissions data for trades in the United States is verified by the Financial Industry Regulatory Authority, a non-governmental regulatory body that provides independent third-party oversight to CCX. Trading is allowed only between members.[12]

The Acid Rain Program is a product of Title IV of the Clean Air Act of 1990. The goal of the program is to reduce specific GHG emissions that contribute to acid rain environmental damage. The system allows emission caps to be met through traditional reductions and fuel switching, as well as taking advantage of available incentives in the free market to reduce emissions. The program is administered under the Environmental Protection Agency.[13]

Companies choose to participate in cap and trade systems for various reasons. The value propositions include: (1) providing credible, third-party-verified GHG emissions reduction results to shareholders; (2) rating agency and regulatory agency compliance; (3) demonstrable corporate social responsibility action; (4) gaining an early track record in GHG emissions reductions (potentially beneficial regarding government legislation); and (5) satisfying other corporate value aspirations.

Conclusion

The reduction of greenhouse gas emissions is a vital component to the lodging industry's sustainability movement. Hotels have the opportunity to educate their guests on how hotels impact CO_2 emissions and how they can reduce their own impact on the environment. As guest demand for green hotel experiences increases, hotels must educate their staffs and develop their own sustainability identities. With mounting global environmental challenges ahead for humanity, tomorrow's travelers will drive even greater demand for lodging that demonstrates measurable, responsible business practices and provides a tangible sustainability experience for guests during their stays.

Endnotes

1. Recent preliminary measurement, pending recalibrations of reference gases and other quality control checks, for November 2010 at Mauna Loa Mauna Loa Observatory in Hawaii, published by the National Oceanic and Atmospheric Administration (NOAA) at www.esrl.noaa.gov/gmd/ccgg/trends/ global.html#global, accessed December 28, 2010. These measurements of atmospheric CO_2 are used for reports by the Intergovernmental Panel on Climate Change and other authoritative information resources on global warming and climate change. Source data is available at ftp://ftp.cmdl.noaa. gov/ccg/ co2/trends/co2_mm_mlo.txt, accessed December 28, 2010.

2. J. E. Hansen, Mki. Sato, P. Kharecha, D. Beerling, R. Berner, V. Masson-Delmotte, M. Pagani, M. Raymo, D. L. Royer, and J. C. Zachos, "Target Atmospheric CO2: Where Should Humanity Aim?" *Open Atmos. Sci. J.,* 2 (2008): 217–231; doi:10.2174/187428230 0802010217.

3. J. Hansen, et al, "Target Atmospheric CO2: Where Should Humanity Aim?"

4. Data from the American Hotel & Lodging Association's website, www.ahla.org.

5. Data from the U.S. Green Building Council's website at www.usgbc.org.

6. An overview of EPA's Portfolio Manager is available at www.energystar.gov/index. cfm?c =evaluate_performance.bus_portfoliomanager.

7. "Greenhouse Gas Inventory and Tracking in Portfolio Manager," Energy Star's greenhouse gas emissions calculations, at www.energystar.gov/ia/business/evaluate_performance/Emissions_ Supporting_Doc.pdf, accessed August 31, 2009.

8. United States Government Accountability Office, August 2008, "Report to Congressional Requesters: Carbon Offsets," at www.gao.gov.

9. Ryan Schuchard and Emma Stewart, Ph.D., July 2007, "Getting Carbon Offsets Right: A Business Brief on Engaging Offset Providers," at www.bsr.org/reports/BSR_Getting-Carbon-Offsets-Right.pdf.

10. Schuchard and Stewart.

11. See Wikipedia, "Emissions Trading," at http://en.wikipedia.org/wiki/ Emissions_trading.

12. See Chicago Climate Exchange website, www.chicagoclimateexchange.com.

13. See "Acid Rain Program SO2 Allowances Fact Sheet," at www.epa.gov/airmarkets/ trading/ factsheet.html, accessed January 3, 2011.

21

Global Hotel Sustainable Development: Drivers and Best Practices

By Ratna Kartadjoemena, Oriol Gimenez, and Alene Sullivan

Ratna Kartadjoemena *was a Consultant at Ernst & Young's Hospitality Advisory Services Practice in the New York office at the time of the writing of this chapter. She has recently transitioned to a new role as a Manager at Starwood Hotels & Resorts' Real Estate Investment Management group in White Plains, New York.*

At Ernst & Young, Ms. Kartadjoemena worked on hotel market feasibility and financial analysis, as well as internal controls and process improvement audits for hospitality businesses. She also has experience in valuation, due diligence, and underwriting for single asset and portfolio transactions for hotels, retail, office, industrial, multi-family, and land. Prior to Ernst & Young, Ms. Kartadjoemena was a Senior Research Manager at The Corporate Executive Board Company, a firm in Washington, D.C., that provides best practices research, benchmarking, and decision-support tools.

Ms. Kartadjoemena is a LEED Accredited Professional and has a Master of Management in Hospitality degree with a concentration in Hospitality Real Estate Finance and Investments from Cornell University. She received a Bachelor of Science degree from Georgetown University's McDonough School of Business, where she majored in International Business and Marketing and minored in Spanish.

Oriol Gimenez *is a Vice President of Acquisitions for Caribbean Property Group, a New York–based real estate investment, development, and asset management firm with investments in the Caribbean and Latin America. His primary responsibilities include property acquisition, property development, debt financing, and strategic planning. Mr. Gimenez was previously a Manager at the Hospitality & Real Estate Advisory Group of Ernst & Young, where he specialized in real estate development, strategic advisory, and transaction due diligence across the Americas. A LEED Accredited Professional, Mr. Gimenez also advised several hotel owners in the pursuit of LEED certification for their facilities.*

Mr. Gimenez received his business undergraduate degree from Pompeu Fabra University in Barcelona, Spain, and graduated with honors from the Cornell University School of Hotel Administration. During his studies at Cornell University, Mr. Gimenez was actively involved, both as a teacher assistant and as an intern, in the planning and development of several sustainable tourism ventures in Europe, Africa, and Latin America through the Center for Sustainable Global Enterprise and the investment and advisory firm La Paz Group.

Alene Sullivan *is a Manager with Ernst & Young's Hospitality Advisory Services Practice. Ms. Sullivan's primary focus is on hospitality and leisure projects in the United States, Latin America, and the Caribbean. She has extensive experience in market feasibility and financial and strategic analyses for proposed hotel, resort, residential, and mixed-use developments as well as operational analyses with a focus on sustainability. Her experience also includes transaction due diligence involving multiple high-profile single asset, portfolio, and entity transactions. Prior to Ernst & Young, Ms. Sullivan acquired considerable international hospitality consulting experience, particularly in market and tourism research in the public and private sectors and operational and strategic advisory. Ms. Sullivan is a contributor and coordinator of the Ernst & Young's quarterly* Global Hospitality Insights *newsletter, among other publications. Ms. Sullivan is a LEED Accredited Professional and holds a Bachelor of Science degree from the School of Hotel Administration at Cornell University.*

IN RECENT YEARS the practice of sustainable hotel development has received increased attention. Recent momentum gained by sustainable hotel development can be traced back to governmental/regulatory pressure to address rising energy consumption and costs, the economic benefits of energy savings, and the positive image associated with environmentally friendly products.

This chapter illustrates sustainability drivers and best practices from various regions of the world, including the Americas, Europe, Asia, and the Middle East, some of which are becoming benchmarks for future operating standards in those regions. The best practices included in this chapter may not be as effective when implemented individually or on an ad hoc basis; however, hotel companies that embrace a truly comprehensive approach to sustainability will be able to develop sustainable competitive advantages and enhance stakeholder support, as well as reap the benefits of price premiums.

Government Pressure to Adopt Sustainable Practices

Governments worldwide are putting increasing pressure on the hospitality industry to invest in sustainable development. Approaches these governments are taking to encourage hotels to adopt sustainable initiatives include implementing legislation, offering various incentives, and creating certification programs.

Global Laws, Agreements, and Mandates to Curb Energy Consumption

To encourage companies to reduce their energy consumption, governments are implementing laws and mandates that promote sustainable growth. Arguably the most influential global agreement to propel environmental awareness is the Kyoto Protocol, which was adopted in Kyoto, Japan, in 1997 and entered into force in February 2005.[1] The European Union, for example, has a 2012 Kyoto goal of reducing greenhouse gas emissions to 8 percent below 1990 levels.[2] Although more recently the December 2009 United Nations Climate Change Conference in Copenhagen failed to make legally binding obligations on developing nations to cut CO_2 emissions, many countries have at least begun to set goals of their own or have ratified legislation to increase the levels of green growth.

The most prominent piece of U.S. legislation passed on this subject over the past few years is the California Assembly Bill 32, also known as the Global Warming Solutions Act of 2006, which aims to reduce California's greenhouse gas emissions by at least 30 percent by 2020 and to further reduce emissions to below 80 percent of 1990 levels by 2050. Since its passing in 2006, the state has implemented many programs to achieve the goals outlined, including the creation of a low-carbon fuel standard, energy efficiency and carbon reduction programs, a cap-and-trade system, and clean car rules. Almost all of the U.S. states have passed legislation to combat global warming, including legislation concerning building codes, which will likely have a strong impact on the hotel industry. Some states have also established their own green tourism programs to certify the environmental efforts of lodging, restaurant, and other hospitality businesses.

Many governments outside the United States have been implementing similar sustainability initiatives. The Chinese green hotel initiative, which began during the country's preparation for the 2008 Summer Olympic Games in Beijing, is one example. In May 2009, Di Jiankai, the director of the Trade Service Division of China's Ministry of Commerce, disclosed that China will try to open a total of 10,000 green hotels by 2012.[3] These hotels are expected to reduce water and electricity consumption by 20 percent and decrease carbon dioxide emissions by 45,000 tons over four years. For the 2016 Summer Olympics in Rio de Janeiro, Brazil, a group was formed to manage a sustainability plan focusing on water conservation, renewable energy, carbon neutrality, ecosystem and soil protection, sustainable design and construction, reforestation, biodiversity, green procurement, waste management, and social responsibility. In July 2008, Dubai launched an eco initiative similar to the one in China to encourage hotels to reduce their carbon emissions by 20 percent by 2011, while the German government passed the Renewable Energies Heat Act (EEWärmeG), which requires owners of newly constructed buildings to use renewable energy sources, such as geothermal, solar, and biomass energy. Jamaica passed the Tourism Enhancement Act in 2005, imposing a $2–$10 fee on all tourists to fund a curriculum for hoteliers regarding sustainable practices, property upgrades to green standards, and community-based beautification projects. To foster transparency and environmental awareness, Australia and New Zealand are encouraging greenhouse gas and energy reporting; in September 2008, Australia's Sustainable Tourism Cooperative Research Centre released its first comprehensive measure of carbon emissions for the tourism industry, "The Carbon Footprint of Australian Tourism" report.[4]

As demonstrated by the various aforementioned legislation, there are many progressive ways in which governments are using laws to encourage environmental preservation. In many cases, governments are pairing their environmental mandates with incentives to encourage environmentally friendly development; examples of this are discussed in the following sections.

Global Trends in Hotel Sustainable Development

The movement toward more sustainable buildings and practices in the lodging sector has gained momentum throughout the world. While a plethora of approaches exist and are being developed and implemented, three trends are prevalent from continent to continent, city to state.

1. Governments are aiding sustainability efforts by:	2. Hotel companies are realizing cost savings through:	3. Customer awareness is growing as companies:
• Mandating carbon emission reduction through targets and reporting • Incentivizing construction and capital expenditures • Establishing public/private cooperative programs • Certifying hotel construction and operations through establishment of sustainability standards and programs	• Sustainable construction • Low certification fees • Operational efficiencies in green design and practices	• Revise travel policies • Install green-meeting site requirements • Produce sustainability policies and reports • Dedicate sustainability staffing and programs • Establish corporate sustainability funds • Create green brand concepts and hotel directories

Incentives to Encourage Sustainable Development

Aside from mandating reductions in energy consumption, governments are also offering incentives to encourage green projects in the private sector. In the United States, for example, green buildings may qualify for state-level tax breaks. Often, qualification for the tax benefits requires Leadership in Energy and Environmental Design (LEED) certification, such as in Howard County, Maryland, where a bill has been adopted that provides a five-year tax credit to "LEED for New Construction (LEED-NC)" and "LEED for Core & Shell (LEED-CS)" certified projects. The credit amounts increase depending on the level of certification; LEED Silver receives 25 percent in credit, LEED Gold receives 50 percent, and LEED Platinum receives 75 percent. Howard County also offers three-year tax credits for buildings certified under "LEED for Existing Buildings (LEED-EB)": LEED Silver receives 10 percent in credit, LEED Gold receives 25 percent, and LEED Platinum receives 50 percent.[5]

In New Mexico, tax breaks range from $9,000 to almost $25,000 per project.[6] In addition, the U.S. government is providing federal tax rebates for using energy-efficient products (i.e., ENERGY STAR–rated products). In Barbados, properties upgrading to achieve Green Globe certification or fulfilling International Organization for Standardization (ISO) 14001 standards may claim a tax write-off of up to 150 percent of the costs.

Many European Union governments incentivize eco-friendly capital expenditures, which for hotel operators may include pipe-work insulation and low-energy refrigeration equipment. In addition to incentives, in the short-term to mid-term it is anticipated that some governments will begin penalizing companies with large carbon footprints.

Governments are also forming public-private cooperative programs to promote sustainability. For instance, in 2008 the Mexican Tourism Board partnered with travel agencies such as Expedia in initiating educational programs supporting conservation and community development at eco-friendly retreats. The State of New York is actively promoting green building development with programs offered by the New York State Energy Research and Development Authority (NYSERDA). NYSERDA helps developers of green buildings with computer modeling, collaborative design and planning workshops, LEED certification processing, obtaining tax credits, selecting green materials, commissioning, and lifecycle costing analysis. NYSERDA also has a program that helps hospitality companies implement sustainable practices.

Globally Recognizable Standards and Certification Programs

To help hospitality and travel companies become more sustainable, the World Travel & Tourism Council, the World Tourism Organization, and the Earth Council Alliance jointly launched an action plan in 1996 entitled "Agenda 21 for the Travel & Tourism Industry: Towards Environmentally Sustainable Development." Subsequently, "Green Globe," a benchmarking, certification, and performance-improvement program based on the Agenda 21 principles, was created. As of March 2010, Green Globe has certified 1,045 businesses throughout the world. In the United States, Green Globe has certified eleven hotel properties as well as tour operators, bus companies, and real estate companies.[7] In addition to Green Globe, governments and private companies have developed an array of regional certification programs and initiatives.

One of the most successful regional sustainability standards is the Costa Rica Tourism Board's Certification for Sustainable Tourism (CST) program. The CST program was developed approximately ten years ago for tourism businesses based on the degree to which they complied with a sustainable model of natural, cultural, and social resource management. Since the implementation of the CST, Costa Rica has been regarded as one of the most successful countries in environmental conservation. In the 2010 Environmental Performance Index report conducted by Yale University and Columbia University, Costa Rica ranked number one in the Americas, scoring 86.4, third only to Iceland (93.5) and Switzerland (89.1). To date, while only one hotel has achieved the CST's highest ranking (Lapa Rios Ecolodge, itself a pioneer in sustainability), many hotels and resorts have made it a priority to adhere to CST standards, most notably the Four Seasons Resort Costa Rica at Peninsula Papagayo, which was awarded high honors, a first among major branded hotel operators in the region. Between 1998 and 2000, total arrivals in Costa Rica increased by 7.2 percent annually, one of the highest growth percentages in Latin America, arguably driven by the country's success in differentiating itself from other regional destinations by marketing itself as a safe, environmentally friendly, nature-based destination.

Other regional groups that have created their own sustainability standards include the Association of Southeast Asian Nations (ASEAN), which in 2008 developed the ASEAN Green Hotel Standards and honors hotels that meet those standards with the ASEAN Green Hotel Recognition Award. Another group, Ecotourism Australia, was formed in 1991 and manages the Advanced Ecotourism Certification, which identifies genuine ecotourism and nature tourism operators in Australia. Another example is the Canada-based Green Key Eco-Rating Program, which expanded its rating program into U.S. territory in 2009 and is a rating system designed to help hotels reduce their environmental impact and operating costs through reduced utility consumption, employee training, and supply chain management.

The aforementioned LEED certification, which is based on the green building standards set by the U.S. Green Building Council (USGBC), is one of the most distinguished and successful sustainability certification programs to date. As of January 2010, there were forty LEED-certified lodging properties worldwide, with a very aggressive growth pipeline that includes 900 lodging projects. Non-lodging hospitality projects, mainly conference and convention centers, also represent an area of growth, with seventeen such properties currently LEED-certified, and an additional eighty-five pursuing certification.[8] USGBC has formed a Hospitality Adaptations Working Group, which comprises industry experts from USGBC-member companies who modify certain LEED credits to better match the environmental impacts of hospitality projects. Starwood's Element hotel is the first major brand that mandates all its properties to pursue LEED certification, while Marriott developed a LEED pre-certified hotel prototype for its Courtyard brand that became available in 2010.

Aside from the United States, other countries that have developed local green building standards include Japan and India. In Japan, the local green building certification was developed by the Japan GreenBuild Council and the Japan Sustainable Building Consortium, and is called the Comprehensive Assessment System for Built Environment Efficiency (CASBEE). India's building standard is called the Energy Conservation Building Code 2007, and specifies the energy performance requirements for all commercial buildings that are constructed in the country.

While a multitude of sustainability standards are available, only some of these standards come with certification programs to assist implementation. Among these certification programs, some are more generic (e.g., ISO 14001) and some focus exclusively on hospitality/tourism (e.g., Green Globe), while others cover the broader real estate sector (e.g., LEED). In addition, some certifications concentrate solely on energy and the environment, while others incorporate other elements of social responsibility. As illustrated by the various examples given previously, some of the standards are global, while others are regional or local. The credibility and amount of rigor placed on assessing, auditing, and subsequently awarding certificates to applicants also vary. Some certifications require a third party to conduct audits on the applicants' operations and some certifications have set standards of performance, while others are based on local/regional performance benchmarks. Hence, hotels must select carefully which certification programs to follow, using the advice of experienced sustainability advisors in the hotel industry.

Certification programs must adhere to consistent and rigorous standards to become effective and have a positive impact on operations as well as on the guest experience. Certifications lose their effectiveness without a way for hoteliers to differentiate comprehensive certification programs from "greenwashing" programs. Hotels in the Americas, however, now have some assistance in selecting credible tourism/hotel-specific certifications through the Sustainable Tourism Certification Network of the Americas. The network is a collaboration among the Rainforest Alliance, the World Tourism Organization, The International Ecotourism Society, and the United Nations Environment Programme. The purpose of this network is to create common standards among the various certification programs in the region and regulate them.

Cost Savings: Reduced Construction Premium and Operational Savings

The movement toward sustainability in the hotel industry is also driven by the significant decrease to the cost premium associated with building sustainably and the increasing evidence of green building operational cost savings. More and more buildings, including hotels, are being constructed with sustainability in mind, not only because of the potential tax rebates, but also because the required capital expenditure to build green has declined. In Europe, several hotel companies are developing faster and more affordable methods of "green" hotel construction; for example, hotel concept citizenM's Industrial, Flexible, Demountable (IFD) building technique allows for hotel rooms to be manufactured in a factory off-site and then shipped to the destination for assembly. Travelodge has adopted a similar technique in the United Kingdom by developing a hotel in London made entirely from modified steel shipping containers, while in the United States, Marriott's LEED prototype is designed to save owners approximately $100,000 and six months in design time.[9]

Green building certification fees are also no longer a barrier to sustainable development. A fall 2009 report by USGBC titled "Cost of Green in NYC" that studied high-rise residential buildings found that there is no statistically significant difference in construction cost between LEED and non-LEED projects. Furthermore, projects with various levels of LEED certification are distributed throughout the range of costs with no apparent pattern. The study also found that the costs associated with certification were not substantial in terms of overall project cost. The median cost of LEED design fees was $0.56 per square foot, the median cost of LEED documentation was $0.30 per square foot, and the median commissioning cost was $1.55 per square foot.[10]

Most importantly, sustainably designed buildings allow operators to save on operational expenses because they are more energy-efficient. LEED-certified buildings have the ability to save 30–50 percent in energy usage, 35 percent in carbon emissions, 40 percent in water emissions, and 70 percent in solid waste; energy savings of 30–50 percent is equivalent to increasing daily savings per occupied room by $1.80 to $3.00 in a limited-service hotel or by $4.00 to $6.75 in a full-service hotel.[11] The LEED Gold–certified Courtyard Portland City Center, which opened at the end of 2009, uses 30 percent less energy and 26 percent less water compared to a typical Courtyard hotel.[12] The Miyako Hybrid Hotel in Torrance, California, which also opened at the end of 2009, received the LEED Silver certification and is anticipated to be 18.4 percent more energy-efficient (based on baseline building costs) and is expected to save many thousands per year in energy costs due to the use of solar panels alone. Furthermore, the hotel is expected to save 2.3 percent in interior lighting and 10.1 percent in exterior lighting costs, as well as reduce emissions by 72 tons per year and decrease water waste by 588,382 gallons per year.[13]

In addition to the cost savings from efficient green construction, hotels can further reduce costs by implementing green operational practices. Hilton hotels across Europe have reportedly saved $9 million since the introduction of its We Care! program in 2006. Hilton was able to achieve such savings through a number of activities that reduced energy use by 15 percent, decreased water consumption by 15 percent, and reduced CO_2 emissions per guest by 11 percent per night.[14]

Guest Demand and a Positive Image Associated with Environmentally Friendly Products

Another driver for the green movement in the hotel industry is customers' growing awareness of and desire for green hotel products (although their willingness to pay a premium for these products is highly debatable). Many corporations are beginning to revise their travel policies to reduce their carbon footprint as part of their corporate social responsibility programs. Corporate meeting planners are also increasingly demanding green policies in the organization and management of in-house events and conferences. Aside from the desire to meet customer expectations, many hotel companies adopt more sustainable practices for public relations benefits, given the recent media focus on sustainability. Many companies are also increasing employee and guest awareness of their sustainability practices. Some companies, such as Starwood Hotels & Resorts and Hilton Hotels & Resorts, have developed company-wide sustainability policies, while other chain hotel companies, such as Sol Meliá Hotels & Resorts and Banyan Tree Hotels & Resorts, and individual hotel properties such as the Willard InterContinental hotel in Washington, D.C., have begun publishing annual sustainability reports.

Many hotel companies have also designed sustainability programs encouraging employee participation. For example, Six Senses Resorts & Spas, which has a company goal to "create innovative and enriching experiences in a sustainable environment," follows a hub-and-spoke model to align corporate sustainability policies with resort-level initiatives.[15] At the corporate level, the company dedicates a social and environment coordinator, an engineer, and an environmental analyst to administering sustainable policies. At the property level, each resort employs a full-time social and environment coordinator to lead the property's sustainability initiatives. Although the company's sustainability department is centralized, line-level resort staff members are the primary project initiators.

Hotels have also created sustainability programs for guests that venture beyond the two major staples of hotel sustainability—the towel reuse program and the key card–controlled guestroom lighting and heating systems. Soneva Fushi by Six Senses created the Eco Centro Waste-to-Wealth Centre, where hotel staff teach guests permaculture methods, such as composting food waste, that guests can replicate at home. Lapa Rios Ecolodge in Costa Rica offers guests guided tours of the rainforest, and the Golfo Dulce Lodge, also in Costa Rica, offers boat excursions within the Golfo Dulce and to the Esquinas River, as well as guided hikes in the rainforest. These tours teach guests about the local biodiversity while simultaneously funding local conservation efforts. Other sustainability guest participation programs include carbon offsetting, voluntourism, and wastewater recycling.

Hotel companies have begun to more actively sponsor social responsibility and environmental conservation programs. For example, Banyan Tree has created programs for Thalassaemia education in the Maldives and Dengue eradication on Indonesia's Bintan Island. The company also supports indigenous artistry through Banyan Tree Gallery, its retail arm that markets local arts and crafts at their hotels. Banyan Tree has developed environmental programs for marine conservation in the Maldives and Seychelles, gibbon rehabilitation in Phuket, and elephant protection in Bangkok. El Nido Resorts in the Philippines actively protects giant clam gardens and supports the reintroduction of endangered cockatoos to the wild. Six Senses initiated a Social and Environmental Responsibility Fund (SERF), in which all resorts contribute approximately 0.5 percent of total revenues to fund sustainability projects. Of the collected funds, 60 percent is spent at the local level and 25 percent is directed to support national non-governmental organizations (NGOs) and other civil groups, while the final 15 percent goes toward international initiatives in climate change, conservation, and environmental education.[16] Other innovative practices include Kimpton's Sustainable Partnership Program, which recognizes members of the community who are working toward sustainability goals by offering up to 20 percent discounts off the best available rates at Kimpton Hotels in the United States and Canada. The Txai Resort in the Bahia region of Brazil partnered with local groups to form a Living Forest program, directing local families toward sustainable farming and away from cutting down timber. The program teaches families sustainable farming and reforestation techniques, and in addition guarantees them a minimum income in exchange for growing native plants such as raffia, coconut, indigenous flowers, and fruit-bearing trees on their own family properties. The program promises to purchase the crop, which is then used by local artisans to make crafts and traditional delicacies.

In light of the sustainable development movement, some hotel companies have begun incorporating strong elements of sustainability into entirely new brand concepts. In North America, such brands include Starwood Hotels & Resorts' Element and the Hyatt Corporation's Andaz. In Thailand, Six Senses plans to push its whole resort portfolio to be zero carbon–emitting by 2020 and to eventually be net carbon-absorbing; the company's newest brand, EVA, was created to be carbon-positive and to have all of its properties LEED Gold–certified. In the Middle East, Coral Hotels & Resorts has launched an eco-friendly budget chain called ECOS Hotels.

With green branding, customers can more easily select green accommodations. Travel search engines have also made it easier for customers to select green products; for example, Travelocity launched a Green Hotel Directory, which lists hotels that have been endorsed by a leading green hotel certification provider, appear in the Rainforest Alliance's Eco-Index of Sustainable Tourism, or are making significant strides in at least three of the four areas of the Tourism Sustainability Council's criteria. Other travel sites offer carbon offsets when customers go to pay for their online travel purchases.

Green master planning is also gaining momentum, aided by both increasingly stringent regulation and differentiation strategies to attract guests who are more and more growing concerned about their health and well-being as well as their travel's impact on local communities. One example of green master planning is the Rosewood Mayakobá, a 1,600-acre development situated along the Riviera Maya in Mexico and surrounded by a delicate mangrove and tropical forest. By securing international luxury lodging operators such as Fairmont, Rosewood, Viceroy, and Banyan Tree, the project demonstrated that some form of sustainable development can co-exist with the needs of high-end brands. Another notable eco-friendly destination is Loreto Bay, an 8,000-acre development in Baja California Sur, Mexico, which markets itself as a sustainable community by emphasizing its green building practices, community initiatives, and nature preserve that covers over 60 percent of the total land area.

Green resort developments are also sprouting in more remote and secluded locations in Latin America. Explora, which offers several lodge-based journeys in remote areas of South America, focuses on the interaction between guests and nature, and has a new property on Rapa Nui (i.e., Easter Island) that has been built according to LEED building standards. The Inkaterra Machu Picchu Pueblo Hotel uses hydroelectricity, as well as indigenous Andean ingredients and treatments, while Morgan's Rock Hacienda and Ecolodge in Nicaragua is part of a 2,500-acre tree-farming and forestation project within a 2,000-acre nature reserve.

Some examples of ambitious and futuristic urban master planning to green standards come from the Middle East, although the harsh water/environmental conditions there beg the question as to whether the siting of these developments is ultimately appropriate or green. Abu Dhabi Future Energy Company is building the world's first zero-carbon, zero-waste city, named "Masdar City." The $22 billion project, which is master-planned by Foster + Partners, is anticipated to house 50,000 people when completed in 2015 and to include an environmentally friendly hotel. Other emirates are also following this trend; in Ras Al Khaimah, for example, the Office for Metropolitan Architecture is developing the "Gateway Eco City" for completion in 2012. The project will be over 400 million square feet and powered by cutting-edge solar power technology. Like Masdar City, Gateway Eco City consists of multiple retail, office, mixed-use, residential, and hotel developments. Dubai has also launched a mammoth ecological project called the Mohammed bin Rashid Gardens. The project, which is scheduled for completion in 2026, is estimated to cost approximately $54.5 billion and to comprise four clusters with approximately 800 million square feet of building construction and greenery in 73 percent of its footprint.[17]

Conclusion

The projects and initiatives discussed in this chapter are examples of ways hotel companies can demonstrate care for the surrounding environment and local communities, but only those companies that are committed to sustainability and take a holistic approach to their sustainability practices can reap lasting benefits. Many hotel chains, such as Six Senses, and eco-lodges, such as Lapa Rios, have created memorable experiences and lasting impressions in the minds of their guests, providing them with some form of goodwill that translates into premium pricing.

Green programs can provide a competitive advantage as long as green practices remain optional. Some green practices are already starting to become a baseline requirement to doing business in the hospitality industry, however, particularly as the cost of nonrenewable energy continues to increase. As such, only those companies with business models that revolve around green practices will have the strongest opportunity to achieve "sustainable" competitive advantages through their green agendas.

Endnotes

1. "Kyoto Protocol," *United Nations Framework Convention on Climate Change,* accessed January 4, 2011; http://unfccc.int/kyoto_protocol/items/2830.php.

2. European Environment Agency, "EU within Reach of Kyoto Targets," press release, November 27, 2007.

3. "China Aims to Build 10,000 Green Hotels in Four Years," *ChinaCSR.com,* May 27, 2009; www.chinacsr.com/en/2009/05/27/5335-china-aims-to-build-10000-green-hotels-in-four-years/.

4. Sustainable Tourism Cooperative Research Centre, "Australian First Tourism Carbon Footprint Report Released," press release, September 8, 2008; www.crctourism.com.au/Media.aspx?id=72.

5. Wes Johnson, "Council to Consider Property Tax Break," *News-Leader,* June 30, 2008.

6. U.S. Green Building Council, *Summary of Government LEED® Incentives,* March 2009.

7. Contact from Green Globe Certification, Hermosa Beach, California.

8. "LEED and the Hospitality Industry," U.S. Green Building Council, last modified January 2010; www.usgbc.org/ShowFile.aspx?DocumentID=5301.

9. Candace Roulo, "Pre-Certified LEED Hotel Prototype Conserves Energy, Water," *Contractormag.com,* January 11, 2010; accessed January 12, 2011, http://contractormag.com/news/pre-certified-leed-hotel-prototype-conserves-energy-water-0365/.

10. Urban Green Council, *Cost of Green in NYC,* Fall 2009.

11. Jim Butler, "The 'Real Economics' Behind GREEN Hotel Development, Conversion and Operation," *Hotel Online,* October 29, 2007; www.hotel-online.com/News/PR2007_4th/Oct07_ShiftToGreen.html.

12. Marriott International, Inc., "Two New Courtyard Hotels 'LEED®' the Way in Eco-Design," press release, September 22, 2009.

13. "California's Miyako Hybrid Hotel Earns LEED Silver Certification," *Hotels,* March 1, 2010.

14. "Hilton's European Hotels Cut Energy Use by 10% in 2007," *Greenopolis,* April 18, 2008.

15. "Six Senses Sustainability Policy," Six Senses Resorts & Spas, accessed January 13, 2011, www.sixsenses.com/Environment/Six-Senses-Sustainability-Policy.php

16. Six Senses Resorts & Spas, *Due Diligence Report,* April 2009.

17. Richard High, "Mohamed Bin Rashid Gardens," *International Construction,* July 18, 2008.